AVIATION IN CANADA

Larry Milberry

McGraw-Hill Ryerson Limited

*Toronto / Montreal / New York / St. Louis / San Francisco
Auckland / Beirut / Bogotá / Düsseldorf / Johannesburg
Lisbon / London / Lucerne / Madrid / Mexico / New Delhi
Panama / Paris / San Juan / São Paulo / Singapore / Sydney / Tokyo*

ISBN 0-07-082778-8

2 3 4 5 6 7 8 9 10 BP 7 6 5 4 3 2 1 0

Printed and bound in Canada

Canadian Cataloguing in Publication Data

Milberry, Larry, date
    Aviation in Canada

Includes index.
ISBN 0-07-082778-8

1. Aeronautics — Canada — History. I. Title.

TL523.M54   629.13'0971   C79-094358-1

Above Head-on view of a CF-100 Mk.IV off the Isle of Wight. *(Hawker Siddeley Canada Ltd., 64005)*

Endpapers For two decades the Norseman fulfilled general purpose duties in the RCAF until replaced by the Otter. Many Norsemen are still in use in Canada. *(Public Archives of Canada, PL49910)*

Page 1 In a montage created by William James, Ralph Johnstone, an American barnstormer, overflies the crowd at the 1910 air meet held at Toronto. *(James Collection, City of Toronto Archives)*

Title page D.H.9 bombers of No.2 Squadron, Canadian Air Force, in England just after World War I. *(Air and Space Division, National Museum of Science and Technology, 1561)*

Contents

Colour Illustrations

Foreword

I was honoured when asked by Larry Milberry to prepare the foreword to *Aviation in Canada*. This book is the first wide coverage of the topic for over a decade and includes much original material.

My own experience in aviation dates back to 1929 and spans such eras as barnstorming, bush flying, early airline operations, and the RCAF in World War II and the postwar years. Later on I retained my close association with flying through such organizations as the Canadian International Air Show, Canada's Aviation Hall of Fame, and the Canadian Aviation Historical Society. Thus have I come to know aviation reasonably well.

As I began reading Larry Milberry's manuscript it dawned on me that there was still plenty of Canadian aviation reading for me to catch up on. *Aviation in Canada* represents a tremendous job of research, going back to the very earliest balloon flights of over a century ago. From there on to the descriptions of the latest developments on the Canadian aviation scene the standard of writing remains high.

The end product is a well refined story of aviation in a country where the airplane has been prominent for so long. *Aviation in Canada* will take its place with the other fine books covering our aviation past.

Z. Lewis Leigh
Group Captain, RCAF (Ret'd)

Preface

Aviation in Canada is a general overview of Canadian aviation history. It gives just a sampling of the events which have occurred since 1840 when the first manned flight took place in this country. It includes much material never before published in a book; but it also includes many well-known stories which, because of their significance, could never be overlooked. With these I have endeavoured to locate new details or give a new slant. On the other hand, a great deal of Canadian aviation history does not appear in this book. This is the case, for example, with military aviation where the volume of history vastly exceeds the space available here.

Aviation in Canada is a photographic as well as a written history. The many photographs shown have originated from the lenses of casual snapshot takers and serious buffs alike. Others are from large private collections, and still others from archives or official sources. They represent the best collection of aircraft photographs available to author and publisher for our mutual objective, the physical limitations of the book considered. Personal credits are given wherever known; otherwise, credits mention the individual who may have provided a picture, the private collection from which it originated, or the archival or other source with reference number given if applicable.

Without the help of hundreds of people, *Aviation in Canada* could never have come about. Some people have provided information, leads, criticism, and support over the long run. Others contributed simple details like a date from

This little Junkers F-13 built in 1923 came to Canada in 1929. It operated on the West Coast and was eventually scrapped in 1938.
Aviation and Space Division, National Museum of Science and Technology (5037)

a log or some other missing link. No matter the degree, everyone's input has been vital. The result is truly a corporate effort wherein my role was primarily scrounger and organizer. To my numerous helpers, thanks!

My chief hope with *Aviation in Canada* is that it will entertain, inform, and perhaps stimulate the reader to delve further into our aviation heritage. I recommend that the reader have nearby a good atlas of Canada. This will assist greatly when names such as Thelon River, Deseronto, Rivière du Loup, and Caniapiscau arise!

I would like to thank these people for their support in providing material and back-up during the preparation of *Aviation in Canada:*

A.L. Berry; W.F. Burgener; J.C. Charleson; Ray Crone; Joanne Culley; John T. Dart; Bill Ewing; N.K. Found; R.H. Fowler; Douglas Froebe; F.W. Hotson; Sheila Jewell; Z.L. Leigh; Wess McIntosh; M.L. McIntyre; Jack McNulty; K.M. Molson; Merlin Reddy; Peter Robertson; A.J. Shortt; Tim Sims; Katharine Sergava Sznycer; L.C. Stevenson; Archie Vanhee; Carl Vincent; Les Wilkinson; as well as the following for their help: Tony Adams; Doug Anderson; Brian Aston; Ernest Ball; Russell Bannock; M.B. Barclay; Bob Beeton; Johnny Bergeron; Arnold H. Bent; Helen Bloor; Bob Bolivar; Denis Bradley; Dave Breese; Harry Bryant; Beth Buchanan; Bruce Campbell; P.D. Campbell; Claude Castonguay; Charlie Catalano; Neil Christenson; Murray Clearwater; Allan Coggon; Gilles Couillard; Joe Czumrik; John Davids; D.J. Davies; Major Al Ditter; Paul Dorfman; Brian Dunn; Captain Tim Dunne; Gath Edward; Frank H. Ellis; Gordon Emberley; Bruce Falkner; E.A. Fallen; Mike Farrell; Dennis Foley; S.R. Found; Claude Fournier; T.P. Fox; George A. Fuller; Ian Geddes; Paddy Gardiner; Walter Gilbert; John Gilpin; Bruce Gowans; Ernie Grant; R.S. Grant; John Griffin; A.T. Griffis; Wm. C. Haines; Robert Halford; Stan Haswell; V.J. Hatton; V.L. Hawkes; Francis Vernon Heakes; Robert Heaslip; Roy A. Heible; F.J. Henley; Harry Holmes; S.W. Horrall; David Hughes; Allan Hunt; Gordon Hunt; J.D. Hunter; Walter Hurst; Gordon Jarrett; Buck Johnson; R.A. Johnson; Phil Jones; S.R. Kaufman;

Captain Clive Ken; Ronald Keith; S.N. Knight; C.M. Konvalinka; Jacques Lacombe; Fred Lake; Jack Lamb; Rocky Laroche; Tony Leriche; Mary Lizette; J.D. Lowe; Charles Luehr; Mel Lundy; Dr. R.D. MacDonald; G.L. MacInnis; Norm Malayney; George Marlow; George Maude; Hugh McCallum; R.S. McCartney; W. McLaughlin; Don McClintock; V.H. McPherson; Sean McRory; Norbert Millar; Carl Millard; Alex. J. Milne; C. Morberg; Dr. A.E. Moss; A.J. Moul; Don Murray; Michael Mushet; Ken Nicolson; Herb Nott; Paul Ostrander; J.F.A. Painter; C.H. Parkin; John N. Paterson; J.S. (Pat) Patterson; H.B. Picken; D. Power; Hans Pulkkinen; Gordon Raynor; Paul Regan; Ross Richardson; Don Rogers; Buck Rogers; Geoff Rowe; K.D. Ruble; Ken Ruel; C.B. Sampson; A.W. Saunders; Peter Scargall; Vic Scheibler; Ivan Schlegel; John Schultz; Gordon Schwartz; H.W. Seagrim; Noreen Searson; Ralph Shapland; D.J. Sheppard; R. Murray Shorthill; R. Simard; Major Rae R. Simpson; Blake Smiley; Jean Smith; W.J.R. Smith; Slim Soule; A.F. Soutar; John Spronk; E.H. Staite; D. Starratt; George Stewart; J. Stubbin; F. Stullen; R.C. Thornber; Col. Bev. Totman; John Timmins; G. Townsend; A.C. Tuttle; Fernando Vachon; Fred Van Brussel; Margaret Van Every; D.J. Veale; Wm. Wheeler; Harry Whereatt; Ron Wiley; Al Wingate; F.G. Winters; Elwood White; Hugh Whittington; Gordon S. Williams; A.D. Wood; S.J. Woodham; C.E. Yauch.

The following archives, firms, government institutions and other organizations have also assisted in the preparation of *Aviation in Canada:* Air Canada; Alberta Forest Service; Archives of Ontario; Bell Aerospace Textron; CAE Industries Ltd.; CP Air; Canada Centre For Remote Sensing; Canadair Ltd.; *Canadian Aviation;* Canadian Aviation Historical Society; Canadian Forces (407, 424, 442, 437 Squadrons, 1 CAG, 116 A.T.U.); City of Toronto Archives; City of Vancouver Archives; Cominco; De Havilland Aircraft of Canada Ltd.; Department of National Defense, Directorate of History; Department of National Defense, Directorate of Information Services; Dominion Pegasus Helicopters Ltd.; Energy, Mines and Resources Canada; Environment Canada;

Glenbow-Alberta Institute; Government of the Yukon Territory; Hawker Siddeley Canada Ltd.; Heli Voyageur Ltd.; *High River Times;* Historical Society of Alberta; Imperial Oil; Imperial War Museum; Kenting Earth Sciences Ltd.; *Kitchener-Waterloo Record;* Labrador Mining and Exploration; Library of Congress; Library of Parliament; Life Picture Service; Lockheed Aircraft; Metropolitan Toronto Library Board; McDonnell Douglas Aircraft; Morrison Knudsen Co. Ltd.; National Air and Space Museum, Smithsonian Institution; National Aeronautical Establishment; National Museum of Science and Technology; National Research Council; New Brunswick Museum; Newfoundland Department of Tourism; Nordair; Okanagan Helicopters Ltd.; Ontario Ministry of Natural Resources; Pacific Western Airlines; Pan American World Airways; Pratt and Whitney Aircraft of Canada Ltd.; Province of Manitoba, Provincial Archives; Province of Saskatchewan, Air Transportation Service; Provincial Archives, British Columbia; Provincial Archives, New Brunswick; Provincial Archives, Prince Edward Island; Provincial Archives of Alberta; Provincial Archives of Nova Scotia; Public Archives Canada; James Richardson and Sons, Ltd.; Royal Canadian Flying Clubs Association; Royal Canadian Mounted Police; Saskatchewan Archives; Société d'Énergie de la Baie James; Saunders Aircraft; Society of Automotive Engineers; Statistics Canada; *Toronto Sun* Publishing Ltd.; Transair; Transport Canada; Trident Aircraft; United States Air Force; United Aircraft, Stratford, Connecticut; Wardair Canada Ltd.; Western Airlines; Western Canada Aviation Museum; Widerøe's; York University, Scott Archives.

I am grateful to the University of Toronto Press for permission to quote on page 22 from *Canada's Flying Heritage* by Frank H. Ellis (copyright Canada 1954 by University of Toronto Press).

Larry Milberry
Toronto, 1979

The Early Days: 1840-1914

J. Strobel's airship at Calgary, July 1908. Jack Dallas made several ascents in it over the city during the Calgary Exhibition but the ship was destroyed by fire during inflation after five days of successful flying displays.

Glenbow-Alberta Institute (NA-423-4)

The Beginnings: Ballooning

From the *New Brunswick Courier,* August 15, 1840:

"Mr. L.A. Lauriat, Professor of Chemistry and Aerostatic Exhibitions, respectfully announces to the Ladies and Gentlemen of St. John, that he will Monday next, 10th Aug., make a Grand Ascension in his splendid Balloon, the 'Star of the East,' within the Barrack Square — being his 36th ascension in America, and his first and only one in this province.

"The lower Barrack Gate will be opened at 1 o'clock, P.M. Inflation to commence at 2, and the Ascension will take place at 5 o'clock precisely. During the inflation, small Pioneer Balloons will be set off, to ascertain the direction of the wind.

"Tickets 2s 6d. Children half price. To be had at the Book Stores, Circulating Library, St. John and Commercial Hotels, and at the Lower Gate of the Barrack Yard.

"The arrangement is such, that those admitted within the enclosed space of ground, will have a full and interesting view of the Chemical Process of generating the prodigious quantity of Hydrogen Gas in the short space of two-and-a-half hours, and also of the whole Chemical Apparatus.

"Should the wind or weather prove unfavourable, the Ascension will take place on the next fair day.

"N.B. Ladies and Gentlemen who may wish to procure comfortable seats, protected from the crowd, for viewing the Inflation of the Balloon and suspension of the Car with its aeronauts, will please secure tickets (4s each) at the Saint John Hotel, Circulating Library and Book Stores. Entrance for the Select Seats by the upper gate, from the parade ground."

From the report in the *Courier,* August 15, Lauriat met with a successful ascension: "A few minutes after 5 o'clock on Monday afternoon, Mr. Lauriat commenced a grand ascension from the Barrack Square with his splendid balloon, 'Star of the East.' The evening was unusually clear, with a gentle breeze from the southwest, and the weather in every respect most propitious for the novel spectacle. The Parade Ground and most of the eminences from which a view of the balloon and its appendages could be obtained, were thronged with anxious spectators. Mr. L. frequently bowed and waved his hat from his fragile car, in acknowledging the plaudits of the gratified crowds. The Balloon took a northerly direction for a short time, and afterwards changed its course more to the east. It was in sight of town for nearly an hour, and the intrepid Aeronaut effected a safe landing in a field on Mr. Van Horne's farm, on the Quaco road, twenty-one miles from the City, in an hour-and-a-quarter from the time of starting. We understand that 7200 feet was the highest altitude which was gained, and that, when at that height, the thermometer, which was at 70 at starting, had fallen to 58.

"We are glad to find, that as the amount received for tickets of admission to witness the process of inflating the Balloon, and the making of other preparations, fell far short of defraying Mr. Lauriat's expenses, a subscription was got on foot and about $100 contributed in a short time. Mr. L. returned to Boston in the steamer *North America* on Thursday."

So it happened that on August 10, 1840, manned flight came to Canada. Louis Anslem Lauriat on that day became the first person to see Canada from the air.

Over the next few years the gas-filled balloon became a feature attraction at celebrations throughout the Canadas and the Atlantic colonies. As a rule, the aeronauts arrived here from the United States. Some were Europeans, and many referred to themselves as "professors."

In 1856 a celebrated French balloonist arrived in Montreal from Boston to conduct a series of flights. This was Eugène Godard, described in the context of his times as "le fondateur de la plus grande dynastie d'aéronautes de tous les temps." Godard had made his first ascent in a hot air balloon in 1847. His appearance in Montreal has been described by G.A. Fuller:

"Under the supervision of the aeronaut and his wife, a new balloon was fabricated in the Bonsecours Market building by a team of seamstresses hired through advertisements in city newspapers. On its completion the balloon *Canada* was placed on exhibition in the City Concert Hall in the same building, which can be called Canada's first aircraft factory.

"On September 8 the balloon was taken to a site adjacent to the City Gas Company works in Griffintown which was to provide the lifting power. Three local gentlemen, the first aerial passengers in Canada, joined Godard in the basket and the *Canada,* serenaded by a band and cheered by a huge crowd, climbed away on a pleasant journey that was to end with a successful landing in St. Mathias parish, Rouville County."

On his return to France, Godard continued his enthusiasm for flight and constructed many balloons. He demonstrated the usefulness of these as observation posts and mail carriers during the Franco-Prussian war, and before his death in 1890 had made over 500 successful ascents in almost every European country, as well as Cuba, the United States, and Canada.

Before long, other communities were being treated to this new rage in urban entertainment. Professor T.C. Lowe made an ascent in Ottawa during July, 1858. The following year that city again played host to balloon artists, but without their balloon! This episode had begun the evening of September 22 when Professor Jno. LaMountain ascended at Watertown, New York. With him aboard the *Atlantic* was a local newspaper editor, John Haddock. The balloon ascended quickly and everything seemed to be proceeding normally. Haddock was soon preoccupied with such things as the scenery below, his ringing ears, the increasing cold, and nausea brought on by escaping gas. Darkness fell, but although little could be seen, the aeronauts could hear barking dogs, wagons rolling over bridges, and locomotive whistles.

Eventually they made a precautionary landing and tied up to a tree in the forest. This didn't seem an ideal place, so, after disposing of most of his excess weight, the Professor was able to get airborne. The *Atlantic,* however, was soon down again, and the two travellers concluded that they were pretty well forest-bound. They had no idea where they were.

After dawn they began making their way through the woods. They carried on for the duration of the day, then rested. Their second day they constructed a crude raft in an attempt to float to civilization. After four days without food, the Professor and his editor friend at last met up with a party of forest surveyors who rescued them from their predicament. As to their whereabouts, the aeronauts discovered that they were 150 miles north of Ottawa!

After recuperating, LaMountain and Haddock set off towards Ottawa, via the Gatineau River system. It was nine days since they had ascended from Watertown. En route to Ottawa they detoured to the site of their landing. There they found the *Atlantic* in tatters. At last they reached Ottawa where, after the locals realized what celebrities they were, LaMountain and Haddock were treated like royalty. Next day they entrained for Prescott, thence on to Watertown where they had been long since given up as dead.

It was easy to determine by the time spent aloft that the balloon had gotten into wind which carried it northward at close to 100 mph! They had flown 300 miles in just four hours, though it had happened unwittingly. This was just the second aerial crossing of the Canada-U.S. border. The first had been made earlier that year by

John Steiner on a flight from Toronto to Oswego County, New York.

In 1861 Professor Lowe returned to carry out several other "grand balloon ascensions" in Canada West aboard the *Enterprize*. The first of these was scheduled for Hamilton on May 24. A big crowd showed up at the launch site, the Crystal Palace. Admission to watch the proceedings was 12-1/2 cents.

To everyone's chagrin, Lowe had to call off the flight because of high winds. Undaunted, he tried again on the twenty-ninth, this time from the Customs House, close by the city's gas supply. Again the crowd gathered for the mid-afternoon ascent, but the gassing up process took longer than expected. This led, predictably, to rumblings among the spectators.

Fortunately, Lowe eventually got off, taking with him R.C. Buscombe as passenger. The *Enterprize* floated up, up, and away. It was carried this way and that by the currents, but finally came to Earth about 20 miles south of Hamilton. The following day Lowe drifted on to St. Catharines where he tried to drum up some more business; but as no group could be found to promote an ascent, Lowe packed up his bag and returned to the United States where he worked as a balloonist in the Union Army.

The following year, 1862, a Professor Ayers carried out six ascents in Canada aboard the *Niagara*. These were at Hamilton, Toronto, London, and Montreal. At one of the two London ascents upwards of 8000 spectators were brought in aboard special excursion trains to witness the gala affair. Twenty-five cents each was paid for that privilege. At Toronto on August 19 Mrs. Ayers went along with her husband on the ascent. She was described as entering the basket "with as much composure as if she were about to take a drive through the streets, and not a sail into the realms of space." This ascent took the pair ten miles east of the city on a 90-minute flight. As was usually the case, the balloonists were greeted by local farmers upon their descent. As appreciation, the balloonist usually offered his helpers tethered ascents in the balloon.

The September 24 ascent from Toronto resulted in the huge balloon drifting out over Lake Ontario. Worse still, it could not gain altitude, forcing Ayers to dump ballast. Before long he was even disposing of items such as his overcoat! Fortunately, the balloon finally began to rise and carried Ayers into New York State.

During these pioneer years of flight in Canada, ballooning was more a spectator's curiosity than anything to be taken seriously, and in time the novelty seems to have worn off. Several more decades were to pass before flying in Canada was to gain any sort of stature.

Throughout this introductory period, there was at least one balloonist operating in Canada interested in the practical application of balloon flight. In August, 1883 Captain H. Elsdale, R.E., took the first aerial photo in Canada. The subject was part of the defences of Halifax, and the picture was taken from a small balloon at a height of 1450 feet. This and similar experiments were funded by Elsdale himself.

Heavier Than Air Machines

December 17, 1903, marked a historic event in man's age-old quest to fly. On that day, the Wright brothers successfully flew the first heavier-than-air flying machine. The Wrights had almost been preempted by Dr. S.P. Langley of the Smithsonian Institute. He had been experimenting with theories of flight and had constructed a powered aircraft. This he attempted to fly on December 8, 1903, but there were problems with the launch mechanism and the machine nosed into the Potomac River without getting airborne.

The Aerial Experiment Association

An associate of Langley's at this time was Alexander Graham Bell. Through Langley, Bell developed a keen interest in flight and had soon established a flight research centre at his home in Baddeck, Nova Scotia. This was not the first such centre in Canada, for in 1902, Wallace Rupert Turnbull had built a wind tunnel at his home near Saint John, New Brunswick. Here he experimented with air foils, hydrofoils, and propellers. This work culminated in Turnbull's greatest invention, the controllable pitch propeller.

In the summer of 1907, Bell started work at Baddeck into the principles of flight. Assisting him were two young college graduates, J.A.D. McCurdy and F.W. "Casey" Baldwin.

At first the would-be aviators experimented with kites towed aloft by a power boat over the waters of Bras d'Or Lake. They constructed a massive tetrahedral kite, *Cygnet* I, and managed to get it airborne on December 6, 1907. Aboard the huge red kite was Lt. Thomas Selfridge of the United States Army. He was present as an official observer of the U.S. government. Selfridge must be admired for his spirit of adventure in riding the *Cygnet* I, for the big glider had no means of control. After seven minutes aloft and soaring as high as 168 feet, down came *Cygnet* I. When it touched, a crewman on the boat was to sever the tow rope. This he failed to do and as it alighted, the glider, with its passenger, went under. Although

Members of the Aerial Experiment Association at Baddeck, N.S. Left to right: G.H. Curtiss of Hammondsport, F.W. Baldwin, C.E., of Toronto, Alexander Graham Bell, Lieutenant Thomas Selfridge, U.S. Army and John A.D. McCurdy, C.E.
Gilbert H. Grosvenor Collection of Alexander Graham Bell Photographs, Library of Congress
(LC-G9-38715-A)

Cygnet I was a total wreck, Selfridge emerged safely from his chilly dunking.

By this time the Bell group was a formal research body, the Aerial Experiment Association. Mrs. Bell had suggested the Association and had even put up $35,000 to finance it. The Association officially came into being in Halifax, September 30, 1907. Its official *raison d'être* was "for the purpose of carrying on experiments relating to aerial locomotion with the special object of constructing a successful aerodrome." This was further explained by Bell as a "co-operative scientific association, not for gain but for the love of the art and doing what we can to help one another."

Having developed and successfully flown kites, the AEA proceeded to the next logical step, to power one of its designs. At the time, aero engines were in a primitive phase of development. There just weren't any really efficient engines that produced ample power, yet were lightweight. With this in mind, the AEA enlisted the expertise of a motorcycle manufacturer from Hammondsport, New York, Glenn H. Curtiss.

That winter, the AEA relocated at Hammondsport, close to Curtiss' shops and with a large lake and suitable flying field nearby. At first the group continued its experiments with gliders, making some 50 flights. Then it was decided that each member should design his own machine for powered flight.

Selfridge's was the first of these and was dubbed *Red Wing*. On March 12, 1908, Baldwin flew the *Red Wing* for a total distance of 318 feet 11 inches. This was a truly historic flight. It was North American's first public demonstration of an airplane flight. Baldwin became the first Canadian and the first British subject to fly an airplane. Bell's remark on this was, "It was fine, but only to think, that it was made by a Canadian and not by an American."

On its second flight, five days later, the *Red Wing* was wrecked, but Baldwin escaped serious injury. His own design, the *White Wing,* came next. It differed from the *Red Wing* in that it employed a novel control feature. This comprised movable wingtip control surfaces for improved lateral stability. Some time later, the famous aviator, Henri Farman, dubbed these "ailerons." The *White Wing* first flew May 18. Later on, the other three flying members of the AEA made their first flights in the *White Wing*.

The *June Bug,* Curtiss' design, was next to fly. On July 4, 1908, the first award of the Scientific American Trophy was made to the AEA when the *June Bug* became the first airplane to fly a straightaway kilometre under test conditions. This was the first official flight of an airplane in North America. The *June Bug* was to complete over a hundred flights before Curtiss converted it into the world's first hydroplane and rechristened it the *Loon*. With this revised edition, the AEA met with little success, as the *Loon* did not get into the air.

The AEA experienced its first serious setback on September 17. That day, Selfridge was at Fort Myer, Virginia.

Orville Wright was demonstrating one of his machines to the U.S. Army. On one flight, with Selfridge as passenger, the plane crashed. Selfridge was killed, thus becoming the world's first aviation fatality. In spite of this loss, the AEA decided to continue its research and to extend its year-long mandate for an additional six months.

The Silver Dart

McCurdy's was the last AEA design to be completed. While the plane was being prepared, Bell and Baldwin returned to Baddeck and continued kite research. McCurdy's plane was named the *Silver Dart*. It had a 49-foot wing span, weighed 800 pounds fully loaded, and was powered by a 35 horse power Curtiss engine. It flew barely a tenth of a mile on December 6, 1908; but before long was being put to all sorts of tests, flying a mile and a half on one occasion.

In January, 1909, the *Silver Dart* was shipped to Baddeck and readied for more testing. There, on February 23, 1909, it took to the air as the first heavier-than-air machine to fly in Canada or in the British Empire. J. A. D. McCurdy was at the wheel for the historic event. His flight covered about half a mile. Of this event Bell wrote, "This may seem to be a small matter at the present moment; but when

The AEA's Drome No. 5 known as *Cygnet* II, seen at Baddeck on February 22, 1909.
Aviation and Space Division, National Museum of Science and Technology (7131)

flying machines have become common, and Aerial Locomotion a well-organized and established mode of transit, the origin of the art in Canada will become a matter of great historical interest, and people will look back to the flight made on February 23, 1909, as the first flight of a flying machine in the Dominion of Canada.'' On March 31, the Aerial Experiment Association was dissolved, as agreed, its chief objectives having been met.

Further Adventures

Over the next year, McCurdy and Baldwin pursued their aviation interests. On March 7, 1910, McCurdy flew *Baddeck No. 2* a distance of 20 miles on two flights totalling 39 minutes. On a flight over New York state, August 27, he transmitted the first ever air-to-ground telegraph message. On October 10 he was awarded Aero Club of America licence number 18.

The following January found McCurdy in Key West preparing for a flight to Havana. An eight thousand dollar prize awaited the first to fly the route. On January 30 he flew a Curtiss biplane off a local beach on a test hop; but no sooner had he become airborne than sightseers poured onto his landing place! On seeing this, McCurdy decided on the spot to push on for Cuba.

Out over the Florida Straits winged the plane, and faded from the view of those watching from the coast. Soon McCurdy was himself out of sight of land, this being another historical first in aviation. True, Bleriot had already crossed the English Channel, but his Calais to Dover course was a mere 18 miles, as compared to McCurdy's course of over 100 miles.

McCurdy was aloft for two hours and was within sight of the Cuban beaches when he ran into trouble. An oil leak forced him to cut his engine and land in the water. He was immediately picked up by a U.S. Navy vessel. President Gomez of Cuba sailed alongside to congratulate McCurdy.

That same day McCurdy put on an air show at Camp Columbia near Havana. Later he was entertained at a lavish dinner and presented with an envelope that was supposed to contain his prize money. Although McCurdy hadn't quite completed the flight, it had nonetheless been agreed to award him the prize. But when he opened the envelope later on, McCurdy found that it contained nothing more than scraps from a Havana newspaper!

McCurdy wasn't particularly downhearted at this trick. His thoughts were still on aviation and its future. Influenced by his Cuba excursion, he was led to comment, "Although not disposed to make any wild calculations . . . I am seriously impressed with the possibility of making intercontinental, transocean flights by aeroplane."

Charles Willard
at Scarborough Beach

McCurdy and Baldwin were just the first of a series of aviators and would-be aviators on the Canadian scene in 1909 and 1910. In 1909 Toronto saw its first airplane when Foster Charles Willard, one of the first Americans to fly, arrived in town with his Curtiss *Golden Flyer*. This was the original airplane to bear the now famous Curtiss name.

Barnstorming was popular in the early part of this century. Stunt flyers and wing walkers would appear at county fairs and carnivals to entertain the crowds. Willard became the first "barnstormer" when he was contracted to travel from New York to Toronto with the *Golden Flyer* to put on a demonstration at Scarborough Beach amusement grounds. There, a rather poor excuse for an airstrip was prepared in anticipation of the flying display.

The plane arrived August 28. That day a local paper reported on the preparation of the runway: "It terminates at the lake front, so when Willard starts the engine going, the aeroplane has either to fly, or he and the machine will get a dunking."

On September 2 an advertisement appeared in the Toronto press, announcing, "Willard Aeroplane Sails from Scarboro Beach to Niagara. To See the Season's Sensation Go to Scarboro Beach." This was a bit of a come-on. Although Willard may have fleetingly considered a lake crossing in the *Golden Flyer,* it was not his serious intent. Even so, the notice in the newspaper made this the first aerial exhibition in North America to be advertised. As it turned out, Willard's flight that evening got him no closer to Niagara than the end of his runway. The *Golden Flyer* failed to develop lift and ended up in Lake Ontario. A terse headline the following day read, "Airship Went Up and Airship Came Down."

Willard tried again on September 7, managing to get off this time. He flew out over the lake on a five-minute flight. It seems that he had planned to alight on the beach, but as this was crowded with sightseers, he was again forced to play amphibian. He set his machine down nicely in the water close to shore.

Willard's last Toronto flight took place September 11. This one was foreshortened by engine trouble, and the *Golden Flyer* was claimed by the lake for a third time! At this, Willard packed it in. In spite of his hard luck, and the disinterest of the Toronto press, Willard had made history. He went on to a famous aviation career that included the dubious honour of being the first aviator ever to be shot down. A farmer, angry at the noise of Willard's machine, fired at it, forcing Willard to land! Willard died in 1977 in California at the age of 93.

The Great Air Meets

The first Canadian air meet was held in Montreal in late June and early July of 1910. It was a widely promoted event and seems to have been well organized and financed. At the site chosen for the meet,

stands were erected to accommodate 10 000 spectators. Special trains were laid on and security arranged. The great French aviator, Count Jacques de Lesseps, and several pilots from the Wright organization arrived in town with their flying machines.

The air meet opened on June 27 with a seven-minute flight by the American, Walter Brookins. From then until July 5, spectators were offered an exciting program of aerial wizardry, including, on June 28, three machines in the air at the same time! More than 20 000 people at a time were on the grounds to witness these feats. With the meet a success, its promoters immediately travelled to Toronto to prepare for a similar extravaganza.

A Toronto headline on July 8 read, "Rapidly Preparing the Big Sky Ships at Weston." The site of the meet was the Trethewey Model Farm just northwest of the city. The arrival of one of de Lesseps' machines was also reported: "The Bleriot machine which came in this morning is covered with soot and dirt. By some unaccountable negligence on somebody's part, it was shipped from Montreal in an open flat car." This also resulted in the wings of the Bleriot being warped.

As at Montreal, the meet organizers were ready for the crowds. Security was to be provided by the Royal Canadian Dragoons who set up an elaborate field camp at the farm. "Not only will they patrol the grounds," reported the press, "but they will watch the surrounding country, to keep outsiders away, and to

prevent crowds from gathering in case any of the aviators come down unexpectedly." The Thiel Detective Agency was also on hand to discourage pickpockets.

De Lesseps and Ralph Johnstone got the air meet off to a start by short flights the evening of July 8. The Count's flight was graphically described in the *Toronto Star:*

"Six men held on to the framework with all their strength. They needed it to hold back the roaring machine which, with more power than any race horse, was straining to be off.

"Finally, the Count raised his hand, the men let go and the Bleriot bounded forward on its three wheels along the ground.

"It had not gone more than ten yards when the Count turned the wheel in front of him which raised the elevating tail at the rear, and the machine began to rise slowly and gracefully."

Each day saw a series of flights conducted by the aviators. There were five flights on July 10, 1910. On one takeoff run, Johnstone experienced trouble: "The machine was released and sped down the track. From the first moment, however, it rocked heavily and about three-quarters of the way down it jumped the track. The

McCurdy's Curtiss biplane being salvaged from the waters off Havana, January 30, 1911.
Aviation and Space Division, National Museum of Science and Technology (001308)

▲

The *Golden Flyer* was the first aircraft to bear Glenn Curtiss' name. It was also the first airplane in North America to be used barnstorming, and flew at Toronto in the summer of 1909.

Aviation and Space Division, National Museum of Science and Technology (10404)

gift of $500 and commented, "I consider that flight the big thing that we had tried in Canada in connection with aerial navigation. The distance travelled by La Scarabée and its intrepid owner last evening was greater than his previous flight across the English Channel."

Readying the airplane flown by McCurdy at the 1911 Toronto air meet. This machine had been built to McCurdy's specifications by the Queens Aeroplane Co. of New York and was powered by a 50 horse power Gnome engine. It was badly damaged by an accident during the Toronto meet.

James Collection, City of Toronto Archives

aviator tried to elevate the machine even as it was, but this was impossible and it simply plowed its way through the dust, and came to a dead stop in the middle of the runway."

One of the novelties the next day was when Johnstone threw a bottle wrapped in cloth out of his machine. When the bottle hit the ground there was a loud explosion. This was an early example of simulated bombing. The explosion was some coordinated pyrotechnics likely provided by the militia.

On July 12 the American aviator Stratton was up in de Lesseps' warped Bleriot when he lost control and crashed. Stratton was not injured, but had to be extricated from a tree, 30 feet above ground.

Next day de Lesseps made the first flight over Toronto, as he had done over Montreal. He was aloft for 28 minutes in his Bleriot, *La Scarabée.* For this achievement, W.G. Trethewey made the Count a

▼

So it went until the meet closed on July 17. Thousands of spectators had come to Trethewey's farm to see airplanes for the first time in their lives. Yet in spite of large crowds, the promoters of the show complained that they lost money, with total expenses running to $35 000.

This same year saw the introduction of flight at other centres across Canada. The aviators were usually barnstormers from south of the border. Charles Hamilton made the first flight in Western Canada on March 25, 1910, when he soared aloft at Minoru Park, Vancouver. His exhibition lasted four days and included a race with a car and one with a horse. Hamilton lost both. On March 26 he made a cross-country flight up the Fraser River to New Westminster and back.

That summer Winnipeggers got their first look at an airplane when Eugene Ely put on a flying display July 15. The day was really too gusty for his flimsy machine, but he went up regardless in order to keep the fee-paying natives from getting too restless. His second flight resulted in a crash. This was reported next day in far-off Toronto as Canada's first serious flying accident. The report had Ely near death,

but in fact he had escaped with only a few scratches.

The following summer saw further exhibitions. There was another air show in Vancouver which resulted in embarrassment for the fliers who suffered a series of unfortunate crackups. Hugh Robinson flew at the Edmonton Horse Show; Bob St. Henry at Saskatoon and Regina. Strobel and Le Van flew Willard's revamped *Golden Flyer* at Calgary. At Winnipeg, Frank Coffyn raced a motorcycle and a car, beating both.

The outstanding events of the 1911 flying circuit were the air meets at Hamilton and Toronto. The Hamilton meet was widely promoted, as illustrated by this invitation in the Toronto papers: "Take the Fine New Steamer Turbinia Tomorrow to Hamilton, 50¢ Return." The initiators of the event were McCurdy, Willard, and J.V. Martin. The meet got under way July 27. McCurdy made a successful flight, but Martin had trouble and made a forced landing some distance from the field. It carried on until August 2, with spectators being treated to many thrills. One of these took place on July 29, a windy day and was reported in the *Globe:* "Charles Willard made an ascent in the evening before the gale had subsided. He was blown about and at one time it was feared that his biplane would be turned on its end and that he would land in a boat on the bay, but he managed to regain the land. He was forced to descend in the marsh a short distance from the bay. The front of the machine was smashed and Willard was cut about the legs."

On the evening of August 2 McCurdy and Willard prepared for a flight to Toronto where they were to perform at another air meet. The resulting flight has

been described as Canada's first air race. While both machines had seven-cylinder 50 horse power Gnome engines, McCurdy's was generally accepted to be the faster. McCurdy gave Willard a headstart towards Toronto. Depending on which Toronto paper one read, different results appeared. The *Globe* made much of the air race story, and placed McCurdy as winner after a 32-minute flight. It reported Willard as arriving in 45 minutes. McCurdy landed on Fisherman's Island at the east end of Toronto Bay, while Willard alighted at the Exhibition grounds.

The *Star* reported Willard as arriving first, making no mention of a race, and suggested that Willard made a headstart in his slower plane to rendezvous with Mc-Curdy over Toronto, so that McCurdy could show him the way to the Donlands Farm landing field. As it turned out, when the two aviators arrived over the city it was so smoggy that the flight to the farm could not be completed. McCurdy reported, "It became so smokey and so dark that I could hardly see anything. I could not see to King Street. I also concluded that it would be folly to attempt to fly up the valley of the Don River and land at Donlands Farm."

The Toronto meet got under way on August 3. The beginning was not too auspicious, for on a takeoff run McCurdy cracked up. The Donlands Farm landing field was rough, and while attempting to take off, "the biplane with the navigator dropped to the right side, the wing striking the ground."

Large crowds turned up the first two days. Nonetheless, the air meet came to a sudden halt when the fliers refused to carry on. The press reported, "The attitude of the McCurdy-Willard Aeroplane Company is that the field which has been secured for

Billy Stark of Vancouver in his Curtiss machine. Stark learned to fly at the Curtiss school in San Diego in 1912. He made his first flight in Canada on April 12, 1912 at Minoru Park. On April 24, sitting on the wing and holding onto the struts, Stark's wife, Olive, went up as a passenger for a six-minute flight. She thus became the first woman to fly in Canada aboard a powered airplane. In this photo Stark is seen at Armstrong, B.C. at Dominion Day celebrations. Some 4000 turned out to see him fly.

Provincial Archives, Victoria, B.C. (33372)

the meet at Donlands Farm was totally unfit for the machines.''

While Willard's Scarborough Beach flights of 1909 had not been too enthusiastically received, within two years such events were drawing huge crowds and headlines in the press. The public was enchanted by flying. At the Donlands Farm meet, Willard was to take passengers for short hops and the press noted, ''The Aviation Committee have received a large number of applications from citizens, and not a few from ladies of the Toronto smart set who are desirous of enjoying the exhilaration of a flight in the air.'' Otherwise, local retailers capitalized on the event. A Simpson's department store advertisement on August 4, 1911, read, ''Heavier than air, yet how it flies. Record flight in furniture selling.''

Barnstormers Across the Land

Barnstorming continued to be popular for the remainder of the pre-war years. George Mestache, a French aviator, performed at Quebec in 1911. His Bleriot was the first airplane to fly over that historic city. Didier Masson was contracted by the *Calgary Herald* to perform. He planned a flight from Calgary to Edmonton. After some preliminary hops, Masson took off October 26, 1911, Edmonton-bound. But his flight was brief. After his gas tank fell on top of him and his propeller broke, he decided to call it quits.

In 1912 Billy Stark of Vancouver emerged as another Canadian barnstormer. He went to San Diego where he learned how to fly at the Curtiss school there. He then bought his own plane, and on April 20 put on his first public demonstration, flying from Minoru Park on Vancouver's Lulu Island. Four days later his wife, sitting on the wing and holding onto the struts for dear life, became the first woman to fly in Canada aboard a heavier-than-air-machine. Stark performed at various shows around British Columbia, and, as seems to have been standard procedure, took his fair share of lumps.

Prairie communities continued to thrill to the antics of the barnstormers. Winnipeggers watched Sam Tickell fly, then come down with unintended

abruptness. Later on, they craned their necks to Hillery Beachey flying Sam's patched up and modified machine. That was on May 24, 1912, the same date Charles Saunders made Canada's first parachute jump from an airplane. That event took place in Vancouver from a plane piloted by Phil Parmalee.

The following year, a husband and wife team also performed at Vancouver. They were Americans, John and Alys Bryant. On July 31, Alys soloed in the plane, thus becoming the first woman pilot to fly in Canada. A few days later, her husband also entered the record book. His plane disintegrated in flight, and he became Canada's first aviation fatality.

John Bryant was one of hundreds of aviators who had lost their lives in early flying accidents. This in spite of the fact that the art was only a decade old, and still a rarity. Frank H. Ellis notes that in 1912, 122 aviators died in flying accidents. World War I, dealt with later, was to put a temporary halt to this form of madness, while introducing a new one.

George Mestach's Morane monoplane, ➤ crashed at Winnipeg after encountering wind gusts on takeoff, July 11, 1912.
Province of Manitoba, Provincial Archives, Foote Collection (893)

Commercial Aviation

Early Commercial Flying: Barnstorming

With World War I over, Canadians overseas began heading home, veterans of the first large-scale modern conflict. They had been trained to handle sophisticated war weapons including, for the first time ever, the airplane. Of Canadian returnees, over 2000 were trained combat pilots.

For most of those affected by demobilization, it was back to Civvy Street. Back to the office, back to school, back to the farm — whatever people had been doing before their normal routines had been so rudely interrupted by war. Of the aviators, not many would ever again listen to the wind in the wires; for neither military nor civil aviation counted for much in Canada in 1919.

Nonetheless, a few managed to get hold of a pair of wings and set off to actually earn a living in the air. This was an extension of the romance that had begun at Deseronto or Long Branch and had taken them in wild *mêlées* over the French countryside, just a short while ago.

At first there was really only one way to earn money flying and that was by barnstorming — picking up where the Willards and McCurdys had left off a few years earlier. What this meant was a lot of dollar-a-minute joy riding, dropping in at fairs and exhibitions anywhere in the country to hustle rides among the crowds. The stunt flying and wing walking of the barnstormers soon became standard fare wherever crowds gathered outdoors. The planes were usually JN-4 Canucks or Avro 504's, hundreds of which were war surplus.

One operation during these times was Canadian Aerial Services which began with an Avro 504. Canadian Aerial Services offered a variety of activities around Montreal including passenger hopping, parachute jumping and racing cars at fairs, and aerial photography. At one point American bootleggers tried to hire its planes to smuggle booze to the United States.

Out West, Harry Fitzsimmons became a famous barnstormer. As with all barnstormers of the day, his operation didn't last too long, but during its short life, many an exciting event occurred including almost losing one JN-4 in a storm; having a prop smashed by a bird strike, followed by a forced landing during which the plane flipped over; and having the plane damaged by a bull at the local rodeo. Fitzsimmons wrote about wing walking in his memoirs, *The Sky Hoboes:* "The reason I started these wing walking feats was that in 1920 we were late getting into the field and I found most of my competitors were bidding for fair contracts. As a newcomer, I had to devise a scheme to beat them to it in order to keep my company in operation. Palmer and I then started to train quietly. One of our favourite places was over Henderson Lake when few people were around. We practiced the top and bottom plane work first and devised a set of signals. As we were both practical airmen, we knew the effect of strain and balance on the wings and how to work together. After I disappeared from sight underneath the plane, Palmer was to give me one minute and a half and if at the end of that time I did not reappear he

would figure that I was exhausted or otherwise unable to get back up. He was then to come down as close to the lake as possible, and pull the plane almost up to a stall. This would allow me to drop in the lake and chances were that I would come out unharmed. That was the plan — if we had used it, which we never did. As I have always been something of an athlete, the balancing and climbing came quite easily to me."

Many a barnstormer ended up with his plane a pile of rubble somewhere in the countryside, but Fitzsimmons managed to wind up his operation with an enviable safety record. He reported that, "During our two years we never had a single instance where a passenger has not left our machine as an enthusiastic booster for aviation."

In Saskatchewan, Stan McClelland reintroduced barnstorming. On April 28, 1919, he loaded Saskatchewan's first passenger, a woman, and roared off across his field. All would have gone nicely had someone not left a car parked in McClelland's path. The Canuck cracked up, but fortunately without injuries. Someone passed the hat and $200 was collected as a downpayment on a replacement aircraft.

Roland Groome was a friendly competitor of McClelland's. Groome had two firsts to his credit. He received the first commercial pilot's licence issued in Canada; and his Jenny, G-CAAA, displayed the first registration allotted by the Canadian Air Board. It was registered on April 20, 1920.

On May 19, Groome flew from Saskatoon to Regina, making stops en route for gas. In his history of Stan Mc-Clelland, Ray H. Crone remarks on one of the incidents of the flight, so typical of the day: "In taking off from Davidson, the plane caught a barbed-wire fence and tore out a number of posts." Perceiving little damage, however, Groome decided to continue southward to Regina.

For two or three seasons, the planes of McClelland and Groome barnstormed across southern Saskatchewan. They introduced aviation to dozens of prairie communities, to places like Eston, Leader, Wilkie, Cutknife, and Unity.

Stan McClelland was involved in another flying venture at the same time he was barnstorming. Between 1919-1922 he operated a flying school to train young Chinese. This was part of a scheme to provide aviators for Sun Yat-sen's forces in China. The program was supported in Canada by the Chinese National League.

An airfield was set up close to Mc-Clelland's field, and a hangar erected with the inscription "Keng Wah Aviation." As recorded by Crone, "Douglas Fraser was hired as the first instructor-pilot to handle the training on the Curtiss JN-4 aircraft which had been ordered through Lieutenant Stan McClelland. Mr. Stanley Bing Mah was to interpret the instructions in theory of flight, airmanship, and aero engines which would be taught the Chinese students." Eventually 17 Chinese fliers were trained at Saskatoon.

During this period, tragedy struck. On October 9, 1921, an American daredevil named Reese was to transfer by rope ladder from one JN-4 to another while flying over downtown Regina. Crone writes, "As Reese climbed up onto the top wing of Groome's JN-4, he was seen to grasp the bottom rung of the rope ladder, float free from the bottom of the aircraft for a moment, then lose his grip on the rope, and plunge to his death some 500 feet below."

McCall's famous landing at the Calgary Exhibition, July 5, 1919. The event was described in the *Calgary Herald,* "With the power suddenly lost from his machine, Capt. McCall was forced to choose as a landing either the race track, on which auto demons were speeding at breakneck speed, or the midway, crowded with thousands, or the centre pole and guy cables of the merry-go-round." Neither pilot nor his two young passengers, Ronald and Herbert Richardson, were injured. The incident prompted the *Herald* to comment that "It was a wonderful exhibition of daring aviation, quick thinking, and pluck."

Glenbow-Alberta Institute (NA-1451-27)

Another early barnstormer was aviator and historian Frank H. Ellis. He has described some of his barnstorming experiences in his well-known book, *Canada's Flying Heritage:*

"When the great day arrived, the whole town was agog, and schools were sometimes closed to give the kids a chance to be on hand. Then as the roar of our engine was heard, and we dropped low, flying at roof-top level along Main Street, the entire populace and all the dogs turned out, racing to the field. In 'tin lizzies,' buggies, and wagons, on horseback, on bicycles, and on foot, they poured along the highway. Usually the first to arrive was a breathless youngster who triumphantly thrust a ragged but precious handbill into the pilot's hand.

"Occasionally we arrived unheralded, and after flying over a few times at a very low level to arouse interest, we selected a suitable landing spot. A crowd arrived like magic, and soon it was all we could do to keep people from swarming all over the plane, while trying to answer a thousand and one questions at the same time.

"Wop" May's JN-4 which he rented from the City of Edmonton for $25 a month, and used to fly newspapers to outlying centres. Like most early attempts to find commercial uses for the airplane in Canada, this one was short-lived. May returned the aircraft to the city then went into partnership with Harry Adair in a venture to fly furs out of the Northland, using a Jenny purchased in the United States.

Provincial Archives of Alberta (Acc. 68.78/10b)

"They were showing war trophies in the old Horse Show Building on Georgia St. That gave me the idea to get an airplane up here to add to the attraction. W.E. Boeing of Seattle came up and thus it came about that the first air mail to leave Canada for the United States left Coal Harbour, Vancouver. It was a stunt of mine, 3rd March, 1919. R.G. (Bob) Macpherson, former M.P., was postmaster. When I asked him if it would be possible for me to send mail to Seattle by airplane he replied, 'Yes, I'll give you a new mail sack; then he can keep it afterwards. The Royal Vancouver Yacht Club gave Mr. Boeing permission to anchor his plane at their float. The Mayor of Vancouver wrote letters to the Mayor of Seattle, and things like that, and we took the new clean white mail sack down, and in the presence of W.A. Turquand, many years manager, Hotel Vancouver; Chief Constable Wm. McRae; and J.T. Little, director, Vancouver Exhibition; and Stuart Thomson, photographer, I handed Mr. Boeing the mail sack; the first air mail out of Canada." Thus did E.S. Knowlton describe Canada's first international air mail flight. This was one of numerous early flights which helped lay a foundation for commercial aviation in Canada. Here pilot Eddie Hubbard and W.E. Boeing prepare to leave Vancouver for their three hour flight to Seattle.

City Archives, Vancouver, B.C.

"At fairs and exhibitions, stunting and wing walking were routine. The latter which was usually the mechanic's role consisted of climbing out of one's seat when the airplane was in flight, and parading back and forth along the front of the wings, on either side of the fuselage . . . . It was necessary to remain in front of the wings as the strong blast of air while flying at approximately 75 mph would have been rather too much for anyone trying to hang onto the back edges of the wings . . . . Sitting astride the fuselage behind the rear seat was another pet exploit of many of us who wished to give the spectators below an added thrill and it did, as we whipped by over their heads at a very low height . . . Many of the more daring of the wing walkers, with stiffer nerves and muscles than I possessed, would climb down from the undercarriage and hang there by both hands as the plane sped over the heads of the crowd below."

Barnstorming was a risky business at the best of times. Pilots were forever killing themselves, and there were even instances when spectators died as aircraft smashed into the ground. In time there was a public outcry against the daredevil pilot. As well, the government soon began tightening up on regulations governing stunt flying. It was only a matter of time before most of the fair-hopping JN-4 pilots were out of business.

An editorial in the *Ottawa Citizen,* September 9, 1920, echoes the sentiments of a concerned public: "The aeroplane crash at Shawville is another reminder that there is a useful place for civil aerial transport, but none for stunting at fairs. Aviation can be demonstrated safe, perhaps as safe as motoring or train

Aeromarine's civilianized F-5-L moored near the Toronto Harbour Commission, May 14, 1921.

Toronto Harbour Commissioners Archives

travelling on properly organized lines of service over distances. But it is no more reasonable to expect the aeroplane to perform stunts at fairs without accidents than it would be to entertain passengers in motor cars by looping the loop, or to carry people on the cowcatcher of a locomotive. Perhaps the Canadian Air Board may find means to head off the possibility of public confidence being destroyed in aviation — as well as to safeguard unwary citizens from unnecessary risk in the air. It should be against the law to perform stunts in an aerial conveyance for hire, as it is to trespass on railway tracks or to speed on thoroughfares.''

Other Ventures

Other ''war surplus'' pilots directed their talents towards ventures less flamboyant than barnstorming. Billy Bishop V.C., wrote *Winged Warfare,* the story of his fighting experiences. He went on the lecture circuit; was offered a job teaching; then one selling cars. He bided his time until W. G. Barker happened along, and the two famous V.C. winners formed a partnership, the Bishop-Barker Company. With two such famous names the company didn't have much trouble raising capital, and was soon operating a used-Canuck

dealership at the old Armour Heights training school. They branched into an early version of charter flying with their air taxi service between Toronto Bay and the Muskoka summer resort region to the north. Curtiss HS-2L flying boats were used, and as many as five passengers at a time were reported to have been crammed into the front cockpit (it was supposed to hold only two or three)! With the sort of airplane being used and the small load factor, plus the fact that one of the Bishop-Barker machines crashed, this gamble soon went by the wayside. We next find the Bishop-Barker concern in the business of painting streetcars for the newly formed Toronto Transit Commission. Unlike the flying end of things, this actually paid!

Among the misfortunes of the Bishop-Barker enterprise were at least two unscheduled landings. A pilot, engineer, and two passengers were on board an HS-2L, G-CADB on the Orillia-Toronto flight which alighted in trees near Brooklin, Ontario on September 10, 1920. Fortunately, no one was badly hurt. One newspaper report of the incident quoted the pilot as claiming that there would have been no problem had the trees not been in the way, as the flying boat was quite capable of landings either on water or on land!

The following May, there was further bad publicity when one of the firm's HS-2L's made a forced landing in Lake Ontario. Of this the *Globe* reported,

''Running out of gasoline, a seaplane belonging to the Bishop-Barker Company, and containing Col. Barker, V.C. and two other occupants, was compelled to light on the lake near Scarboro Bluffs and about a mile off shore yesterday afternoon. The party was bound for Belleville on a trial trip. The plane was one of the latest acquisitions of the company. It was thought that there was sufficient petrol to carry it to Oshawa for replenishment.

''The supply, however, gave out when the machine was over the lake but fortunately near enough to land to be observed by Constable Stevens, who telephoned the Life Saving Station at Ward's Island.''

Toronto recorded another early milestone in commercial aviation on May 14, 1921, when an Aeromarine 75 ''Flying Cruiser'' landed on Toronto Bay. It was en route from Havana to Detroit via Washington, New York and Montreal. The pilot of the plane was Theodore L. Tibbs, an ex-Torontonian. Over the previous winter he had operated between Havana and Key West, completing 96 trips.

The ''Flying Cruiser'' was a great attraction during its brief stopover in Toronto. One headline read, ''Giant Air Cruiser Visits Toronto, Makes Trip From Belleville in One Hour and Forty Minutes.'' It was described in detail for the benefit of those for whom ''giant air cruisers'' were a novelty: ''There are two cabins on the Santa Maria, and the ap-

pointments are luxurious the interior being finished in mahogany and silver. There are six comfortable reclining chairs in the forward cabin, while the after cabin is fitted up as a lounge and smoking room with seating accommodation for five and conveniences for card-playing or writing.''

Before leaving for Buffalo Tibbs commented, ''We would start a service between Toronto and Buffalo if Toronto were wet.''

Tibbs' company, Aeromarine West Indies Airways, is credited as America's first genuine airline. It had begun operations in October, 1920 using six modified F-5-L flying boats, first used on the Key West-Havana run. By 1922 the airline was also operating on the Great Lakes, flying between Cleveland and Detroit.

Historic Firsts

In 1920, the Canadian Air Board was constituted. It promised to bring order and rationale to the country's small commercial flying ventures and began immediately to licence pilots and register aircraft.

During these boom days of aviation in Canada, various noteworthy ''firsts'' were recorded. On August 7, 1919, Captain Earnest Hoy flew in a JN-4 from Minoru Park in Vancouver, to Calgary, where he

alighted 16 hours, 42 minutes later. Over 12-1/2 hours had been spent in the air. Thus, for the first time, Canada's western mountain region had been traversed by air.

In 1920, the Air Board sponsored a project to conduct the first-ever trans-Canada flight. The Air Board was anxious to determine the feasibility of such flights, as it was already investigating the possibility of future air mail and passenger operations. A proving flight would give valuable experience in route planning, and in dealing with the peculiarities of weather and topography in the various regions overflown. It was also hoped that public interest in aviation might be fired up by a trans-Canada flight. In the long run, this was important if the public was ever to accept flying as a viable means of travel.

The actual flight got under way October 7, 1920 from Halifax, with a Fairey seaplane piloted by Lt. Col. Leckie and Major Hobbs. Their leg of the trip was cut short after a forced landing at St. John, New Brunswick. An HS-2L was brought in to replace the Fairey. Leckie and Hobbs then carried on to Rivière du Loup where a landing was made in pitch darkness on the St. Lawrence.

From there an F.3 flying boat carried pilots and engineer across the rugged Canadian Shield to Winnipeg via Ottawa,

The F.3 flying boat on the Red River at St. Vital, Manitoba, October 1920. Leckie and Hobbs had flown this aircraft on the Rivière du Loup-Winnipeg section of the first trans-Canada flight.

DND (AH-88)

North Bay, Sault Ste. Marie, Kenora, and Selkirk.

At this point the seaplane was exchanged for three D.H.9 landplanes, as the land of lakes was now behind, and the dry, flat plains lay ahead. After various setbacks, one of the D.H.9's made it to Calgary on the eleventh. Two days later, pilots Tylee and Thompson bucked heavy winds to make Revelstoke where they were weathered in until the fifteenth. That day, again wind-buffeted, they were able to reach Merritt in the British Columbia interior. On the seventeenth, plane and crew, all three well worn, finally made it to Vancouver. Eleven days had passed, 45 hours spent aloft, and 3265 miles covered! Canada's first transcontinental flight was history. To air-minded people of the day, it would now be only a matter of time before practical flights across the country became reality.

During this same busy time, the visionaries could see the beginnings of air links on an intercontinental scale. The year

1919 saw three historic trans-Atlantic crossings. On May 8, three Navy-Curtiss flying boats set course from Far Rockaway, New York, for Trepassey Bay, Newfoundland. This was the first leg of an attempted Atlantic crossing. All three machines eventually arrived in Newfoundland and pushed on for the Azores. This was to be a near-disastrous leg, for one aircraft was sunk after a precautionary landing; and another was badly damaged by heavy seas. It managed to taxi safely to the Azores. The third aircraft was the only one to reach Lisbon, then Plymouth, where the adventure terminated. This aircraft, the NC-4, thus became the first aircraft to fly the Atlantic. The following month saw the first ever non-stop aerial crossing of the Atlantic. On June 14 two British aviators, Alcock and Brown, took off from Quidi Vidi, Newfoundland, in their Vickers Vimy. Sixteen hours, 12 minutes later they landed in Ireland, winners of the £ 10 000 *London Daily Mail* prize for the first aviators to fly the Atlantic non-stop.

The Vickers Vimy at Quidi Vidi, Newfoundland, June, 1919. Captain John Alcock and Lieutenant Arthur Whitten Brown flew this aircraft to Ireland on the first non-stop flight across the Atlantic Ocean of a heavier-than-air machine.

Public Archives of Canada (PA 72433)

The same year, the first east-west aerial crossing of the Atlantic was made. On July 2, the R-34 airship left England, and 108 hours later moored at Mineola, Long Island. These were the first successful Atlantic crossings, the first of a series of flights and attempted flights that were to capture the headlines in the years ahead.

The Airplane Goes North

Immediately after the war, the first concerted efforts to find a civilian use for the airplane were undertaken. The focus of this venture was the vast timber tracts along the north shore of the St. Lawrence River and its tributaries. Over these forests, the art of aerial surveying was to be introduced. In Labrador, a beginning had already been made in this field. There, in 1919, a Canadian firm, H.V. Green Aerial Survey Co. Ltd., conducted a forest survey for the Southern Labrador Pulp and Paper Co. of Boston.

The expedition was assembled at Annapolis, Nova Scotia, and in early July sailed aboard the steamer *Granville* under Daniel Owen, an RFC veteran. After arriving in Labrador and setting up camp, two JN-4's were put to work. Five American pilots were employed. Flying conditions were favourable, and within ten days, the job was complete. Some 15 000 aerial photos had been taken.

Just at this time, the Canadian forest industry was beginning to consider the uses of the airplane in forestry patrol work. In March of 1919 the Canadian Forestry Journal was lamenting that Quebec's plan to introduce airplanes was not being encouraged by Ottawa, "even though public-owned hydro-planes are lying useless in their hangars in Nova Scotia and skilled pilots are kicking their heels and aching for some form of active service." The Quebec proposals soon led to the formation of the St. Maurice Forestry Protective Association. It succeeded in acquiring two of the surplus ex U.S. Navy HS-2L's stored at Dartmouth and had them ferried by Stuart Graham to Lac à la Tortue near Grandmère. The two planes were placed in service during 1920. Crews were kept busy over the season spotting for forest fires and with aerial sketching, photography, and transporting fire-fighters and their gear.

It was soon obvious that such uses of the airplane could provide the industry with vital services which, using traditional means of getting around, took much longer to perform or, in cases, were out of the question. For example, a sweep over a tract of forest provided the aerial surveyor with an immediate bird's eye view of what lay below — the general character of the forest, its extent and accessibility. Maps could be sketched and photos taken, classifying tracts by tree type and degree of

maturity. Future camp and plant sites could also be determined, and gravel deposits and water storage areas located and plotted. Routes for future roads, railroads, and transmission lines could also be much more readily determined from the air. As well, the airplane extended the surveyor's reach into areas never before explored. The forest companies in Quebec were quickly sold on this new concept and aerial surveying there began expanding.

The original St. Maurice operation gave way to Laurentide Air Service Ltd. In 1922 Laurentide won a big Ontario government contract. The following year twelve H-boats were employed in forestry patrol, covering 20 000 square miles of

resource management led to the development of other operations. From 1920 to 1923 Price Brothers operated three Martinsyde biplanes on forest service flights.

Chief pilot for Price Brothers was H.S. Quigley. Before long, he set out on his own and formed Dominion Aerial Exploration, flying HS-2L's. About the same time, the Ontario Paper Company was using aircraft along the North Shore, and another firm, Fairchild Aerial Surveys of Canada, had come onto the scene. Although hard times were soon to beset aviation, it was these pioneer ventures which laid a solid grounding for commercial aviation in Canada.

owned or chartered by the big oil companies are an everyday sight in the North. Those who fly the Twin Otters or 737's, though, were predated by a handful of pioneers. Interestingly enough, the locale for their flying was the Mackenzie River Valley. This region had been legendary for its oil deposits since the 1800s and the oil had been known to the Native People of the region in pre-history.

Big oil finds had been made along the Mackenzie River right after World War I, setting off a mad rush of fortune seekers into the region. "Black gold" had them tripping over one another in their enthusiasm to share in the bonanza. Chief of the oil properties to be developed along the

The Dayton-Wright F.P.2 seen at Biscotasing, northern Ontario during 1922. It was the only F.P.2 ever built and had been designed expressly for aerial surveying. Registered N-CAED, it operated for the Spanish River Pulp and Paper Co. The aircraft was wrecked at Michipicoten Harbour on Lake Superior on September 28, 1922 when a float gave way on takeoff.

Province of Ontario, Ministry of Natural Resources

forest in a vast territory stretching from Lake-of-the-Woods to James Bay. Some 550 passengers were carried and 400 forest fires reported. Otherwise, Laurentide surveyed 39 000 square miles of Northern Ontario timber for the Spanish River Pulp and Paper Company.

In Quebec, use of the airplane in forest

Oil Exploration Down the Mackenzie

Today no one questions the need for airplanes in resource development. Mineral surveying, remote sensing, transport back-up for oil exploration or some big scheme like James Bay — these are everyday services provided by the airplane in Canada. The tendency is to associate these uses with modern times but their roots actually lie over half a century ago. Even in 1920 there were some grandiose schemes to put commercial aviation on a large-scale, money-making basis.

Recently much Northern flying has been spurred by exploration and development of energy resources. Aircraft

river were those of Imperial Oil near Fort Norman.

Newspapers headlined activities in the oil fields — they were wildly optimistic! "Great Oil Field Found in Northland," "Gas for 500 Years," and, "Run Pipe Line to Bering Sea, Ambitious Project to Get Oil from Mackenzie Basin." The latter, a CP dispatch of December 8, 1920, went: "Conveyance of the oil products of the Mackenzie River Basin to the Bering Sea by pipe line, from where it would be carried by tankers to the markets of the world, is an ambitious project for which sanction will be sought by a bill to be considered by Parliament at the approaching session."

Equally attracted as the prospectors were by the smell of oil were those who specialized in transportation services. The oil rush created an overnight boom for the steamship companies which plied the lakes and rivers from McMurray down; but the possibility for cashing in on the northward movement of men and supplies didn't elude those who saw a future for the airplane in Canada. In February, 1921, the following article appeared in the press, "Air Routes to Far North Oil Belt Proposed: F.G. Ericson, the Toronto birdman, has announced his intentions of operating a flying service between Great Slave Lake and Fort Norman on a commercial basis." Ericson was well known in aviation circles, having been chief engineer at Canadian Aeroplanes, and thereafter a dealer in surplus airplanes and a member of the Air Board. The news article proceeded to outline the proposed scheme of another experienced aviation figure of the day, E.L. Janney. This was the same fellow who, in 1914, had become Canada's first military aviator. His was a rather imaginative scheme: "A dirigible capable of carrying about thirty passengers will be put on the Edmonton-Mackenzie route, according to Captain Janney's plan, in March." The fare was quoted at $1500 for the return trip from Fort McMurray.

Two other notable proposals were publicized about the same time. One was to be operated by a firm headed by F.R. McCall, an ex-fighter ace with 37 enemy planes to his credit. The firm's newspaper advertisement read as follows, "Fly to Fort Norman in absolute safety and comfort for what it costs to hire guides and buy outfit. Flying time about eight hours each way. Two six-passenger Flying Boats of a stable, safe type, approved by the British Air Board, to be placed in scheduled service between Peace River and Fort Norman the first day of May. Capt. Fred Robert McCall, D.S.O., M.C., D.F.C. in charge of actual flying."

Yet another hopeful was "Wop" May. He and his associates hoped to commence a flying boat service out of McLennan, in the Lesser Slave Lake region, with Fort Norman being their northern-most terminus. Operations were to begin in June, 1921, under the title "Great Northern Service." Numerous schemes indeed, and all ambitious; but history doesn't record the commencement of even one of them. For as yet, there were simply too many difficulties and question marks surrounding the launching of a large-scale commercial flying operation, especially one in the remote Northland.

The complexity of any such scheme is well illustrated in the study made by a Toronto mining concern into the feasibility of a full-scale aerial expedition down the Mackenzie in 1921. The promoter in charge of the study was Frank Egerton Davison. Davison was an experienced mining man who had taken part in the Yukon gold rush of '98. He was one of those archetypal entrepreneurs people associate with this mad-cap era of mineral exploration and development. From the turn of the century onward, Davidson's name appears in connection with such mining interests as the Ballarat Mining Company, Universal Gas and Oil, Precambrian Exploration and Development, Raymore Gold Mines, Quesnel Mining, and the Yukon-Alaska Exploration and Development Syndicate. Mining was in his blood, as were the future means of technology which would make the industry more flexible and prosperous.

One of Davison's many interests was Mackenzie River Oil Ltd., a company formed in 1921 to explore for oil in the Mackenzie River basin. The firm was capitalized at five million dollars, and Davison bought into it by trading 44 oil leases he held in the Peace River country for 200 000 shares in Mackenzie River Oil. His first concern was to organize a major geological expedition down the Mackenzie, and it occurred to him that air transport could become part of the venture. In fact, he mused, it could even become the key to the entire expedition! But as no one to date had conducted a large-scale aerial expedition to the North, Davison sought expert advice.

He approached R.H. Mulock to obtain a detailed report on just how feasible the scheme was. Mulock was well qualified to speak on the topic. He was a noted World War I flying veteran, and was later to rise to important positions with Canadian Vickers and Canadian Airways. He submitted his assessment of the situation in a letter dated April 18, 1921. The report began on a positive note: "The proposition must stand on its own feet from an earning point of view as far as fast transportation is concerned. The scheme proposes to sell high speed service and, if the traffic is available, should pay large returns; as speed is worth high prices and the public are always willing to pay for it within reason."

Mulock suggested that the expedition be equipped with F.3 flying boats. Though an ex-military design, the F.3 was thought suitable enough, as it was big, and capable of a 2000 pound revenue load. This meant that ten passengers could be accommodated. The F.3 had two 360 hp Rolls-Royce engines, could "get off" in 20 seconds, climb to 9000 feet in 56 minutes, cruise at 70 mph and fly non-stop for 800 miles. All of these facts were acceptable for the sort of plane required on an airlift between Peace River and Fort Norman.

Mulock went on to recommend costs and other factors. He suggested a fleet of five aircraft, three line and two spare; eight pilots and eight mechanics at a per season rate of $4000 and $3000 respectively. Other specialized help would cost $7400, while food for 36 men for 180 days at $2 per day would run to a further $13 000. Fuel for 106 round trips at 1440 gallons per trip would cost $152 640; oil, $15 264; and $76 000 for maintenance and administration.

So went the budget. To it would be tacked on $205 000 to cover other items such as the cost of boats, buildings, tools, an H-boat for the superintendent, and so on. Along with a contingency fund, financing of the venture totalled $500 000.

Mulock, though, was careful to point out that for the sake of practicality, he had built in a reserve cushion of 25 percent. Money could be saved by efficient operations. For example, he budgeted 18 hours for each one way flight, noting that, all going well, it could be flown in 11. Theoretically, the half million could be reduced to $375 000.

Mulock then proceeded to compare these costs with those of the steamship companies. The per passenger fare by boat from Peace River to Fort Norman was $77, as quoted by the Alberta and Arctic Transportation Company. It was cheap by F.3 standards, which Mulock didn't see being much less than $300 a head. Where the flying venture made up, however, was in time. The boat trip to Fort Norman was a 5-1/2 day trip downbound, 9 days coming back, while the flying boat service offered trips in as short as 11 hours.

The report was an exhaustive exercise, and indication enough that somewhere in the future, there was a vital role to be played by the airplane in the development of Canada; but for Davison in 1921, Mulock's estimates must simply have been too high, in spite of the obvious benefits of air travel. The geological survey of 1921 was completed by Mackenzie River Oil, but using traditional means of transportation. Its connections with aviation were limited to the fact that one of the geologists was "Doc" Oaks, an ex-fighter pilot destined for bush-flying fame; and that in the field reports there appear photos of one of Imperial Oil's Junkers aircraft lying damaged at Fort Simpson. Curiously enough, it's really with this little plane and its mate that the story of flying in northern Canada really begins in earnest. The Mulock report, though, serves well to illustrate how, over 50 years ago, people were seriously planning to put aircraft to work on large-scale civilian projects.

"Mammoth Monoplanes Are Being Fitted With Skis"

While Davison temporarily set aside his interests in aviation, a rival oil company was preparing to send aircraft into the same region, the Mackenzie Valley. Imperial Oil had brought in the first oil along the Mackenzie and was anxious to consolidate its operations in the region. As transportation and communications between the North and the outside were slow and unpredictable, the company decided to experiment with airplanes as a possible means of relieving this handicap. Thus it organized an aerial expedition north beyond the sixtieth parallel. This was to be the first such undertaking in Canada.

In 1920, Imperial Oil ordered two Junkers-Larsen JL-6 monoplanes; and in November of that year, "Wop" May and George Gorman journeyed to New York, took delivery of the planes, and ferried them back to Edmonton. An operations base was established at Peace River Crossing where the planes arrived March 5, 1921. The *Edmonton Journal* announced, "Mammoth Monoplanes Are Being Fitted with Skis at Peace River." One of the planes was partially dismantled and hangared: "The operation of shoving the wingless monster into its northern shelter was expedited by the volunteered assistance of a score of Peace River school children who undauntedly contrived to be present on the memorable occasion." The paper also noted that it was intended that each plane fly with a carrier pigeon on board to serve as a message relay in case of emergency.

The planes had been registered and christened. One, G-CADP was *Vic;* the other, G-CADQ, was *Rene.* Personnel on the trip were to include George Gorman, pilot of *Rene;* E.G. Fullerton, pilot of *Vic;* William Hill and Peter Derbyshire, mechanics; H.W. Waddell, surveyor; and Sgt. Hubert Thorne of the RCMP. Hill described the latter as, "guide, philosopher, friend and liaison man."

Thorne was to become the first member of the RCMP to use the airplane in the course of duty.

Fuel was to be a key to the success of the Imperial Oil enterprise. Wherever the planes were scheduled to set down, there had to be a fuel cache. At Fort Norman, the crew could count on a fuel supply, as a suitable grade of aviation spirits was being distilled there. On March 22, Gorman and Fullerton made a haul of 100 gallons each to Hay River to establish a cache. The return trip was completed in one day, uneventful except that Indians below, never having seen airplanes, took pot shots at them! Fullerton's plane was hit, but no damage, aside from a few holes, was done. Two days later, the expedition was off in earnest, winging its way north over a landscape rarely traversed by the white man. Prior journeys there had been confined to the occasional hardy adventurer like Samuel Hearne or Alexander Mackenzie.

No one aboard *Vic* or *Rene* had much of an idea of what to expect once they waved goodbye to Peace River; only two hours out some may have been having second thoughts about their eagerness, for they were in the teeth of a raging blizzard. Both planes descended to 500 feet and groped along until a safe arrival was made at the Hudson's Bay Company post at Fort Vermilion.

It wasn't until the twenty-seventh that the weather again cooperated, allowing the Junkers to continue on to Fort Providence. It was here that the fliers got their first look at Mackenzie River ice. It had been hoped that the river would be suitable for landings, but this hope vanished as the airmen studied the surface below, which, as later reported, was "for miles and miles, a jumble of piled up, contorted and hummocky ice and crusted snow which promised inevitable disaster as the consequences of any attempt to land."

Vic and *Rene* at Edmonton prior to their first trip north. Those in the foreground left to right are: Elmer Fullerton, H.S. (Dick) Meyers, Mrs. McQueen, Charles E. Taylor, George Gorman, and William Hill.
Glenbow-Alberta Institute (NA-2303-1)

On March 30, the planes flew the 140 miles to Fort Simpson, logged in 1 hour, 42 minutes. Once overhead, the planes circled, looking for a safe landing place. Then *Rene* approached to land. On touchdown it settled into deep snow and nosed over, breaking its propeller and a ski. *Vic* came in safely. Of their arrival Hill later wrote, "This was real serious business, 50 percent of our aircraft out of commission, no spares within 500 miles and 300 miles short of our objective." *Vic* was soon flown out to a safer landing place on the river. *Rene* then borrowed *Vic's* propeller and skis, thus becoming the more airworthy of the duo, as *Vic's* engine needed servicing.

The party then decided to attempt a hop to Fort Norman, a further 350 miles northward. Before this was done, however, word arrived that no suitable fuel had been refined there after all. With a mere 75 gallons remaining at Fort Simpson, the expedition was on shaky ground. Then more trouble! On a takeoff run, *Rene* faltered, and a second propeller was splintered. This, luckily, was just at the time that Hill and a Hudson's Bay Company man named Johnson had completed work on a hand-made propeller, an achievement that goes down as one of the early examples of a flier's ingenuity.

With the cooperation of a local missionary who had tools and a workshop, Hill and Johnson assembled oak sleigh runners and made up their own glue from moose ingredients. Hill described what went on: "We collected bolts from boats, jacks from river steamers, and everything that could be pressed into clamping service. We built a roaring fire in the shop stove and worked like mad in order to get our blank together while wood and glue were hot . . . . The result was satisfactory. While the blank was drying, I set up a bench to act as a general template table and rigid bed on which to carve out the propeller. The templates were made from sheet steel which had once served as a smoke stack on a small steamer on the river. I fitted a complete template every six inches from boss to tip, so placed in slots in the workbench that quick and accurate gauging could be done with the minimum amount of error . . . . The work of chopping with hatchet and carving with drawknife and spokeshave went on daily, and we began to have a propeller that seemed adequate enough.'' The hand-made propeller was very satisfactory, and with *Rene* now in further trouble, work immediately started on a second.

While all this had been going on, the weather had been changing, and in the early morning darkness of April 24, all hands were suddenly rousted out of bed and down to the river. The Mackenzie was breaking up and the two Junkers had to be readied and flown to safety. *Rene* was taxied out but broke a tail skid. By fast action, its propeller was switched to *Vic* which got away, barely clearing blocks of ice heaving out of the river. It landed safely on a nearby lake.

Rene was then hauled ashore by a team of oxen. Next day Gorman, Fullerton, Hill, and Waddell took off for Peace River, and flew the 510 miles in six hours, non-stop. This feat alone was enough to convince Imperial Oil that aviation had a definite place in the North. The company's report noted that, ''Between the points the airplane spanned in its six-hour flight, the fastest time by dog team is forty-five days. Air travel will be done.''

Vic was soon back in service for the

Rene after its accident at Fort Simpson, March, 1921.

Public Archives of Canada (C 36390)

company. On May 27, this time on floats, it was en route ''down north.'' Fullerton, Hill, and Waddell were aboard, as was a geologist, Theo Link, and spare parts needed to repair *Rene*. Of the first leg of the trip Link reported, ''The trip from Peace River to Fort Vermilion was made in 2 hours and 35 minutes. Last year I made the same trip by boat in 33 hours running time.''

Next day, shortly after takeoff, an exhaust stack cracked. Back to Fort Vermilion went *Vic*. Fullerton and Hill then ferried to home base for repairs and were back to collect Waddell and Link on the thirtieth, then northward again. Link busily recorded geologic formations, forest fires, buffalo herds, wide-swinging meanders that were more recent than known maps showed, and a splendid view of the Vermilion Chutes. That evening *Vic* set down at Fort Smith.

June 1 saw the fliers safely arrived at Fort Simpson and just after 5 P.M. next day they were preparing to land at Fort Norman. Here misfortune awaited, for at touchdown, a float separated and a wing was badly damaged. Fortunately, no one was hurt, and work began to salvage the plane. It was rafted 50 miles downstream to the Imperial Oil site, and there, by August, was once again fit for service. Off went *Vic* to join *Rene* at Fort Simpson, and on June 21, both veterans flew home to Peace River. The flight was routine, but on landing, *Rene* crashed and was wrecked once and for all.

Shortly after this, *Vic* was sold and went to British Columbia to fly with a mining concern. During this time not only did *Vic* fly unlicenced, but its pilot was himself unlicenced! This era in the plane's history is recalled by Leigh Brintnell of Western Canada Airways in a letter to the Controller of Civil Aviation, June, 1929:

''We are operating at the present time at 6 Mile Lake, 12 miles from Prince George and while there noted that the old

Junkers F.13, which the Imperial Oil used to have, has been reconditioned and is now flying again. Do not wish to make this an official complaint but would like to submit these suggestions to you so that you can take care of them if you deem it advisable.

''The machine has no official licence and I believe its former licence was G-CADP. The pilot flying it is an old time German war pilot and has no licence either. We have kept our engineers from examining this machine officially as we did not wish to be implicated in any way in the event of a crash. Unofficially we feel that this machine is very unsafe to fly, as half an aileron pulled away in the air the day before I arrived.''

Brintnell went on to comment that the pilot seemed of doubtful ability; however, correspondence from this chap, a Mr. Jorse, to the Civil Aviation Branch does not indicate this. Perhaps Brintnell was merely trying to protect the interests of his own firm. An RCMP report on the matter of the Junkers suggested Brintnell's complaint was perhaps just the result of ''professional jealousy.'' Eventually a government inspector got around to looking over *Vic*. The old crate was condemned, and left beached on Stuart Lake in 1929, there to rot and be picked apart by the locals.

As to the propellers hewn by Hill and Johnson, they disappeared for a long time. One was eventually located with the Oblate missionaries and, in 1938, donated to the National Research Council. In 1945, after much detective work, Frank H. Ellis, noted aviation historian, discovered that the other was still in the possession of the Gorman family. Today both these famous artifacts are on display in the National Museum of Science and Technology, Ottawa.

William Hill with the new propeller he helped fashion for *Vic*. This picture was taken at Fort Simpson, April 1921.

Public Archives of Canada (C 36391)

Viking Prospector

Another early probe into the North was conducted by the Vickers Viking, G-CAEB, a Laurentide machine. In 1924, pilot R.S. Grandy and engineer B. McClatchey journeyed up the west shore of James Bay as far as Attawapiskat. The purpose was to carry an Indian Affairs official to various Reservations so that Treaty money could be paid out, a job which took about two weeks. Usually months of arduous canoe travel were necessary on this annual undertaking.

The following year G-CAEB flew west under charter to a mineral exploration syndicate. The area of operation was the remote and mysterious northern interior of British Columbia and the Yukon. On this contract, nearly a hundred flying hours were logged, and the northern prospecting expedition by air was safely concluded.

In 1926 the Viking was again at work, this time over the godforsaken hinterland to the north of Lake Athabaska. G-CAEB was this time in the hands of two flying veterans, Jack Caldwell and Irenée Vachon. Over the off-season, their plane had been overhauled at Sault Ste. Marie, then shipped west to Edmonton where the crew overhauled the engine. Then the Viking went north by rail to Lac la Biche, Alberta, launching point for the expedition. The entire mineral search was based on tales heard of a rich gold deposit "somewhere" to the east of Great Slave Lake. No gold ever materialized, but from a flying point of view, the venture was a success. The Viking enabled the prospectors to cover more territory, and faster, than they had ever imagined possible.

For some time afterward, G-CAEB lay dormant at High River; but was eventually purchased and freighted to Jericho Beach, British Columbia where it was checked out and flown. Soon, though, it was found that its Napier Lion engine was in sad condition, and the famous old Viking was again mothballed. Then, in 1932, a Captain Fred Clarke purchased it for mining operations he had in view. G-CAEB was meticulously overhauled, and by late summer was again in the air.

On September 16, fate closed the books on the old Viking. While cruising over the Strait of Georgia, its engine took fire when a fuel line broke. A safe emergency landing was made, but the plane was lost.

The Ontario Provincial Air Service

The Ontario government made early investigations into the use of aircraft in forestry patrol. In 1919 it cooperated with

the Canadian Air Force to study this possibility. Results suggested a plan to patrol some 30 000 sq. mi. at a cost over the season of $12.50 per square mile and a total budget requirement of $700 000. This included purchasing 18 aircraft. Like Mackenzie Oil's scheme, this was felt to be too grandiose for implementation.

Ontario first employed aircraft in forestry work in 1920, and through the following years large tracts of Shield country were sketched and photographed from the air. Sketching and photography soon became vital activities in the province's forest resources management program. From his perch in the nose of an HS-2L, a sketcher, who was usually a trained forester, had a bird's eye view of the forestscape for miles around. As he studied this view, he would begin to transfer it onto his mapsheet. Besides obvious features such as lakes and rivers he sketched in the limits of various forest types lying below. Occasionally the pilot would set down so that the forester might examine random areas in closer detail. Once a sketch was completed, the aircraft returned to base. The sketcher submitted his work which later became the raw material for detailed topographic maps prepared by the government.

On one such mission in 1921 forester R.N. Johnston spotted a forest fire in the Sioux Lookout area. This was reported and, before long, fire control measures were taken, with a fire ranger being flown into the site. As a result, Ontario's Department of Lands and Forests began to consider more earnestly the merits of aircraft. In following years the province contracted with firms like Laurentide for aerial surveys and fire patrol work.

G-CAEB, the famous Vickers Viking Mk. IV photographed at Remi Lake in northern Ontario.
Aviation and Space Division, National Museum of Science and Technology (001741)

Ultimately, the Ontario Provincial Air Service came into being in 1924.

Formation of the OPAS amounted, more or less, to the transfer of personnel and aircraft from Laurentide Air Service Ltd. to the Ontario government. Roy Maxwell, a famous pioneer in northern flying and pilot for Laurentide, became the first Director of the newly formed service. After the war, Maxwell, who was an RFC veteran, barnstormed and did aerial filming with the Canadian Aero Film Company at Hamilton. In the summer of 1920 he had conducted a series of flights by HS-2L into the James Bay area, the first time anyone had visited that region by air.

Maxwell set about to equip, staff, and organize an air services that would be second to none. He spared none of his experience, talents, nor a penny from his budget to achieve perfection in his operation. Sixteen pilots, 19 engineers, and 13 HS-2L flying boats were immediately taken on strength. Though not particularly ideal in non-military roles, the HS-2L's were available from war surplus stocks, and at low enough prices to guarantee them a place on the civil aircraft market.

In the first year of OPAS operations, the HS-2L's logged 866 patrols and some 2600 hours in the air. They proved efficient enough in spite of their mechanical idiosyncrasy. It became almost routine for HS-2L's to go overdue on flights, so much so that those awaiting the arrival of a flight learned not to become overly apprehensive.

A Curtiss HS-2L at the Ontario Lands and Forests base, Sault Ste. Marie. This machine was built in 1918 and joined Lands and Forests in May 1924. It was taken off strength nine years later.
Aviation and Space Division, National Museum of Science and Technology (11920)

If an H-boat was late arriving, it was no doubt floating on a lake somewhere, with the crew making repairs to its Liberty engine and its accountrements. Eventually, plane and crew would turn up.

The HS-2L was no hot performer. Those who flew it often joked how it took off, cruised and landed at one speed, 65 mph! Pilots for this reason or that sometimes found themselves in rather cramped quarters. This may have been on account of a hasty emergency landing on a small lake. Repairs made, taking off could present a challenge. Jack Dillon, an old OPAS hand, described just such a predicament:

"One such incident necessitated this plan: the H-boat needed more takeoff run than the lake provided, so we simply had to create room. To accomplish this, an axe crew moved in to cut a swath through the standing timber on the opposite shoreline wide enough for the boat to fly through, with some space to spare. This meant dropping every tree for about a quarter of a mile along a 200-foot wide strip.

"While this axe work was in progress, the boat was pulled, tail up, nose in the water and pointed toward the opening being created. Then a two-inch rope was firmly attached to the bowsprit, threading back through the fuselage, out the tail assembly and tied to a spruce tree about chest height. Then, using the most accurate map available to estimate flying time to the nearest large lake, the right amount of gas was carefully measured into the tank, with allowance made for warm-up. Every item of equipment that could possibly be removed from the craft was dismantled and just enough water was left in the radiator. Once the larger lake was reached, all replacements would be carried out. The pilot then selected for the takeoff was picked because he was competent and did not weigh too much . . . .

"When all was ready the motor was started. A ranger with a razor-sharp axe was stationed at the tree anchor. The pilot would hand-signal when he was ready and the restraining rope would be severed.

"As the revs increased to takeoff power, the spruce bowed and waved from the pull and prop backwash. The rope was cut and, with a few skips and bounces, the lightened boat skimmed across the lake, passed through the trough in the trees and lifted into the sky."

The HS-2L's were obsolete when purchased by Maxwell in 1924, and as the years passed, they began, inevitably, to tire. New types were tried out, but of these, only one was to have a major impact on the OPAS at this time. This was the de Havilland Moth, a fleet of which was acquired starting in 1928. By 1932 the last of the old H-boats was disposed of.

In 1934 the Liberal government of Mitch Hepburn swept into power in Ontario and immediately set about to do a bit of "house-cleaning." High on the list of priorities was an investigation into the operations of the OPAS. An inquiry was opened, with Maxwell the chief target. In spite of the tremendous record of his department, it seemed that all was not exactly 100 per cent.

Commissioner Lang spent days listening to testimony from all sorts of witnesses, both for and against Maxwell. Few faulted him either personally or as an administrator, but certain irregularities did crop up. For example, the H-boats purchased in 1924 came from the company with which Maxwell had recently been manager. They were sold to Ontario at $5500 apiece, while Laurentide, the main Canadian dealer in H-boats, had purchased them for as little as $3000 from United States government surplus. They were also sold to Ontario as new, but later on six were found to have been used.

Maxwell purchased Liberty engines for the flying boats from his friend, F.G. Ericson, at $2850 each, engines which Ericson had purchased for just $300 each! Some of these were delivered to the OPAS with the warning "not to be flown," and hence had to be reconditioned at an additional $2000 each. Maxwell was also accused of overbuying parts for the Liberties at a time when the HS-2L was nearing the end of its usefulness. So it went, the Liberals having a field day embarrassing their Conservative opponents in Queen's Park. The outcome saw Maxwell retire his post, even though not all the accusations against him held up. As new Director of the OPAS, Hepburn then chose his close friend and chauffeur, G.E. Ponsford.

THE FOREST WATCHER

Over lake and pine-clad forest,
Over river flashing by,
Sails the white-winged forest watcher,
Softly in a cloud-swept sky.

Softly drones the distant engine,
Over virgin timberland,
Speaking peace unto the forest,
Where the mighty giants stand.

Onward then o'er tracts scarce charted,
Over cataracts asweep,
Over mountain, plain and valley,
Over glades that lie asleep.

Far into the western twilight,
Flashing wings against the sun,
Hums the softening song of engine,
Throbbing until day is done.

Flight Lt. F.V. Heakes, RCAF, 1928

The three-seat JN-4, G-CAFS. This aircraft was used by J.V. Elliot in the Red Lake region during the spring of 1926.
Aviation and Space Division, National Museum of Science and Technology (08074)

Mining Spurs Commercial Flying

Around the turn of the century, prospectors began crisscrossing the rugged landscape of the Canadian Shield in search of mineral wealth. Impressive strikes were made in northwestern Quebec around Rouyn and Amos, and in adjacent parts of Ontario. It wasn't long before this region was attracting aviators, for the airplane seemed a natural solution to travel difficulties in this wild and inaccessible country.

In 1924 Laurentide Air Service established a flying boat operation out of Haileybury, Ontario, on Lake Timiskaming, serving points throughout the gold belt on a daily basis. This was Canada's first scheduled commercial flying service. The fare to Rouyn, a bit over a hundred miles, was $60 one way. Baggage over 25 pounds was charged at the rate of 20¢ a pound. The service was popular enough, but returns were marginal and operations did not resume the following year.

About the same time two prospectors were striking pay dirt at the opposite end of Ontario. These were the Howey brothers of Red Lake. News of their good fortune soon reached around the world and triggered a wild rush into this remote area. Adventurers could make it by rail to a point well south of Red Lake; but from there it was difficult to reach the gold fields, which were at least 80 miles away. Many actually walked this distance. In winter, the fortunate travelled by dog team and could make Red Lake in six days. One of those eager to try commercial flying in the region

was J.V. Elliot, a veteran flier from Hamilton where he ran a flying school and shops refurbishing JN-4's.

In 1926, Elliot freighted two of his JN-4's northward to Sioux Lookout. There they were assembled and flown to a base at Hudson. Service to Red Lake began immediately. Business was brisk, for most dreaded the thought of hoofing or mushing it into Red Lake over miles of rugged shieldscape in the dead of winter. During the winter flying season, Elliot's ski-equipped planes carried 587 passengers and nearly a ton and a half of freight and mail. Elliot's was one of a number of flying outfits in the late twenties that was granted permission to issue its own air mail stamps. The service to Red Lake was short lived, however, as the JN-4 was not adaptable to floats. At spring breakup Elliot ceased operations in the North.

Others soon followed in Elliot's slipstream. In 1925, F.E. Davison was back on the aviation scene. He set up a firm known as Patricia Airways and Exploration on the basis of 1000 shares, each worth $100. Davison was chief shareholder, but others included such names as Sir Henry Pellatt, Roy Maxwell, and H.A. "Doc" Oaks. Oaks became chief pilot for the new company.

The Curtiss Lark of Patricia Airways and Exploration Ltd. In 1927 this little aircraft flew nearly 50 000 miles in the remote wilds of northwestern Ontario.
Aviation and Space Division, National Museum of Science and Technology (001923)

The operation began with a single plane, and considerable fanfare accompanied its delivery flight to Red Lake. The plane was a Curtiss Lark. On March 21 it was ferried from the Curtiss plant on Long Island to Buffalo by Curtiss' famous pilot Charles S. "Casey" Jones. From Buffalo, Roy Maxwell flew the Lark to Toronto's Leaside aerodrome, accompanied by *Toronto Star* reporter Frederick Griffin. Griffin was later to submit daily reports covering, in dramatic style, the Lark's progress as it battled its way northward. From Leaside, the Lark departed on a non-stop flight to Sudbury, where a safe landing was made on the ice of Ramsey Lake. From that point on it was rough going, but at last, on April 12, the plane and occupants arrived safely at Sioux Lookout, 1500 miles northwest of Long Island, 23 days after departure from the plant. The Lark was immediately readied for service and soon began operations. The one-way fare via Lark, Sioux Lookout to Red Lake, was $120.

Performance of No. 2 Stinson
Under Pilot W.N. Cumming
Installed in service at Haileybury
on March 29th 1927
In service 18 days out of 19 days

Total flights	105
Passengers carried	160
Baggage	2076 lb
Express	81 lb
Mail	51 lb
Hours flying	50 lb
Gas used	689 gal
Oil used	19 gal
Total flying hours for	
machine	55 hr 42 min
Total engine hours	73 hr 39 min
Total mileage flown with	
machine	5565 mi
Revenue miles flown	5000 mi
Total revenue	$3502.50

Patricia Airways soon expanded with the addition of Stinson Detroiter cabin aircraft in both the Red Lake and Quebec goldfields on the Haileybury-Rouyn route. The Lark continued as a good revenue earner, until September 12, 1927, when it cracked up and sank while landing at Hudson. Pilot J.R. Ross managed to escape as the plane went under, but three passengers, employees of Jackson Manion Mines, had to struggle desperately under water to get out. Fortunately all survived. The Lark was shipped to Canadian Vickers for repairs, but was declared too badly damaged and was junked.

Western Canada Airways

The northern scene was a changeable one for bush fliers. Employment opportunities changed rapidly, with pilots and engineers readily moving from job to job. Everything was so new in their field that there was simply no settling down anywhere. Oaks, as it turned out, was not one to sit tight for long, especially if he sensed an opportunity. In late 1926 he journeyed to Winnipeg for he had heard that one of that city's entrepreneurs was planning to set up a flying business. This was James A. Richardson.

Oaks was hired as the pilot for Richardson's newly formed company, Western Canada Airways. He and engineer Al Cheesman were soon on their way to New York to collect the company's first plane, a five place Fokker Universal, G-CAGD, *City of Winnipeg*. On Christmas Day the plane was delivered to Hudson in Northern Ontario and two days later was out earning revenue. In January, its first full month at work, it flew over 87 hours and carried 78 passengers along with about 5 tons of cargo.

In March of 1927 WCA landed its first big contract. The federal government was conducting a study into the possibility of establishing a seaport on Hudson Bay. This would provide a short route to Europe for prairie grain. Sites at Port Nelson and Fort Churchill were under consideration, and engineers were anxious to conduct drilling through the ice at the latter place before spring breakup. RCAF Fairchilds were put to work on the project, but to speed things along it was decided to airlift equipment and supplies from the rail head on the Hudson Bay Railroad, about 200 miles south of Fort Churchill. Western Canada Airways took this contract, but it came at a difficult time. Two of its planes were unserviceable due to accidents, but help in the form of some Fokker personnel, including Bernt Balchen, soon had things set straight and a pair of Universals took off for Cache Lake, base for the airlift.

For the next month, the two planes kept up a hectic pace shuttling back and forth with men and equipment. For the whole period, the mercury never rose above 45 degrees below zero. Some minor difficulties were experienced, including two forced landings by Fred Stevenson, but by April 20, the job was completed. A dozen passengers and eight tons of mixed cargo had been carried during 102 hours of flying. As it turned out, WCA's ability to undertake and successfully complete this job directly influenced the government's choice of Fort Churchill over Port Nelson as site of the proposed harbour.

Later in the year, WCA took on work in the Senneterre region of northwestern Quebec, as well as a big job hauling freight for Sherritt Gordon Mines which was diamond drilling north of The Pas. By October 4, 23 tons and 58 passengers had been carried on the job. This was the biggest airlift to date in North America and had been entirely handled by Fred Stevenson flying the Universal, G-CAGE. The airplane was certainly proving its worth as a dependable means of transportation in the North.

One of Western Canada Airways' Fokker Universals on a northern lake. This machine joined the Western Canada fleet in January 1928. It was destroyed in a takeoff accident at Peace River, Alberta December 15, 1931. The Universal was powered by a 200 horse power Wright J-4 Whirlwind engine. Its payload was about 1500 pounds. Z.L. Leigh has described the Universal: "The passenger cabin had four seats and was separated from the pilot's cockpit by a wooden wall with a small peep door through which the pilot could look every now and then to be sure that all was well in the cabin."

Via Ralph Shapland

On January 5, 1928, Stevenson, newly assigned to the WCA base at The Pas, took off in G-CAGE on a local test hop. What was to have been so routine suddenly turned into disaster, for the Universal unexpectedly went into a spin and crashed. The pilot, one of the finest in the North, died instantly, thus becoming Canada's first fatality in commercial bush flying. That year, Stevenson was posthumously awarded the Harmon Trophy for Canada.

Through 1928, Richardson's airline continued to expand. It opened a flying school at Winnipeg and absorbed D.R. MacLaren's company, Pacific Airways. MacLaren joined Western Canada Airways, bringing along his HS-2L. Soon WCA's new West Coast division expanded with the addition of two Boeing and two Vedette flying boats. These were mainly for use on fisheries, forestry, and customs patrols and on their first season chalked up 445 flights.

One of those flying on those operations was Walter Gilbert. Like many of his compatriots he was an ex-RFC fighter pilot, having flown S.E.5's over France with 32 Squadron and 52 Squadron. After the war he had done some flying with the Canadian Air Force and in 1928 had joined WCA. At first he had operated out of Cranberry Portage flying Universals, but was soon posted to the West Coast on fisheries patrol.

Fisheries patrols were flown to insure that boats were fishing within boundary limits and within specified distances from the mouths of streams; that fish were being taken within season; that nets in use were legal in terms of length and webbing. The planes were used to inspect spawning grounds and for general transportation of fisheries personnel as well. It was claimed that a single fisheries patrol plane could do the work of 40 patrol boats!

During a 1967 interview, Walter Gilbert recalled his early West Coast flying. "I spent about ten months in all there during which time I had the remarkable experience of going into every hole and corner on the British Columbia coast. I covered as much ground in that respect as one could on the surface, I guess, in years and years. The fisheries patrol was just in its infancy then. Don MacLaren was superintendent of the Western Canada Airways B.C. division and we had a very, very pleasant life, and quite a lot of fun. The salmon poachers had been having their own way with surface craft because practically every fishing boat was faster than the old patrol boats the fisheries officers had at that time. They could recognize them coming miles away by the sound of their engines and they'd im-

mediately take in their nets and get out of the prohibited areas until the boats went away again. It was very easy.

"Well, we beat that situation by taking advantage of the deep inlets that make up most of the B.C. coast. We knew where they were poaching. We'd come up the next inlet, perhaps five or six miles away just on the other side of the mountain range that separated the two, then climb quickly and just suddenly appear over the top. We carried an eight by ten roll-film oblique camera and we'd catch them cold.

"We'd photograph the poachers from reasonably low elevation with some known object in the background. Then we'd land and take their papers away from them. They soon became used to that, and they teamed up to make it a little more difficult for us.

"Then we started another racket. One of the fisheries patrol boats, if the weather was calm, just lay to, well off shore. We would spend the night tied up to her, and leave just at the first gray dawn, and come in and repeat our performance. We let the word be spread around that we had new equipment and were flying all night. That practically squelched the poaching for that year."

The McKee Trophy

In 1927, "Doc" Oaks became the first recipient of the McKee Trophy. The trophy had been instituted in commemoration of the famous flight across Canada in 1926, the first crossing by a single aircraft. J. Dalzell McKee, son of a prominent Philadelphia family, had proposed a flight to Hudson Bay.

Eventually McKee abandoned his scheme and opted instead for another route. As he had wanted to get his Douglas 0-2B float plane back to its California manufacturer for some modifications, he chose to fly the plane there, charting a course straight across Canada. Such a flight had never before been made using a single aircraft. McKee was joined on his venture by Squadron Leader A.E. Godfrey of the RCAF. As McKee had wanted a knowledgeable companion along, and as Godfrey was on leave at the time, the two formed a team.

McKee and Godfrey took off from Montreal on September 11, 1926, and flew to Ottawa. Next day they headed for Sudbury but were forced down by low cloud. It was the thirteenth when they reached their first destination. Within two more days they had passed through Sioux Lookout and arrived at Lac du Bonnet, but not totally unassisted. Unsure of the route to Lac du Bonnet, the aviators had come

down on a lake near an Indian Reservation where inhabitants accurately pointed them on their way. On September 19, McKee and Godfrey arrived safely at the RCAF station, Jericho Beach in Vancouver. In appreciation to Canada for help given along the way by the RCAF, the OPAS and the Controller of Civil Aviation, McKee donated the now famous trophy. It has been awarded almost every year since to the Canadian contributing most significantly to the progress of aviation in Canada.

McKee planned an even more ambitious flight for 1927. He hoped to fly from Montreal to Edmonton, head north to Herschel Island, across Alaska, down the Pacific coast to Vancouver and eastward back to Montreal. The flight was never taken, for McKee was killed on June 9, 1927, when one of the two Vedettes acquired for the expedition crashed while alighting on Lac la Peche, north of Montreal.

More Northern Episodes

Throughout this period, commercial aviation continued to pick up. Aviation and forestry had certainly found each other. Statistics from 1926 indicate the growing importance of this association. Over 59 000 square miles were photographed from the air at the request of the Topographical Surveys Branch of the Department of the Interior. Some 58 000 000 acres were patrolled, 259 fires detected; and 256 of these were suppressed with the assistance of aircraft. Meanwhile, prospectors, trappers, missionaries, and other people of the North were coming more and more to depend on the bush pilot.

In 1928, Northern Aerial Mineral Exploration began operations. It offered specialized service to the mining industry and was similar to two other firms in that respect, Dominion Explorers Ltd., and the aviation branch of Consolidated Mining and Smelting. NAME's first annual report indicates the scale of the commitment and the daring of those involved in such flying ventures. In part, the document reads, "The flying was done in practically all parts of northern Canada, from Ungava to the Yukon, planes usually working in pairs. Thirty-seven gas caches have been established throughout the north, which will meet our requirement for 1929." As a footnote it is mentioned, "During the season we had only one major engine failure, a broken crank shaft, which has been replaced by the manufacturers." To operate over such a vast hinterland, completely out of touch with civilization for months at a time, would be challenge enough even by today's standards.

A 1929 Boeing B-1E of Western Canada Airways moored off the B.C. coast. Powered by a 420 horse power Pratt and Whitney Wasp engine this little flying boat would cruise at 95 mph and was ideal for fisheries patrols. According to Walter Gilbert, "It was a very useful, quite high-performance boat."

Aviation and Space Division, National Museum of Science and Technology (1080)

NAME's routes extended from Landing Lake in the Yukon, south and across to Sudbury, and around to Fort Harrison on the east coast of Hudson Bay. Its eight pilots as listed in the report were F.B. Barager, A.M. Berry, H.A. Oaks, C.A. Cheesman, W.J. McDonough, T.M. Reid, C.A. Schiller, and J.D. Vance. Six were ex-RFC, one ex-RNAS, and one came from an American operator, Aeromarine Airways. It is of interest that James A. Richardson had provided 25 per cent of NAME's capital on start up. Clearly, he had more than a passing interest in the flying business.

There are few still living who can relate first hand what it was like flying in the far North in the late twenties. Fortunately, though, enough original material has survived to let the reader today share in and appreciate the excitement as well as the anxieties, dangers, and disappointments of those pioneers of the sky.

A.M. Berry

In late 1928, A.M. "Matt" Berry took part in a mineral exploration trip as a pilot for NAME. Of this undertaking, Berry, who died in 1970, has left a good account in his diary. This diary gives an informative look behind the scenes into the life of the early bush pilot. The entries begin on July 15 where we find Berry and Cheesman en route for Long Lac from Sudbury. The entry shows the two fliers temporarily lost and groping about for the railroad — their "iron compass": "Leaving town Cheesman overlooked the railway and we flew too far to the South and were temporarily lost. He kept trying to pick up the road by a course slightly South of West until I was convinced we were well South of the track and suggested flying due North until we picked it up. This we did and had no other difficulty. We arrived at Long Lac at 8:30 P.M. and docked at the Provincial Air Station where Capt. Dawson was in charge."

The next day Berry and Cheesman pushed on to Hudson: "We reached Hudson at 3:00 and docked at Western Canada Airways. Fred Greaves, the veteran cook for the company, shouted to us to come up for a lunch and gave us a dandy too. I was given a bed to sleep in but am to board at the Western Canada camp. A fine bunch of boys."

This was a new experience for Berry. Like many World War I veterans, he was just getting back into aviation, for to this time there had been little demand for commercial pilots. Berry was impressed by the experiences of his first few days in the North. Part of his entry for the sixteenth reads, "Looking back over the trip out it certainly was a marvellous experience. Until one takes such a journey by air they can have no conception of the immensity of this country of ours. I was particularly struck with the mining possibilities of the district from Sudbury out as it seems incredible that such a tremendous stretch of rough rocky country can't be chuck full of minerals."

Berry's first operational flight was into Favourable Lake, July 17. Two prospectors up there, Murray and Stewart, had made a strike that looked promising and Berry wrote, "I wanted to see them and also take in some grub. It was 260 miles up so I needed a big load of gas but nevertheless the Fokker took off nicely. I got my first view of the country over which I expected to be flying shortly and it certainly presents a lot of difficulties to the inexperienced pilot. A few such trips and I think I will be quite O.K. as I am getting onto the hang of following the waterways . . . . We found Murray and Stewart in good spirits but looking for mail which we didn't have. Ken had some wonderful samples of lead and silver ores, tremendously rich, but he was not very enthusiastic. Thinks the body of ore not large enough to get excited about. Al took him up in the Fokker to look at the territory north where he's going shortly. He is convinced he is in the right district and will have a mine shortly. Al let me fly the ship both ways and I had a great time. We ran into a lot of smoke and had to come down to 500 ft. to see the ground. We passed over one big fire at Deer Lake and had a wonderful view of it. We were flying at 3000 ft. and great columns of smoke were at least a thousand ft. above us."

On the nineteenth, W.J. McDonough arrived in a Fairchild along with his engineer, Tom Caddick: "Both glad to get back to civilization and good things to eat. Cheesman told McDonough that he was picked to go on the Mackenzie River expedition so Mac [McDonough] is all upset and trying to work things so he can get hold of the Wasp Fairchild that Doc Oaks is bringing out and leave me with this crock of a Wright that he has used up in work here. I am sitting tight to see what happens."

On the twenty-second, J.E. Hammell, president of NAME, and "Doc" Oaks, assistant manager and chief pilot, were in Hudson. Hammell wanted to check into

exploration under way at the time: "Oaks in bad humour this A.M. Hammell wanted to get to Red Lake so McDonough loaded R.E. [G-CARE] with two of them and heavy baggage, about 700 lbs. Stiff breeze blowing and tried twice to get off water and couldn't. Porpoised her tremendously. Oaks very sore at display. Transferred passengers and load to R.J. and Doc flew them in himself. In the evening flew R.E. into Sioux Lookout with practically same load as in morning and gave Mc a lecture on taking off. Mc peeved."

For the next few weeks things went along routinely at the NAME base. As the engine in G-CARE had been shipped to Winnipeg for overhaul, Berry and the others spent a lot of time with such things as improving their docking facilities. There was some excitement August 15, though: "Famous Loening arrived at Hudson with Younger at helm and Duke Schiller and Paul Feloon as passengers. Very odd looking kite but has wonderful performance. Great interest in this addition to our fleet. Al flew it down to Sioux Lookout in evening to show it around."

The twenty-first found Berry in Winnipeg about to fly north on exploration work. Five days later he was at Churchill.

August 27: "Paul and I up at 3:00 A.M. to get ship off beach at high tide intending to leave for Pas to get remainder of grub.

Turned out wet and blustery just as we were cranking up so Pat thought we had better stay put. Turned out better in morning so we got away at 2:00 when tide was up again. Arrived Pas at 7:30 on nonstop flight, tired and stiff and ready for bed."

August 29: "Ready to start but timing it so as to reach Churchill at high tide. Took a real hot bath, had lunch and pushed off at 12:00. No sign of Vance and R.E. before we left. Got in just right and found Pat and Duke in just ahead of us. Made a terrible landing close in and was relieved to find no one saw us coming in so didn't mention it."

August 30: "Got away for Chesterfield at 7:30 and had to fly at 250 feet to keep under the mist and low clouds. Very forbidding looking shore line, rocks everywhere and very little shelter. Most barren looking country imaginable, not a sign of life anywhere except for gulls, geese, ducks, and white whales."

August 31 [Baker Lake area]: "All a

G-CATM, the Loening Amphibian referred to in Matt Berry's diary. This rugged design would carry six people. ATM was wrecked in an accident at Thicket Portage on August 25, 1929. Pilot "Duke" Schiller was uninjured.

Aviation and Space Division, National Museum of Science and Technology (002814)

Pilots and engineers of Northern Aerial Minerals Exploration Ltd, posed with an FC-2 at Winnipeg in 1928. Standing left to right are: W.J. McDonough, C.A. Schiller, J.D. Vance, H.A. Oaks, A.M. Berry, F.B. Barager, J.D. Culliton, G.M. Wadds, and F.H. Fisher. Those seated are J.R. Humble, S.A. Cheesman, T. Caddick and C.F.K. Mews.

Manitoba Provincial Archives, Western Canada Aviation Museum (W.C.A.M. 13)

very desolate looking place and one wonders how any human could eke out an existence on such an inhospitable stretch of barren rock. My admiration for the Husky [Inuit] increases daily as I see what he has been up against.''

September 3 [Baker Lake]: "Beached plane at Revillon Frères and found Dickins with Super Fokker ahead of me. He and Col. McAlpine as passenger touring the country. Had come up from Mistake Bay by Ferguson and Kazan rivers and were going to Lake Athabaska via Thelon river then back to Winnipeg. We had the honor of having the first plane in Baker Lake last trip and Dickins is second.''

September 6 [Baker Lake]: "Very strong winds from the S.W. Not fit for plane on the water so as we think Leith was delayed by rain and wind I didn't pull out but left buss [plane] on the beach. Tides are receding and leaving her high and dry. Tried to stop a leak in a pontoon yesterday by using rosin mixed with seal oil and I think it worked.''

September 7 [re. prospectors] "Tom and Joe [two prospectors] blew in this afternoon. Couldn't get up the [Thelon] river with boat so going to leave it here and have me put them up stream where they will walk back. Took Bill and St. Paul for a tour of inspection up the Princess river and the upper lakes. Pretty fast water but they are going to try it with the canoe.''

September 10: "Took Dick Reid away up the Quoich river taking the right hand branch to the first big lake where I left him with all his equipment. Very rough country covered with light fall of snow but to me it looks like a marvellous place for prospecting. Very rocky shores so we had to assemble canoe from plane and paddle stuff to shore. Dick seemed quite content but I hated to leave him alone in such a place.''

In the meantime, all had been awaiting the arrival of the supply vessel *Pat and Mike.* It was long overdue to this date, being at Chesterfield without a pilot to take it to Baker Lake.

September 13: "Joe and Tom want to go up to Wager Bay and I don't want to chance it except on a clear day with good visibility.''

September 14: "Got a good start and took Bill and Shearer about 40 miles North into a good big lake where the formation looked good. We got off with them and found lots of mineralization and formation even better than we hoped for. Crushed some rock and found excellent tailings. Lowe thinks it's gold. Everything looks so good we think it best to bring Tom and Joe in to make a thorough search. Quite calm after dinner and we couldn't get off the water. First time R.J. had refused to take a load for me. Dumped Lowe and our grub and a lot of equipment and got off.''

September 21: "Gales from the N.W. with practically steady snowfall all morning. Temperature just below freezing. Not fit for flying at all. Arthur and I went hunting ptarmigan about 10:00 and came back with fifteen of them. Had loads of fun though it was very hard work tramping through the soft snow. Thought of trying to make Joe's camp in the afternoon but the wind was very high and the visibility poor so we thought better of it. Still no sign of schooner and everyone is worried.

Arthur imagines all manner of catastrophes have overtaken her but I fancy the captain is still just delaying purposefully. This is making it very hard to get our camp together for the winter and it looks as if we will have to bring in the prospectors for unloading the schooner and erecting the hut. In a little over a week we will have to be thinking of beating it back to civilization . . . . [Arthur] suggested yesterday that if Hammel sends in a plane this winter that I come back with it. Am not so sure I would like the job particularly as there would be no hangar or even nose hangar for taking care of the ship and it would be a big undertaking to put up anything after the snow comes.''

September 22: ''Worked on engine all day. No luck until we tried changing one set of plugs and then got her rolling at 6:00 P.M.''

September 24: ''Got off water by 2:00 and ran for Joe's camp. Missed their lake and landed in one farther North. Finally got to their camp and discovered they had flown. Found note saying they had started to walk for Baker Lake on twenty-first. Can't understand why they were out of fuel as we took up seven gals. and they were only in camp seven days. Gathered up their equipment and beat it for Bill and Shearer. Lowe had a hell of a time — got his feet wet and hands very cold and was thoroughly miserable. Found Bill and Shearer rolled up in their eiderdowns and quite comfortable — lots to eat but reduced to burning their tent poles for fuel. Mighty rough on the lake but the ship took off nicely with a big load. Rather rotten landing in Baker Lake. Joe and Tom haven't come in yet.''

September 25: ''No sign of Joe and Tom and we are worried. I think we should take a couple of Huskies [Inuit] to the old camp and let them follow the old tracks South.''

September 26: ''Fog and low mist this A.M. but we took the buss and went up the Thelon looking for Joe and Tom. Dick and Bill came along with Lowe. Went up the river 30 or 40 miles then inland East. Engine cut over first lake and we came down to find a plug had worked loose and blown out. Soon made repairs and got off again but fog got so bad we were forced to return without seeing any sign of the boys. Decided to let Bill go out with a native and try to trail them back.''

September 29: ''Up early for a good start [for Chesterfield] but there was a heavy fog over the lake and we couldn't get off. Tried to make it at 10:30 but couldn't get through so came back and worked on the motor. Parson Smith asked us for lunch and we were just about going when

Paul saw someone on the shore. We watched through the glass but couldn't make out who it was till he was quite close and then it was Tom — all alone! He was in bad shape and broke down telling us Joe had died three days out of camp or on Sept. 24th. He realizes now how very foolish they were in ever leaving the tent in such weather. Says it was Joe's idea as he seemed determined to get back. . . . Lowe upset. Expects Hammell in on the plane coming through. They find the schooner's back is broken and she is doomed. Cargo nearly all off and a day or two will finish it . . . . Bill and the Huskies came into camp. They had lost the tracks at the North end of big lake and hadn't seen Joe's body but had found Tom's rifle and compass.''

September 30: ''Beautiful day, first we have had for a long time. Got Bill and Toopic ready to go and find Joe's body but when tried to crank the buss the starter broke. Tried swinging prop by hand and with a rope but couldn't get a kick out of her . . . . Staff and Bill got pie-eyed on Bob's rum and Bill had Toopic running amuck and speaking lots of English. Staff cooked a bannock and we got two tins of beefsteak and onions out of the store and had dinner at Bob's.''

October 1: '' . . . . Saw Tom in the evening and he appeared much better and quite cheerful. His feet are bad yet but the parson says they are improving steadily. Wore my new koolitang for the first time and don't find it any warmer than my old canvas coat. Good protection for the face however.''

By October 4, the party was seriously considering breaking camp. Holes in the floats of the plane were patched up, and by the ninth, Berry was again back at Churchill.

October 10 [about to fly to The Pas]: ''Cook gave us breakfast at 6:00 and the boys looked after Tom. Started at 7:00 but the DISASTER complete. The engine picked up a spray and quit and when we settled in the water the right pontoon sank almost immediately. Plane rapidly settled tail first so I got the boys out on the front of left pontoon which helped some. Saw motor boat shoot out from dock and was mightily relieved. Sinking fast when they pulled up to us and tried to take us in tow. Pulled Tom through window as door was locked. He protested loudly but plane was straight on end by this time.''

The plane was pulled to shore. Oaks arrived on the twelfth and flew out Tom, while Berry and the others spent the next few days stripping down the damaged plane for shipment south.

October 17: ''Nice mild quiet day but I didn't do much except hang around camp

and mend some socks and underwear. Going to wash but Bob wanted the tub. Paul and Shearer were out along the beach and found my ivory crib board, a bunch of tools, two pictures, the crank and gas hose.'' These were items washed up which had been lost when Berry's plane sank.

October 19: ''Paul and Shearer found my camera in the sand and also my safety razor and old army knife as well as 51 cartridges for the 32. I went down later and found Arthur's thermos bottle about 20 yards off shore. Cleaned up camera in evening and it appears in fine shape and will be O.K. if shutter is not injured. Luck is surely with us and I still hope to find Tom's and Paul's bags.''

October 21: ''Had the ptarmigan for dinner today and they were fine. The boys seemed to enjoy everything. We had ptarmigan and gravy with lots of dressing, mashed potatoes, creamed green peas, lemon pie, strawberry preserves, currant bread and cake and tea. Pretty fair chuck for the Barren Lands say I.''

On November 16 Berry was flown out to Deer Lake from where he caught the train to the Pas and Winnipeg. Next week he was in Toronto, already working on plans for the next year's expedition to the North.

Another 1928 venture had been organized by Lt. Colonel C. D. H. MacAlpine, head of Dominion Explorers. MacAlpine planned an aerial survey along the west coast of Hudson Bay, chartering a Super Universal from Western Canada Airways. The plane was G-CASK and its pilot C.H. Dickins. For plane and pilot MacAlpine agreed to pay $75 a day plus $1.50 per mile.

The flight departed from Winnipeg August 28 and flew north to Norway House, Churchill, Rankin Inlet, inland to Lake Athabaska, Stony Rapids, Cold Lake to the north of The Pas, and back to Winnipeg by September 9. The party had travelled some 4000 miles during 37 hours aloft, averaging about 107 mph. Over most of the route, the expedition was traversing Barren Lands never before seen by the white man. For his achievements on this expedition, Dickins was awarded the McKee Trophy for 1928. Over that year he had logged 1035 hours in the air.

Another noteworthy flight of 1928 was completed by T.M. Reid of NAME. Starting out at Baker Lake in one of the company Loenings, Reid flew south to Moose Factory, thence northward to the Richmond Gulf in the area of the Belcher Islands. By so doing, Reid became the first to fly right around the shoreline of Hudson and James Bays.

The MacAlpine Expedition

The most dramatic aviation incident in Canada during the late twenties had its beginnings on August 24, 1929, when a Dominion Explorers party headed by Lt. Col. MacAlpine flew North from Winnipeg on a mineral exploration venture. It was equipped with its own Fairchild piloted by Stan McMillan with Alex Milne as engineer; and a Fokker of Western Canada Airways piloted by G.A. Thompson with D.A. Goodwin as engineer. Also in the party were Richard Pearce and E.A. Boadway, two mining men. There were early difficulties, with the Fokker being lost in the strong tide at Churchill. At the same time word arrived that the expedition's supply ship had sunk in Hudson Bay.

The lost airplane was quickly replaced by G-CASK and on September 9 both planes rendezvoused at Beverley Lake to the west of Baker Lake where Major Robert Baker had joined the party. That day they set off for the Arctic coast hoping to strike it along Bathurst Inlet, but poor weather closed in. Nonetheless, the expedition pushed on and, as fuel dwindled, reached the coast, though uncertain exactly where.

The aircraft set down and the party began to evaluate its situation. It was soon visited by a group of Island Inuit, eight adults, and some children. These were friendly, and informed them that they were not far from a white settlement located across open water. On September 12 an attempt was made to locate this place using the Fokker. Engine trouble prevented it getting airborne, and its remaining fuel was transferred to the Fairchild which then took off with Stan McMillan, Alex Milne, Major Baker and the Inuit called Joe. They flew a short reconnoitre but could not discern any land in the direction indicated by the Inuit. After this flight there was very little fuel left, and MacAlpine's party realized that it was stranded. It was out of contact with civilization, with only its limited survival kit, and the Arctic winter was about to set in.

As it was between seasons it would be several weeks before the sea was frozen enough to permit an overland trek; so the party set about building a shelter. This was built from sod with a tarp for the roof, and a large tent as the entrance way. The problem of food was later described by one of the party:

"The party was divided into hunters, fishers, and fuel gatherers. Fortunately, we were provided with plenty of ammunition. We also had a fish net but we caught only two fish. The season for the salmon run was long over. There were not many sea fish and the rivers soon froze over.

"For the first two weeks we were able to shoot a considerable number of ptarmigan but the flocks soon migrated south. Ground squirrels were obtained until the snow came during the first week in October. These, together with dried fish given to us by the Eskimos, formed our main diet with a small ration of the white man's food we had with us for variety.

"Not knowing how much fish the Eskimos would be able to supply us with we voluntarily went on very strict rations from the tenth September to the twelfth October. Checking our consumption afterwards it worked out at 6-1/2 oz. of food per man each day."

Some other details were recently provided by Alex Milne. He recalls that the fish net they had set in the nearby river was largely shredded and devoured by crab-like creatures; and that the ptarmigan's combination of white camouflage and high speed made them very difficult targets. As for the Inuit, he makes it very clear that their generosity saved the day. They provided fish and plenty of seal blubber. In doling out fish, they would smell the portions; then give the best ones to the visitors, while keeping the bad-smelling ones for themselves. Alex relates how eating Inuit fare took some getting used to and that seal blubber was at first violently rejected by the stomach.

Towards late September some more Inuit came into camp, one of whom spoke English. He informed the MacAlpine group that they were located on Queen Maud Gulf well east of their intended point of arrival; and that the neighbouring settlement was Cambridge Bay. On October 21 the whole party set out for

The MacAlpine party at Dease Point. Left to right are: E.A. Boadway, S.R.M. McMillan, D.A. Goodwin, A.J. Milne, Col. C.H.D. MacAlpine, "Joe" (an Inuit), G.A. Thompson and Maj. R.F. Baker.

R. Pearce

Cambridge Bay across the ice, travelling in three dog teams. At first good progress was made but then things slowed down. Stopovers were necessary so that everyone could rest, and to wait for bad weather to clear. Open water forced another halt and, as food was dwindling, one of the teams had to backtrack to the old camp for replenishment. It was five days before it rejoined the main party, and on November 2 the arduous trek resumed.

At day's end, the party was played out. Their native companions built snow houses for the overnight stop. Next day they were again off across the ice and at 7:30 in the evening, November 3, Cambridge Bay was reached. News of this was radioed to the outside via the steamships *Bay Maud* and *Fort St. James*.

In the meantime, a search and rescue operation had been under way, centred around a large fleet of aircraft used in search, supply, and backup roles. Other supplies were freighted to Churchill by rail, thence by boat to Baker Lake. Search efforts were hampered by a number of factors, including limited fuel supplies, the need to change over to skis, and several costly accidents. Besides these, few of the air crew had had experience flying over the Barren Lands. One who was experienced was "Punch" Dickins who began searching this forbidding terrain on September 26.

In mid October the five planes at Baker Lake were drawn out of the water for the changeover to skis. This was a major effort as the usual gear and facilities were not available. Part of the operation has been described by T.W. Siers: "When an attempt was made to fit skis on the Fairchild it was found that the shock absorber struts were missing so the mechanics set to and made struts out of a radio mast. The mast was made of 3 in. galvanized pipe. The ends were heated and flattened, then a piece of keel strip was taken from an old motor boat and driven into the flattened ends and bolted into place and holes drilled for attaching to the machine. We were fortunate in locating a 1/2 in. post drill at Dominion Explorers' base and the drilling was not so difficult as one would imagine. The struts fitted without using force and the circumstances considered, this spoke well of the men who made them."

On October 25 four planes took off for Bathurst Inlet. They landed some distance from the Dominion Explorers camp at the Burnside River. Here trouble cropped up when a Fokker went through the ice. The other planes spent several days, weather permitting, scouring the landscape for the MacAlpine party. One of them overflew Dease Point where the two stranded MacAlpine planes lay buried in snow. Then on November 5 an Inuit arrived at the search base with news that the lost men had arrived safely at Cambridge Bay. The search was over but not so the woes of the searchers.

In organizing to get back south a Fairchild was damaged at Muskox Lake, and Roy Brown's Fokker was wrecked at Aylmer Lake. Another Fokker was laid up at Fort Reliance with a cracked cylinder. With these set-backs it took until December 4 for the MacAlpine party and most of the searchers to arrive at Cranberry Portage near Flin Flon.

A tribute to the Inuit who assisted the MacAlpine party was later written by G.A. Thompson:

"No account of our stay at Dease Point could be complete without a eulogy on Eskimos. They are probably considered heathens by the churches, but personally I have never met truer Christians nor more truthful, honest, generous people.

"On our arrival at Dease Point we explained our situation to them and we promised that they would be well rewarded if they would look after us and take us to Cambridge Bay. They had nothing but our word for this but if we had been their own children they could not have mothered us with greater care. When luxuries such as tobacco, tea, and sugar ran low they shared their meagre store with us. Even our lack of suitable clothing that caused us the greatest discomfort they did their best to supply."

In Search of Franklin

The following year G-CASK was recovered at Dease Point and flown south, and its mate, G-CASM assigned to carry an expedition under Major L.T. Burwash to investigate the location of the magnetic north pole and to search for evidence of the ill-fated Franklin expedition of the mid 1840s. This aircraft, however, developed engine trouble and G-CASK was called in as replacement. On September 4, 1930 Walter Gilbert flew it from Coppermine on Coronation Gulf headed for King William Land via Cambridge Bay. Next day the expedition flew up the west side of the Boothia Peninsula as far as Franklin Strait, the area of the magnetic pole. Returning southward, stops were made along the top side of King William Land where some Franklin artifacts were discovered in a cairn. Stan Knight, the engineer, described the find: "In the bottom of the cairn which, it appeared, had been rifled since it was set up, was a piece of serge from what was apparently a navy coat, a piece of hemp rope, a gadget for tightening a guy rope on the side of a tent, and a piece of Cardiff coal. These may seem like insignificant things, but they were completely foreign to that area and obviously had been left by the party when they landed."

On September 7, G-CASK was again back at Coppermine having pushed to new limits the northern presence of the airplane in Canada. During the trip, Stan Knight photographed much of the country, and his photos later proved valuable in making up maps of the region. For his efforts on the trip, and other contributions to Canadian aviation, Walter Gilbert won the 1933 McKee Trophy.

One of Canada's most famous pioneer bushplanes, the Fokker Universal, G-CASK seen here at the Gilbert Labine Camp, Echo Bay, Great Bear Lake, Christmas 1931. On all operations in the NWT, Canadian Airways aircraft like ASK were crewed by both pilot and air engineer.

Walter Gilbert

Walter Gilbert standing by a Western Canada Airways Universal in 1928.
James Richardson and Sons, Ltd.

The Air Mail

Aviation in southern Canada may not have been as exciting or as risky as in the North. But it was steadily growing. While it was timber, minerals, furs, and fish that were keeping bush fliers active, in the populated south it was the mail sack that to a large extent made commercial flying viable.

In the late twenties the federal government decided to experiment with air mail, and set aside $75 000 for this in 1927. Air mail was already big in the United States, the transcontinental air mail system having been completed in September, 1920. In Canada, official air mail had its beginnings May 10, 1927, when under a Canadian Government contract, J.F. Stevenson of Western Canada Airways flew mail from Rolling Portage to Gold Pines to Red Lake return. Other inaugural flights followed that year. One took place on September 9 when pilot J.H. Tudhope and crewman G. La Grave loaded mail at Rimouski for the first of a series of proving flights.

They were to fly in a Vickers Vanessa to Montreal with 500 pounds of mail transferred from the Canadian Pacific liner *Empress of France*. Unfortunately the Vanessa cracked up while taking off from the choppy St. Lawrence. Crew and mail

were rescued, the mail not arriving at its destination until some days after the *Empress* had docked at Montreal! The Post Office was not deterred by this accident and soon regular flights were being made between Montreal and Rimouski, speeding inbound and outbound mail to its destinations. These flights saved from one to four days on delivery.

Besides the mail run along the steamer route, Ottawa tried other new air mail routes. One of its "firsts" was the December 23, 1927, flight when Romeo Vachon flew 753 pounds of mail from Lac Ste. Agnes near La Malbaie to communities along the North Shore of the St. Lawrence as far down as Sept Îles, and returned to base on the same day. His success was added evidence that the airplane had a valuable contribution to make in Canada's more isolated regions.

Before long, flying mailmen were visiting more such out-of-the-way places. On February 8, 1928, Vachon carried the first air mail to Anticosti Island. The Magdalens, and Pelee Island in Lake Erie were also soon benefiting from this new concept. In winter such places were normally cut off from the rest of the country. For Pelee Islanders the winter mails had traditionally arrived via sled-equipped

boat, manhandled across Pelee Passage by the local mail contractor and his helpers. This hardy crew braved ice, snow, and wind for twelve hours in crossing to or from the island. The airplane relieved them of this difficult routine, and over the winter 1927-1928, London Air Transport carried eight tons of mail on the Pelee Island service, completing 63 flights.

The air mail was like manna from heaven for Canada's ever-struggling flying operations. Guaranteed revenue earned on government mail contracts helped pay the bills to provide the impetus for expansion. The air mail led to the opening up of new airways in many parts of the country, and notable flights were commonplace. In 1928 the first trans Canada air mail was carried. S/L A.E. Godfrey and Sgt. Major Graham took off from Ottawa in an FC-2 on

A Fairchild FC-2W2 of Canadian Colonial Airways inaugurating Canada-U.S. air mail service at St. Hubert, October 1, 1928. Canadian Colonial was controlled by the Aviation Corporation of Delaware, an organization bidding at the time to take control of commercial aviation in eastern Canada. AVL was destroyed in a hangar fire at Newark, New Jersey, in August 1930.

Public Archives of Canada (PA 59962)

Three aircraft of "Wop" May's Commercial Airways fleet. The all red trio are a pair of Bellanca CH-300 Pacemakers and a Lockheed Vega. The Commercial Airways fleet began hauling four tons of mail down the Mackenzie Valley on Dec. 10, 1929. Seventeen days were required to complete the job.

Aviation and Space Division, National Museum of Science and Technology (7168)

September 5, and after 32 hours of flight arrived at Vancouver on the eighth. The first air mail to wing into the far North was carried by "Punch" Dickins. Flying a Western Canada Airways plane he flew from Ft. McMurray on January 23, 1929 heading "down north" along the Mackenzie. Three days and 850 miles later Dickens delivered the mail to Fort Simpson. Later that year "Wop" May of Commercial Airways carried the first official mail to the Arctic with a load that reached Aklavik on December 30. To Western Canada Airways' chagrin, May had been able to win the Mackenzie Valley air mail contract in 1929.

No matter where airplanes were being flown in Canada, operators had to use their ingenuity to make flying pay. The worst thing was to have planes idle. Thus, even in the North, where mail, furs, mining equipment, and other loads were the mainstay of bush flying, the ancient art of barnstorming was still practiced. In one of his reports to WCA, "Punch" Dickins wrote, "At Aklavik there were about 300 Eskimos that had never seen a plane and together with about 300 dogs tied up, the din when I shut off the engine and got out,

G-CAJT, the D.H. 61 Giant Moth loaned by Canadian Vickers to Western Canada Airways for mail route evaluation on the Prairies. The first of these flights was flown between Winnipeg and Calgary September 13-20, 1928. AJT was destroyed by fire near Calgary the following month.

James Richardson and Sons, Ltd.

was astounding. The Eskimos were very curious and I took some 35 of them up in the machine at $10 each for about 10 minutes. I could have taken more, but by the time I had made seven trips with 42 persons all told, I was too tired and called it a day about 11 P.M. This revenue helped the trip considerably."

Besides the boost given commercial aviation in the late twenties, there were other changes being felt on the commercial flying scene in Canada. Existing air operators began coming under the influence of syndicates. New names appeared, such as International Airways and Interprovincial Airways. In 1929, Canadian Airways and Canadian Transcontinental Airways came under the umbrella of the Aviation Corporation of Canada with control over a wide network of airmail routes in eastern Canada. Once again James A. Richardson was involved in these changes. He was one of several influential Canadians who was keenly aware of moves afoot by American interests to take over commercial flying in southern

Canada and was anxious to prevent this from coming about. One large American operation was already doing well in Canada. This was Colonial Airways which flew mail between Albany, New York, and Montreal.

On June 25, 1929, Western Canada Airways was awarded the Prairie air mail route. The airline was already prepared for this big contract having invested considerably in route-proving the year before. The contract necessitated additions to the fleet, and six Fokker F.14's were ordered. These were to serve as combination mail/passenger aircraft. The service, as worked out, was to operate at night, and officially got under way March 30, 1930. Although eventually to be cut as part of the government's Depression years austerity planning, it again affirmed the capability of the airplane as an effective means of transport in Canada. Over 90 per cent of WCA scheduled air mail flights were completed on time during the duration of the Prairie service.

This sort of development was indeed a

hopeful sign that commercial aviation in Canada was coming of age. Yet overall, Canada still lagged internationally. Europe, Russia, and the United States were all ahead of Canada in commercial aviation developments. About this the Aerial League of Canada editorialized, "The Dominion finds herself in the anamalous position of being a pygmy among giants in the matter of civil aviation."

Long Distance Flying

A major trend of the late twenties and the thirties was long distance flying. The many flights made were motivated by personal and national pride with enticing prizes often being put up by private or corporate interests. Whatever the reason, the romance and excitement of record-making flights that followed World War I returned in 1927 when Charles Lindbergh amazed the world with his solo flight across the Atlantic. In 33-1/2 hours he covered some 3600 miles between New York and Paris. With this, the rush was on to share in the

fame and laurels that awaited the successful long distance flier.

Many of these flights originated from the famous landing strip at Harbour Grace, Newfoundland. Adventurer after adventurer lifted off from here to disappear from view within minutes over the vast Atlantic seascape. Americans, British, Italians, Germans, Danes, Hungarians, Canadians, the French — everyone seemed to be involved. Some were to succeed but for others the last heard of them was the fading drone of their motors as they winged out over the Atlantic. Among the successful was Amelia Earhart who, in June of 1928, became the first woman to fly the Atlantic. In October the following year, Erroll Boyd, with H.P. Connor navigating, became the first Canadian to make the crossing, flying from Newfoundland to England in a Bellanca called *Maple Leaf*.

During this era, Canada provided considerable assistance to many of the long distance fliers. Information concerning landing places, weather, fuel caches, and so

on was made available on request. Thus did Flight Lieutenant Francis Chichester receive detailed information regarding his proposed 1931 flight across the Arctic en route from New Zealand to England. Distances between landing points were accurately listed, warnings were given about dangerous waters for his seaplane to avoid. A letter to the German flier Von Gronau informed him of fuel caches, including one at Sugluk Inlet: "4 drums, approximating 160 gallons, which is stored in a small bay to the west of the Inlet. Information on this can be obtained from the Trading Post."

The RCAF also provided assistance to Charles Ulm. In 1934 he had his Airspeed Envoy at St. Hubert making preparations for a trans-Pacific flight. At this time, the RCAF sent J.D. Hunter to St. Hubert to set up Ulm's auto pilot. Hunter had conducted the tests of the first auto pilot in Canada which had been installed in an Air Force Bellanca. After completing work on Ulm's auto pilot, a test flight was conducted under fully loaded conditions and all went well. Ulm later flew to California, but on the first leg of his trip, flying from San Franscisco to Hawaii, he and his crew became lost and were never heard from again.

Two Canadians were lost on a transAtlantic attempt. Terrence Tully and James Medcalf, both of the OPAS, entered as crew in the London, Ontario — London, England flight promoted by Carling

Commercial Airways' Avro Avian at Peace River, Alberta, during its famous mercy flight to Fort Vermilion. "Wop" May and Vic Horner had flown it there in January 1929 with a cargo of antitoxin needed in Little Red River where diphtheria had broken out. The determination of an Indian musher who had brought word of the epidemic and the quick reaction of medical and aviation interests in Edmonton saved Little Red River from possible disaster.
Glenbow-Alberta Institute (NA-1258-62)

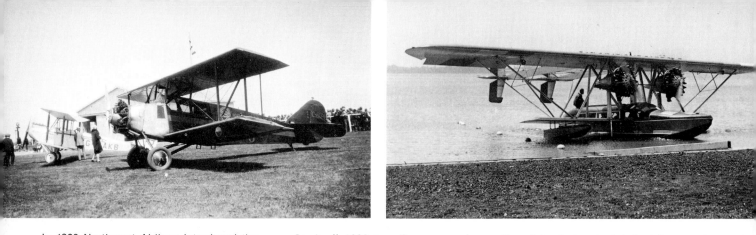

In 1926 Northwest Airlines introduced the Stinson Detroiter on its Minneapolis-Chicago run becoming the first airline in America to use a closed-cabin landplane. Northwest's first route extension was Minneapolis-Winnipeg via Fargo. One of its Detroiters is seen here at Winnipeg in 1928. A Winnipeg Flying Club Cirrus Moth is in the background.

Neil Christenson

Breweries. Carling provided the airplane, a Stinson Detroiter, and in a rousing send-off the pair set off for England, August 28, 1927. They made their way to Harbour Grace and on September 7 headed eastward for England. They and their plane, the *Sir John Carling,* disappeared forever. An OPAS colleague of Tully and Medcalf, "Duke" Schiller searched far out over the Atlantic for his friends, flying in the Detroiter *Royal Windsor.* This was the plane in which he and Phil Wood had planned to fly the Atlantic, but after the disappearance of the *Sir John Carling,* they prudently abandoned their scheme.

The first large modern commercial airliner in regular service in Canada was this Ford Trimotor of B.C. Airways. It was placed in service between Vancouver and Seattle in early August 1928 but crashed disastrously into Puget Sound on the twenty-fifth of that month. The plane had taken off in poor visability, forcing the pilot to fly low over the water. All seven aboard died in the crash.

Provincial Archives, Victoria, B.C. (76745)

In April 1928 two Germans and an Irishman took off from Dublin in a Junkers W.33 called the *Bremen.* They headed westward for New York in their attempt to become the first ever to fly an airplane non-stop east to west across the Atlantic. This was to be a more challenging flight than those which flew the Atlantic from west to east for it set the Junkers in the face of the Westerly winds.

While the first half of their trip was routine, the trio ran into bad weather approaching Canada. It appears that they were forced off course towards the north, crossed the Labrador coast, then turned southward apparently searching for habitation and a safe place to land. After some 37 hours aloft they reached Greenly Island in the Strait of Belle Isle. Here they made an immediate landing, fearing that their fuel was too low to continue safely. Upon landing, the aircraft was slightly damaged but the crew was safe.

Word soon reached the media that the *Bremen* had landed and a mad rush ensued to be first to "scoop" the story. First on the scene was "Duke" Schiller who flew down the rugged North Shore from Lac Ste. Agnes near Murray Bay. For the next few weeks he was to be the reporter of events for the *Toronto Star.* After Schiller's arrival, a small army of reporters, photographers, and aviators streamed to Greenly Island. Notables included Romeo Vachon, Floyd Bennett, and Bernt Balchen in a Ford Trimotor, and Hugo

Toronto's first scheduled airline service began in June 1929 with downtown-to-downtown flights between Toronto and Buffalo. Canadian Colonial Airways, used Sikorsky S-38's on the run. Return fare was $30. The service was popular during that year's Canadian National Exhibition but business dropped off when summer ended and was never resumed. In this view, NC9138, later christened *Nonokas* is seen arriving at the Toronto air harbour located at the foot of Yonge Street.

Reprinted by Permission of the Toronto Sun Ltd.

Junkers' daughter. When Bennett became ill and was hospitalized at Quebec, Charles Lindbergh flew to Quebec with medication. Upon Bennett's death, however, interest shifted from Greenly Island to Washington where Bennett was buried; and to New York where the crew of the *Bremen* was honoured.

Some time after, a U.S. Army team undertook to repair the *Bremen* which by then had been removed to nearby Blanc Sablone. With repairs completed, a takeoff over rugged terrain was attempted, but the *Bremen* cracked up, sustaining extensive damage. After this it was was removed by steamship and eventually repaired and put on display in the United States, finally ending up at the Ford Museum, Dearborn, Michigan, where it may be seen today. The complete story of the *Bremen* has been documented by F.W. Hotson of the Canadian Aviation Historical Society.

Another famous event during these hectic years of spanning oceans and

The *Bremen* stranded on Greenly Island, with repairs under way. At the right is Dr. Cucsenier of Canadian Transcontinental Airways who had accompanied "Duke" Schiller on the initial flight to rescue the downed fliers.

Via Fred Hotson

continents was the trans-Atlantic crossing of the airship R-100. The great vessel slipped its moorings at Cardington, England, on July 29, 1930, cruising westward in the wake of the R-34 which had made the first non-stop aerial crossing of the Atlantic in 1919. On the evening of July 30, the R-100 arrived over Montreal and next morning docked at St. Hubert. For two weeks, the R-100 cruised the skies of southern Quebec and Ontario as far inland as Niagara Falls. It was hoped that the flight of the R-100 would be a prelude to a new mode of trans-Atlantic passenger travel and link all parts of the Empire; but when the R-100 set off for home on August 13 it was the last time Canada would host such a vessel. Calamities struck several of the big airships over the next few years and this unique kind of Jumbo-style travel fell into disfavour.

Several globe-encircling flights also involved Canada during the early thirties. The famous Wiley Post flew into Edmonton on June 30, 1931, from Fairbanks, homeward bound on his New York to New York flight. He found Edmonton's Blatchford Field unserviceable, as his arrival there had been preceded by heavy rains. A safe departure seemed impossible. But while Post and his navigator, Harold Gatty, slept, airport manager Jimmy Bell put crews to work taking down overhead wires along a two-mile stretch of paved road adjacent to the airport. Come morning, Post taxied onto the road and took off uneventfully for New York. June 30 - July 1, 1933 Post was again in Edmonton on another of his world flights.

For years after his historic flight to Paris, Charles Lindbergh continued his interest in long range flying. In part these were conducted as route-proving operations for Pan American Airways. One of these in 1933 took him and his wife on a 30 000 mile flight around the rim of the Atlantic. Another during the same period took them around the world, with part of the route being across Canada's Barren Land. Another flight of note during these years was that of Leonard Reid and James Ayling who became the first ever to fly non-stop from Canadian to British soil.

The R-100 moored at St. Hubert after its crossing from Cardington. The St. Hubert tower, intended as part of an Empire-wide chain of airship bases, was 207 feet high.

York University, Scott Archives

James R. Ayling and Leonard G. Reid with their D.H. Dragon and Ford sedan just prior to departing for Baghdad from Wasaga Beach.

Reprinted by permission of the Toronto Sun Ltd.

Their flight, originally intended to reach Baghdad, commenced at Wasaga Beach on Georgian Bay, August 8, 1934. It terminated 30 hours, 55 minutes later in Middlesex with throttle control problems.

Also of interest during this period were three flying boat flights conducted by the German, Wolfgang Von Gronau. The purpose of these was "by means of systematic investigation more precisely to determine the suitability of the northern air route to North America." In August 1930, Von Gronau and his three crewmen flew from northern Germany. They reached Cartwright, Labrador, via the Faeroes, Iceland, and Greenland. On their eighth day they reached Halifax. Next day, August 26, they flew on to New York; thence they sailed home via steamship.

Commander Wolfgang Von Gronau's Dornier Wal pictured during a stop-over at Lac du Bonet, Manitoba in August 1932.

Via Ralph Shapland

The following year, Von Gronau flew to Iceland, Greenland, directly over the Greenland ice cap, and southward to Povungnituk on Hudson Bay. The expedition next reached Longlac in northern Ontario where 90 gallons of fuel were taken from the RCAF's fuel cache there. Next day, Von Gronau pushed on to Chicago, then to New York where crew and airplane again took ship for home.

In 1932, Von Gronau again traced the North Atlantic route. From Cartwright he flew across North America with stops at Montreal, Windsor, Chicago, Minneapolis, Lac du Bonet, Cormorant Lake, Lac la Biche, and Prince Rupert. From there, the Germans flew northward to Alaska and out over the Pacific to complete the first "round-the-world" flight by flying boat.

Even though the excitement of long-distance flying was in the public eye almost constantly after 1927, this phenomenon in aviation ought to be placed in perspective. Such flights were still rare by the mid thirties, and between 1919-1930, only 21 trans-Atlantic crossings had been made.

While the world so carefully noted these daring flights, Canada itself did not seem to be much involved directly in the competition. But although its aviators were not hailed in ticker tape parades in New York they were hardly slackers when it came to great feats in the air. Theirs were more practical and work-a-day accomplishments, yet the territory overflown was no less awesome or unforgiving than the murky Atlantic. And though it wasn't spectacular headline news, the McKee Trophy continued to be awarded annually as by far the most meaningful tribute in recognition of Canadian aviators.

Through the Depression

Although the Depression was hard on aviation in Canada, most firms were able to carry on. Aerial surveying went on, Depression or no. In 1932 Toronto became

Two of General Italo Balbo's 24 Savoia-Marchettis alighting at Shediac, New Brunswick in July 1933. This was the second time Balbo, Italy's Air Minister, had led a mass formation of flying boats across the Atlantic. Such escapades won world-wide recognition for the countries concerned and further emphasized the possibilities of flight.

DND (HC-6594)

the first Canadian city to use aerial photography to secure the detail required to produce a city map to scale. A Puss Moth of Skyways Ltd. was used for this project. On clear days pilot L. Sellar and photographer W.F. Shaylor would climb to 3600 feet. Sellar would fly a preselected course holding his speed and altitude steady. Shaylor would begin clicking his shutter at precise intervals, overlapping each exposure. Scale of the photos was 300 feet to the inch. Once processed these were enlarged to 100 feet to the inch and carefully worked into the base map already drawn by ground surveyors using existing maps. These were generally old, outdated, and drawn to various scales. Details such as individual structures, house numbers,

Wiley Post's Lockheed Vega, *Winnie May* at Edmonton's Blatchford Field in 1933. During this globe-encircling flight Post was alone, but equipped with an auto pilot and radio direction finder. The trip was completed in 7 days, 18 hours, 19 minutes.

Provincial Archives of Alberta, Alfred Blyth Collection. (BLY. 137/1)

fence and lot lines, streetcar tracks and hydro lines were then added by draftsmen using the aerial photos as their references. An engineer on the project noted, "In two hours Mr. Sellar and Mr. Shaylor do work that would take four surveyors over a year to perform, securing the same information by actual house-by-house measurement."

Though on a reduced scale, mining also continued to provide flying contracts. There was a gold rush in 1933 in the Caribou Mountains of British Columbia. The trip overland from Vancouver to the goldfields took two days. Many prospectors, however, took advantage of charter aircraft which covered the distance in two or three hours. One report of the day noted that the gold rush had caused

"the most sudden awakening to the merits of air travel in B.C.."

With the general slump in business during the Depression, fliers frequently resorted to their old standby, barnstorming. They scoured the countryside for farmers' fields, fair grounds, resorts or wherever else there was the chance of hustling passengers for five- or ten-minute rides. To each pilot the motto "Anyone with five bucks is my personal friend" fitted exactly. That finding the clients with five dollars to spend was not all that easy is reflected by Jack Charleson's comment that, "Piloting aircraft in those days was a very dangerous and hazardous profession as the risk of starving to death was ever present."

Murray Shorthill has recalled these times in the *Journal of the Canadian Aviation Historical Society:* "Then we used to have the cent-a-pound weekends at Edmonton quite often, usually with parachute drops as an added attraction . . . .

"We usually did quite well financially on these special events and somehow the 'cent-a-pound' idea seemed to be quite attractive to the public. We never lost one passenger or even injured one seriously in the thousands we carried. Great credit must go to the pilots who initiated the public out of its apathy towards flying. Only once did we have a near fatal accident — the J-5's on McConachie's Trimotor were just ticking over when a woman walked right through the turning port propeller without a scratch. Both Grant and I jumped at the same time to grab her, but she was already through. She sure was lucky.

"We often had wing tips dig in, machines up on their noses, flat tires, low grade gas which overheated the engines, short field problems, and many little

unexplainable things. But in the final run, I feel that we always gave good value for the customer's dollar — which can't be said for many other forms of amusement and service to the general public."

Canadian Airways

During this period American interests continued attempts to gain control of commercial aviation in Canada. Because of this, Canadian business strengthened its position through the Aviation Corporation of Canada, but something more important occurred on November 25, 1930, when the two national railroads formed Canadian Airways, with James A. Richardson as president. The new airline was divided into two operational districts, Eastern Lines and Western Lines. With operations from coast to coast, Canadian Airways was a logical step towards the day when a full trans-Canada airline would be a reality.

Canadian Airways was more a series of regional operations and the various parts of Canada served were not interconnected. An important result of Canadian Airways coming into existence, though, was the reduction of cut-throat competition that had existed in commercial flying over the previous few years. With the new airline forming, operators such as Western Canada Airways, the original Canadian Airways, and Transcontinental Airways were brought together in a cooperative venture. Of course there continued to be competition. Along the Mackenzie, there were companies like Mackenzie Air Service and Spence-McDonough Air Transport; and along the river, RCAF aircraft were depriving commercial operators of badly needed revenue by operating flights for various civil government departments.

Canadian Airways expanded considerably in the months following its inception, both in terms of new aircraft and new business. Its most famous aircraft was acquired in the fall of 1931. This was the Junkers 52, CF-ARM. The biggest airplane in Canada at the time, it was much heralded, though plagued for years with technical gremlins. Not until it was reengined in 1937 with a Rolls-Royce Buzzard did it come into its own as a revenue-earning freighter.

Canadian Airways also purchased a number of smaller Junkers bush planes in the early thirties. These had a good payload, were unusually trouble free, and reflected low operating costs. They were to serve the airline and its successor for many years to come.

The slow Fokker F.14 mail planes were eventually replaced by speedier Boeings and Stearmans, and for a time

CF-AWR, the Bellanca 66-70 Air Cruiser brought to Canada by Mackenzie Air Service in 1935 to haul uranium concentrate from Great Bear Lake to Edmonton. This busy scene is at Cameron Bay on Great Bear. AWR survived until January 1947 when it was wrecked in a crash in north-western Ontario.
Aviation and Space Division, National Museum of Science and Technology (4710)

Canadian Airways prospered. But inevitably the Depression caught up with commercial flying. In early 1931 the R.B. Bennett government began cutting back on air mail contracts, and the following spring cancelled outright Canadian Airways' Prairie air mail service. This forced the company to tighten its belt. There were lay-offs and pay cuts affecting many employees. Adding to these woes, air mail on some routes was taken over by the RCAF; and the lucrative forestry patrols provided by civil operators in Manitoba were lost when the RCAF sold the province a

Two famous types used in the Canadian bush, both shown in their winter ski apparel. CF-BIM was a Stinson SR-9F Reliant owned originally by McIntyre-Porcupine Mines, which imported it in 1938. CF-BIF was the Beech C-17R of Starratt Airways and Transportation seen here on Uchi Lake, Ontario. It was later taken over by CPA and sold in Alaska in 1944.
Via Gath Edward and Jean Smith

number of old Vedettes at a dollar apiece giving rise to the Manitoba Government Air Service.

In spite of such setbacks, Canadian Airways managed to keep the props ticking over. Its statistics for 1935 show 17 869 hours logged. This compares with the 16 059 hours flown that year by the RCAF. The company carried 5 275 745 pounds of express, 817 678 pounds of mail, and 14 542 passengers. The full Canadian Airways story may be read in K.M. Molson's *Pioneering in Canadian Air Transport*.

Mackenzie Air Service

Canadian Airways' competitors during this period included such firms as Explorers Air Transport and Mackenzie Air Service, the latter being founded by Leigh Brintnell. Brintnell had been a World War I flier and had joined Western Canada Airways in 1927. His pioneering spirit had soon taken him farther into the North than most bush pilots had dared yet venture. In 1929 he conducted an extensive survey flight. Leaving Winnipeg he flew to The Pas, Waterways, down the Mackenzie to Great Bear Lake where he let off a prospector, Gilbert Labine, and on to Aklavik. From there he flew to Dawson across the rugged Richardson Mountains and crossed other Yukon ranges over which the airplane had not yet flown. The flight continued to

One of Leigh Brintnell's Fokker Super Universals, brought to Canada in late 1932. It is seen during changeover to floats at Fort Saskatchewan. CF-ATW was wrecked at Cambridge Bay April 20, 1934 while making a forced landing due to fuel exhaustion.
Public Archives of Canada, Matt Berry Collection (PA 90895)

Whitehorse, Skagway, Prince Rupert, Prince George, Edmonton, The Pas, and Winnipeg. This incredible trip took Brintnell over 9000 miles in 94 hours of flying.

Before long, Brintnell was general manager of Western Canada Airways, and a driving force behind that operation. Regarding an early trip down the Mackenzie, he pointed out to "Punch" Dickins, who had had some difficulties along the way, "We do not see that the Mackenzie River is such a hazardous place to fly as you have a certain amount of dog team travel up and down the river with occasional cabins and a post every 150 miles or so. Conditions are really much worse north of Gold Pines or north of The Pas as there are no definite routes of travel and no one is in the country." Here was a real man of the North.

In 1932 Brintnell established Mackenzie Air Service, in direct formidable competition with his previous employer. Through the thirties, he built up a business

specializing in service to the mining industry. Brintnell's staff, from truck driver Archie Watt to capable and respected pilots like Stan McMillan, Matt Berry, Gil McLaren, Marlow Kennedy and Bob Randall were intensely loyal, and proud to be associated with him.

Mackenzie's fleet originally included the standard Fairchild 71's such as CF-AKN; and Super Universals such as CF-ATJ. The big Fokker AF-14A, CF-AUD, was another early type. It crashed in Edmonton in May 1934 killing a mechanic and injuring pilot Matt Berry. In time the fleet was updated. New aircraft included the Fairchild 82's CF-AXM, 'XN and 'XQ; the Norseman's CF-AZA, CF-BAM and CF-BFR; the Beech 17, CF-BBB (Brintnell's Bastard Beech); and the Bellanca Air Cruisers CF-AWR, CF-BKV and CF-BTW. CF-AWR was operated for Eldorado Mines, hauling pitchblende concentrate from Great Bear Lake, south to Edmonton. The origin of this connection was the 1929 flight when Brintnell flew a prospector, Gilbert Labine, to the shores of Great Bear. Labine struck it rich, discovering vast deposits of pitchblende, the ore of radium and uranium. Thus did aviation play a direct role in the discovery and development of one of the world's greatest pitchblende deposits.

When it came to Canada in 1930 this Junkers Ju.52 was the largest aircraft in the country. It was 60 feet long with a wing span of 96 feet 9 inches. All up weight was over 15 000 pounds. Registered CF-ARM, it became famous freighting in many parts of Canadian Airways domain. In this photo it is shown refuelling at Beauchene on Lake Onatchiway, northern Quebec. At the time it was hauling freight between there and Manouane Lake 100 miles to the northeast where a dam was being constructed for the aluminum foundry at Arvida.

S.J. Woodham

A new Stinson SR-5A clearing Customs at the Toronto Air Harbour October 15, 1934 on its delivery flight to Canada. CF-AWO was owned by General Airways of Toronto. On April 7, 1936 it was unloading at the Siscoe gold mine in northern Ontario when a deplaning passenger accidentally hit the throttle. AWO then took off on its own, climbed to about 200 feet then, as stated in a letter from General Airways to the Controller of Civil Aviation, "connected with the surface of the lake, left wing first."

Reprinted by permission of the Toronto Sun Ltd.

The Trans-Canada Airway

In spite of its growth, aviation in Canada was still in its infancy during the mid to late thirties. Few aircraft in service were in the airline category. Those few were a handful of Ford Trimotors, Barkley-Grows, and Lockheed 10's. Standard equipment was still the Fokker, Junkers, and Fairchild bushplanes. Without more up-to-date equipment there was little hope of Canada beginning transcontinental airline operations.

A trans-Canada airway had been under discussion for many years. The trans-Canada flight of 1920 had actually anticipated such a route, and since the late twenties the Aerial League had been steadily plugging the concept and studying potential routes. These could be no more than conceptual, for across the land there were very few airports and hardly any navigation aids. On the positive side, though, more than one group of influential Canadians were considering backing a

transcontinental airline. One of these was headed by James A. Richardson.

Ironically it was the Depression which gave concrete hope for the establishment of a trans-Canada airway. On October 8, 1932, Major-General A.G.L. McNaughton, encouraged by J.A. Wilson, Controller of Civil Aviation, submitted a proposal to Prime Minister Bennett to employ some of the country's unemployed. The plan was to put 2000 single, homeless men to work on a series of relief projects that included building landing fields for a coast-to-coast airway. Bennett immediately adopted the scheme. Detailed plans were worked out and before long camps were going up all along the 3108 miles of proposed airway. Forests rang with the

sound of axe and saw as upwards of 2600 relief workers at a time began carving out airstrips in parts of the country often remote from civilization. The airstrips were for the most part designated as emergency strips. They were additional to existing municipal airports, more and more of which had been appearing throughout the thirties. The new fields added to the ones already existing along the airway meant a landing field about every 25 miles along the route.

Actual selection of airport sites was an exacting responsibility, especially where the Canadian Shield or B.C. mountain region was concerned. Siting was finalized after aerial survey and evaluation by crews on the ground. In cases where land was privately owned, or its timber or mineral rights held, negotiations were necessary before the government could take possession. Clearing, draining, and grading of each site was followed by runway construction, there usually being two runways 3000 by 600 feet in dimension. Key airfields were to be equipped with hangars, and refuelling and meteorological facilities. Strategic ones were to have radio broadcasting stations and beacons. Intermediate strips would have a resident caretaker plus some lighting and communications facilities. Lighting could include a revolving beacon, with generator if required; obstruction lights; ground approach lights; and white boundary lights.

In 1934, J.A. Wilson went on an inspection tour of the complete trans-Canada airway. After attending the opening of the new Summerside airport on Prince Edward Island he headed west. His

Woes in the bush. A Canadian Airways Fairchild 71 being salvaged after a mishap.

Via N.K. Found

trip ended up six weeks later on the West Coast. Some 15 000 miles had been covered, 9000 by air. Included had been a side trip down the Mackenzie River with Walter Gilbert, as far as Cameron Bay on Great Slave Lake.

The Relief Projects had been designed to create as many man-hours of labour as possible. While teams of horses, trucks, and other machinery were available when

One of the toughest bushplanes ever, the Junkers W-34. Several of these aircraft operated in Canada from the early thirties onward. ATF joined the Canadian Airways fleet in late 1932 and 28 years later was still in commercial service, by that time with Pacific Wings Ltd. In 1962 it was donated to the National Aviation Museum where it is now on display.
Aviation and Space Division, National Museum of Science and Technology (001479)

needed, old-fashioned elbow grease was the order of the day. Relief workers received 20 cents a day for their efforts, giving rise to their unofficial title, the Royal Twenty Centers. By the time the program was phased out in mid 1936, some 170 000 men had spent an average of 3.5 months each working in the many camps across the land.

All these efforts to build airports couldn't have come at a better time, for technology was about to bring great things to civil aviation. Developments in aircraft design were soon to change the whole concept of commercial air travel. Aircraft manufacturers in the United States were just introducing a new generation of airliners. These were fast all-metal aircraft. The first was the Boeing 247. In its slipstream came the even more revolutionary

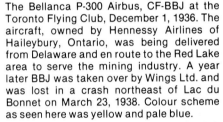

The Bellanca P-300 Airbus, CF-BBJ at the Toronto Flying Club, December 1, 1936. The aircraft, owned by Hennessy Airlines of Haileybury, Ontario, was being delivered from Delaware and en route to the Red Lake area to serve the mining industry. A year later BBJ was taken over by Wings Ltd. and was lost in a crash northeast of Lac du Bonnet on March 23, 1938. Colour scheme as seen here was yellow and pale blue.
Reprinted by permission of the Toronto Sun Ltd.

Douglas DC-1, first flown July 1, 1933. It went into production as the improved DC-2. Airlines in the United States were soon operating large fleets of these airliners. United purchased 60 Boeings; TWA purchased a big fleet of DC-2's. At the same time, Lockheed was producing the first of its modern airliners, the Model 10. Canada's new airway, once just a distant dream of men like James MacBrien, J.A. Wilson and James Richardson was being completed in time to benefit from these exciting developments.

This era in air travel was introduced into Canada with aircraft bearing the colours of American operators, and the travelling public was quick to take advantage of their services. Vancouver was first to benefit from 247 service. On Dominion Day, 1934, a United Airlines 247 opened service between Seattle and Vancouver, accompanied by plenty of press coverage. *Canadian Aviation* magazine reported the occasion:

"It was hailed by the mayor and others as an event of major significance in the transportation history of the city, giving as it does, direct connection with the

Workers preparing stumps for pulling at DND Relief Project site No. 5, Megantic, Quebec, May 1935.

Public Archives of Canada (PA-34544)

Trans-Atlantic Flights Stage Through Canada

During the thirties interest in a trans-Atlantic air service developed. The British experimented with plans to use airships like the R-100. The Germans launched the Dornier X flying boat, a white elephant which struggled across the Atlantic in 1930 but was unable to return for over a year! Much more successful was the stately

The Controller of Civil Aviation's Stearman 4C being refuelled at Diver, Ontario, during an inspection tour of airport construction there October 1934.

Public Archives of Canada (PA-34696)

network of airlines which extend from Seattle to all parts of the North and South American Continents.

"The latest and finest equipment of the company has been placed on the run — the twin-engined, ten-passenger, 180 miles per hour Boeing 247's. There are two uniformed pilots and a hostess on each ship and each arrival or departure is witnessed by an admiring crowd of sightseers." The planes with their uniformed crews were soon busier than expected, whisking travellers between the two centres in a mere 55 minutes. From Seattle passengers could fly on to Montreal but the route lay completely through the United States. It would still be several years before Canadians would be flying their own national airline.

Modern airliners at Vancouver in the mid thirties. NC13348 is a 10-passenger Boeing 247 of United Air Lines, CF-AVJ, an 8-passenger de Havilland Rapide operated by Canadian Airways. The 247 linked Vancouver with the rest of the continent via Seattle, while the Rapide flew between Vancouver, Seattle and Victoria. The 247 had first flown in February 1933 and became the world's first modern airliner. It reduced U.S. transcontinental flying time to 16 hours. The Rapide made its first flight early the following year.

Gordon S. Williams

German airship, *Hindenburg,* which completed many crossings to America. During its period of operation it was possible for a passenger to fly from Hawaii to San Francisco on a Pan American Clipper, thence to New York via domestic carrier. American Airlines provided a shuttle between New York and Lakehurst, New Jersey, where the *Hindenburg* docked. In as little as 80 hours since departure from mid-Pacific, the passenger could be in Europe!

At the same time, Pan American was conducting survey flights between New York and Southampton. These staged through Canada at Shediac, New Brunswick, from where they carried on to Botwood, Newfoundland; Foynes, Ireland;

A Pan American Airways Sikorsky S-42 of the type used during the late thirties on experimental trans-Atlantic route proving. NC16736 is seen here in the River Shannon at Foynes after a crossing from Botwood. On a July 28/29 crossing in 1937 Capt. Harold E. Gray flew this aircraft from New York to Shediac in 6 hours 1 minute, Shediac to Botwood in 2 hours 53 minutes, and Botwood to Foynes in 12 hours 44 minutes for a total trans-Atlantic time of 21 hours 38 minutes.

York University, Scott Archives

and Southampton. Sikorsky S-42 flying boats were used. Meanwhile, Imperial Airways was flying similar trips with the Short S.23. Overall, the older S-42 proved a more practical passenger plane with its greater range, payload and all-up weight. The S.23 reached as far inland as Toronto in 1937.

By the late thirties, American flying boat technology had surpassed that of Britain. The Boeing B-314 entered scheduled trans-Atlantic service in May,

1939. The inaugural passenger flight on June 24 carried 20 passengers from New York to Southampton, again touching at Shediac for fuel.

Also during this period, Britain decided to develop two major airports, one at Shannon, Ireland, and the other in Newfoundland. Work on these began in 1936. Grass runways 600 and 1200 feet wide were constructed, but Britain did not simultaneously develop a trans-Atlantic landplane to use these exotic facilities. The first aircraft to use the Newfoundland base was a tiny Fox Moth! This airport, Gander, would not come into its own until World War II and the years thereafter when land-based passenger planes finally replaced the flying boat on the Atlantic routes. Pan American ceased operations at Shediac October 27, 1945.

A National Airline

Just what form the soon-to-be-established trans-Canada airway would take was still a

matter of discussion midway through the decade. For some years James A. Richardson had been promoting Canadian Airways as the best company for the job as it was the largest and most experienced airline in the country. Thus, with a certain amount of confidence, he began preparing for the eventuality that Canadian Airways would be designated Canada's national airline.

His staff drew up a detailed route system, 3445 miles in length, and proposed a fleet of a dozen Lockheed 10 Electras for the job. Experiments were begun on new routes with routes from Vancouver to Victoria and Vancouver to Seattle being developed. Canadian Airways introduced Lockheed 10 Electras on these routes in direct competition with United Airlines' Boeings. At the same time, the company began a program to qualify its pilots on instruments. Z.L. Leigh, Canada's first fully qualified instrument-rated airline pilot, spent a year training aircrew in a specially-instrumented Laird biplane, as part of Canadian Airways' program to be ready for the day when it would be designated as Canada's major airline flying coast to coast.

Then, in 1937, Ottawa made its plans known on the issue of a national airline. The year before the Department of Railways and Canals had merged with the Department of Marine to form the Department of Transport. Control of civil aviation was transferred from the Department of National Defence to the new DOT. Other developments were reviewed by C.D. Howe some years later: "On being appointed Minister of Transport, I lost no time in laying plans for an expansion of civil aviation in Canada. To acquire a background for doing so, I visited the United States, and travelled over its airlines for the purpose of making a study of air transport, and the facilities required in that connection. To provide a grouping of services directly related to transport by air, the air services branch of the Department of Transport was created, to include the newly acquired civil aviation division, and the meteorological division and the radio division of the former Department of Marine. The new branch was placed under the direction of a capable officer of the department, who was instructed to expand all three services to meet the requirements of a coast to coast interurban air transport service, following the latest American practice.''

The government now proposed that the Canadian National Railways, Canadian Pacific Railway Company and Canadian Airways become joint owners of a new airline. This was a disappointment

Passengers, crew and others concerned with the dawn-to-dusk flight of July 30, 1937, photographed prior to departure for Vancouver. From left to right are D.W. Saunders, L. Parmenter, F.I. Banghart, W.H. Hobbs, H.J. Symington, C.D. Howe, J.H. Tudhope, C.P. Edwards, J.D. Hunter, J.A. Wilson, George Wakeman, D.R. MacLaren.

Public Archives of Canada (C 63377)

for Richardson, particularly as he would not have an equal say with the government parties in policy decisions. This was evident in one of the administrative proposals — a nine-seat board of directors on which the CPR and Canadian Airways would have only two members each.

Trans-Canada Air Lines

As it happened, the CPR and Canadian Airways decided not to participate in the government's proposed airline scheme. On April 10, 1937, then, Trans-Canada Air Lines came into existence as a wholly-owned subsidiary of the CNR. With this, Canadian Airways reorganized. It dropped its Vancouver-Seattle run, turning it over to TCA along with two Lockheed 10's and a Stearman mailplane. These became TCA's first aircraft and on September 1 the same year the new airline operated its first revenue flight, on a previous Canadian Airways route, using an ex-Canadian Airways airliner, the Lockheed 10A, CF-AZY. Pilots E.P.H. Wells and F.M. McGregor were also from Canadian Airways. Two passengers, both TCA officials, were carried. The *Seattle Post Intelligence* noted, "Trans-Canada Air Lines, destined to become one of the most important links in a British aviation system

which is expected to encircle the globe, became a reality yesterday . . . ."

A formidable challenge faced the new airline. It had to establish an integrated air service across thousands of miles of countryside, from Atlantic to Pacific. Airports along the entire route had to be brought up to standard immediately, even though TCA had only two modern aircraft at the time. Native talent to deal with the organization of a proper infrastructure was scarce, a predicament which led C.D. Howe to seek out and import personnel from the United States. A number of key individuals, mainly from United Airlines, accepted Howe's invitation. These included P.G. Johnson, TCA's first Vice President of Operations; D.B. Coyler, Chief Technical Adviser; O.T. Larsen, Technical Adviser, Meteorology and Dispatch; H.O. West, Technical Adviser, Maintenance and Overhaul; H.T. "Slim" Lewis, Technical Adviser, Pilots and Flight Training. Although these and other Americans had all returned to the United States by 1945, they contributed immeasurably to the establishment of TCA as a modern, successful airline.

TCA soon ordered new equipment, increasing its fleet of Electras to five. Bigger Lockheed 14's were also added to the fleet. TCA was soon piling up thousands of hours winging over the Prairies on training flights between Winnipeg, Regina, Lethbridge and Vancouver. This was the most intensive aspect of getting ready for actual passenger operations. Pilots were instructed in a variety of areas, from the mechanical aspects of their aircraft; to basic flying characteristics; instrument flying; local

radio range, night, and cross-country flying.

Many of the early TCA pilots came to the airline directly from the bush. These included Z.L. Leigh of Canadian Airways, Gil McLaren from Mackenzie Air Service, and Herb Seagrim from Wings Ltd. Leigh was the first Canadian pilot hired by TCA. He started with the company Aug. 20, 1937. That they so readily adapted from the old bush planes to the modern Lockheeds indicates the high degree of flying ability of the Canadian bush pilot.

On July 30, 1937, C.D. Howe flew the new airway from Montreal to Vancouver. Besides gaining personal first hand experience, Howe hoped that the flight would help create a feeling of confidence in transcontinental flying in Canada. He boarded a DOT Lockheed along with his deputy, C.P. Edwards; TCA Director, H.J. Symington; pilots J.H. Tudhope and J.D. Hunter; and engineer L. Parmenter. The flight initially departed St. Hubert at 0300, but deteriorating weather forced it to return at 0330. It got away again at 0420 and made Gillies, Ontario, at 0640. Gillies' departure was at 0710 with arrival at Sioux Lookout at 1055. Forty minutes later the Lockheed was again in the air, en route to Winnipeg where it landed at 1155 (Central). It left Winnipeg at 1235 and landed at Regina two hours five minutes later. After only 20 minutes on the ground there it carried on to Lethbridge where it landed at 1610 (Mountain). The flight departed Lethbridge at 1640 and landed in Vancouver at 1830 (Pacific), after 14 hours 30 minutes of actual flight. Thus was completed the first ever dawn-to-dusk trans-Canada flight.

Canadian Pacific Air Lines

While TCA was getting under way, another airline was in the making. Since 1919 the Canadian Pacific Railway had had in its charter the right to operate an air service. It exercised this right in 1929 by joining a syndicate to control commercial aviation in eastern Canada. The syndicate resulted in the formation of the Aviation Corporation of Canada. When Canadian Airways was formed in 1930 one of its Vice Presidents was E.W. Beatty, President of the CPR. Thus did the railway foster an interest in commercial flying. In 1939 it surveyed many smaller air services to further determine the feasibility of expanding its aviation interests. Most of these companies were found to be in financial doldrums and the CPR made deals to buy several of them. During 1940-41 ten companies were consolidated, and in May, 1942, they were formally amalgamated into Canadian Pacific Air Lines.

Typical of the companies taken over was Grant McConachie's Yukon Southern Air Transport. McConachie had started flying for a living in the early thirties. He formed United Air Transport and was no doubt pleased when he landed his first job, odd as it may have seemed. The job was to fly an enthusiastic professor and his flock of yellow-tinted crows south from Edmonton. The professor had a bird migration theory he was trying to validate. Before long, McConachie was established as a fish hauler in northern Alberta. This meant bread and butter, more or less. In the off season there was the inevitable barnstorming and special contracts such as one supporting a prospecting venture in the wilds of B.C.'s Stikine Mountains.

The Lockheed 14 CF-TCX after crash landing at Malton one night. Just as the aircraft was getting airborne, both engines quit. With only landing lights to assist him, the captain did an admirable job of setting down in a ploughed field. Although there were no injuries, TCX was a write-off.

Air Canada

McConachie pioneered with flights north from Edmonton to Whitehorse. In the summer of 1938 he flew the first air mail on this route and a month later introduced air mail between Vancouver and Whitehorse. By this time he had teamed up with Ginger Coote to form Yukon Southern Air Transport. Northern routes had always intrigued McConachie, for the farther north he got the closer he came to realizing an old dream, that of flying to the Orient by a shortcut. He was convinced that a northerly route would prove to be just such a shortcut.

McConachie was brash and optimistic. Otherwise he might not have survived in such a competitive field. There are many examples of his famous personality, one being how he supposedly conned Sir Harry Oakes, an eccentric millionaire, out of a Ford Trimotor for a mere $2500. Later on, he succeeded in relieving Canadian Car of three new Barkley-Grow airliners committing no more than a dollar each for them and a promise to make up the difference when he could. This deal was concluded January 3, 1939. Had the railroad not taken over Yukon Southern shortly afterwards, Canadian Car may have had trouble realizing the $169 367.94 owing on the three planes!

Another example of McConachie's famous way of doing things occurred during a period in which he was in trouble with his insurers over a rash of accidents. As the story goes, he was in Chicago in early 1939 parlaying over insurance. Apparently he had convinced his insurers that he wasn't all that great a risk and they agreed to cover his latest acquisition, the Fleet Freighter, CF-BJT.

After closing the deal, McConachie had the businessmen out to Glenview Airport to see their new asset. He showed them around then climbed into the cockpit to start up. Within a few minutes the Fleet was a smouldering wreck! Leaking fuel had ignited as McConachie started his engines and the fabric-covered plane went up like a

mini *Hindenburg.*

The usual story about this incident is that the Fleet had caught fire and, after McConachie had abandoned it, had careened around the ramp like a flaming pinwheel, ending up a mass of rubble. This was typical of many stories surrounding McConachie. There was often a bit of hyperbole embellishing the mundane truth. A look at the picture of the Fleet taken just after the fire shows the chocks in place and the plane still quite recognizable.

By the time World War II had begun, Yukon Southern was operating a large fleet of airplanes, and a far-reaching route system. But like most other commercial flying operations in Canada at the time, it was on the verge of financial ruin. The war put a halt to much of the mineral exploration and led to a slowdown in other basic northern flying activities.

McConachie's credit was the only thing keeping his planes airborne, and with little or no cash flow from month to month, credit was running out. When the chance came to bail out and join CPA, McConachie didn't hesitate.

The CPA deal enabled many a fish hauler to extricate himself from hopeless debt. Besides, overnight it made him a respectable employee, if not an actual executive, with an airline backed by the biggest private corporation in Canada. Somewhat ironically, the deal also brought together bush pilots who, for a decade or more, had been ferocious competitors. Now these old hands — McConachie, May, Dickins, and the rest were all members of the same big club!

In one sense, CPA had created a kind of monster for itself. It was now master of a far-reaching network of routes serving many parts of northern and western Canada, plus some in the east. These represented a nightmarish hodge-podge, far from the tailor-made routes of TCA. Canadian Pacific's fleet was another headache — 14 different types of aircraft, not to mention engines, and most of this equipment outdated.

The new airline immediately began work in support of the war effort. It established the trans-Atlantic Ferry Command; operated Elementary Flying Training Schools and Air Observer Schools within the British Commonwealth Air Training Plan; major aircraft and aero engine maintenance bases; and flew vital missions over the Northwest Staging Route from Edmonton. This activity made up for the reduction of civilian flying brought about by war; although regular services were kept up along the more important routes.

One of these was CPA's passenger

operations between Montreal, Quebec, and Bagotville, using, at various times earlier in the war, a Barkley-Grow, Boeing 247, and Hudson. CPA pilot Don Murray recalls one flight in the Hudson:

"We had taken off from Quebec to fly to Montreal. There wasn't supposed to be really anything wrong with the weather at all, but when we got up near Montreal it had dropped to below VFR limits. There was nothing to do but turn back to Quebec.

"Then Quebec came on to report they were 300 feet and half a mile in heavy snow! Quebec was my only alternative and there was only enough gas left for four or five quick approaches.

"The radio range had just been installed at Quebec; and although it wasn't yet commissioned, we could use it. The runway was at this time, I think, only 3500 feet long. They did have the ends rolled down, but there were no approach lights. So what happened is that we would get the range and catch a glimpse of the field, but at 300 feet it was gone in a moment. There didn't seem to be a hope in heck! We tried two that way and missed them both. With the third we were getting to the point where it was no longer funny, and we were starting to think in terms of gear up.

"Then I called the tower and requested

McConachie's Fleet Freighter as it burned at Glenview Airport, Chicago.

Via M.L. McIntyre

that when we crossed the range next time they start firing flares, any colour they liked, and every few seconds. This they did, and sure enough we saw one, two — this was something to go on and we broke out over the end of the runway OK.

"About half way down the runway we still had a lot of speed and I knew we were going to go off the end, so I was ready to retract the gear. The brakes were on full and it was all we could handle. We did end up off the end about 200 feet but simply turned around and taxied back."

All this, of course, had to be reported to North Sawle who was in charge of CPA operations at Quebec. Just what the crew had gone through getting the plane down is indicated by Don Murray's remark to Sawle, "Last night I really felt I was in the wrong business. I hate to say this but I seriously thought that if I ever got the plane down, I'd go back to being an engineer."

Sawle was pretty reassuring about the incident, telling about some of his own close calls. One of these involved a Lockheed he was flying from Calgary to Vancouver. Just after reaching 15 000 feet, the plane began to ice up severely. Even with full power it started losing height and speed.

"Any time," cracked Sawle to the co-pilot; then a stoic, "That's it," as the plane went into a violent spin. But as luck would have it, the plane broke into clear weather at 7000 feet and shed ice. Sawle regained

control and the flight carried on to Vancouver.

As the war continued, both TCA and CPA acquired more up-to-date aircraft. In the early forties, Lockheed 18 Lodestars came onto the scene. TCA ordered 12 at $130 000 each. CPA received several on a priority basis given the vital operations it was performing on the Northwest Staging Route. These arrived in Canada in U.S. Army camouflage.

The CGTAS

A landmark during these years occurred July 23, 1943, when TCA began operating the Canadian Government Trans Atlantic Air Service, flying mail and priority passengers between Canada and Britain. For this task a number of Lancasters were civilianized.

The rationale for this service was expressed by C.D. Howe: "The growing strength of the Canadian armed forces and their increased activities have made it necessary to establish this quick and effective means of communications with the United Kingdom for men and materials. The need for a speedy and regular troops air mail service is particularly pressing. Over a quarter of a million members of the Canadian forces are now in the United Kingdom . . . . "

The CGTAS had its beginnings in the summer of 1942 when TCA sent three crews to the Ferry Command ground

school at Dorval. From there the crews were checked out on BOAC Liberators while awaiting their own aircraft. The first of these was an RAF Lancaster, R5727. It had been in the United States being flown on a publicity tour by Clyde Pangborn. At the end of the tour it flew to Malton where turrets and other military hardware were removed. Re-registered as CF-CMS, it was then handed over to TCA. Subsequent aircraft came off the Victory production line.

Although primarily intended as fast mailplanes, the civilianized Lancasters could carry 8 - 10 passengers. Crew were Captain, First Officer, Navigator, and Radio Operator. Passengers were usually VIP's, but westbound frequently were return ferry pilots. Eastbound, planes departed Dorval and usually continued non-stop to Prestwick on what was a 12-hour run. They returned via Iceland or the Azores and Bermuda.

Captains on this pioneer service across the Atlantic included M.B. "Jock" Barclay, J.R. Bowker, S.R. Found, George Lothian, Gil McLaren, and Lindy Rood. For the most part they held little affection for their aircraft. With TCA they had been spoiled by the modern, comfortable Lockheed airliners. Even the BOAC Liberators impressed them more than the noisy, cold Lancasters.

There were frequent mechanical problems as well. On one trip, Captain Lothian had just departed Dorval when a dinghy accidentally jettisonned. The hatch cover which flew off damaged the tail and consequently the flight returned. Mail was transferred to a spare aircraft which took off, but was forced back by severe weather over the Maritimes. On the third attempt a propeller blade failed, forcing another turn around. The fourth attempt succeeded in reaching Prestwick. Another pilot recalls making 21 crossings in the Lancasters with the first 20 having problems of one sort or another. Only the final trip was completely smooth!

Two TCA Lancasters were lost during the CGTAS era. One, commanded by Captain Maurice Gauthier, disappeared into the Atlantic at Long.40W while flying east. The other burned out after a crash landing at Dorval. During the war, the Lancasters completed some 500 trans-Atlantic crossings carrying 1 500 000 pounds of mail.

Post-War Expansion

Once the war was over, TCA and CPA undertook to modernize with the DC-3. As these entered service, older aircraft were disposed of. These went to the four winds, some like the famous CF-ARM, to the scrap heap; others to take up new careers elsewhere.

TCA's Lockheeds had by this time flown a million passengers for 60 000 000 miles; yet there was still a ready market for them. Some continued on as airliners with smaller operators such as Associated Airways and Southern Provincial Airlines. Others became corporate and aero-survey aircraft. As corporate machines, they became Canada's first really exotic private planes, and were to remain popular into the sixties.

Canada's aircraft industry was geared for military production during World War II; but as soon as the war ended, attention turned again to civil production and to commercial flying. More than ever the Canadian public was air minded. The exploits of Canadian airmen overseas had done much to create an atmosphere more sympathetic to flying than had previously existed. C.D. Howe made the point in Parliament: "The urgency of war production has caused many businessmen who were formerly unfamiliar with air travel, to become new customers for our commercial airlines." This new atmosphere gave TCA and CPA cause for post-war optimism.

BALLAD OF A BUSH PILOT

In days gone by I used to fly
A Fairchild eighty-two,
And was it fair or stormy air
We'd always muddle through.
For hours I'd sit upon the bit
Of Kapok-padded seat,
My knees tucked in beneath my chin
In comfort, hard to beat!
The instruments, the cowling dents,
The grease spots on the glass,
I still recall them one and all
As through the years I pass.

I see also, in passing show,
The day my motor quit;
While taking off, it gave a cough.
There was no place to sit
But in the trees; and I said "Please
Don't fail me now, old chum!"
With groan and crack she broke her back,
But I just cut my thumb!
My head I felt, undid my belt,
And said, with logic true:
"Two motors would, if they were good,
Have carried us on through!"

Things happen strange, and courses
    change,
And soon there came a day,
In Sioux Lookout, when I took out
A Beechcraft "Eighteen A."
You'll never know, nor can I show
The ecstasy I knew:
As days went by, I found that I
forgot my Eighty-two!
I threw away my shirt so gay,
I shaved my face each morn,
In navy blue, brass buttons, too,
A Captain I was born.

Things happen strange and courses change,
As I have said before;
The joy for me was short, you see,

For that year came the war!
They took away my "Eighteen A,"
My uniform so fair
I hung aside, and then I tried
To fly a Travelair!
I missed indeed twin-motor speed
That I had known so well.
It lured me north and I went forth
Beneath the Yukon spell.

"Strange things are done 'neath midnight
    sun"
Twas said in days gone by.
That still is true in forty-two
For malemutes now fly!
The Northern Lights still see queer
    sights —
I've flown o'er Dawson's Trail,
(Where dog teams plied and strong men
    died)
A Condor full of mail!
The mountain'd marge of Lake Laberge
I found akin to Heaven,
And Whitehorse Field, is where I wheeled
A Boeing Two Four Seven!

I've carried boats and smelly goats
In Junkers thirty-fours;
I froze my toes in Barkley Grows
On Great Bear's rocky shores.
In summer heat and winter sleet
I've flown them old and new;
With radio beams and endless streams —
I still just muddle through.
Throughout the years of sweat and tears
This wish has come to me —
Before I die, I want to fly
A Douglas DC-3!

Capt. Charles R. Robinson
Composed in Boeing 247 CF-BVT while flying down the Mackenzie River, Sept. 21, 1942

One of the Canadian Pacific Airlines Lockheed 18 Lodestars still in its U.S. military camouflage paint. Lockheed airliners were the mainstay of TCA and CPA until fleet modernization began after World War II. CF-CPA was built in 1942 and handed over to CPA by the U.S. Army for use along the Northwest Staging Route. It later became CPA's VIP aircraft, then was sold for $16 000 to Labrador Mining and Exploration. It ended its career in 1960 in a crash in Labrador while operating as a survey aircraft.

CP Air

The North Star

To this point neither airline had long range capability, a deficiency that had to be corrected for the world's major commercial operators were beginning to extend routes into the intercontinental area. Of Canada's airlines, only TCA had direct experience at this, having operated its fleet of Lancasters between Canada and Britain during the war.

TCA's trans-Atlantic service continued after the war and was scheduled on a daily basis as of September 1, 1946. But the old Lancasters were quite unsuitable as civil airliners. More appropriate equipment was needed. This appeared in the form of the North Star, introduced by Canadair in 1946. A Canadianized DC-4, the new airliner was soon the centre of public

controversy, and the issue provided the opposition Conservative party with ammunition during federal election campaigning. Among other complaints, there were aspersions against the Merlin engines which critics felt did not belong in a civil aircraft as they had been developed for military needs. Nonetheless C.D. Howe in his inimitable style carried the day and the North Star went on to a long career as the backbone of TCA's fleet in the fifties.

In actual fact, the North Star was not all that it was supposed to be. It suffered serious teething problems which cost the government a great deal of money to get ironed out. Howe, the Liberals, and TCA were determined to make a success of the North Star at any cost.

TCA began North Star operations April 15, 1947 on the Montreal-London route. Captain on the first trip was Gil McLaren. During its career on the Atlantic route, the North Star would sometimes make nonstop crossings, but more often than not, the trip was, as one pilot described it, "around" the ocean rather than across it. Goose Bay, Gander, Reykjavik, and Shannon were frequent refuelling points for the North Stars.

By mid 1948 North Stars were also flying to Bermuda and Chicago and communities all along the airline's route system, offering Canadians their first real

taste of modern long range air travel. By the end of 1948, North Stars had flown the Atlantic over 2000 times and in 20 months of service logged 27 000 hours. The Bahamas, Jamaica, Trinidad, the Barbados, Tampa, Shannon, Prestwick, London, Paris, and Düsseldorf were other North Star ports of call by 1952. The type was eventually to provide TCA with 14 years of service, logging 193 000 000 miles before its retirement.

CPA Reaches the Orient

Canadian Pacific introduced North Stars in July, 1949. It had purchased three as a condition for obtaining permission to fly to the Orient. The initial flight left Vancouver for Sydney via San Francisco, Fiji, and Auckland, and was the realization of Grant McConachie's pipedream from United Air Transport days. That pioneer flight carried just one fare-paying passenger, T.M. "Pat" Reid of Imperial Oil. How could McConachie have hoped to build a successful airline at that rate? The situation must have had the cynics chuckling, but with his unique way of doing things McConachie forged on. At first he refused even to advertise the new Pacific service, commenting that, "Flying CPA should be like getting religion, with every happy customer a convert for spreading the good word." Sure enough, the airline's trans-Pacific routes were to become famous. Before long, CPA's North Stars were flying all the way to Tokyo, thirty hours aloft from Vancouver. Return fare was $1437.50; and the routes were actually starting to catch on. Their ultimate success, though, was linked to two unexpected factors. One was the shuttling of Chinese immigrants from Hong Kong to Vancouver, at the going rate of $798.60, first class only!

The other bonanza was CPA's involvement in the Korean War airlift. Between August 1950 and March 1955 it completed 703 return trips Vancouver - Tokyo over the Great Circle route via the Aleutians. For the 39 000 passengers carried it was, as usual, nothing but the best in service, and word of this spread among GI's being ferried to and from the East. As a result, the CPA charters soon

CF-CMT, one of TCA's Lancaster Mk. X PP mail/passenger planes used by the Canadian Government Trans Atlantic Air Service.

Air Canada

became top-heavy with high ranking officers, leaving the GI's to make their way across the Pacific in less exotic fashion.

The excitement of these years is recalled by one of CPA's pilots, Captain L.C. "Craig" Stevenson. He remembers Canadian Pacific getting ready to begin operations across the Pacific:

"A course in air navigation was begun in late January of 1949 which was to last well into the month of April. This course was conducted by an ex-BOAC crew member, F.D.P. 'Fred' Wicker, ably assisted by navigator Pat Roy on loan from TCA. After sweating out this course, we began pilot training on two North Star M1 series aircraft borrowed from the RCAF. Our own North Star C4's were in the late stages of construction at Canadair.

"After this training was completed, the first survey flight was organized. Booked onto it was an almost full load of pilot and navigator trainees under the direction of Captains Pentland and Sawle, and navigators Wicker and Roy. During this flight we all had a go at navigating as well as taking turns at the controls. The major airports surveyed were Anchorage

The cramped passenger compartment of a CGTAS Lancaster. Seated on the left are M.B. (Jock) Barclay of TCA and Roy Dobson of Victory Aircraft. On the right are Romeo Vachon of TCA and Jack Skull of the CNR.

Public Archives of Canada (C 63383)

and Shemya in Alaska; Tokyo, then known as Haneda; Lungwha Airport, Shanghai; and, of course, Hong Kong. Many other routes along the way were surveyed for alternate and refuelling purposes. This operation took 10 to 12 days to complete. We carried a spare engine in mid-cabin due to the fact that there were no spare Merlins in the Orient at that time.

"An interesting feature of the flight was our visit to Shanghai around April 25. Due to the impending Communist takeover of mainland China, we refuelled there as quickly as possible, took on some packages of Canadian diplomatic papers, held a conference with the Canadian Attaché, and left for Hong Kong rather hurriedly. The Communist troops were reportedly only

Backbone of the post-war TCA and CPA fleets was the Douglas DC-3. CF-TES and CF-TDT were the last TCA DC-3's and served on the Prairies "milk run" from their Winnipeg base as late as 1961. Standard configuration for these aircraft was for 21 passengers.
Aviation and Space Division, National Museum of Science and Technology (5573)

ten miles from the airport and no one expressed any real desire to stay there, though most regretted not being able to have a look at the famous city. The evacuation of Shanghai and other parts of China was just beginning and Kai Tak Airport in Hong Kong was plenty busy during the four days we spent there." Time logged on CF-TEP for the extensive Vancouver-Shanghai-Vancouver trip was 63 hours 16 minutes.

"After returning to Vancouver, more training was carried out, this time on our own North Stars. There was a world of difference between the earlier M1 aircraft and the new C4's. The M1 had no pressurization; no noise suppression insulation; had open exhaust stacks; and was without doubt the noisiest and most uncomfortable aircraft it was my misfortune to be associated with. By comparison, the C4 was a veritable 'Queen of the Air,' as it was pressurized, had reasonably good insulation against noise, as well as manifold-covered exhaust stacks.

"However, the C4's still proved to be too noisy for comfortable travel. Also, as

they were limited in payload and range for the long Pacific routes, all flights had to be routed through San Francisco, instead of direct Vancouver-Honolulu. A few such flights were made, but only with exceptional tailwinds.

"The North Star's maximum seating capacity was 36, and this made it a very uneconomical aircraft for the Pacific. These were the reasons the North Stars were dealt off to TCA as soon as possible. Our pilots welcomed the 'new' DC-4's purchased from Pan Am as interim aircraft until delivery of our DC-6B's. Although the DC-4 was unpressurized, it was more suitable for our route structure, having much better range and payload carrying capability."

Captain Stevenson was aboard the first CPA North Star flight to the South Pacific, sharing flying duties on the trip with Captain Vanhee. Also aboard was Captain Pentland as company supervisor. The flight departed Vancouver July 13, 1949. Later on, Captain Stevenson flew the North Pacific route, about which he also has some personal comments:

CF-TFN, a TCA Canadair DC-4M2 North Star taxiing at Malton, June 29, 1960. TFN was initially delivered to TCA March 5, 1948. The North Star cruised at 240 knots and carried between 40 and 62 passengers depending on configuration.

Larry Milberry

"Shemya became our refuelling and crew lay-over point on the North Pacific route. This was a bleak, windswept island. While there, CPA used the facilities of Northwest Airlines. Due to Shemya's location, the weather there left much to be desired. With the cold Bering Sea to the north and the warm Japanese Current to the south, fog was prevalent, and ceilings of 200 feet and half a mile visibility were more the rule than the exception. Coupled with strong winds (usually cross winds) these conditions called for some rather interesting approaches. The U.S. Air Force, however, maintained at Shemya what were probably their best-trained GCA operators.

"One of these, a Sergeant Gates, was superb. A Southerner, his drawl would come over the air when the aircraft was approaching the minimum altitude and one's knuckles might be getting a little white on the wheel. 'You ah slidin dawn the ole wiah,' he'd report, meaning you were right on glideslope and perfectly lined up with the runway centreline. This would nearly always relieve any tension that might be mounting and enable a pilot to relax and do a much better job flying.

Often, though, one would make two or three approaches and pull-ups before getting everything buttoned up and completing the landing.

"One anecdote I remember about McConachie's optimism was a pep talk he gave while we were in the preliminary navigation class, to the effect that Shemya was a piece of cake to operate through due to the runway length and width, plus the adequate GCA unit there. In this he was correct, but his statement that, although the summer cloud ceilings were 200 feet and even sometimes lower, one could almost see Shemya from the north end of Vancouver Island on a clear day, did raise a few smiles.

"McConachie was ever the optimist. All of us were grateful that a man of his optimism, faith, and salesmanship was guiding the company during these sometimes difficult but always interesting times. Although we did not always share his unlimited optimism, we always heartily endorsed his vision, drive and courage."

Jetliners on the Horizon

These were also the years when Canadian airlines began considering commercial jet operations. TCA had initiated a project in WW II which in 1949 resulted in the spectacular Avro Jetliner. It proved out well in tests and was for sale at $850 000 per aircraft. It would have suited TCA's internal routes; but lacked the range required by CPA. Instead, CPA, con-

vinced by Grant McConachie, chose the de Havilland Comet. An order for two Comets was announced by McConachie on December 15, 1949.

But the government and TCA lost interest in the Jetliner. The project languished and died. CPA came closer to actually pioneering jet travel, as its two aircraft were constructed and ready for delivery. Of this venture veteran CPA captain, Archie Vanhee, has written, "I was one of a group of CPA pilots who attended a Comet course in Vancouver given by D.H. instructors from Hatfield, England. Our first Comet was scheduled to be delivered soon after completion of our ground school. But delays occurred. Finally, Captains Pentland and Sawle were to ferry the first Comet to Australia and I was to wait at Hatfield for Sawle's return and ferry the second one with him." Captain Vanhee was to then take over Comet instructing at CPA's Sydney base.

Suddenly the scheme dissolved like a mirage. On March 3, 1953 in the early morning darkness, CF-CUN, *Empress of Hawaii,* prepared to take off from Karachi for Sydney. It roared off down the runway. The nose lifted, but apparently the nose-up attitude was too great. Even though speed increased, the wing remained stalled. The aircraft crashed furiously off the runway. No one survived. A combination of design peculiarities and the aircrew's unfamiliarity with the Comet had brought CPA's Comet scheme to an end. It was to be another decade before Canada's airlines

"Wop" May, Grant McConachie and "Punch" Dickins prior to takeoff of CPA's pre-inaugural North Star flight to Australia. This photo was taken at Vancouver, July 10, 1949. The North Star was soon found to be unsuitable for CPA's trans-Pacific operations and replaced by DC-4's.

Vancouver City Archives

Airline luxury in 1949. This view shows the passenger cabin of a CPA North Star.

Canadian Pacific Railway Co.

Captain Archie Vanhee works on navigation exercises aided by Fred Wicker. Describing the training of CPA crews prior to the inauguration of trans-Pacific passenger service from Vancouver, Captain Vanhee has noted, "I doubt if any group of pilots had ever received more or better training prior to commencing a regular air service anywhere. We were ready, primed up, and looking forward to the job ahead."

Canadian Pacific Railway Co.

One of the two de Havilland Comet jetliners built for CPA but kept from service by tragic design flaws.

Hawker Siddeley Canada Ltd. (6481C)

would see the reintroduction of jet airliners.

During this period, TCA was entering a new era of administration. In 1948 Gordon R. McGregor took over as the airline's first full-time president. McGregor had learned to fly at the Kingston Flying Club in 1932. His enthusiasm for flying can be gauged by the fact that three times during the thirties he won the Webster Trophy, awarded annually to the pilot showing the greatest skill and competence among Canada's flying clubs.

McGregor joined 115 Sqdn (Auxiliary) at Montreal in 1938, and before much longer was overseas. He distinguished himself as a fighter pilot during the Battle of Britain, and eventually came to command 126 Fighter Wing, obtaining his discharge at the war's end with the rank of Group Captain.

After its brief experience with the Comet, CPA chose the Douglas DC-6 for its long-range routes. The DC-6 proved reliable, and became many a pilot's all-time favourite airplane. CPA introduced its first DC-8's in 1961, and immediately began selling off its DC-6's. CF-CZV was sold in Scandanavia where it operated for several years. This photo was taken at Dorval, May 22, 1961.

Larry Milberry

He joined TCA in 1945, first as General Traffic Manager, then as president. He held this position for 20 years. By the time McGregor retired, his airline had grown to include over 100 turbine powered airliners, and over 16 000 employees.

Regional Operations

While TCA and CPA were, by 1950, large well-established airlines, they didn't offer service in all parts of Canada. Many routes that would have been uneconomical for them were left to smaller airlines in the various regions. These airlines had struggled through the early post-war years, then prospered and expanded during construction of the Distant Early Warning Line in the mid fifties. But once that project was completed, business dropped off and these smaller companies suffered. Some went broke. In response to this situation, Ottawa stepped in with a new policy to aid these so-called regional airlines. Since that time, the regionals have grown, with each being equipped today with fleets of modern airliners and offering a variety of services.

Maritime Central Airlines

Typical of the regionals in the pre-DEW Line days, was Maritime Central Airlines. MCA had been founded in 1941 with scheduled runs between Charlottetown, Summerside, Moncton, and St. John. This

service had long been the dream of Carl Burke, a native of Prince Edward Island. As a youth, Burke had hopped passengers to and from the mainland across the Northumberland Strait, for $50 a head. Eventually Burke and a partner, Josiah Anderson, founded Maritime Central Airlines. Not long after, Anderson lost his life flying with Ferry Command.

MCA's inaugural flight occurred December 7, 1941. The original fleet comprised a Boeing 247, a Barkley-Grow and a Fairchild 24. Conditions weren't always the best either. MCA's service to Fredericton was in and out of a farmer's field. Once the new airport was opened up, MCA lost its right to land in Fredericton, and TCA took over. The first year of operation was a credible one for MCA with over 9000 passengers carried.

One of Maritime Central's more historic operations during World War II involved the Barkley-Grow. In December of 1942 it was chartered by the U.S. government to take part in a search and rescue mission over Greenland where a B-17 was lost.

Pilots Wade of MCA and Moe of the USAAF ferried CF-BMV to Greenland, but on December 23, while landing on sea ice in poor weather conditions, the aircraft broke through the ice. While the plane was still afloat, the crew salvaged what they could. They were understandably apprehensive, for they had little idea where they were.

CF-BZH, a DC-3 acquired by Maritime Central in 1946, loading freight at Saint John, New Brunswick. Carl Burke originally purchased BZH from the U.S. government for $20 000. Later, while serving with Arctic Wings, it was damaged at a DEW Line site. While being ferried to Mt. Joli for repairs on February 14, 1956 it was destroyed in a crash.

Via Canadian Aviation

They spent the first few days huddled in their life raft not venturing towards shore on account of thin ice. By the twenty-seventh, however, they had finally made it the 400 yards to shore. On that day, for the second day in a row, they sighted a B-17 flying patterns nearby, no doubt searching for them. They went unnoticed, but two days later were lucky to fall in with a party of Inuit. Wade later detailed this happy event:

"It was a glorious feeling to think that we had been seen, and that in such an apparent wasteland and so far from human habitation someone should come along as if by chance to give us help. We were thankful and delighted to meet the Eskimos.

"We gave them a drink of our coffee-flavoured water and some biscuits and all began dragging the boat and equipment up the fiord to where the dog teams were waiting. When about halfway to their sledges, Otouk, the other Eskimo who had been left with the dogs, came to our assistance. After a noisy greeting and much handshaking, we proceeded on our way. Very soon another driver came in sight with a powerful team to which we attached our boat so that it could be dragged closer to

the waiting dog team. Our equipment was quickly distributed among the sleds and we were soon on our way to the Eskimo village of Tederitik at the head of Ikerasarssuak Sound.

"It was then snowing very hard and the Eskimos were anxious to reach the village as soon as possible. It was apparent to the Eskimos that a terrific storm was approaching. After a fast and thrilling sled ride of about five-and-one-half hours, we reached the village. We were met some five miles out by other teams and Eskimo boys on foot. The boys ran for miles behind our sled without tiring.

"By this time the snow had stopped and the stars appeared. It was really a thrilling sight. We were heartily and enthusiastically welcomed to the village and given a supper of boiled seal meat. We enjoyed the hospitality of this Eskimo village from December 29th until January 2nd, 1943."

After their narrow escape, Wade and Moe were taken to the U.S. Army post at Angmagssalik where they learned that they had been given up for lost! Had it not been for the Inuit once again coming to the rescue of downed aviators, the story might not have had such a happy ending.

By 1946, MCA had made considerable headway, 32 000 passengers being carried that year. Burke's basic concept of providing airline service to the Maritimes really seemed to be catching on. The fleet was expanding and included such types as the Rapide, Lockheed 10, Crane and DC-3, adequate for Burke's needs. A number of Cansos were bought from War Assets, from Mount Pleasant, P.E.I. These were

bought for their engines, but as the air frames were found to be in good shape, the aircraft were completely refurbished.

One day, pilot H.S. Jones and chief engineer Gordon R. Raynor flew in the Rapide to the ice off the Magdalen Islands. There they loaded skins from seal hunters. From that day on, no matter what Gordon tried, the Rapide smelled of seal.

The same aircraft, CF-BNJ, went up on a wing while landing. Both lower wing spars were broken. Gordon called de Havilland in Toronto for replacement parts, but all that was available were drawings and a supply of wood! These were gladly accepted, but the heavy work of fashioning spars proved too much for MCA's diminutive woodworker. Gordon himself ended up doing most of the work. Fortunately his career at fixing broken airplanes dated to the early twenties when wood was a key ingredient.

Once sold by MCA, the Rapide flew for a while with other operators, Spartan Air Services included. Eventually it was grounded, and seems to have met an undeserved fate at the hands of an irate mother. She was apprehensive about the way local children had adopted the Rapide as a big toy, and put a match to it!

Besides regular passenger runs, MCA sought revenue in other likely and unlikely ways: mail contracts were operated; special flights originated in Charlottetown and Yarmouth hauling lobsters and strawberries to Boston and New York; seal surveys were flown over the Gulf of St. Lawrence and off the Newfoundland and Labrador coasts; service was provided twice weekly to the isolated Magdalen

Islands; and ice patrols were flown for the federal government.

For 1948, nearly two million pounds of freight and mail were carried, and the fleet had grown to include three DC-3's, a Canso, four Lockheed 10's, a Rapide, two Cranes, and two small Stinsons. Five years later MCA had become third in Canada for airline revenue earned, being next only to TCA and CPA. Sixty-five thousand passengers and 4245 tons of goods were carried that year.

MCA's service to St. Pierre off the Newfoundland coast came about in typical Burke fashion. While holidaying, he had dropped into the little French island. The inhabitants, Burke soon determined, were keen to have an air link with the mainland. The island had the remnants of an airstrip begun but never completed. This was enough for Burke!

He quickly organized workers and equipment to level the strip, and at noon the next day an MCA DC-3 touched down on St. Pierre, to the jubilation of the local inhabitants. Since that day, they have enjoyed daily service to and from Sydney on Cape Breton Island, 200 miles southwest.

Maritime Central's greatest period of growth took place in the mid fifties. By then northern operations had been added, with flights having reached as far up as Labrador and Ungava. The Labrador story is itself a major one in Canadian aviation history.

Iron Ore and Airplanes: Aviation in Labrador/New Quebec

Labrador/New Quebec represents one of the least hospitable natural regions in Canada. A bleak, barren landscape, it has been for ages the home of nomadic hunters and fishermen, the Naskapi and Inuit. On rare occasions in the past, it was visited by European adventurers, fur traders, and missionaries. One of these, the Oblate missionary, Louis Babel, knew of the presence of iron in the region as early as 1870. Later this was confirmed by A.P. Low of the Canadian Geological Survey, who recorded iron ore deposits in his report of 1895. Because these deposits were so remote, it would be many years until they could be worked. Remoteness, though, was no deterrent to the prospectors who crisscrossed Labrador over the next few decades.

In 1929, Doctors Gill and James conducted a mineral survey, including some of the Schefferville deposits. On this occasion they made use of the airplane, this possibly being the first time prospectors

and geologists had flown in the region. Three times during the thirties Professor Alexander Forbes of the Harvard Medical School led scientific expeditions to Labrador and used aircraft for transport, reconnaissance, and aerial photography. The results of his work are recorded in "Northernmost Labrador Mapped from the Air" published by the American Geographical Society in 1938.

Large-Scale Exploration

By 1936, the climate for mineral exploration in Labrador which had been dampened by the Depression began improving. At that time, two Montreal mining concerns, McKay Exploration, and Weaver Minerals cooperated in the formation of Labrador Mining and Exploration. This resulted in large-scale, organized mineral exploration, with the airplane figuring importantly in the general picture. The most important development at this time in aviation was the formation of Newfoundland Skyways, a subsidiary of Dominion Skyways of Rouyn, Quebec. Two Bellancas were sent to transport men and supplies into Labrador, Moisie on the St. Lawrence being their operations base. Some of the details of the first summer's work are recorded by Tim Sims, Newfoundland Skyways' chief pilot:

"The Bellancas cruised at 105 mph and with maximum fuel would have a payload of 1000 pounds and an endurance of 4 hours. About 50 percent of our flights were for the purpose of transporting fuel and oil, and laying down caches in the bush. Canoes, sometimes two at a time, were tied to the floats. In this condition the take-off distance was not greatly affected, but the rate of climb was drastically reduced.

"The first interior base camp was established at Lake Ashuanipi, about 200 miles north. Teams consisting of a geologist and prospector then fanned out across the country and were resupplied with food perhaps once a fortnight. Sometimes it was difficult to locate these parties as they may have moved faster or slower than expected. A smoke signal or a strip of red cloth stretched over their tent usually solved the problem.

"The aircraft were not equipped with radio and, as only crude maps were available, navigation could be a problem. Avoiding becoming lost, except temporarily, required making sketch maps as one flew along, and keeping an eye on the direction of the watersheds. On fine days the spray rising from Hamilton Falls could be seen for perhaps 50 miles.

"Low clouds were often down on the mountains about 50 miles north of Moisie,

but no instrument flying was undertaken. When the clouds were too low to follow the Moise River Gorge, a landing would be made for perhaps an overnight stay until conditions improved. Many of the forced landing lakes were full of speckled trout, and supper was never a problem. Every visit to a new lake held the possibility of submerged rocks, but close scrutiny and a low pass before landing kept you out of trouble . . . . ''

For the next season, the Bellancas were based at North West River on Hamilton Inlet, and an inland camp was established at Sandgirt Lake. These points were connected by radio. Chief geologist on the expedition was Dr. Joe Retty. One day he was approached by an Indian, Chief Mathieu André, who showed him a rich ore sample. Of this Tim Sims has noted, "He was supposed to direct us to a spot where he found promising samples. Although he knew his way by canoe, he could not recognize the terrain from the air. After several tries, the right spot was located and the hunt for iron ore was on in earnest."

Before too long, the mineral explorers realized that the local people had much to offer. Labrador Mining and Exploration's geologist, Dr. Gustaffson, made a point of this in one of his reports: "Chief Sylvestre Mackenzie and most of his family were flown to Wishart Lake where they pointed out new iron-bearing rocks. Dominique Doctor and his family were flown to what we called Dominique Lake in the Quebec concession, 24 miles N.N.E. of the first big north bend in the West Branch of the George River. Within a radius of eight miles he pointed out four places where heavy pyritization occurs. These places open up the possibility of a big new mineralization zone in schists. We also flew some of Mathieu André's goods to a lake near Grand Falls (while on a trip there anyway) and gave him some flour and lard."

Over each summer for the next few years Labrador Mining and Exploration put men into the field to continue to search for iron ore. With each year, further experience was gained in the use of aircraft. To a large extent, the annual expeditions depended on bushplanes for supply and most transportation needs. In his 1939 preliminary report on operations in the New Quebec concession, Dr. Retty suggested this dependence: "The execution of the work was greatly hampered by the disappearance of the Bellanca Skyrocket and its occupants, Pilot C. Frechette and Radio Operator Edward Gaynor."

The Bellanca had made a forced landing on a lake while flying from Sandgirt Lake to Moisie, July 3. As no help

Pilot Don Murray with the Quebec Airways Bellanca CH-300 Pacemaker he flew over the 1942 season in Labrador.

Via Don Murray

turned up, the two fliers decided to strike out through the bush for the St. Lawrence. They both perished. The lake on which their plane was eventually located is today known as Bellanca Lake; there are also Lakes Frechette and Gaynor in the area.

Through their persistence, Retty and his staff began to detail the extent and quality of iron ore deposits in the Labrador/New Quebec region. The potential appeared to be immense. Major expeditions were mounted in 1941 and 1942 employing the Quebec Airways fleet. Aircraft used included the Fairchild 71, CF-BJE; the Fairchild 82's, CF-AXE and CF-AXF; the Junkers W-34, CF-ATF; the Bellanca CH-300, CF-BFA; the Beech 18's, CF-BQG, CF-BQH, and CF-BQQ, and two or three Rapides including CF-AYE. These usually operated from Seven Islands and Havre St. Pierre, and sometimes from Rimouski and Mt. Joli.

An excerpt from Dr. Gustaffson's 1942 report to Labrador Mining and Exploration gives a good indication of just how important the airplane had become to the exploration operation: "The first few flights in 1942 over the general region from André Lake in the northwest part of the Labrador concession to McNeil Lake revealed a very large area in which numerous rusty red zones — obviously gossans — could be seen from the air. Gradually aerial sketches were completed and enough was known about the drainage and about the locations of gossans to start placing prospectors in the mineralized area. As more and more prospecting teams were placed in the country, reconnaissance flights reached out farther and farther and kept extending the limits of the mineralized belt. The limits are still unknown . . . .

The belt is at least 12 miles wide and may be 50 miles wide . . . . ''

Dr. Gustaffson also recorded in detail other aspects of the summer's flying:

"The flying was separated into two categories: (1) freighting of goods and supplies and transportation of men and luggage into Sandgirt from Havre St. Pierre and out again to Havre St. Pierre or Seven Islands, and (2) interior flying comprising flights for the purpose of (a) placing prospecting and geological parties and their supplies and equipment in the field, shifting them from place to place, and ultimately returning them to Sandgirt, (b) provisioning and supervising field parties, (c) sketching new country, and sizing it up for the purpose of planning work in it, (d) visiting places of geological and other interest.''

His notes also indicate the cost involved in chartering bushplanes: "All freight including personal luggage came in to Sandgirt from Havre St. Pierre at $0.47 per pound, except canoes which were charged at $140 each. Passengers were flown in at $80 per person plus war tax of 10 per cent. Passengers or freight could be flown out free provided they were flown out in airplanes which had brought in a minimum payload of 800 pounds. Gasoline in 10 and 45 gallon drums for the interior flying was reckoned at 10 pounds to the gallon or at a freighting cost of $4.70 per gallon on the invoices presented to us. We were to provide food and lodgings for Airways men while engaged on freighting.''

Relations through the season were not always the best between Labrador Mining and Explorations, and Quebec Airways, as Gustaffson's report notes, "many 10 gallon gasoline drums contained only 6 to 8 gallons of gasoline, often along with nearly a gallon of water and some sand.''

Hourly rates for aircraft were $50 for the Bellanca, $65 for the Fairchild 71, $105 for the Beech 18. No rosy picture is given of aircraft serviceability in Gustaffson's report: "Much of the time the aircraft were not strictly fit to fly and were not being properly looked after. We experienced considerable engine trouble while in the air. On one occasion the starter shaft fell out while in flight. On another occasion the airplane landed in flames . . . . The one bright spot in the interior flying picture was Don Murray, our regular pilot. His skill, good humour, and strenuous effort to do a good job for us were greatly appreciated.''

Over the whole 1942 season, 89 719 pounds of freight were carried by the Quebec Airways aircraft, for a total of 178.45 hours flown.

In spite of the big iron ore finds made up to 1942, Dr. Gustaffson was not too optimistic about the future of mineral development in Labrador. He concluded his annual report, "An unhappy result of our failure to discover quickly mineable deposits of strategic minerals is the dimming of any chance that the Labrador and Quebec concessions can contribute metals or other minerals to the war effort. The remoteness of the area and the difficulties of operating there under wartime limitations on civilian aircraft, aircraft personnel, and radio equipment make it very doubtful in my mind whether further expeditions should be attempted until after the war. We stretched our luck too thin last summer operating as we did with old patched-up, poorly serviced aircraft and with wholly inadequate radio communication. Unless definite improvement in airplanes, radio, and personnel can be guaranteed, the profit motive alone is inadequate to justify the inevitable risks. Only if high-grade iron ore is wanted badly enough by the Canadian or United States governments to make them willing to start building a railroad now (or as soon as a given tonnage of ore is proved up) is it worthwhile in my opinion to proceed with another expedition before the war's end.''

Nonetheless, exploration continued through the war. In 1944 Labrador Mining and Exploration entered a new phase in aviation by purchasing three of its own aircraft. These were the Fleet Finch, CF-BXJ which operated on floats; the Fleet 50 Freighter, CF-BXP; and the Stranraer, CF-BXO. D.J. (Don) McClintock, presently chief pilot for Labrador Mining and Exploration, wrote of CF-BXP, "The Fleet had a life of exactly ten days. It crashed on takeoff from Sandgirt Lake with a pilot by the name of Duffy getting credit for the kill.''

Dr. R.D. MacDonald, a geologist with

The Canadian Vickers-built Stranraer owned by Labrador Mining and Exploration. This aircraft is now preserved in the Royal Air Force museum at Hendon, U.K.
Dr. A.E. Moss

Labrador Mining and Exploration, recalls that the Stranraer was a big asset in that "it could carry a sizeable load in comparison to other available aircraft such as the Junkers, Fairchild, and de Havilland Rapide . . . . As to the use that was made of BXO in Labrador and New Quebec, it was mainly used for freighting men and materials from Sept Îles to bases at Sandgirt Lake and Iron Arm of Petitsikapau Lake. A minor amount of inland flying was also done in servicing field parties.

"The main reason for its short life in the Labrador-New Quebec area were: 1) The Stranraer was not amphibious and therefore was restricted solely to open water periods. 2) The loading hatch was small and restricted the size of materials that could be loaded. An even smaller interior structure restricted sizeable freight to the rear of the aircraft, thus limiting carrying capacity. 3) When the amphibious Canso became available towards the end of the war, the Stranraer could not compete as to carrying capacity, versatility, availability of engines, and airframe parts, etc."

Dr. MacDonald notes two occasions when CF-BXO almost came to grief. He writes that in 1944 it "almost flooded and drowned at Boucheville en route to Sept Îles. Someone used the urinal tube and left the funnel below water level rather than hanging up as any flying-boat man would surely have done . . . . In 1945 CPA took over the flying operation of BXO. Again, many minor incidents occurred, including smashing of wing floats, but also

including a flooding and sinking caused by hitting a submerged rock. It took an ingenious group of 'Bushmen' to refloat and repair it."

Early Post-War Activity

In 1946 development of the Labrador/New Quebec iron ore properties was intensified. Larger aircraft were immediately brought into play and air transport operations were handed over to Canadian Pacific Air Lines. Aircraft available during this time were the DC-3, Canso, Anson, and Norseman. One of the first DC-3 trips involved flying a small tractor and roller to Hollinger Lake, a few miles east of Knob Lake. This equipment was needed to maintain the ice strip there. The DC-3 used was equipped with a set of non-retractable plywood skis.

Captain John T. Dart was one of CPA's pilots flying charters for Labrador Mining and Exploration during this period and he writes:

"In the summer of 1946 we had a float operation into Hollinger Lake and later Knob Lake. I had a new Mark V Norseman, CF-BHZ. Hank Gates had a Fairchild 71 and he was based at Hollinger Lake servicing geologists in the area. I was doing other flying in the St. Lawrence - Seven Islands area, but did some trips to Hollinger Lake. The ice was slow to go in the north that year. My engineer, Tommy Moore, and I made a trip on June 21.

"Hollinger Lake was still frozen, so we landed in Timmins Bay in a strip of open water and unloaded our passengers into canoes. I was afraid to stay over night in case the ice moved, so we left immediately, and had just time to get to Sandgirt Lake, about 100 miles east, before dark. The next morning we went to Ashuanipi, our gas cache, and sat there for

a week waiting for good weather in Seven Islands. When it got good there it would be bad at Ashuanipi.

"When we did get back, we loaded up and went right back to Hollinger. I see by my log that we stayed there for five days taking parties out and during that time I landed once in the famous Knob Lake. I remember turning around to taxi back and seeing the 'knob' at the south end."

During this time, two unusual aircraft made their appearance over Labrador on proving flights. One was the Bristol Freighter, G-AGVC. It had been in North and South America on an extensive sales tour and was used briefly by CPA which had a contract to fly 250 tons of freight from Mt. Joli and Seven Islands to Knob Lake. Most of the freight was equipment needed to build the Knob Lake airstrip — a small tractor, two trucks, grading equipment, building supplies, and fuel. Tim Sims did all the flying on the Bristol.

The other aircraft was the Canadian Car Loadmaster, CF-BEL. This was the Canadian-built prototype of the famous Burnelli "flying wing." It was flown on a few demonstration flights to Knob Lake under command of V. J. Hatton; but no sales interest developed in the Loadmaster and it was exported to the United States.

Hollinger Ungava Transport

By the mid forties, huge quantities of iron ore had been proven by Labrador Mining and Exploration, enough in fact to justify the opening up of a transportation corridor from the St. Lawrence River to the Labrador Trough where the ore lay. Thus in 1947, Hollinger Mining, parent company of Labrador Mining and Exploration, established the Quebec, North Shore and Labrador Railway. The

Two workhorses at Sept Îles on July 10, 1952. In the foreground is CF-DXO, one of HUT's DC-3's. Behind it is CF-FBJ, the C-46E used by Dorval Air Transport on the cement lift to Menihek. The C-46 carried 12 000 pounds, twice the payload of the DC-3.

Aviation and Space Division, National Museum of Science and Technology (12656)

proposed line would link Sept Îles and Knob Lake. This was the beginning of a grand-scale operation that would see not just a railroad, but also towns, mines, dams, and a major seaport built. An airline was also to be established around which the whole undertaking was to revolve.

Those interested in the scheme to open up the Labrador interior included such American firms as M.A. Hanna, Armco, National Steel, Wheeling Steel, Republic Steel, and Youngstown Steel. These were to supply the capital required to see the project through. In 1949 Hollinger and the American interests formed the Iron Ore Company of Canada; on September 21, 1950 the contract was signed to build the 357 mile railroad to Knob Lake. From then on the motto of the huge venture became "Ore by fifty-four."

Hollinger had concluded early after the war that it could likely save money, and provide the service it required if it controlled its own flying operation. In 1948, it formed Hollinger Ugava Transport to provide its aviation needs. This signalled the end of CPA's involvement along the route to Knob Lake.

Hollinger Ungava Transport began operations in 1948 with two DC-3's (CF-DXO, CF-DXR), two Norsemans, a Bellanca Skyrocket and a Stinson 108. The job of organizing all the flying went to C.W. (Charlie) Hoyt. He had previously been C.O. of 164 Transport Squadron, Moncton, the unit providing logistical support for such bases as Goose Bay and Gander. He was to become the driving force behind HUT. Other original personnel with the airline were pilots J.B.

(Jack) Scott and W.H. (Wess) McIntosh; and engineers John Luty, Ernie Grant, and Tony Leriche, all widely experienced and competent men.

The first big job faced by HUT was the siting of airstrips north of Sept Îles. This was conducted first by aerial spotting from one of the bushplanes. Sites were chosen to be as near as possible to future construction camps. Initial phase of airstrip construction involved moving a small tractor and ground party to the site by bush plane. The tractor would then be used to plough out a rough strip just adequate for the DC-3. This meant that supplies and heavier equipment could be brought in to improve the strip and install facilities. In this way, a dozen airstrips were carved in the landscape north of Sept Îles.

The HUT operation opened up flying opportunities for many Canadians who, on account of an oversupply in Canada of aircrew in the immediate post-war period, had had to take jobs overseas. One of these was Wess McIntosh. In 1948, he was flying DC-4's in Argentina for Flota Aerea Mercante. One day while relaxing in his favourite café in Buenos Aires he received a long distance phone call. It was Charlie Hoyt offering Wess a job in Labrador, 10 000 miles north, and wondering if he could start next morning! Wess was soon on his way home. Others followed, including Don McLintock who left his job flying with BOAC; and Allan Coggon, and Ralph McKnight who had been flying for KLM. Other pilots soon plying the airway north from Sept Îles included the well-known RAF fighter pilot Reg Reynolds; Paul Ostrander who had flown Spitfires in Burma and had recently become Canada's third certified helicopter pilot; and such "greenhorns" to the flying business as John Timmins, Willy McLaughlin and Claude Castonguay. In all, some 116 pilots were to fly for HUT. HUT's first trip, Mt. Joli to Knob Lake, took place June 9, 1948. The aircraft was the DC-3, CF-DXR piloted by Hoyt and McIntosh. Flight time was 2:42 hours and the landing at Knob

Lake was on the ice. From that first day, operations grew steadily, with HUT's two DC-3's completing 233 trips by year's end, and logging 1365 hours. Most of the flying was connected with the pressing need to prove more and more iron ore. The pace of flying for individual pilots may be reckoned by the figure 994.23 total hours flown by Wess McIntosh for 1950.

Initially the base for DC-3 operations was Mt. Joli on the South Shore of the St. Lawrence as Sept Îles could not handle the scale of logistics called for. As yet its port had not been expanded, whereas Mt. Joli was a major rail hub through which material could be funnelled. Once Sept Îles was developed, however, it became the southern terminus for air freighting. Ships began arriving there to unload cargoes which were then moved by truck to a large compound. Here they were sorted and assembled onto pallets for the flight north.

To keep the flow of goods and passengers moving, aircraft had to be kept at a peak of serviceability. All routine maintenance was done at Mt. Joli, where engine changes were completed in six or seven hours, and 75 hour checks within a day. But there was also servicing in the field resulting from breakdowns and minor mishaps. During one year this meant 19 unscheduled engine changes. One such change took place at Baie Comeau, and kept Tony Leriche busy for four days with only the cook from a local resort to help him.

Airport serviceability was just as vital to the operation. Airports were interconnected with a teletype system that provided up-to-the-minute weather information; all were equipped with DOT approved beacons. Runways were kept serviceable at all times, even during blizzards when big triangular wooden frames weighted with stones were dragged up and down them by tractor. Using this technique, runways were ready for use as soon as a storm abated.

One of HUT's biggest challenges was the cement haul to Menihek where a hydro dam was being constructed. Originally it

A dramatic view of Don McVicar's Lancaster Mk. I tanker. This picture was taken at Sept Îles by John A. Rodriguez in August 1952.

Morrison-Knudsen Co., Boise, Idaho

The same aircraft after its crash at Menihek.

Fred Van Brussel

had been planned to haul the cement in winter over a tote road aboard tractor-drawn sleds. As it turned out, however, no cement arrived at the dam site this way. Climate and terrain decreed that sleds would turn over, or disappear into the muskeg; that tractors would break down in the middle of nowhere; and that men would curse the day they went to Labrador.

As with everything else that went north, the cement was flown in. In 1953 dam construction was in full swing and the DC-3's were hauling 600 tons a week to Menihek. Each load meant 6000 pounds, or 80 bags of cement. This averaged out to 200 DC-3 arrivals per week. By the time the operation was history, 190 000 bags of cement had been flown to Menihek. During the cement lift, one DC-3 logged 422 hours in a single month.

Pilots recall many an anecdote from these hectic days. One set a record by not leaving his cockpit for a straight 12 hours. Another memory is of how pilots on finishing a shift headed for the bunkhouse, rousted the next pilot out of bed, and pointed him in the direction of the waiting DC-3. While one bleary-eyed fellow was settling down in the warm, just-vacated bunk, the other was taxiing out for takeoff.

Fuel was another major item airlifted from Sept Îles. At its peak, Menihek required 7000 gallons a day. Two DC-3's were assigned to haul fuel, usually on weekends. Each one was fitted with an 800 or 1000 gallon removable tank. On one arrival at Knob Lake the ground crew came out to decant the load only to find the tank empty! The captain had felt his plane a bit light on takeoff, but the truth of the matter did not occur to him at the time. An even

more frustrating event occurred at Menihek when 10 000 gallons of precious fuel oil was accidentally leaked into the local river through a damaged pipeline.

HUT's fleet also logged thousands of hours hauling building materials north. There were aircraft full of tar paper, plywood, and prefabricated sections of buildings custom made to just fit a DC-3's cargo doors. Supplies of acetylene, oxygen, dynamite, beef, bread, beer, even tranquillized horses, and bulldozers cut into sections — everything went in by air. The heaviest and most ungainly single item transported by DC-3 were booms for 3/4 yard power shovels. These weighed 7000 pounds and invariably dinged the airplane while being loaded and unloaded.

Midst the movement of freight, HUT also had to make room for thousands of passengers a year. These were efficiently and safely accommodated; but amenities were few. Any passenger expecting special treatment was soon awakened to the rude facts of flying HUT.

While DC-3's were the main workhorse on the HUT operation, many other types of aircraft were used. HUT operated two Cansos, a Lodestar, a Cessna T-50, and two Bell 47's. The Lodestar was the company's VIP aircraft, having been purchased from CPA in 1950 for $16 000. The T-50 was used to keep pilots proficient

on instruments. The Bells, flown by Hank Gates and Paul Ostrander, were used primarily to transport medical cases from remote locations. As the original HUT bushplanes aged, they were replaced by Beavers.

Many non-HUT aircraft were also used during the construction of the Quebec, North Shore, and Labrador Railway. There were C-46's of Slick Airways and Dorval Air Transport; World Wide Airways' Lancaster I tanker; and even an Avro Tudor. The Lancaster, CF-GBA, crashed and burned at Menihek on July 28, 1953, while transporting 3250 gallons of fuel. The pilot, A.R. Iba, later recalled that he knew his landing had not worked out perfectly when he caught sight of one of his main wheels bouncing down the runway in front of him!

The Tudor had been purchased by Montreal interests which hoped to put it to work on the cement haul. Registered CF-FCY, it was flown to Sept Îles, thence to Menihek. Air Vice Marshal D.C.T. Bennett, noted expert on the Tudor, was along to supervise the operation, and decided the Menihek strip was too short for the Tudor to use safely. Consequently, CF-FCY did no freighting in Labrador. Instead, it was taken over by Lome Airways and operated briefly as a freighter between Toronto and the West Indies,

"McIntosh's Folly" at Sept Îles, October 19, 1951. Though never again to fly, this aircraft continued to serve HUT as a source of spare parts for its DC-3 fleet.

Morrison-Knudsen Co., Boise, Idaho

CF-FCY, the Avro Tudor Mk.V at Sept Îles while being evaluated for use on the cement haul to Menihek.

Morrison-Knudsen Co., Boise, Idaho

hauling meat from Toronto and bringing back loads of fruit.

In 1951 a USAF C-119 Flying Boxcar was loaned to the Iron Ore Company to fly heavy equipment to Knob Lake. This was Operation Ungava, successfully completed but for considerable wear and tear on the airplane. The operation lasted 49 days, with as many as five return trips per day being flown from Sept Îles.

On another occasion a backlog piled up at Sept Îles. This resulted in Operation Overload with several RCAF North Stars of 426 Squadron coming to the rescue to move freight to Mile 224.

The intensity of flying between Sept Îles and Knob Lake throughout this period can be best appreciated only by those who were there; but statistics do help inform the armchair enthusiast. HUT's airstrips were extremely busy places. On a single day, Mile 224 logged 96 aircraft arrivals. For 1953 HUT moved 34 047 tons, 69 590 passengers, completed over 10 000 flights, and chalked up over 18 000 hours in the air. To the point a year later when the railroad was completed, the whole flying operation had been fatality free, with the exception of a child who had disappeared out the window of a DC-3 in flight.

This is not to say that there were no flying accidents. The operation was open to countless hazards, yet HUT suffered only two aircraft lost until the opening of the railroad.

On October 19, 1951, pilots McIntosh and Mackie were preparing to take off from Sept Îles in CF-DXR. Aboard was 7974 pounds of 3/8 inch corrugated steel plates, eight feet in length. Just as the plane was about to lift from the runway, the cargo tie-downs gave way and the heavy load shifted aft. McIntosh later reported on the frightening moment: "With normal power the tail rose to takeoff position momentarily. At this point the aircraft went into a violent climb. In spite of both pilots pushing forward on the wheels, and the trim tab being moved forward, we were unable to stop the aircraft from climbing to approximately 100-150 feet. The aircraft was in the stalled position with no control when it hit the ground. The aircraft hit the ground on the tail wheel and the left wing."

HUT's Canso, CF-DIK, was sunk some time after the crash of the DC-3. While touching down, a float dug in and the aircraft slammed into the water, split open and sank. Pilots Van Brussel and Packer were uninjured.

Another incident involved HUT's Lodestar, CF-CPA. After transporting a polio victim, it had to be disinfected. This was done using a slow burning fumigator.

After a while, someone noticed large quantities of smoke pouring from the plane. The fumigator had ignited and the Lodestar was gutted inside before the fire could be doused.

By early 1954 the massive Labrador - New Quebec development project was nearing completion. On February 13, Jules R. Timmins drove the last spike, and on July 31 a ceremony was held at Schefferville declaring the Quebec, North Shore, and Labrador Railway officially opened. The first ore train left for Sept Îles that day. The whole undertaking had been made possible by those hundred or so pilots and their unfailing DC-3's. Over 81 000 tons of cargo and 169 603 passengers had been carried, and over 1 500 000 ton miles flown. Safety considered, it is unlikely that this sort of record had ever been achieved in world aviation history.

Before long, HUT was being phased out. Aircrew, groundcrew, and aircraft began to disperse. One of these aircraft was the C-46, CF-FBJ of Dorval Air Transport. It had worked hard on the cement lift to Menihek. Towards the end of the HUT operation, CF-FBJ made a heavy landing at Frobisher which resulted in one engine dropping off the aircraft. Further damage was caused in attempting to control the C-46, and the owners almost wrote it off. Eventually, though, it was decided to rebuild CF-FBJ and in the subsequent overhaul hundreds of pounds of fine cement powder were discovered in the belly of the aircraft, the legacy of its days flying to Menihek. When CF-FBJ was put back into service, pilots noticed improvement in performance as the aircraft was now much lighter.

Once the job is done, its significance seems to fade as people go on to new things. But memories last. Captain John T. Dart remembers well his days over Labrador, even before HUT came along, "I left Seven Islands at the end of October, 1948. In later years, while on overseas flights from northern Europe, we would flight plan in over the north, bound for Montreal or Toronto. The route sometimes took us over Knob Lake. On the chart it is known as Schefferville, but the radio facility designator is unchanged — KL. Occasionally too, it would be clear, and after having known it from away back when, it always seemed to be a miracle from 35 000 feet — roads, railroads, power lines, and towns in place of what I had known. It was unbelievable."

The Distant Early Warning Line

Not long after World War II had ended and the Cold War begun, North American defence experts concluded that the most important means of protecting their continent would be to establish a chain of radar stations along its northern flank, designed to pick up Soviet aircraft which might, in the future, attack. Three defence lines were planned, one in the far North, the Distant Early Warning Line along the seventieth parallel; one further down, the Mid Canada Line; and one along the U.S. - Canada border, the Pinetree Line.

Building these lines was to be a huge undertaking. In the case of the DEW Line, the challenge was to be all the more complex since most of the sites were accessible only by air. In 1951, Maritime Central Airlines had bid on and won the supply contract for the eastern portion of the Pinetree Line. Revenue and experience gained on this job stood MCA in good stead when the big DEW Line contracts came up later.

The announcement to build the DEW Line was made in March of 1955, and Carl Burke's airline received a big chunk of the airlift business. MCA's job was to provide air transport for 17 of the 42 new radar stations. Except for a few sites which could be supplied during the summer sealift, virtually everything had to come in by air. As with the HUT operation, the DC-3 was to be important to the DEW Line, but many other types were to fit into the picture, notably the Curtiss C-46. Other MCA types to serve were the Canso, Bristol Freighter, DC-4, and Avro York. In time, the airline which had begun so humbly in 1941 was to log 28 000 flights and haul 81 000 tons on the DEW Line, all in just 29 months.

The scope of DEW Line operations is indicated by the fact that in early 1955, 60 Canadian civil air transports were involved on the job. As well, there were dozens of smaller bush planes employed across the North; plus a big fleet of USAF, U.S. civil and RCAF transports.

The locale for the flying stretched from Labrador to Alaska. Conditions were worse than those faced by HUT. Keeping aircraft in readiness against adverse weather was to test the patience and ingenuity of ground crew. Added to grim weather was the dearth of radio and navigation aids and marginal airport facilities.

Typical of many DEW Line episodes was one involving a small tractor required to clear snowdrifts at one of the sites. A John Deere tractor was flown to the site, but unloading gear failed to turn up in a second DC-3. Rather than return to base with the tractor, the crew decided to unload. A snow ramp was built up to the DC-3's door; but in the process the floor of the plane became slippery. As the tractor was being eased towards the door, it slid loose and careened to the rear, cutting three of the plane's fuselage ribs. Eventually it was unloaded, and the DC-3 was ferried south for major repairs. As to the John Deere, it proved no match for the snowdrifts, and two bulldozers were called in.

The bulldozers arrived over the site to be paradropped from C-119's. As the chutes opened, however, their nylon shrouds snapped in the cold and the big machines crashed through thick ice. This sort of difficulty was part of the daily challenge to the DEW Liners. Solutions were rarely long in coming. In this case two more bulldozers were flown north, this time with parachutes equipped with cold resistant silk shrouds.

One of those flying on the DEW Line was G.L. MacInnis. For his contributions on the big job he was awarded the McKee Trophy for 1956. MacInnis flew the initial survey for the 17 sites to be established in the eastern Arctic. This task involved flying back and forth along the line of proposed sites looking for safe landing places; for natural features that might hinder or prevent access between base camp and radar site; for sources of fresh water and of gravel for future construction. The latter usually meant spotting for leftovers from the last Ice Age — eskers, kames, and other deposits rich in naturally sorted sand and gravel.

Pinpointing most of the sites was fairly easy going, but for some there were holdups. One of these was Site 30, code-named Foxe. MacInnis and his copilot David Hoyte had often circled over it scouring the whiteness for a place to set down. To March 23, 1955, they'd had no luck; but on that day, a stretch of ice with some potential appeared. The crew flew low over the ice, figuring it to be about 6000 feet long. Then they set down. Leaving engines idling, they walked to shore, where they discovered a deposit of limestone gravel, ideal for construction.

Marking the runway with a flag atop an old broom, MacInnis and Hoyte took off for Coral Harbour to deliver the news. Within hours of their arrival a massive airlift had been organized, and a fleet of transports was winging out of Coral with equipment and supplies for Foxe.

Prior to this departure, the MCA pilots briefed all flight crew. In typical DEW Line fashion MacInnis notes, ''We explained to the crews that at dawn we would take off at thirty minute intervals, cross to the north shore of Southampton Isle and then follow the anchor ice to Foxe, 300 miles further north, where they would see a yellow flag.'' After warning of ice hummocks ten to twenty feet high and a tip that the flag was at the upwind end of the strip, the freighters were off.

Conditions at DEW Line airstrips were not always the best. Site 27 was reportedly in service in the spring of 1955. The first aircraft arrived April 10 piloted by J.S. Patterson of Dorval Air Transport. On touchdown, his C-46 immediately sank into deep snow, making a STOL roll out. The strip had not been properly prepared and compacted, forcing the crew to carry out its own measures by bulldozing down the runway under full power in order to clear a path through the snow.

Some sites, Resolution for example, had no airstrips initially. Supplies arrived by sea during the brief summer, but by paradrop in winter. DC-3's were the standard drop planes used and parachutes were kicked out at 400 - 500 feet at 120 mph for best results. Once the cook at Resolution jokingly complained about three broken eggs out of his shipment of 30 dozen. For his irreverence in the presence of airline personnel he was reminded that his next 30 dozen could accidentally arrive with a few blasting caps mixed in!

Many DEW Line stories include a human touch. On a survey flight one day, a DC-3 crew landed to inspect a possible site. On returning to their plane, the crew was surprised to find that an Inuit mother had laid claim to one of the DC-3's wheels. Resting back against it, she was nursing her baby. If she had stayed too long the engines could have frozen up, but with due respect, the fliers waited until mother and baby were quite finished and on their way before they started engines.

Dew Line Woes

The DEW Line airlift was not without its flying mishaps. Some were disastrous, as was the crash of an Associated Airways York, CF-HMY, at Edmonton in May, 1955. Many accidents, though, did not result in serious human consequences. Such was the case with N90407, a United States Overseas Airlines DC-4. On May 9, 1955 it

DEW Line freighters at Frobisher Bay, April 18, 1955. Running up is "ol' Shakey," a USAF C-124 Globemaster. To the right is Maritime Central's DC-3, CF-FKQ, equipped with wheel-skis.

United States Air Force

had departed from North Bay on a cargo flight to a DEW Line site, Cam 4. There were 12 hours of fuel on board. The aircraft arrived at Cam 4 and unloaded. Next day it departed without refuelling, intending to do this at Coral Harbour. En route, the pilot learned that there was no fuel there, so decided to push on for Churchill. Twelve hours and 30 minutes since the North Bay departure, his four engines quit! The pilot landed on the ice of Hudson Bay, 25 miles northeast of Churchill. Although the crew claimed severe headwinds had been encountered en route to Churchill, weather officially was discounted as a factor contributing to the mishap.

It had been an early spring on Hudson Bay, and Lloyds of London, considering all the salvage factors, decided to write off N90407. They paid the owners $500 000. At the same time, though, Ralph Cox of Overseas thought the aircraft was recoverable. He purchased salvage rights for $5000 and started work to save the plane.

First priority was to preserve the ice on which the DC-4 was sitting. This was done with a thick layer of sawdust and hay

N90407 as the ice melted from under it in Hudson Bay.

John Dominis, Life Magazine

CF-IQQ at Dorval, July 26, 1959, rebuilt after its near-disastrous collision with Wheeler's DC-4 at Val d'Or. The C-46 has all but disappeared from use in Canada. Two were still flying in Canada in 1979.

Larry Milberry

spread on the ice. Next, inflatable pontoons were positioned under the aircraft in case the ice eventually did melt. Finally, the whole aircraft was cocooned in plastic to preserve it from sea water. Some Inuit were hired to try to tow the ice flow to shore with their boats. This failed, and by July 2 it had melted away totally. Two days later, supported on its pontoons, the DC-4 arrived at Churchill. It was lifted from the water, disassembled and loaded onto five flatcars. It was next shipped to Overseas' base in New Jersey where it was decided that it was too badly damaged for repairs to be done there. It carried on to Pan Am's Brownsville, Texas base and on December

20, 1957, returned to the Overseas fleet completely refurbished. The project had cost just over half a million dollars. In the meantime, the resale value of the DC-4 had dropped to $300 000! Apparently Lloyds knew its business.

Another mishap involved the USAF C-124, 51-5176, of the 53rd Troop Carrier Squadron, Donaldson Air Force Base, South Carolina. It was one of the many Globemasters providing heavy lift capability on the DEW Line when it came to grief on April 2, 1957.

This particular Globemaster had loaded a fuel tender and a six-by-six truck at Churchill to fly to Cambridge Bay where the RCAF awaited delivery. While on final at Cambridge Bay, the big transport landed short, and hit a sharp bump. This was more than "ol' shakey" could stand and she immediately shed both wings!

The fuselage continued down the runway and slithered to a stop. All eight

crewmembers walked away, and the Military Air Transport Service of the USAF was again proud to have been of service. Both trucks were delivered safely, on schedule!

Another incident during these years of building radar lines involved two aircraft, one belonging to World Wide Airways; the other to Wheeler Airlines, Dorval-based carriers.

On May 21, 1956, World Wide's C-46, CF-IQQ, loaded with dynamite, was on a night time resupply run. En route there was engine trouble and an emergency landing with one engine out was made at Val d'or. The plane remained on the runway awaiting assistance.

Meanwhile, Wheeler's DC-4, CF-ILI, also loaded with dynamite, was awaiting takeoff at the opposite end of the runway! Seconds later it was under way. Then, to the horror of its pilots there was the C-46 directly in front of them. This was a desperate situation for there was no chance to abort takeoff and hardly enough speed to lift off. The captain opted for a quick pull up. He pulled back on the yoke and got airborne. There was a jolt as the DC-4 skimmed past the C-46. The plane was safely aloft, but all was not right. The captain declared an emergency and circled for a landing but was delayed while the World Wide plane was cleared from the runway. That jolt felt in the cockpit of the DC-4 had been plane bumping plane! The DC-4 had come out best while the C-46 had lost its tail and part of a wing. For such a potentially explosive situation, the outcome had been a lucky one.

MCA Branches Out

MCA faired well financially on the DEW Line. This enabled expansion into other areas. Its fleet grew to include the DC-6 and Viscount. Overseas charters were begun in the mid fifties, many carrying refugees to Canada and the United States from the Hungarian uprising of 1956. Many other flights were operated bringing Rhesus monkeys from India for the production in Canada of Salk vaccine. Tragedy struck the airline August 11, 1957, when one of its DC-4's crashed near Quebec. The plane was carrying holidayers back from the U.K. All 79 aboard were killed.

In 1957 MCA set up a subsidiary based at Dorval. This was Nordair, formed from the combined assets of Mont Laurier Aviation and Boreal Airways. Nordair was soon flying DEW Line contracts, and scheduled operations that terminated at Frobisher, 1300 miles north of Dorval.

Quebecair and Eastern Provincial Airlines

Two other airlines operated in eastern Canada after the war. Quebecair evolved from Rimouski Airlines, serving communities along the St. Lawrence Valley and elsewhere in Quebec. In 1958 it became the first of the Regionals to fly turbine-powered aircraft when it purchased a fleet of Fairchild F.27 Friendships.

Eastern Provincial Airlines formed in 1949 to become Newfoundland's first modern airline. It served the province's larger centres but also brought air travel to

Nordair's Herald, CF-NAF at Malton in 1962 while flying the airline's short-lived "Seaway" route. NAF later went to Maritime Central. On March 17, 1965, it was en route from Halifax to Sydney when it disintegrated in flight near Upper Musquodoboit, Nova Scotia. All eight aboard perished. Cause of the accident was skin corrosion resulting over a period of time from leaking acid.

Larry Milberry

many of its isolated outports. In the early sixties it had branched out throughout Labrador and was even serving communities in Greenland with an Otter and Canso. In 1963 Eastern Provincial bought out MCA to become the major airline in Atlantic Canada.

Regionals in the West

Elsewhere, other regional airlines were experiencing growth attributable to DEW Line construction and resupply contracts. On the West Coast, Queen Charlotte Airlines had begun operations just after the war, flying scheduled and charter services to coastal communities as well as to mining, fishing and logging camps. One of its first big contracts was flying on the Alcan project at Kitimat and Kemano in Northern B.C. during the early fifties. The Rapide, Anson, Stranraer, Canso, and DC-4 appeared in QCA markings.

Pacific Western Airlines

The other major B.C. airline during this period was Central B.C. Airways. It had been founded by Russell L. Baker. He had migrated to the Coast from Winnipeg in 1935 to fly with Ginger Coote during the Bridge River gold rush. Later on, he flew with Canadian Airways and CPA. The lore and, to some extent, plight of the bush pilot are portrayed by Baker in this excerpt from a letter he addressed to "Punch" Dickins in 1938:

"We had bad weather on police charter and did not return to Fort St. James until Sunday. All passes north of Aiken Lake were plugged tight. However, in a way it was fortunate as I landed at Bear Lake, and in the course of our stay there got a ten-ton contract from Carl Hanniwal, a trader at this point. His supplies are to be moved in in June. I also landed at Takla and on the twelfth of this month am to move a ton and a half into McConnell Lake, so although I missed some business at the Fort I have more than made up for it.

"De Ganahl is also moving quite a number of men into Germantown next week and I am getting my share of this business.

"Molly wired me from Vancouver about a charter from Prince George to Dawson, Yukon on the 15th of March and I have quoted price and am awaiting his reply . . . .

"I would also appreciate your advising me re Arnett's and my expenses while at Fort St. James. I have placed Arnett in a suitable boarding house at $7 per month rent plus 40¢ per meal. I am looking around for a small cabin.

"I am carrying out the instructions you left me, although my flight reports may be delayed at times owing to my operating in an area north of here where the mail service is poor.

"I am trying to keep down expenses as much as possible and have made a deal with Fraser to use his garage as a storage shed in return for boarding Arnett at his brother's place . . . . "

In 1946 Baker formed Central B.C. Airways in partnership with Walter Gilbert. He purchased three war surplus T-50 Cranes and two old Junkers from CPA. From a pile of spares he came up with a third Junkers. As with other small post-war operators, business was slow, but Baker procured a forestry patrol contract with the B.C. government. It was renewed for several years following, helping to keep him solvent.

In 1948, Baker purchased the prototype Beaver, CF-FHB and within a year was running a major operation that focused on the Alcan development. Growth continued and in 1953 he renamed his company Pacific Western Airlines. Two years later, he absorbed QCA, then

One of Quebecair's Fairchild F-27 Friendships seen at Dorval on September 5, 1961. It had joined the Quebecair fleet in 1958 and was still in service 21 years later.

Larry Milberry

Associated Airways to give PWA a fleet of some 60 aircraft.

During this period, Baker was pioneering in the air bus field. At first Ottawa would have none of this scheme which saw passengers boarding aircraft much as they do a bus, no reservations needed. Finally, in 1955, the Vancouver-Powell River air bus was approved. It was inaugurated with fares 25 percent below normal. The trip took 25 minutes by DC-3, versus six hours by bus, and was soon the popular choice of those travelling between the two centres.

Russell Baker on the wing of one of his Junkers bush planes at Ft. St. James, B.C. in 1947.

Public Archives of Canada (PA 102385)

Associated Airways

Edmonton-based Associated Airways also had post-war beginnings. It was founded in 1945 by T.P. ''Tommy'' Fox and David C. Dyck. Fox had earned his wings in 1930, and two years later built his own aircraft, a Pietenpol Air Camper, CF-ATU. During World War II he served with No. 3 AOS, Edmonton; and with Ferry Command.

Associated began humbly, with the Tiger Moth, CF-BEN; and the Dragonfly, CF-BZA, one of the old RCMP machines. Business initially consisted of flight training, passenger hopping, fish hauling, mercy flights and even rain making.

One of the aircraft used on the fish haul was an Anson. During one landing on Lake Chipewyan, 360 miles north of Edmonton, its starboard wing was damaged. Fox quickly appraised the situation. He needed the aircraft to fulfill his contract, and concluded that one way or the other the Anson would have to be repaired.

In -50°F weather he began work on the aircraft. This amounted more to surgery! Using a saw, the damaged wingtip was trimmed up. This left it 9-1/2 feet shorter than that of the usual Anson. To balance things off, Fox simply amputated 9-1/2 feet from the port wing. After sealing up the wingtips, he then took off for Fort McMurray.

As the aircraft would not fly well at less than full throttle, Fox soon ran out of fuel. He landed on the Athabaska River 30 miles short of his destination. Here he waited two days for fuel to be flown in, then carried on.

At Fort McMurray the Anson switched from skis to wheels and was then ferried to Edmonton for repairs. For his efforts, Fox got his aircraft back on the active list but also suffered the inconvenience of being temporarily grounded by the DOT.

One of Associated's numerous mercy flights took Fox, Dyck, a patient and nurse all the way from Edmonton to Rochester, Minnesota, in the Dragonfly. Another took serum to Old Crow in the Yukon where a diphtheria outbreak threatened an Indian community.

In 1950, encouraged by oil exploration that the big Leduc find had spurred, Fox decided to pioneer in helicopters. He set up Associated Helicopters and acquired his first machine, the Bell 47, CF-GSL. It was soon at work in the Lesser Slave Lake region.

Further growth occurred the following year when Associated took over Matt Berry's Territories Air Services and Yellowknife Airways in which Berry and Max Ward were partners. This gave the company a solid foothold in the North. In 1952 it acquired the first Canadian-owned Bristol Freighter. This was soon on the airlift of men and supplies to and from the big uranium development around Beaver Lodge on Lake Athabaska, and to other mining properties. The Bristol was ideal as it could haul up to 6-1/2 tons over a 300-mile distance and featured clamshell doors for drive-on, drive-off operations.

By 1955 Associated's fleet included the Beaver, Norseman, Skyrocket, Bonanza, Anson, Barkley-Grow, Lockheed 14, DC-3, DC-4, Avro York and Bristol Freighter.

CF-EKO, Tommy Fox's clipped wing Anson Mk.V. Bush flier's ingenuity at its height!

John Davids

One of Associated Airways' Avro York freighters on the ramp at Edmonton. The York appeared in Canada during the DEW Line construction era. One York, CF-HAS, was in service with Transair as late as 1961.

Pacific Western Airlines

DEW Line contracts were being flown, with Associated the major contractor for the western section. There was so much work to be done that Associated was actually subcontracting out some of the work to its competitors. The Bristol was a major asset throughout this period as it could haul such items as bulldozers without these having to be cut apart.

Then, in the midst of all this activity, trouble appeared. The airline experienced a series of flying mishaps. The Bristol, two Yorks, the Lockheed and a Cessna 180 were all lost in accidents. Not long after these setbacks, Associated was approached by Russ Baker of PWA who made an offer to buy the company. In November, 1956 a deal was struck by which Associated's air transport operation became part of PWA, though Associated Helicopters remained independent and still under Fox's control. Apart from the long-term benefits of Associated's northern bases and route structure, PWA was obviously interested in the short-term benefits of becoming the prime DEW Line contractor in the region, two factors which explain Baker's desire to buy out Fox. Following the sale, Fox continued to run PWA's northern division and was for a time a Director and Vice-Chairman of the airline.

Associated Helicopters remained an independent operation for over 20 years after the PWA takeover. By 1977 when it was sold to Okanagan Helicopters it was still staffed by some of its original employees.

Transair

Transair had its beginnings in the post-war years as Central Northern Airways. Milt Ashton and Roy Brown, two World War I fliers, had pooled their resources even earlier to form Wings Ltd. It disappeared in the CPA shuffle of 1941, but after the war, Ashton and Brown were back in business. They took over CPA's hodge-podge of routes in Northwestern Ontario and northern Manitoba. With six Norsemans and two Bellancas, Central Northern began operations from bases at Pickle Crow, Sioux Lookout, Lac du Bonnet, Sherridon, and Flin Flon. It prospered when the DEW Line came along and the fleet expanded to include types like the Canso, C-46, York, and Bristol Freighter. In 1955 Central Northern merged with Arctic Wings, Spartan's air transport subsidiary to become Transair. Once the DEW Line construction phase

was completed, Transair was hit by a painful recession. It failed to win any of the initial vertical resupply contracts, and lost money for a period of years beginning in 1957. It did open up a Mid Canada Line resupply service, though, operating a DC-4, CF-JEA, between Churchill, Winisk, Ottawa, and Montreal. In 1961, the pendulum swung back in favour of the Winnipeg airline when it won the biggest DEW Line resupply contract ever awarded. Before long, it was operating five DC-4's north from Churchill to Cape Dyer, Cambridge Bay and Cape Perry.

Wardair

In 1946, Max Ward established a flying operation at Yellowknife with a Fox Moth, CF-DJB. This had cost him $12 500, about three times his actual worth at the time. His company, Polaris Charter, specialized in service to the booming mining industry in and around Yellowknife.

Forerunner of Transair was Wings Ltd., formed in the thirties. Seen here is one of Wings' aircraft, the Fairchild 82, CF-AXF. It was photographed in 1937 at Tavani in the Northwest Territories while freighting for Hudson Bay Mining and Smelting between there and Padlei, a trip of about two hours each way. Pilot on the contract was Jack Faries and engineer was Ralph Shapland. CF-AXF later served with Canadian Pacific Air Lines and Dominion Skyways. It was wrecked September 12, 1942 during takeoff from Lac Pipmuacan, Quebec.

Ralph Shapland

At first things did not work out, and Ward had to temporarily give up being an entrepreneur. For a time he flew for Tommy Fox, but in 1953 was again running his own company, this time known as Wardair. He purchased an Otter, the first of its type in the Territories. When business picked up, he added two more, followed by the Bristol Freighters being disposed of by TCA in 1957. These proved

Wardair's Bristol Freighter CF-TFX loading a de Havilland Beaver. TFX, originally owned by TCA, is now a historic monument at Yellowknife airport. It was the first wheel-equipped aircraft ever to land at the North Pole.

·De Havilland Aircraft of Canada Ltd. (8671)

Max Ward in his first aircraft, a Canadian-built Fox Moth.

Wardair Canada Ltd.

ideal in handling bulky and heavy items associated with mining.

In the early sixties Ward decided to experiment in the international air charters field, at the time a real frontier. In 1962 he leased a DC-6 from CPA and, at a loss of $270 000, ran eight overseas flights. Next year he purchased a DC-6 from KLM.

Overseas charters began to gain in popularity, and the DC-6 was soon earning its keep. It was also kept busy carrying passengers and freight on both the International Upper Mantle Project in the Coppermine area and the Polar Continental Shelf Project. On another Arctic job it was fitted with a magnetometer used to record the Earth's magnetic field over an area of 2-1/2 million square miles.

Growth of the Trunk Carriers

Trans-Canada Air Lines and Canadian Pacific Air Lines kept pace with air transport developments throughout the post-war era. A major advance for TCA was its order for Lockheed L.1049 Super Constellations. The first of these was delivered in February, 1954 by Captain George Lothian. He took off from Burbank, California, and 7 hours 55 minutes later touched down at Dorval. With its 4000 mile range the "Connie" became Canada's first truly transcontinental airliner.

The Super Constellation enabled further extensions of TCA's international routes with Zurich, Brussels, and Vienna being added to the system. It also gave Western Canada direct access to Europe. Passengers could now fly from Winnipeg to London via Gander.

Gander was in its heyday during this period. It had boomed during World War II when it became the jump off point for some 17 000 aircraft flown to Britain by Ferry Command. After the war when trans-Atlantic passenger service began to develop, it was a vital refuelling base. In 1956 Gander handled 650 000 passengers. In 1958 12 000 international flights stopped there.

Long-range jetliners began overflying Gander in the early sixties and today it is a relatively quiet airport. In 1977 only 133 international scheduled airliners landed there, carrying just 19 525 passengers.

Also in 1954 TCA began trans-Canada air freight when it introduced the Bristol Freighter. This turned out to be premature, however, and the Bristols were sold off. Some time later, three North Stars were converted to freighters with 18 000 pounds payload. These served until 1961.

During this same period CPA was introducing its new long-range airliner, the Douglas DC-6B. Its first proving flight was to Honolulu, on January 24, 1953. A month later, service began on the North Pacific between Vancouver and Tokyo.

The DC-6B was to prove an outstanding airliner. It seated 64 and could fly over 4000 miles at speeds over 300 mph. CPA opened up other new services at this time, flying south from Vancouver to touch at Mexico City, Lima, Rio de Janeiro, Santiago, and Buenos Aires. Toronto-Mexico flights began in November, 1955. That year also saw the start of trans-polar flights between Vancouver and Amsterdam. Toronto and Montreal to Lisbon were being operated by 1957.

CF-TEV, an L.1049G Super Constellation belonging to TCA. In all, 14 "Super Connies" were operated by TCA. None was ever involved in a fatal accident, though two were wrecked in crash landings, one at Brampton and one at Malton. Seating for this famous aircraft varied between 48 and 63.

Lockheed Aircraft (AL4112)

The 1950s also saw CPA heavily involved on the DEW Line. Its main responsibility was the supply of fuel from Norman Wells to points between Herschel Island and Shepherd Bay at the base of the Boothia Peninsula. Eight C-46's, five DC-3's and two DC-4's worked these contracts. Forty-two two-man crews were required, flying out of Edmonton, Fort Nelson, Norman Wells, and Yellowknife. Pilots were given an annual quota of 1020 hours, and at 100 hours every eight to ten days, a pilot could nicely wind up his year by

An unflattering view of a TCA Viscount. CF-TGY was written off in this accident at Malton October 3, 1959. It landed short during a heavy squall, but all 40 on board survived. The TCA Viscount carried up to 54 passengers.

Larry Milberry/Merlin Reddy

October and be on his way south with a neat bank roll!

CPA never suffered a serious mishap during these busy years. The workhorse on the job turned out to be the oft-maligned C-46; yet the entire CPA fleet survived to the end of the operation, thanks to capable pilots, and, a first-rate maintenance program.

Up until 1953, CPA operated DC-3's on its shorter internal routes, but that year introduced the Convair 240. The Convair boasted such features as pressurized cabin and reverse pitch propellers. First flights were on the Vancouver-Whitehorse run, but places like Penticton, Castlegar, Cranbrook, and Calgary were soon hosting the new planes. The Convairs were to provide reliable service for over a decade.

A major event in commercial aviation in the mid fifties was the introduction of turbine-powered airliners. This new era began with the Vickers Viscount. With this type TCA brought turbine power to the North American airline scene. The first of many routes to enjoy Viscount service was Montreal-Toronto-Ft. William-Winnipeg. The Viscount had the effect of increasing the number of passengers flying with the

CF-WCO, one of Millardair's DC-3's at ▶ Terminal 1, Toronto International Airport on January 4, 1974. The DC-3 is the world's most famous airliner and is still widely used in Canada, especially in the North. This veteran type has survived efforts of aircraft manufacturers to replace it with more modern designs.

Larry Milberry

airline and was to evoke universal popularity with aircrew, groundcrew, and the travelling public alike. Fifty-one were eventually purchased. The Viscount did its share to push TCA over the 10 000 000 passengers-carried mark in 1955.

With the Viscount, the jet age had arrived or, if we recall the Avro Jetliner, rearrived in Canada. CPA purchased its first turboprops in 1958. These were Bristol Britannias, and they were soon taking over from the DC-6B's. They first operated Vancouver-Tokyo, then Vancouver-Honolulu. By 1959 they were flying the company's hard-won Vancouver-Winnipeg-Toronto-Montreal service, for the first time offering direct competition on TCA's transcontinental route. This resulted from the decision of the Air Transport Board to allow CPA one such flight per day to allow it to interconnect its Atlantic and Pacific routes.

Older Types Retire

In 1960 and 1961 both Canada's trunk airlines again invested heavily in new equipment. TCA ordered 23 Vickers Vanguards to replace the North Stars. But the really big move was into pure jets. Both companies had ordered Douglas DC-8's as new long range equipment.

Reequipment meant that the days of the aging piston-pounders were numbered. Evidence of this was the retirement of the North Star on June 30, 1961. The DC-3 and Super Constellation were sold off by late 1963 by which time TCA was operating an all-turbine fleet. CPA retained its DC-3's and DC-6B's on passenger service through to 1969, but held on to its last DC-3, CF-CRX until 1974.

Inevitably, even the still modern turbine aircraft faced retirement. Air Canada operated its last Vanguard passenger flight on October 31, 1971; the last freight flight was on May 26 the following year. The Viscount, though still used around the world today, was retired April 27, 1974, after nearly 20 years of safe reliable operations. The Viscount fleet had logged a million and a half flying hours.

Backbone of Air Canada's domestic fleet is ▶ the DC-9. One of the world's most successful airliners, over 1000 have been sold since it was first flown in 1965. More than 40 are in service with Air Canada.

Robin Brass

Veteran Airliners Sold Off

For all practical purposes, the era of the piston-powered airliner was over by the mid sixties. For a while, though, a handful of ex-TCA and RCAF North Stars did linger on, wearing the national markings of countries like Mexico, Venezuela, the United States, Panama, and Italy.

Some remained in Canada where it was hoped they would operate a service between Toronto and Havana for International Air Freighters. This scheme was short lived. A number of flights were made to Cuba hauling pigs and chicks, but business failed and the North Stars were scrapped. Another old North Star, CF-TFM, gained some notoriety. In April, 1966 it was reported sold to the King of Burundi. Later, however, it was known to have taken on a load of machine guns at Rotterdam under the company name Silver Lane. Bearing an Italian registration it departed for West Africa. On October 11 it crashed in the Cameroons. CF-TFM was the last ex-TCA North Star known to have operated anywhere.

TCA's Super Constellations were mostly taken in as trades by Douglas when the airline bought its DC-8's. Like the North Stars, most were cannibalized and scrapped but a few did carry on for a while. CF-TEX, bearing Ghanian markings, was arrested at Malta for gun running; CF-TGF was used by a series of U.S. cargo airlines including Capitol, Standard, and American Flyers; CF-TGB went to Standard Airways in whose service it crashed when number three propeller reversed pitch while the plane was on final approach at Manhattan, Kansas; CF-TEZ, involved in a previous accident at Malton, was rebuilt at Dorval using parts from CF-TGC, and eventually burned out in an accident at San Francisco in 1963.

Viscounts disposed of by TCA ended up with such far distant operators as Air Inter in France, and Air India. One went to

One of Air Canada's Vickers Vanguards approaching to land at Toronto. TCA's Vanguards carried up to 108 passengers.
Larry Milberry

the Department of Transport, one to Transair, another to United Aircraft as a flying test bed. Many of those retired at Winnipeg were scrapped when no buyers could be found, though as recently as 1978 a number were still lying here and there around the airport. The Vanguards went off to serve with smaller airlines from Britain and France, to Iceland and Indonesia.

CPA's DC-6B's were also scattered around the globe. CF-CZZ continued on with PWA, Wardair, as a fire bomber with Conair, and with Northwest Territorial Airlines as recently as 1978. Others gave service to Air Micronesia, World Airways, and Union de Transports Aeriens. The company's Britannias carried on for Caledonian Airways, African Air Safari, Transglobe, and Cunard Eagle.

Persistent Airliner

While older types were being phased out of service, one airliner has persisted over the years, even though it has been superseded regularly by newer designs. This aircraft is the DC-3, some 3000 of which still operate globally. In Canada, as elsewhere, the DC-3 has actually outlived some of its replacements. Eastern Provincial Airways and Nordair each purchased Dart Heralds in the early sixties as DC-3 replacements and flew them for several years. The Heralds were gone by the mid seventies, but both airlines were still flying the DC-3. Oddly enough, today, 40 years after the DC-3 first entered production, it is at its peak as a commercial transport in Canada, with over 150 currently in service. CF-TDJ is still operating as Goodyear Tire and Rubber's executive plane. It had originally joined the TCA fleet in 1945 as that airline's first DC-3.

Mishaps

Safety has always been paramount with Canada's big airlines. The types of aircraft chosen for use proved to be among the finest available, and safety records were only occasionally marred by accidents. TCA lost two North Stars. One of these went down following a mid air collision with a Harvard over Moose Jaw in 1954. The other crashed into Mount Slesse near Hope, B.C. in 1956. No lives were lost in Super Constellation accidents. There were no major Viscount or Vanguard disasters though these types were occasionally involved in accidents. Shortly after leaving Victoria for Vancouver on March 1, 1970, Viscount, CF-THY, collided with an Ercoupe. The little two-seater went down but the Viscount landed safely with its 29 passengers. There was another near disaster at Bagotville when a taxiing Viscount had its fuselage split open and tail wiped off by an RCAF Voodoo that was just getting airborne. The fighter's crew safely ejected but a flight attendant on the Viscount was killed. Vanguard, CF-TKV, encountered turbulence over Rocky Mountain House during a 1963 flight with the result that one passenger died and 12 were badly injured.

In 1949, a CPA DC-3 went down in Quebec and in 1965 its DC-6B, CF-CUQ, crashed in northern B.C. In both cases all aboard died, and it was later determined that the airliners had been bombed. CPA's North Star, *Empress of Vancouver,* was lost at Tokyo in 1950 and its Britannia, CF-CZB, at Honolulu in 1962 while attempting a three-engined go around. Both airlines have also lost DC-8's in serious accidents. One of CPA's crashed at Tokyo; while Air Canada DC-8's have crashed near Ottawa, Montreal, and Toronto.

Canadian Freighters in Africa

In the late sixties, Nordair was still operating Super Constellations. These were sold to Canairelief for use on the food lift to Biafra during the Nigerian civil war. Three aircraft were based offshore on the Portuguese island of São Tomé, and were flown and maintained by Nordair personnel. The first flight was made January 23, 1969, in CF-NAJ. The crew on this occasion were J.S. Patterson (Captain), Paul Waldorf (First Officer), Vincent Wakling (Engineer), and Fred Smyth (Load Master).

All Canairelief operations were at night, with each "Connie" hauling about 16 tons of food per trip to the makeshift airstrip at Uli. Each aircraft averaged three trips per night, completing each leg in 1 hour and 15 minutes at 260 knots.

Navigation was via two beacons and approaches were made on instruments with runway lights coming up when the aircraft was on final at 400 feet. As soon as propellers were reversed, the lights went off. This was necessary as a Nigerian night intruder was usually in the area awaiting a chance to bomb the airstrip.

During the operation one crew was lost when its aircraft flew into a hill attempting to land. Another was destroyed on the ground after taking a hit from a Nigerian bomber. The last Canairelief trip took place January 17, 1970. At this time the "Connie" barely got away from Uli which was under heavy fire and about to fall to the federal troops. On this occasion

Captain Pat Patterson leans out the cockpit window of a Canairelief Super Constellation on São Tomé. The occasion was the first relief flight into Biafra, January 23, 1969. The aircraft, CF-NAJ, was previously owned by Nordair.

Via J.S. Patterson

the aircraft was under command of Captain Peter Knox.

The pace of the food lift was hectic. During its brief duration, Captain Patterson himself made 152 trips to Uli in less than seven months. Overall, Canairelief "Connies" hauled 10 000 tons of food, providing life for an estimated one million starving Biafrans.

Pure Jet Fleets

In 1965 TCA became Air Canada. That year its jet fleet numbered 16 DC-8's and passengers were riding them between Montreal and Vancouver in five hours non-stop, a great improvement over the 11 hours they had had to restlessly while away aboard the "Connies." On shorter intercity runs, DC-9's and Boeing 737's were gradually to take over. Speed, comfort, safety, and reliability reached new peaks with these aircraft.

DC-9's began taking over from prop-jets on Air Canada's routes in 1966,

One of the six Bristol Britannia 314's operated in the sixties by CPA. This one, CF-CZB, is seen loading at Winnipeg in 1960. CZB was later involved in a serious landing accident at Honolulu in which 27 of the 40 on board lost their lives.

Province of Manitoba, Provincial Archives (Industry and Commerce Collection 376)

operating domestically as 72-seaters. Eventually 53 were in service including a 107-seat stretched version. 737's in CP Air's bright orange colours now fly the route so well served for years by DC-3's, Convairs, and DC-6 B's. These are today a familiar sight at airports from Vancouver to Montreal.

With the phasing out of the Viscount in 1974 by Air Canada, both Canada's major airline fleets were pure jet. There were regular and stretched DC-8's, DC-9's, and 727's; 737's, 747 Jumbo's, and Tristars for a combined fleet of over 140 aircraft. Passenger service continually grows with Air Canada's and CP Air's passengers-carried statistics for 1977 being 10.9 million and 2.6 million respectively. Air freight for Air Canada totalled 247 000 000 ton miles and for CP Air 86 446 000 ton miles.

With the age of the commercial jet entering its third decade, the earlier generation of jets is already disappearing from Canadian skies. Older Air Canada aircraft have been leased to Air Jamaica and Cubana. Two of the Cubana aircraft have already come to grief. One collided with a military transport; another was bombed in flight. Two other Air Canada DC-8's, CF-TJB and CF-TFC, were sold for scrap in 1977. Such aircraft have been replaced gradually with the latest generation of Boeing, Lockheed and McDonnell Douglas airliners, new examples of which are regularly joining the fleet.

The Regionals Update

While fleet modernization was beginning in the early sixties, other changes were occurring on the air transport scene. In 1963, Eastern Provincial Airways took over Maritime Central Airlines. The following year, Nordair, by that time independent of MCA, absorbed Wheeler Airlines' heavy transport division. Other names disappeared, as did World Wide Airways. With EPA, Nordair, Transair, and PWA, the Boeing 737 became the standard workhorse. Quebecair reequipped with the Friendship and BAC-111. The regionals were now modern airlines which

had entered an era of general prosperity and sophistication.

Besides DEW Line resupply contracts still operated by the regionals, scheduled service throughout the North and charters in support of oil and gas exploration are very important in regional operations. Scheduled flights into Resolute indicate the vitality of the regionals in the North. Resolute, at 74° 43′N is Canada's most northerly commercial airport. In 1978 this community of just 550 people was being served twice weekly by a Nordair 737 (Montreal / Frobisher / Resolute), PWA 727 or 737 (Edmonton / Yellowknife / Resolute)

U.S. airlines began operating prop-jets on their Canadian routes in the late fifties. One of these was the much-heralded Lockheed Electra. This picture of American Airlines *Flagship Philadelphia* was taken April 10, 1960. The aircraft was just touching down at Malton after its one-hour flight from New York. This aircraft has recently been flying with the Mexican government as XC-HDA.

Larry Milberry

Three generations of airliners in Air Canada service: a Viscount, two DC-8's and a Boeing 747, photographed at Terminal 1, Toronto.

Larry Milberry

The Lockheed L.1011 Tristar, the most recent design to join Air Canada's all-jet fleet.

Air Canada

and a Transair 737 (Winnipeg/Churchill/Resolute). Total aircraft movements for Resolute in 1977 were 9968.

Aircraft operated by the regionals today include a variety of other types. There are 707's, H.S.748's, YS-11A's, DC-3's and Twin Otters. Besides regular operations they also provide specialized ones. Nordair flies ice reconnaissance for Environment Canada using modified Electras. PWA is in the global freight business using Hercules. These can turn up anywhere in the world with a load of heavy cargo. They've flown out of Lagos on relief missions to drought-stricken Niger; flown oil exploration support throughout the Canadian Arctic and in Ethiopia; freighted on the James Bay hydro development; and flown resupply to the diamond mining centre of Dundo in Angola. Flying from Benguela and Sã da Bandeira, the PWA "Hercs" supplied Dundo with the endless requirements for that centre of 100 000.

Such operations occasionally present difficulties. At Dundo, natives habitually made off with the flare pots used to mark runways for night landings. It was eventually decided to update with electric lights. These were duly installed atop tall metal poles at the runway's edge; but someone failed to consider wingspan and the first "Herc" down had a light standard wrapped around a wing!

In 1979 PWA received a three year contract to transport CF-104's between Edmonton and West Germany. The CF-104's are to be overhauled by Northwest Industries at Edmonton to keep them updated until the New Fighter Aircraft is put into service by the Canadian Forces. Using

a stretched L-100-30 Hercules, PWA will make one trip a month from West Germany to Edmonton carrying two CF-104's.

Charter flying began developing in a big way during the sixties, and the regionals were eager participants. They soon added larger though interim types to meet a growing market. DC-6's, DC-7's and Super Constellations being phased out in the big world airlines provided a ready supply of cheap long range aircraft for PWA, Transair, Wardair, Nordair, and World Wide Airways. With experience gained on these older aircraft and the charter market growing, the regionals were soon moving to jets and operating package holidays to the Caribbean, Latin America, Hawaii, destinations in Europe and elsewhere.

Currently all the Regionals are involved in charter flying. Boeing 707's, 727's, and 737's serve on the holiday routes, as do Quebecair's BAC 111's and Nordair's DC-8's. As the vacation market expands, wide body aircraft are on the horizon for the Regionals.

Typical of the short haul charters was one operated by Nordair on April 7, 1978. Its 737, CF-NAB, flew 113 passengers from Toronto to West End in the Bahamas. As one group of holidayers was taking up residence at the Grand Bahamas Hotel, another was boarding NAB for its return trip to Toronto. In all, 226 passengers had been moved that day in 5-1/2 hours flying time, with 4648 gallons of fuel being burned — just 20 gallons per passenger! CF-NAB is by now one of the world's high time 737's, with over 27 000 hours logged to late 1978. It joined the Nordair fleet in the autumn of 1968.

Through 1977 Canada's five regional airlines carried a total of 5.2 million passengers compared to 4.5 million the previous year. A significant event among these airlines was the approval early in 1978 by the Air Transport Committee of

the takeover by Alberta-owned PWA of Transair. Transair had for several years been experiencing financial hard times. Later in the year the Canadian Transport Commission approved the Air Canada takeover of Nordair, though later ordered its resale to private enterprize. Route changes involved in these decisions were granting Transair permission to serve Regina, Saskatoon, Calgary, and Edmonton; Nordair was granted permission to take over Transair's previous service between Toronto, Sault Ste. Marie, Thunder Bay, Dryden, and Winnipeg.

Wardair Expands

The Canadian airline par excellence in the charter field is Wardair. With a history dating back to its old Fox Moth it has become a global operation. After succeeding with his DC-6 charters in the early sixties, Max Ward arranged the purchase of a Boeing 727 in 1967. Suitably registered CF-FUN, the 727 was christened *Cy Becker* after a bush flying pioneer who had worked with "Wop" May in the early days.

CF-FUN was the first Boeing jetliner registered in Canada and as such was well supported by Boeing. The world's leader in manufacturing airliners was anxious to make a favourable impression in Canada. The airplane turned out well for both Boeing and Wardair. It proved ideal on the airline's European charters and during seven years in Wardair colours averaged 10.5 hours per day aloft, for a total of some 25 000 hours. In its first year of operation it completed 125 trans-Atlantic crossings, 58 of which were made in the peak July travel period.

In 1973 Max Ward received the McKee Trophy. In part the official citation describing Ward and his airline read:

"During the last ten years, the company has established a reputation second to none anywhere in the world for

Part of CP Air's famous "Orange is Beautiful" fleet. The *Empress of Canada* is being pushed back from Terminal 1 at Toronto for a flight overseas. The airline presently operates four 747's, 11 DC-8's, 10 737's and 2 DC-10's. Two more DC-10's are on order.

Larry Milberry

Many foreign airlines link Canada with the rest of the world. Here Alitalia's DC-10, *Benvenuto Cellini* taxis to the terminal at Toronto after a flight from Rome. Arriving behind are an Air Canada 727 and a Beech 18.

Larry Milberry

efficient operations and service to the travelling public. From an aircraft utilization standpoint, the company has achieved utilization rates which are among the highest recorded for the various aircraft operated. Servicing and maintenance of the company's fleet have been maintained at the highest levels, and the company's safety record has been outstanding.

"The personal dedication and leadership demonstrated by Mr. Ward in making these notable achievements possible have without doubt been largely responsible for the success of the enterprise. By his ability to lead and to inspire others, he has created an efficient team of enthusiasts, dedicated to the pursuit of excellence in every facet of the company's operations, and the results of this are evident for all to see."

Wardair's fleet has continually expanded, first with two 707's, then two 747's. In the spring of 1977 an order worth over 234 million dollars was announced by the airline. This was for two more 747's and two DC-10's, a move calculated to further maximize efficiency. With delivery of these, the hard-working 707's were sold, one in Kuwait and the other in Austria. Other signs of growth of the airline have included the formation of Wardair Canada Ltd. on January 1, 1976, and Wardair International the following June as parent company to the airline. International Vacations Ltd. (Intervac) was also formed as the marketing outlet for Wardair vacation packages.

For 1977 Wardair's average daily fleet utilization was 11.6 hours per aircraft, an exceptionally high figure. Load factors were also high, and over two billion passenger miles were flown, more than double the 1973 figure. For 1978 seven

A Pacific Western Airlines Boeing 737 at Vancouver International Airport.

Larry Milberry

During their formative years, Canada's regional airlines operated small as well as larger types. As the regionals grew they turned exclusively to airliners and sold off their bushplanes and lesser routes. This PWA FBA-2C is just taxiing out for takeoff from a West Coast seaplane base.

S.R. Found Via A.J. Moul

The scene at Boeing Aircraft on the occasion of Wardair accepting its first Boeing 747. On hand for the day were Wardair's famous 727, CF-FUN, and one of its 707's as well as a replica of Max Ward's original Fox Moth.

Wardair Canada Ltd.

Canadian cities were being served by the Wardair fleet.

Even though Wardair concentrates on international charters, it still retains its Northern operations. These are carried out with six Twin Otters, but in the summer of 1978 these were joined by the first of two Dash 7's. These will be used as freighters, but may later become the basis of a northern package tours operation.

A recent entry in the charter field has been that of Ontario Worldair. Airborne after years of effort by its founders, Ontario Worldair began operations in late 1978. Its first aircraft, an ex-Quantas Boeing 707, arrived in Canada on November 28 and soon began operations to southern holiday points. The 707's first charter was to Montego Bay, Jamaica, on December 1.

Third Level Carriers

While the big commercial jets are crisscrossing Canada daily, smaller aircraft are operating at much lower flight levels.

These belong to the third level carriers, companies with names like Air Gaspé, Atlantic Central Airlines, Austin Airways, Lambair, Time Air, and Northern Thunderbird Air. The communities they serve are frequently off the beaten track or along routes abandoned by the larger airlines as uneconomical. Aircraft in use are a mixed bag of Beechcraft, DC-3's, Islanders, Mallards, Saunders, Shorts, and Twin Otters.

St. Andrews Airways, serving a district in northern Manitoba, began operations in the early seventies interconnecting various centres in the Island Lake region. Operations began with a Beech 18 and three well-used Found FBA-2C's. Eventually a class three licence was obtained permitting the airline to operate into St. Andrews airport just north of Winnipeg, and providing a rationale for new equipment. Saunders ST-27's were acquired giving the firm real airline status

and the capability of fast transportation between the southern and the remote northern parts of Manitoba.

A West Coast third level operator is Air West, equipped primarily with Twin Otters. Air West dates from 1959 when Norman Gold formed Powell River Airways with a Cessna 172. Within two years he had four planes and was operating to numerous centres along the Coast. Business grew with the absorbing of two small rivals and in 1967 the company was renamed Air West.

The real plum for Air West became its Vancouver-Victoria commuter route, a downtown-to-downtown service. Almost fifty years ago this was a popular Canadian Airways route served by a 10-passenger Sikorsky S-38C flying boat. Today it is flown mainly by the float-equipped Twin Otters, with over 100 000 passengers annually travelling the route. This represents over half of Air West's customers.

Air West's fleet in 1978 included nine Twin Otters, two turboprop Grumman Goose, three Turbo Beavers and a variety of other light aircraft.

Northwest Territorial Airways is the North's largest indigenous third level operator. Based at Yellowknife it provides scheduled and charter services using DC-3's, DC-6's, and an Electra as of 1978. It is part of a transport system which includes a trucking operation that connects to Edmonton. The two modes are integrated through an infrastructure of warehousing, handling, and packaging. In 1978, Northwest Territorial became the first Canadian operator of the Lockheed L-100-30 Super Hercules freighter.

Otonabee Airways is a small third-level carrier in Southern Ontario. It began as a charter operation in 1970 equipped with a Cessna 310. This was augmented by a Cessna 402 and in early 1975 by a Saunders ST-27. The Saunders was put into service along a route that included Toronto Island Airport, Peterborough, Kingston, Ottawa, and Montreal. The service was very slow to develop, but picked up in 1978 with an Otonabee deal to take over the assets of Saunders Aircraft Corporation. This gave Otonabee five more ST-27's with several others available and the frequency of service was immediately expanded. Extension of the route system included daily flights to Syracuse, N.Y., and throughout 1978, business increased steadily. To date, Otonabee has been able to offer a service between Ottawa and downtown Toronto via Kingston for $69 same day return, as compared to Air Canada's $101.50. Otonabee's flight takes about the same time as Air Canada's, if one includes in the latter flight the time spent travelling to and from Toronto International Airport. In 1979 the company changed its name to Air Atonabee.

Montmagny Air Services is a Quebec operator located on the South Shore. Founded by Gilles Couillard in 1954, it is today one of North America's shortest airlines with a scheduled service seven miles

Rosella Bjornson, became Canada's first woman airline pilot when hired by Transair in 1973 as First Officer on the F.28 Fellowship. At the time, she also became the first woman in North America to fly a commercial jet on a scheduled airline.

Transair

long between Montmagny airport and the airport on Île aux Grues in the St. Lawrence River downstream from Île d'Orléans. Aircraft used are two 1948 Aeronca Sedans modified with 180 horsepower Lycoming engines. This modification, along with oversized tires and other small changes, has created an economical high performance aircraft for the short gravel strips used. Montmagny also operates a Cessna 180 but due to the fine qualities of the ancient Aeroncas, it is used only as a reserve aircraft.

Montmagny serves the small farming population on Île aux Grues carrying about 3000 passengers per year on the eight-minute crossing. Fare one way in 1978 was $7, but this is reduced to $5 in winter when the ferry *Majorlaine* cannot operate.

The ferry runs two or three times daily making a 20 minute crossing with a fare of $1 per passenger.

Montmagny also carries many passengers on a charter basis. Most of these are hunters who converge on Île aux Grues in the autumn to shoot Canada geese, snow geese, and varieties of ducks that pass through on their southward migration. The Aeroncas also provide exclusive air service to Grosse-Île, that small island in the St. Lawrence infamous for the thousands of Irish immigrants who perished there from cholera over a century ago. Today it is a quarantined federal government agricultural research centre.

Austin Airways

The most historic of Canada's third level carriers is Austin Airways of Timmins. Initially Toronto-based, Austin Airways was founded in 1934 by two brothers, Charles and Jack Austin. Their firm was soon involved in a variety of activities in northern Ontario using Waco, Moth, and Fleet aircraft. In time operations expanded to bases throughout northern Ontario including around the James Bay shore and all the way up the east coast of Hudson Bay.

In 1974 White River Air Service took over Austin Airways. The following year Jack Austin received the McKee Trophy. To 1979, the Austin fleet included four H.S. 748's used on freight/passenger operations. These gradually have taken over from Austin Airways' DC-3's and Canso's. Only one DC-3 remains in service. The 748's are in use at such distant centres as Pickle Lake in northwestern Ontario and Sugluk on Hudson Strait. Eight Twin

Passengers deplaning from an Otonabee Airways ST-27 at Toronto Island Airport after a flight from Kingston in June 1978. At the time, passengers flying Otonabee were being offered a same-day return ticket Ottawa-Toronto for $69 compared to the $102 ticket for those travelling Air Canada. CNT had previously been XR 391 of the RAF, Queen's Flight.

Larry Milberry

Two Air West Twin Otters at Vancouver's downtown seaplane base. Air West carries over 100 000 passengers a year between this base and downtown Victoria.

Larry Milberry

Gilles Couillard delivers passengers on a trip to Îles aux Grues in the St. Lawrence.
Larry Milberry

Otters and a variety of light twins and bushplanes are also in service. A recent addition has been a Cessna Citation for use as a high speed air ambulance. It has been fitted with an oversized door to facilitate loading stretchers. Air ambulance service was originally introduced by Austin Airways' in the mid thirties using a modified Waco.

Austin Airways has employed many famous aviators. The well-known Leigh Capreol was the first pilot hired by the Austins. Today the ranks of its pilots include Rusty Blakey, with 40 years of bush flying to his credit. Another veteran is Training Captain Archie Vanhee who, in 1978, celebrated 50 years of flying! Archie soloed in 1928 at the Montreal Flying Club.

Millardair is Canada's largest privately owned charter airline. Its fleet includes 10 DC-3's and 6 DC-4's. The DC-4's were put into service in 1978 as freighters. C-GQIA is seen at Quebec loading nine tons of auto parts for Windsor. Owner Carl Millard, in the airline business since he joined TCA in 1940, has specialized in service to the auto industry since he founded his own company in 1955.
Larry Milberry

Since that time Archie Vanhee spent considerable time in the bush including as a pilot with Mackenzie Air Service; then in the RCAF in World War II. During that period he was primarily involved as a flying boat instructor on the West Coast, and instructing on Hudsons on the East Coast. For a time he was Commanding Officer of 160 Sqdn, a coastal command squadron flying Cansos. After the war Archie flew extensively with CPA, but in 1960 was grounded on account of vision problems. When Canada adopted international eyesight standards for pilots, his licence was reinstated and Archie resumed his flying career. In 1972 he joined White River Air Service and became chief pilot for IFR including for Norontair. Sometime after, he became involved with CIDA and travelled to West Africa where he trained pilots on the Twin Otter in countries like Senegal and Upper Volta. In January 1979 he was again back in West Africa upgrading Twin Otter crews.

Building Dams by Air

One of the great air lifts in Canadian history has been under way in northern Quebec since the early seventies. The locale is the James Bay region, an area 600 miles north of Montreal stretching east-west for 400 miles between Fort George on James

Atlantic Central's six-passenger Piper Navajo departs the ramp at Saint John, New Brunswick, July 7, 1978, while an EPA 737 is just arriving.
Larry Milberry

Bay and Caniapiscau to the east. Traditionally the home of nomadic hunters and trappers, it is today a place where massive dams, dikes, reservoirs, and powerhouses are taking shape. The outcome will be a doubling of Quebec's hydroelectric capacity by 1985.

Although the region's hydroelectric potential had been known for many years, it wasn't until 1971 that work to develop it was initiated, when la Société d'énergie de la Baie James was formed and exploration began. This early phase depended exclusively on bush planes and helicopters. In

Archie Vanhee in the rear cockpit of the Montreal Flying Club JN-4 in which he soloed in 1928. In 1980 Archie will celebrate half a century in commercial aviation. He has flown such historic aircraft as the Fairchild 82, Norseman, Vedette, Vancouver, Shark, Hudson, DC-3, Canso, and North Star. His all-time favourite was the DC-6B. Archie became interested in aviation during World War I when exposed to the air battles that raged near the town in Belgium where he lived as a boy.
Archie Vanhee

that first year 21 fixed wing aircraft and 25 helicopters were under contract to SEBJ.

Within a year, aviation requirements advanced a stage when SEBJ decided to develop sites along the La Grande River. A major exploration program was organized requiring an airlift of fuel and supplies. A contract was let to Nordair and flown in three parts during March, 1972. DC-3's, DC-4's and C-46's flew from Val d'Or to frozen Lac Carbillet near the future LG-2; eight DC-3's flew from Schefferville to lakes lying between Caniapiscau and the future LG-4; and a PWA Hercules operated between Val d'Or and Fort George. In all, over 1500 tons were moved including some 5000 fuel drums.

This operation had been supervised by Nordair's Vice President, Operations, F.J. Henley. Once it was complete, he left Nordair to become air transport consultant to SEBJ. His first task was an economic study of transportation east of LG-2 resulting in the decision to purchase an aircraft large enough to support the build-up of exploration and development there. In 1973 an L382E Hercules was acquired.

Registered CF-DSX, the Hercules made its first revenue flight on September 26, 1973. Since then it has become increasingly vital to the operation, and has logged some 8000 hours to late 1978. It has been claimed that had strikes, the 1974 labour disturbance at LG-2, and budget restrictions caused by the Montreal Olympics not interfered, CF-DSX would have had the entire project a year ahead of schedule.

SEBJ's rugged Hercules on one of the ice strips used throughout the James Bay complex before modern airports had been constructed there.

Société d'Energie de la Baie James

At first CF-DSX operated like any other bush plane. There were few airstrips and little in the way of navigation aids. In winter the Hercules took to the ice with the Beavers and DC-3's. Its first ice landing was made at LG-3 on February 5, 1974, when Captain Ken Ruel brought it in on a runway 4500 feet long by 150 feet wide by 42 inches thick. This was the farthest south in Canada that a Hercules had ever landed on ice.

LG-3 was one of five ice strips in use that winter. Construction of such a strip began by flying in a small farm tractor and a snowblower that attached to it. Snow was cleared and holes drilled in the ice. Through these, water was pumped up and used to flood the runway in 400-foot lengths. Using this process 6 inches of new ice could be laid over the full length of the runway every 24 hours.

For the first year of ice strip operations fuel and supplies were carried in to support exploration, but the following winter, heavy machinery was delivered and used that summer to construct gravel runways adequate for Hercules operations. At the same time, radio beacons and other improvements were installed at the new strips.

While today's Hercules operations are quite sophisticated, in the beginning support equipment was scarce. Although food was handled in igloo containers, there were no skid pallets or trailers to handle them. Loading construction wood took up to three hours; it took two hours to off-load. These are now 15- to 20-minute operations. There were other difficulties as well, like the 24 hours it could take to deice CF-DSX using a small hand pump, in Arctic conditions.

Utilization has steadily risen over the

Hercules' four years on the project. In 1974 it logged 1104 hours. Through 1977 it was averaging 250 hours per month. Its freight-delivered statistics to the end of 1977 were over 50 000 tons. This figure is edging closer each day to the 81 000 ton total figure for the entire Hollinger Ungava operation.

Some camps on the James Bay complex depend almost entirely on CF-DSX. One is Caniapiscau. Its only transportation link to the outside is a 5800-foot gravel runway. As a camp of 1100 in 1977, its daily requirements included 15 000 pounds of food; 17 000 gallons of fuel and 40 000 pounds of explosives. The Hercules is the pipeline for these and whatever else is needed at Caniapiscau.

Between July 1 and July 8, 1977, CF-DSX delivered 51 loads to Caniapiscau for a total of 1 704 187 pounds. A typical load included aluminum motor boats, pipes and fittings, firefighting gear, and food, all weighing 42 000 pounds. Another load was a mixture of explosives and crates of eggs!

Fuel arrives at Caniapiscau in a special tank carried by the Hercules, 26 feet long by 7 feet in diameter with a 6300-gallon capacity. This is a vast improvement over the early days when the same aircraft hauled fuel in drums, 127 per trip. Fuel for the various sites is airlifted in from Schefferville, 125 miles east of Caniapiscau.

Once the basic infrastrucure was in place throughout the James Bay complex, and work begun on the major facilities, a study was made to determine air transport requirements of the 17 000 people who would be living and working in the region by 1978. Commercial airlines could not provide the necessary service to move these vertically to and from the south, and horizontally from site to site, so SEBJ decided to set up its own airline operation. Six Convair 580's were acquired from North Central Airlines of Minneapolis. Quebecair signed a five year contract to fly and service the fleet, and on July 10, 1976, the first Convair revenue flight was logged. Today, the 50-seat Convairs fly a route that originates at Dorval, and touches at Quebec, Bagotville, Caniapiscau, LG-4, LG-3, LG-2, Opinaca, and Val d'Or.

Other fixed wing aircraft operate throughout James Bay. These include DC-3's, Caribous, Navajos, and a few bushplanes. Nordair and Quebecair operate to LG-2 with 737's and BAC-111's; and helicopters continue to be indispensable to the overall operation. The collective efforts of all these will be the addition to Quebec's energy reserves of over 10 million kilowatts of electricity by 1985.

Surveying, Spraying, and Fire-Fighting

Early aerial photography in Canada. Photographer William James occupies the rear cockpit of a JN-3 at Toronto. Note his camera mount! Up front, also well prepared for a cold flight, is the famous pilot Bert Acosta.

James Collection, City of Toronto Archives

Aerial surveying in Canada dates to the World War I era. This Huff-Daland HD-19 Petrel 5 was used from 1924-1926 by Fairchild Aerial Surveys of Grand 'Mère. Pilot Ken Saunders is seen passing a camera to his wife.
Aviation and Space Division, National Museum of Science and Technology (001958)

The Golden Era: Lightnings and Mosquitos

Conditions after World War II favoured a resurgence in aerial surveying. Thousands of skilled pilots, navigators, engineers, and camera operators were home. They constituted a reservoir for aerial survey firms like Spartan Air Services and the Photographic Survey Corporation which formed immediately after the war. Initially, surplus aircraft like the Anson, Hudson, and Canso were readily available at low prices and were easy to adapt to surveying standards.

The aerial surveyors' bonanza at this time was Canada's program to update existing topographic maps and to map previously uncharted zones like the Arctic. This was to result in a ten-year project demanding all the resources of civilian and military aerial surveyors. Besides this, the Canada Forestry Act of 1947 called for a complete inventory of the nation's forests, a task that could be accomplished only from the air. There was also an increased demand for aerial surveying to assist in new highway, railway, and pipeline construction, hydro and irrigation projects, municipal zoning, and so on.

While aircraft like the Anson were well suited to survey work, high altitude aircraft were soon being sought. This was because the costs of mapmaking are directly proportional to the number of photos taken. With this in mind, Spartan procured its first P-38 Lightnings in 1950. Jack-of-all-trades Weldy Phipps directed the modification of these two aircraft and in 1951 he and R.H. (Bob) Fowler flew these aircraft to the Yukon on their first high altitude contract. The aircraft were CF-GSP and CF-GSQ. Camera operators for the job were Gene Benoit and Joe Kohut; and the two mechanics were Len McHale and Bill Doherty.

The aircraft were based at Dawson and were supported by an Anson which shuttled supplies from Edmonton. They immediately set to work flying lines between Dawson and the Arctic coast. These were flown at 35 000 feet from where a single exposure covered 100 square miles. The Lightnings could carry a pair of 165 gallon drop tanks, but their weight made it difficult for the aircraft to reach altitude. Because of this, drop tanks were used only when ferrying. This meant that pilots had to manage their fuel very carefully. Generally an endurance of three hours at 400 mph was normal. Entries in pilots' logs during this contract show many flights of 2 hours and 45 minutes, even one of 3 hours and 10 minutes. This was expecting a lot of the Lightnings but the remuneration system encouraged pilots to push their luck. Besides a fixed salary, there was a high altitude bonus, plus 27 cents for every mile flown. On July 31, 1953, a Spartan Lightning, CF-GKH, crashed while approaching Dawson, killing both crewmen. Its tanks had run dry — perhaps the result of trying to stretch the fuel too far.

As the weather around Dawson deteriorated mid way through the summer of 1951, one of the Spartan Lightnings moved to Vancouver to carry out photo survey work between Comox, B.C., and Calgary. On August 1, Bob Fowler was taking off from Vancouver when one engine began burning furiously. A quick turn around and downwind landing brought the Lightning down safely. The aircraft was in poor shape, but with hard work on the part of engineer and pilot, it was flying again in three days! Work out of Vancouver continued, and if the entries in Bob Fowler's log for August 18 are any indication, the pace was hectic. That day Bob flew 8 hours and 20 minutes. This was gruelling work. Upon landing for fuel and film magazines, the crew often stayed on oxygen, ready to zip off as soon as possible. Fatigue inevitably resulted, and attacks of the bends sometimes forced a pilot to abort his mission. Boredom and loneliness were other problems. Because of this, Bob Fowler made an opening in his instrument panel in order just to see his fellow crewman in the nose!

The Lightning was well liked by Spartan crews. Rocky Laroche joined Spartan one morning in 1954 and the same day was flying a Lightning at 38 000 feet between the Soo and the Lakehead on a survey flight. To him this aircraft was always a joy to fly.

Spartan tried one other high performance aircraft at this time. This was CF-GUO, a de Havilland Sea Hornet. The British had been testing it at RCAF Station Namao. Once tests were completed, they decided to dispose of the aircraft. A Spartan pilot, Bill Ferderber, bought it along with a quantity of spares. After a brief period with Spartan during which Ferderber performed low, medium, and high altitude photography, the Sea Hornet was traded to Photographic Survey for a pair of Mk. 26 Mosquitos. These were CF-GKK and CF-GKL, and were used by Spartan in crew training and equipment evaluation pending delivery of a batch of Mk. 35's from Britain.

Photographic Survey used the Sea

Hornet for one season operating it from Prince George, B.C. At the end of the season it was abandoned at Terrace, B.C., with a blown engine.

In 1954 Spartan purchased 10 Mk. 35 Mosquitos in Britain. These were to be the mainstay of Spartan's high altitude operations until 1960. Once in Canada, the Mosquitos were modified. A fuel tank was fitted in the bomb bay and the bomb doors replaced with a moulded plywood panel. For aircraft not already so equipped, a Plexiglass nose was fitted, and the canopies were modified to improve visibility. Bulkheads aft of the wing had to be removed to make way for the Wild RC-8 aerial camera and camera ports were installed in the belly. These were of optically correct glass calibrated by the National Research Council.

A door was fitted on the starboard side aft of the wing to allow entry by the camera operator, or, as in one case, his hasty exit, rip cord in hand. CF-HML was equipped with dual controls as a training and pilot proficiency aircraft. All these modifications were done at the Spartan shops at Uplands Airport, Ottawa.

The Mosquitos were in service by 1955 with the earliest operations being from Fort Smith and from Pelly Lake in the Northwest Territories where they flew from a graded sand bar. From here the pattern of operations became two 5-1/2 hour sorties per day, weather permitting. The

Spartan's P-38 CF-GKE at Fort Smith, N.W.T. in 1955. The original Lightnings as flown by Bob Fowler had more streamlined noses.

Bob Bolivar

first international contract for the Spartan Mosquitos was one in Colombia with R. Laroche, B. Bolivar and B. Cox as crew. Another involved three Mosquitos which flew from Colombia to El Paso in the spring of 1957. From that base they conducted a survey over Mexico, flying on 39 consecutive days and covering 92 000 line miles. The weather was exceptional. Normally cloud could be expected to restrict operations, sometimes saddling air crew with days of inactivity.

Although nice to fly, the Mosquito wasn't for every pilot. While the Lightning was relatively easy to handle, the Mosquito required a bit of learning. As one Spartan pilot expressed it, the Mosquito flew the pilot for the first 25 hours. If he persisted, the pilot eventually became master.

Over the years, several Mosquitos were involved in accidents. On an early Colombian contract, CF-HMN was wrecked at Techo Airport, Bogotá. It was making an emergency approach on one engine when the pilot noticed a DC-4 taxiing on the runway. He overshot but on the next approach there was another aircraft on the runway! At this point, the pilot had had enough. He veered off and crash landed on the grass.

For low and medium altitude, survey companies in Canada continued using war surplus aircraft for many years. These included Ansons, Beech AT-11's, Hudsons, Lockheed 14's, Cansos, DC-3's, and Lancasters. A typical low altitude job took a Photographic Survey Canso to New Guinea to survey and record variations in the Earth's magnetic field. The Canso flew 113 000 miles and covered 80 000 square miles. In 1958 one of Kenting's B-17's flew

The Avro Anson V was one of the most widely used aircraft in the post-war aerial surveying period. The primary operators of this type were Spartan and Photographic Survey (Kenting). These three pictures show a minor mishap that befell CF-GRN at North Bay March 20, 1950. The Anson got away from pilots Bill Ferderber and Bob Fowler during their landing.

R.H. Fowler

a magnetic survey over 42 000 square miles in Canada, and the Pacific on an international project to help update air and marine navigation charts. The B-17 flew from Canada's West Coast to San Francisco, Hawaii, Christmas Island, Tahiti, Samoa, Fiji, New Zealand, Australia, the Philippines, Japan, the Aleutian Islands, and home. A P-38 and B-17 surveyed 60 000 square miles of Venezuela, and a Canso surveyed Reykjavik, Iceland, to determine the shortest drill routes to pools of geothermal water required by that city's heating system. A contract on Canada's east coast kept a Hudson busy on a seal count.

A photo-survey Lancaster of 408 Sqdn over Ellesmere Island in the high Arctic.

DND (PL 86695)

Mosquito's engines, for example, had a practical life of just 400 hours. At the same time, more modern and efficient survey aircraft like the Cessna 310 and Aero Commander were becoming available.

The last of the old fighters to serve in Canada were the bright orange P-38, CF-JJA, and the dark blue one, CF-NMW. Previously of Fairchild Aerial Surveys, Los Angeles, CF-JJA had been purchased for $35 000 in 1956 by Survey Aircraft Ltd. of Vancouver. It flew with them until 1961 when it was exported to Argentina.

CF-NMW was owned by Bradley Air Service, Carp, Ontario. It flew the last P-38 aero survey contract in this country. This was a historic event as it brought together three old aero survey hands — pilots Weldy Phipps and Russ Bradley, and navigator/camera operator Bob Bolivar.

The aircraft was picked up at Philadelphia and ferried to Watson Lake in the Yukon. Between July and mid September 1961, the crew did photo work from there, using Fort Simpson as a refuelling stop. Some 30 000 photos were taken during the contract. The P-38 was surplus after this job, and ended up in a short-lived aviation museum in Niagara Falls, Ontario.

Three of the Spartan Mosquitos appear to have survived as relics and may all eventually be restored. CF-HML is one of these and has been under restoration by the Air Cadets in Kapuskasing, Ontario, for several years. Other types have disappeared, though Cansos and DC-3's are still favorite survey types. One Anson, INCO's CF-HOT, was still operating in 1979, all others in Canada having long since gone. A letter from Spartan to the DOT in 1965 suggests an ending typical of those faced by such old machines. It reads in part, "We do not intend to reactivate this aircraft and it is only a matter of time until we turn it over to the RCAF Fire Fighting School at Ottawa."

World Wide Specialists

Canada is more than ever a world leader in aerial surveying. One of its internationally operating firms is Geoterrex of Ottawa. Through 1978 it operated Cansos in France, Germany, Ireland, Ivory Coast, Kenya, Qatar and Wisconsin; a DC-3 in Iran; a Lodestar in Colombia; an Otter and Aero Commander in northern Canada; and helicopters on various jobs in Europe, Africa, and the United States. Generally aircraft were kept to busy flying schedules as indicated by its DC-3, CF-ITH, which logged some 900 hours for the year.

The tri-camera system aboard a Lancaster: two obliques and one vertical. Notice the operator's sparse furnishings and his heating system.

DND (RE 3986-7)

These many and varied projects provided a legacy of human interest stories. One is of the Canso, CF-JJG, which landed one day in Surinam. As he taxied in, the pilot shut down his engines and coasted towards the ramp. This resulted in a loss of hydraulic power and, hence, no brakes. The Canso rolled on and through the window of the airport bar. Undaunted, the slightly embarrassed pilot stepped from the plane and ordered himself a beer.

An offshoot of Canadian aerial surveying expertise was the training of surveyors and technicians in foreign countries. Throughout the world, Spartan and Photographic Survey set up subsidiary survey companies. Canadians at first did the actual surveying, but trained local people in the art. In time, these subsidiary companies became independent.

Inevitably, the war surplus survey aircraft faced retirement. Their maintenance became increasingly difficult. The

CF-GKK and CF-GKL were two Mosquitos used briefly by Photographic Survey and later by Spartan. Both were ex-RCAF aircraft KA244 and KA204 respectively.

R.H. Fowler

Arctic Operations

Canadian aircraft have spent over 30 years surveying in the Arctic. Initially there was the task of photo-mapping the entire region, an undertaking shared by the RCAF and civil operators. Later on the job of conducting airborne magnetometer surveys of the Arctic was begun. The first of these was carried out from 1953-1963 by the Dominion Observatory. This was the Phase One coverage, and included the entire country. Phase Two extended from 1969-1976 and featured closer line spacing with emphasis on the Earth's shorter

CF-JJG, one of the real veterans of aero surveying still flying in Canada. This Canso has operated on contracts all around the world since 1957, and was photographed at Malton on February 26, 1961.

Larry Milberry

wavelength magnetic field. Once again, all of Canada was surveyed. The DC-6 was the primary aircraft type employed, being provided over the years by Conair, Northwest Territorial Airways, PWA, and Wardair. On one contract, a Wardair DC-6 equipped with the Dominion Observatory's specially designed magnetometer operated for 17 days with flights averaging 13 hours. Some 2 500 000 square miles were surveyed. Aboard each flight were a seven-man flight crew plus five scientific personnel. Wardair's over-the-Pole experience with DC-6's was a valued asset in navigation for such an operation.

Since 1962 the National Aeronautical Establishment operated a North Star on electronic surveys. The aircraft, CF-SVP-X, was involved on such projects as researching the aeromagnetic detection of submarines, and techniques for identifying possible oil bearing formations in the Polar continental shelf. Sedimentary deposits up to 40 000 feet thick were located off Labrador, in Baffin Bay, Melville Bay and

The most exotic of high performance survey aircraft used in Canada during the fifties was this de Havilland Sea Hornet.

Via R.H. Fowler

elsewhere. These finds led to active oil exploration in places.

The North Star also mapped the magnetic patterns of ocean floor rock as investigations into the theory of continental drift; the results demonstrated for the first time how this process had occurred between North America and Greenland.

CF-SVP-X served with the NAE until April, 1977 when its last survey, one in the region of the Gulf of Boothia, was made. Upon return to Ottawa it was decommissioned, then ferried to CFB Trenton. This was the last North Star to have operated anywhere in the world. It

Hudson Bay Air Transport's DC-3 with its 4m transmitter loop, part of its electromagnetic equipment used in searching out mineral deposits.

Larry Milberry

CAPITAL AIR SURVEYS LIMITED
BONNECHERE AIRPORT R.R. NO.5 KILLALOE ONTARIO

QUEBEC CITY PQ· SCALE 1·100000   SEPT. 3/76 ZEISS RMK 8·5/23

Aerial survey imagery in use today ranges from low-level photographs to those taken by satellites such as ERTS (Earth Resources Technology Satellite). This is a typical high altitude photo, showing Quebec City and its environs. After over 300 years, the ancient strip farming patterns of New France are still visible. The photo was taken from Capital Air Survey's Lear Jet flying at 38 000 feet.

Capital Air Surveys Ltd.

A Kenting DC-4 ice patrol aircraft departing Malton for Thule, Greenland, May 17, 1971. The observation bubble is the canopy from an F-86 Sabre.

Larry Milberry

In Canada today much aerial surveying is performed by light twins like the Aero Commander, Aztec, Queen Air, Navajo, and Cessna 310. CF-RYZ is a Cessna 310J currently operating with Northway Survey of Toronto.

Larry Milberry

had logged 20 075 hours, 4612 of these for the NAE. CF-SVP-X was replaced by a Convair 580.

The Canada Centre for Remote Sensing

Airborne surveillance is currently being conducted by the Canada Centre for Remote Sensing. It operates a fleet of flying laboratories from Uplands Airport — two DC-3's, a Dassault Falcon and a Convair 580. The Centre dates to 1970 when it first became operational as the Canadian Forces Airborne Sensing Unit. Its first aircraft, the CF-100, 18767, flew in support of 12 projects that year. Other aircraft were added but the unit was disbanded November 1, 1975, and reorganized in its present form.

Activities of the Centre are varied. They include the analysis of data collected by aircraft and satellites such as LANDSAT (U.S. remote sensing satellites). In the late seventies the Centre was conducting vegetation studies. Included were forest fire mapping and crop monitoring as with Project Spud-Op designed to institute a workable potato monitoring system for New Brunswick. Also included was a study in Southern Ontario of yield losses from bacterial blight of field beans. Measurable levels of blight were detected by aerial photography in 49 of 59 fields in a test area of 15 square miles. On another project, corn aphid infestation was detected on infrared film and methodology was developed to determine amounts of infestation on a field basis.

In Alberta and Manitoba, rangeland surveys have been conducted to determine the nature and extent of grazing lands; throughout the country various forest inventory experiments involve the centre each year.

Other than vegetation studies, it works in such other areas as hydrology, oceanography, and ice studies. Between April 1 and December 31, 1976, its aircraft flew a total of 13 203 miles on 86 different tasks. These were in support of projects developed by federal and provincial government ministries, universities and industry. Lines were flown at heights up to 36 800 feet.

Each of the four current CCRS aircraft, or sensor platforms as they are known, has a variety of equipment. The Dakota, C-GRSB, carries four 70 mm cameras for measuring solar reflected energy of Earth features; a Wild Heerbrugg RC-8 9 inch by 9 inch and an RC-9 9 inch by 9 inch aerial survey camera; a Barnes PRT-5 Radiometre to measure the Earth's infrared radiation; a Daedalus 2-Channel Line Scanner to record energy reflected or emitted from the Earth's surface; and a CCTV camera with video and audio record capability. The aircraft flies with three flight crew and up to six sensor operators.

Dakota C-GRSA is dedicated to equipment testing and evaluation. New equipment so tested has included the Laserfluorosensor, an active night-time profiling device for distribution, identification, and concentration monitoring of oil spills, water pollution, chlorophyll, algae, and tracer dyes. It operates by exciting and detecting the characteristic fluorescence emissions from these substances.

The Laserbathymeter has also been evaluated. This is a remote water depth measuring device for use over relatively clear and/or shallow lakes, rivers, or coastal waters, and operates by measuring the time interval between surface and bottom back-reflected pulses.

Ice Patrols

Parts of Canada's Arctic are perpetually icebound, with ice from the Arctic spreading well south even in summer. Icebergs float south past Newfoundland, and ice floes as far south in Hudson Bay as Churchill are common through mid July each year. The Great Lakes partially freeze over in winter.

Ever since the *Titanic* collided with an iceberg and went down in 1912, the U.S. Coast Guard has been plotting icebergs and warning ships of their presence off the east coast. The objective of the Hudson Strait Expedition in 1927 was to study ice conditions in the Hudson Strait. In the 1940s, the job of monitoring and forecasting ice conditions in Canada was assigned to the Canadian Meteorological Service. In the mid 1950s, its ice observers provided reports to those involved in the sealift of DEW Line supplies. They spotted from Lancasters of 407 Sqdn at Comox, and 408 Sqdn at Rockcliffe. In 1959, civilian aircraft took over from the Lancasters.

The first specially equipped ice reconnaissance aircraft in Canada were two DC-4's put into service by Kenting Aviation on government contract. Each had advanced navigation equipment, plus terrain mapping radar that provided 360° coverage of the ground below to enable the detailed surveying of ice conditions. The DC-4's served until 1972 when they were replaced by two even more sophisticated Lockheed Electras operated by Nordair. These operate with a flight crew of four plus six ice observers. Patrols are eight to ten hours long and are flown five days a week. Patrol altitudes vary from 500 to 2500 feet except in areas where icebergs are known. Then 600 feet becomes the minimum.

Information gathered from Electra patrols can be fed immediately in chart form to vessels equipped to receive it, and is otherwise forwarded to Ottawa for wider distribution.

As well as along the sea coasts, ice is also monitored on the Great Lakes, St.

Westland Spraying Services' Lysander CF-FOA spraying the Luehr farm at Taber, Alberta in 1949.

Art Luehr Via Charles Luehr

Lawrence River, and Gulf of St. Lawrence, where winter navigation is growing in importance. DC-3's and helicopters of the Coast Guard are involved at this level. These will be joined in 1980 by two Dash 7R Ranger surveillance aircraft ordered in June, 1978.

Agricultural Lysanders at Work

Since the early twenties, aircraft in Canada have been used in many natural resource oriented roles. Of these, forestry is historically most significant, though aircraft found early applications in mineral exploration, agriculture and other resource areas. These activities blossomed during the post World War II era and are now integral with Canada's natural resource based industries.

A historic agricultural venture in the forties was Westland Dusting Service of Edmonton. This firm had been set up in 1946 by E.S. (Ted) Holmes, using surplus Lysanders. These were acquired from War Assets at Swift Current and Suffield for between $50 and $250 each. The first of these, CF-DGI-X, became a prototype for Holmes' eventual fleet of four aircraft. The basic modification required was to arrange for a tank to carry liquid chemical agricultural spray. Holmes' solution was straightforward. The standard 95 gallon Lysander fuel tank was given over to the chemical, while a 44-46 gallon fuel tank was fitted in the centre section behind the pilot.

All Holmes' engineering changes were duly approved by the Department of Transport and three other aircraft were converted, the work being done at Northwest Industries. CF-DGI-X made its first test flight after conversion on May 1, 1946. The other Lysanders were CF-DRL, CF-FOA, and CF-GFJ. Before long, they were spraying throughout southern Alberta, under the motto "Weed 'Em and Reap"! In January, 1948 Holmes sold his company which then became Westland Spraying Services, at High River.

The Lysander spraying operation was set up on a sophisticated basis. Each aircraft operated with a mobile ground crew which included field manager, pilot, truck driver, and field marker; each was equipped with a car, a truck and a house trailer. As such, the team was self contained and ready to operate wherever business called. The truck carried fuel and spares for its Lysander, as well as chemical spray ingredients.

The field manager's job was to line up jobs, then brief the pilot about fields to spray, those to avoid, and obstacles to watch for; while the field marker's job was to pace off 120 feet between Lysander passes. This was not an enviable job, and on one occasion a field marker was knocked unconscious when struck by a passing Lysander. Spray runs were optimally made at eight feet and 140 mph. This fact prompted Holmes to write the DOT concerning its requirement that his pilots carry parachutes. Holmes pointed out that, " . . . 90 per cent of our flying is done below ten feet . . . where parachutes would be quite useless." The DOT accepted his argument.

Holmes had transformed the airplane into an effective agricultural implement, but at this time there wasn't sufficient interest to support a successful operation. This is evident by looking at the hours logged by CF-FOA between May 14, 1948, and May 16, 1950. These totalled a mere 52 hours. CF-GFJ logged 40 hours 5 minutes between May 16, 1949, and May 16, 1950. The most recent entry in the file for CF-DRL is dated May 16, 1950, and includes the DOT inspector's comment "found in good condition and considered airworthy," but shortly after this, Westland Spraying Services and its aircraft disappeared from the aviation and agricultural scene.

"Ag" Flying Today

Since the early fifties, agricultural spraying in Canada has increased annually. In 1976, 2 653 581 acres were reported treated in the fight to control weeds, plant disease, and insects, and to attain efficiency in fertilizer and seed application. A total of 36 451 hours were flown on these operations. On the Prairies where most of the agricultural flying was done, average per acre cost to the farmer from commercial operators was $1.97, or $225 per hour flown. Some 465 aircraft were reported used in agricultural flying for the year, with most being converted to take a hopper/tank with spray booms. Each year, however, more and more especially designed "ag" planes operate in Canada.

Spraying the Forests

Of the various aerial spray operations begun after the war, by far the most significant was the one directed against the spruce bud worm in the forests of New Brunswick and the Gaspé. By 1951 the destruction caused by the bud worm was nearly disastrous. Losses to the forest industry were growing annually. To combat this situation, a consortium of federal and provincial government interests plus members of the forest industries decided in 1951 to experiment with an aerial spray campaign in order to stave off further losses.

A fleet of 20 spray aircraft was assembled, and during a two-week operation the following June, 192 000 acres were treated with pesticide. The results proved worthwhile, and thereafter, Operation Budworm became an annual event in the region.

In 1957, the operation began on June 4, with 212 aircraft available. These had been assembled by the chief contractor, Wheeler Airlines, which brought together no less than 190 Stearman sprayers and 22 other aircraft for use on inspection and communications duties. Most of the Stearmans came from the United States. Twenty-two airstrips were in service, 20

Avengers of Skyways Ltd., Langley, B.C. running up at Cartierville May 22, 1961. They were en route to Fredericton to participate in the annual spruce bud worm spraying operation in New Brunswick.

Larry Milberry

having been constructed expressly for the budworm fleet. These were either U- or V-shaped, with one runway for takeoffs and one for landings. As the operation progressed, aircraft hopped from strip to strip until July 4 when the last acre was sprayed. In one month, 6.3 million acres had been treated, and 23 000 sorties flown.

Beginning in the early sixties, the Stearman was replaced by a more versatile type, the Grumman Avenger. The Avenger had been retired from RCN service in the late fifties and was procured by civilian operators through Crown Assets. Its ability to utilize 3000-foot strips; its good high speed cruise and low speed handling characteristics; its 1950 hp Wright engine and rugged undercarriage; and its 500-gallon capacity versus the 150-gallon capacity of the Stearman, all made the Avenger a desirable "next generation" spray plane.

The Avengers were fitted with a big tank partially recessed in the bomb bay, and could serve either as a spray or fire fighting aircraft. In the spray role, they could dispense chemicals at the rate of 120 gpm. Over the years, the Avenger has proven a valuable work horse in the fight against the bud worm. The 1975 season brought 33 of them to the forests of Eastern Canada, from as far away as British Columbia.

Although there are still some 35 Avengers active in Canada, it is clear that

the old "Turkey," as it has been lovingly called for decades, is itself about to give way to advances in technology. In 1973, four Conair DC-6's bore the brunt of Operation Budworm. On a 14-day operation, these aircraft, equipped with their 2500-gallon tanks, and DECCA Navigation System for precise tracking, sprayed 6 000 000 acres in Eastern Canada. In 1977 Conair sold its last eight Avengers to a New Brunswick operator.

Fire-Fighting from the Air

In the immediate post World War I period, the forest industry began employing aircraft to patrol forest tracts to spot for fires, and when fires occurred, to assist in their suppression by flying rangers and equipment to the fires. In time these operations grew and provinces began establishing their own forest protection services. Ontario led the way with the Ontario Provincial Air Service formed in 1924.

In the late forties, the Saskatchewan government introduced smoke jumpers in its forest protection service. These were fire-fighters who parachuted directly to the fire scene. The smoke jumpers arrived quickly and were not worn out by hours or days of backpacking and canoeing through the woods to reach a fire. The government set up a training base at Prince Albert where jumpers learned gymnastics, map reading and compass use, radio operation, first aid, fire-fighting, and parachuting. When jumping to a fire, the smoke jumpers wore heavy canvas flying suits and wire mesh face masks. Jumps were made from a Norseman from 1500-2000 feet. The Norseman then came around to drop gear from 300 feet. Jumpers immediately went

to work on the fire, supported by the Norseman which used the nearest lake as a base. As late as 1960, Saskatchewan still had 16 smoke jumpers at work.

Another fire-fighting technique introduced in the late forties was water bombing. At first this was not too sophisticated, and involved such experiments as bombing fires with bags of water. Trial and error, however, led to refined techniques, through the joint efforts of government and industry. The OPAS conducted the first operational attack on a forest fire September 9, 1950, when a Beaver dropped 2800 pounds of water in five gallon bags on a fire north of Sault Ste. Marie. By the mid fifties, the OPAS was operating a large fleet of Beavers and Otters and developing increasingly effective water bombing techniques.

There were 90-gallon float-mounted tanks which could be rapidly refilled via scoop while the aircraft planed along the water. This gave way to a belly-mounted tank on the Otter; and finally to a float designed to carry water internally. These floats eventually equipped the government's Turbo Beavers, Otters, and Twin Otters, respective capacities being 140, 200, and 450 gallons.

Field Aviation of Toronto, under Knox Hawkshaw, has specialized in the design and installation of aerial fire-fighting equipment. During the late sixties, Field developed a system that is by now world famous. The firm collaborated with many operators to come up with a water bomber conversion of the Canso. By virtue of its ruggedness and amphibious nature, the Canso worked out as an ideal fire-fighter. The conversion centred around the installation of twin 400-gallon tanks mounted side by side on the centre of gravity, a probe system for taking on water, and a water dumping system comprising a pair of doors in the bottom of the hull. Over thirty such Cansos have been converted by Field to date, and these have operated around the world. In 1968-1969 two Canadian Cansos flew to Chile, a 52-hour ferry flight, to fight forest fires there. Earlier, Cansos had gone into service with the Quebec and Newfoundland governments, and in Spain and France.

Field has developed another drop system. This is a membrane tank system. The membrane tank, mounted in the belly of an aircraft, is slit open by a rapidly moving knife. This allows for a water release with minimal break-up of the drop by wind blast, and therefore greater impact on the fire. The system was evaluated in a Twin Otter, but as yet has not seen wide use.

Hawaii Mars, one of two Martin JRM-3 Mars operated by Forest Industries Flying Tankers from its Sproat Lake base on Vancouver Island. At over 80 tons gross weight, the Mars is the world's largest flying boat and fire-fighting aircraft.

Larry Milberry

Other systems designed under Mr. Hawkshaw have included that used in the OPAS's fleet of Grumman Trackers, as well as the system used by the Canadair CL-215. The OPAS Trackers entered service in 1972. Ontario acquired six of these 800-gallon tankers. Saskatchewan has recently procured a similar fleet of Trackers. The CL-215 is widely used by the Quebec Government which operates 15. Manitoba became the second province to operate the CL-215 when it purchased one in 1977.

Parallelling the design of water and retardant delivery systems has been the development of a wide range of fire retardants. While water is the basic fire-fighting agent for planes like the Otter and Canso, land-based types generally use chemical retardants. In this case, water is the medium for delivering the chemicals. These act to immediately suppress fire, and also to prevent it in future by their long-term fire retardant qualities. As the retardant deteriorates, it becomes a fertilizer.

Many types of aircraft are currently employed fighting forest fires in Canada. Besides the actual bombers, some are used to spot fires. Spotting is done visually, but also with airborne infrared sensing equipment.

When a fire is under attack, "bird dogs" are used. These are fast single and twin-engined aircraft used to direct the bombers as to hot spots requiring strikes, wind direction, best approach to the target and so on.

Few Avengers operate on the fire-fighting scene any longer. Instead, the trend has been towards larger aircraft. The A-26 Invader has generally replaced the Avenger. It has twin-engine speed and safety, and a 900-gallon capacity. In the same class are the Trackers.

Two other World War II vintage aircraft converted as chemical bombers in Canada have included the North American B-25, used in small numbers; and a lone Avro Lancaster CF-TQC, experimentally fitted with a 2200-gallon tank. It served briefly with Northwestern Air Lease in Alberta, but is now part of the Strathallan Collection in Scotland.

The biggest land-based bomber in Canada is the Douglas DC-6B. Conair operates a fleet of these and has designed its own external belly tank of 2500-gallon capacity. This system features a choice of 15 different drop patterns, depending on the nature of the fire.

The Conair fleet of DC-6's has proven to be a versatile one. Not only are the aircraft used for fire-fighting, but have also operated as geophysical platforms, bud worm sprayers, and in fertilizing salmon breeding waters in B.C. In the latter role, one DC-6 was used extensively in 1977. Fertilizer was applied in designated waters in order to stimulate algae growth. The increase in algae was calculated to increase the supply of plankton on which salmon feed.

The latest fire bomber conversion in Canada is that done by Conair on the CS2F Tracker. Known as the Firecat, the conversion is 3000 pounds lighter than the standard Tracker and has an 800-gallon fire retardant capacity. The Firecat was introduced in early 1978.

The mightiest water bomber in the world is the Martin JRM-3 Mars. Two of these flying boats operate from Sproat Lake on Vancouver Island. Theirs is one of the distinctive stories in the evolution of fire-fighting aircraft.

The Mars had its beginning as a military transport and made its first flight in July, 1942. The prototype performed impressively, but as the war was ending by the time production had begun, only five more aircraft were completed. These entered service with the U.S. Navy in 1946. For the next decade, they operated on the San Francisco-Honolulu route.

The Mars was a giant for its day and logged numerous historic flights. One of these was a non-stop Honolulu-Chicago flight by *Caroline Mars* with a 14 049 pound payload. Another was from Patuxent River, Maryland, to Cleveland, Ohio, with 68 263 pounds, twice the payload of today's C-130E Hercules! On a trip between San Diego and Alameda

Naval Air Station, *Marshall Mars* carried 301 passengers and seven crew.

In 1956, the four surviving Mars were retired from service and purchased by Mars Metal Corporation. About this time, though, D.E. McIvor, a flier from British Columbia, heard about the Mars and approached his firm with a proposal to consider buying the Mars and converting them to water bombers.

The idea was accepted, and in order to finance the venture, a consortium of six forest industry companies was established — Forest Industries Flying Tankers.

The first aircraft arrived at Victoria on August 19, 1959. Plans were immediately made to bring the Mars up to DOT standards and for converting one to water bomber configuration with the installation of tanks, intake probes and dumping doors. This work was all done by Ferry Aviation. The converted aircraft flew its initial trial on March 8, 1960. Six thousand gallons of water were scooped up in 15 seconds on this occasion.

The system designed for the Mars included a 6000-gallon 4-compartment plywood tank over the CG; twin probes of 6 3/4 inch diameter with 16 inch travel which deploy while the aircraft is planing along the water; and four side-dumping doors. The last aircraft converted had part of its own fuel tankage adapted for the water load, eliminating the need for the big plywood tank.

Of the four aircraft brought to Canada, CF-LYK and CF-LYL remained in service to 1978. CF-LYJ crashed June 23, 1961; while CF-LYM was wrecked in a

storm at Victoria in November, 1962.

Interesting facts about the Mars include its 120-foot length, 200-foot wing span and 162 000-pound gross weight. It is powered by four 18-cylinder 2500-horse power Wright Cyclones, has a cruise speed of 175 mph, drop speed of 140 mph and touchdown speed of 80 mph. It carries 11 000 gallons of fuel, burned at a rate of 650 gph while on operations. Water is thickened with a gelling agent prior to drops. These are made at 150-200 feet and a single drop may cover four acres. The Mars is capable of flying to the Queen Charlotte Islands on the north coast of British Columbia; operating on fire suppression all day; and returning to base without having refueled. No one expects the two Mars to operate indefinitely. Within the next decade they are bound to be phased out, as spare parts become increasingly hard to get. There is no airplane in the world which could replace the Mars on a one-to-one basis, so Forest Industries Flying Tankers is currently considering alternate approaches to fire control on the B.C. coast. A real possibility is more intensive use of helicopters.

The important role played in Canada by aircraft in forest fire control is evident by 1977 statistics from Alberta's department of Energy and Natural Resources. Fifty-three fixed-wing aircraft were chartered for fire work including light twins, 33 single-engined Cessnas of various models, two DC-3's, a Dornier 28 and Twin Otter. Thirty-eight helicopters were chartered, from the Hughes 500C to the Sikorsky S-61. Chartered aircraft logged 1903.2 hours. As well, government-owned and contracted aircraft were used. Government aircraft logged 3861.7 hours and contract aircraft 3341.9 hours, for a total for the year of 9106.8 hours. Of these 5688.3 hours were flown by helicopters, indicating the particular importance of these in fire control.

Fixed-wing tankers used were six B-26 and four Cansos which flew 657.7 hours and dropped 440 625 gallons of water and retardant. Twenty-one helitankers dropped 551 756 gallons, with the Bell 205A being most widely used for a total of 82 840 gallons. Helitankers logged 161.9 hours.

In 1977, aircraft were used to make 6258 drops in Ontario. Aircraft included the Ministry of Natural Resources' fleet of Turbo Beavers, Otters, Twin Otters, and Trackers; as well as many chartered and contracted types. Overall these aircraft dropped 1 409 965 gallons of water and retardant. The Otters, with 456 870 gallons dropped, were the most widely used aircraft, followed by the Trackers, Twin Otters, and Turbo Beavers.

Smoke jumpers descending from a Norseman of Saskatchewan Government Airways near Prince Albert, September, 1952.
Public Archives of Canada (NFB 64309)

Canada's Aircraft Industry

The *Baddeck No. 1* at Petawawa in 1909.
Public Archives of Canada (C10999)

The Canadian Aerodrome Company

While aircraft manufacturing in Canada dates to World War I its roots actually go back further, to the Aerial Experiment Association. After Alexander Graham Bell had satisfied himself that the AEA had achieved its objectives, the organization was dissolved; but Bell encouraged McCurdy and Baldwin to carry the venture further. He thought that they should look into the practical application of flight, and suggested they construct additional machines with an eye to marketing them. This seemed logical enough, so Canada's first test pilots turned salesmen and the Canadian Aerodrome Company was established to advance their aims.

During July and August, 1909, two Canadian Aerodrome machines were shipped to the Militia camp at Petawawa, where arrangements had been made to demonstrate them. Unfortunately, misfortunes plagued the aviators, and both machines were wrecked in crashes. This did not help in enlightening the military to the need for an aviation corps, and no machines were ordered.

McCurdy and Baldwin returned to Baddeck to pursue their business activities. They shortly afterwards received their first commercial order, this being for a small monoplane from Mr. G. Hubbard of Boston. This aircraft, known as *Mike,* was the first Canadian-built aircraft ever to be exported. At the same time, the spring of 1910, there were four other aircraft at Baddeck: the rebuilt *Baddeck No. 1, Baddeck No. 2,* and two powered kites, *Cygnet* and *Oionos.* There was a lot of activity centring around these aircraft, but without financial backing there was little chance for McCurdy and Baldwin to succeed. Government support was sought, primarily through Major G.S. Maunsell who foresaw a future in Canada for military flying, but his pleas fell on deaf ears in Ottawa. The Canadian Aerodrome Co. ceased operations later in 1910.

There was a flurry of airborne activities in the following years in Canada, but no attempts were made to manufacture aircraft. The market would not support such a specialized enterprise, not, that is, until World War I.

Curtiss Aeroplanes and Motors Ltd.

The war did not suddenly create an aircraft industry. It took time for people to realize that airplanes could serve the military. At first they were used to observe the enemy, as balloons had been in previous decades. Inevitably, though, they were put to more destructive uses and before long the skies

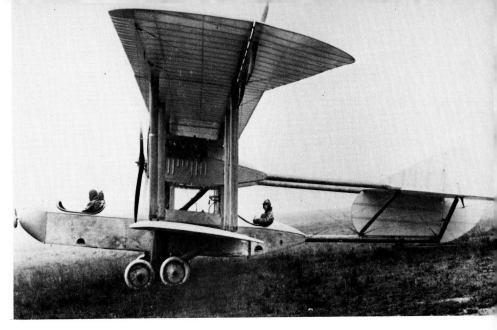

The Curtiss Canada prototype during trials in England. Conceived before the advent of fighter aircraft, its designers did not take the need for defensive armament into consideration. Hence, the Canada was obsolete before it could enter service.
Aviation and Space Division, National Museum of Science and Technology (A 1286)

over France were speckled with airborne warriors weaving this way and that in deadly combat. The scale of such activity grew, putting a great strain upon those who built aircraft and trained air crew. To alleviate this situation, Britain turned to Canada which was remote enough so that manufacturing and training could go on without enemy interference. In Canada, however, Glenn H. Curtiss had already set up his own aircraft manufacturing operation, Curtiss Aeroplanes and Motors Ltd. in Toronto. This complemented his other operations in Toronto, namely a flying boat school at Hanlan's Point on Toronto Bay, and a school for land planes at nearby Long Branch.

The Curtiss manufacturing facility, located on Strachan Avenue, turned out a small number of JN-3 trainers and 12 Curtiss Canadas. The Canada was the first Canadian-designed military aircraft, Canada's first multi-engined aircraft and its first military aircraft to be exported. It was also the first and the last Canadian-designed bomber. Design on the Canada was begun in 1915 directed by Curtiss' chief engineer F.G. Ericson. The first aircraft was test flown at Long Branch that July. It was later shipped to England. Eleven other Canadas were built but not sent overseas, as it was evident that the type, not designed to carry any defensive armament, had been eclipsed by developments in aerial warfare.

The Curtiss flying schools trained pilots most of whom, after paying their own tuition, went overseas to join the

Royal Flying Corps or the Royal Naval Air Service. To this point, the Canadian government had no flying training program.

Canadian Aeroplanes Ltd.

In late 1916, Britain and Canada devised a scheme to train aviators and aviation technicians, through the Royal Flying Corps, Canada. High on the list of priorities was the mass production of training aircraft. The government established Canadian Aeroplanes Ltd. which bought out the Curtiss plant. Construction of a new factory on Dufferin Street began immediately and by May, 1917 it had been completed and was turning out a modified JN-3, the JN-4 Canuck.

The RFC, Canada had settled on the JN-4 mainly because of its straightforward design. It presented no particular manufacturing problems. At the same time, it wasn't the easiest plane to fly, a point considered to be an asset as it would be more demanding of those flying it.

The Canadian Aeroplane's JN-4 was not built to precise Curtiss specifications. Some of the modifications introduced were a stick to replace the standard wheel-type control; a metal tube tail structure instead of the usual wooden frame; and skis for winter operations.

The Canadian Aeroplanes operation was a formidable one, from the assembly of raw materials onward. At first wings were covered with Irish linen, but U-boats interrupted its delivery. A substitute, milled cotton, was provided by the Wabasso Cotton Co. at Trois Rivières. Wood was another essential raw material. Ash was needed for longerons, spruce for wings, oak for propellers. To insure supplies, the Imperial Munitions Board acquired its own timber stands on the British Columbia coast. Curtiss provided OX-5, 90 hp engines from the U.S.

Production of JN-4's accelerated to a peak in February 1917 when 350 aircraft were built. Over 21 months enough airframes for 2900 complete Canucks were manufactured, the total value being $14 000 000.

Besides manufacturing Canucks, Canadian Airplanes also built 30 F-5-L flying boats for the United States Navy. These big aircraft had a wing span of 102 feet and weighed seven tons. A lone D.H.6 was also built, as were two Avro 504K's. The latter type had been intended to replace the JN-4's had the war continued much longer.

These achievements clearly demonstrated Canada's ability to produce aircraft on a large scale; but they didn't help much when the war ended, and military aircraft were no longer required. As quickly as it had come into existence, Canadian Aeroplanes Ltd. folded up. Canada's booming aircraft industry was wiped out over night.

Post-War Beginnings: Pioneer Firms

Throughout the early twenties, the aviation scene in Canada was quiet. The airplane had proven itself in war, but as yet, no significant civilian role had emerged for it. What need there was for aircraft in post-war Canada was adequately served by large stocks of war surplus aircraft. There were also plenty of ex-military crews around to do what flying there was. For some years JN-4's and HS-2L's almost monopolized aviation in Canada, becoming the Model T's of the sky.

But people realized that such types would not satisfy aviation needs indefinitely. This is illustrated by R.H. Mulock in a letter to F.E. Davison on the matter of Davison's proposed aerial expedition down the Mackenzie River in 1921. Mulock wrote, "The only large types of machines available for work this season are those designed primarily for war duty. In the design of these machines, first cost, operating cost, fuel consumption, low maintenance cost, accessibility of repairs, life of machine and engines, etc. were all sacrificed for fighting efficiency; and now when we use them commercially where dividends instead of fighting efficiency are the main object, we must face the high cost of maintenance and operation . . . . "

At this time, though, enterprising aircraft manufacturers were beginning to introduce aircraft designed for commercial operations. These were evident in the post-war efforts of the Junkers and Fokker companies in Europe. Gradually, aircraft were coming on to the market that were smaller, capable of much improved

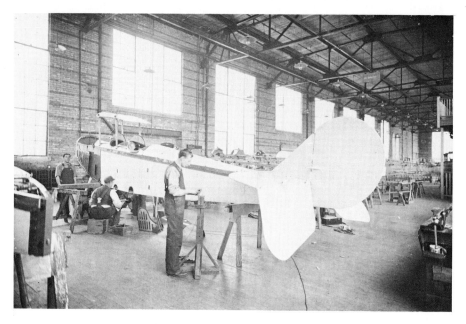

A Curtiss JN-4 Canuck fuselage at the Canadian Aeroplanes Ltd. plant in Toronto. At its busiest, the plant employed 2400 workers.

Public Archives of Canada (PA 25168)

payloads, and generally more efficient than war surplus types. At the end of his letter to Davison, Mulock urged, "One of the first duties of the management should be to look into the type more suitable for the Northern work and place orders." This advice Davison did eventually follow when he set up his commercial flying operation a few years later.

The first Canadian manufacturer to enter the post-war market was Canadian Vickers of Montreal. Based on a contract awarded in 1923 for flying boats to do aerial surveying in Manitoba, Canadian Vickers built six British-designed Viking flying boats. As experience was gained on these aircraft and other types like the HS-2L's, it was possible for Canadian Vickers to create a design that embodied more features particularly suitable to the Canadian environment. The result was the Vickers Vedette, first flown November 4, 1925.

The Vedette soon gained popularity with the RCAF and other operators. Sixty were built, and six were actually exported to Chile. In the late thirties a few were still in use by the RCAF and Manitoba government. Vickers could not be content with just one design, and soon became the first Canadian aircraft manufacturer to make available a range of products. It built a number of Avro 504 and 552 trainers for the RCAF and otherwise broadened its design interests. These resulted in several notably unsuccessful aircraft, but each of these added to the company's experience and capabilities.

As an aircraft manufacturer, Canadian Vickers was at first on its own in Canada, but in the late twenties, was joined by several other firms. This expansion was in response to the growing interest in flying at the government, commercial, and flying club levels.

Government had become interested in aviation for a variety of reasons: forestry patrol, fisheries patrol, postal delivery, defence and training included. The mining boom on the Canadian Shield spurred interest in commercial flying. The Aerial League, with its aim of a coast to coast network of flying clubs created a need for training aircraft. Besides these factors, time was catching up on the old war surplus types that had for nearly a decade carried much of the load in Canada. Those interested in the future of Canadian aviation were not unduly concerned about the continued operation of aircraft such as the HS-2L. One comment at the time read, "Government inspection is gradually eliminating these planes, but it rests also with the public to decry the use of such antiquated equipment."

Thus Canada's aviation expertise began to evolve. Names such as Boeing, Curtiss-Reid, de Havilland, Fairchild, and Ottawa Car appeared on the scene. The establishment of these companies meant, at last, that there would be new designs in good variety available to Canadian operators. Overall, an optimistic outlook prevailed throughout the industry on the eve of the Depression. A glance at the intentions of Canadian Vickers early in 1929 indicated this, for its plans called for the construction of 18 Vedettes, one Vista, one Vancouver as well as various Fokker designs to be built under licence — 10 Universals, 20 Super Universals, and six Trimotors.

One of the F-5-L flying boats under construction at Canadian Aeroplanes Ltd. This type was powered by twin 400 horse power Liberty engines and carried a crew of six.

Public Archives of Canada (PA 25199)

Fairchild Aircraft

The Fairchild name had come to Canada in 1922 after Ellwood Wilson had met in New York with Sherman Fairchild. Wilson was chief forester with the Laurentide Pulp and Paper Co. and had been instrumental in the formation of the St. Maurice Forestry Protective Association just after the war. Fairchild had just introduced his revolutionary new aerial camera.

Upon Wilson's suggestion, Fairchild set up Fairchild Aerial Survey (of Canada) Ltd. From 1922 onward, the new company strove to build up business and to convince foresters that the future of forest surveying lay with the aerial camera.

Eventually Fairchild diversified his Canadian interests. In 1926, in partnership with J.V. Elliot, his firm conducted a passenger, mail, and freight operation between Hudson and Red Lake in Northwestern Ontario, and ran a similar service between Haileybury and Rouyn. Neither venture, however, survived beyond the first season. The following year, Fairchild conducted some experimental mail flights for the Post Office, flying the Ottawa-Rimouski route in connection with the trans-Atlantic mails; but when contracts were let in 1928, Fairchild was overlooked. It seems that being a largely U.S.-owned business, it did not qualify, in spite of its experience and its low bids.

Sherman Fairchild had perfected the aerial camera of the day, but was not satisfied with the types of aircraft available as camera platforms. To rectify this, he designed his own plane especially for aerial photography. This was the FC-1, first flown in 1926 and soon, in its production form, to become the best all round utility plane available at the time in North America. Three of these, FC-2's, were soon in the hands of Fairchild at Longueuil near Montreal. Canadian operators were quick to place orders and the FC-2 became to the Canadian bush what the Norseman and Beaver were to become in later years. As demand for the type increased, Canadian Vickers began licence manufacture of the FC-2.

Although Sherman Fairchild's Canadian operation was doing well, it was sold out to a group headed by James A. Richardson of Winnipeg. It was thought that Fairchild made this decision based on the fact that he would not likely ever win mail contracts in Canada but Fairchild invested money in a new Montreal-based company, Fairchild Aircraft Ltd.

Canadian Vickers subsequently lost its right to build the FC-2, and Fairchild set about to update the type. Meanwhile, Canadian Vickers continued turning out Super Universals, 15 in all. These competed directly with the Fairchild but were not as desirable to users, as the Canadian government had forced design changes in it that upped its gross weight and lowered its useful load. Hence, the Super Universals

Canadian Vickers first indigenous design, the Vedette, in this case a Mk. II. Notice the wire mesh between the struts behind the cockpit. This helped prevent foreign matter flying back into the propeller. The Vedette was used extensively on forestry and photographic patrols during the twenties and thirties.

DND (HC1552)

The one and only Vickers Velos aero survey aircraft built by Canadian Vickers of Montreal in 1927. An aerodynamically unsuccessful design, the Velos sank at its moorings at Montreal the following year. It is seen here in RCAF markings registered G-CYZX. Moored behind it is the famous Fokker Universal, G-CASK.

DND (RE 11710-33)

The design that brought de Havilland Aircraft to Canada in 1928 — the Gipsy Moth. This one was registered to the Ontario Provincial Air Service in June, 1929 and remained in service for 17 years. In this view taken in September 1933, CF-OAA was visiting Amesdale, Ontario, site of an unemployment relief work camp.

Public Archives of Canada (PA 34860)

Two RCAF de Havilland D.H. 75A Hawk Moth utility aircraft at Toronto, October 1930. Only three Hawk Moths served in Canada. As with many de Havilland aircraft of the day, these were not built in Canada, but assembled from knocked-down aircraft shipped from Britain.

De Havilland Aircraft of Canada Ltd.

sold at a slow rate. Meanwhile, in 1930, Canadian Vickers built six Bellanca CH-300's for the RCAF for use as general purpose aircraft.

The availability of sturdy, reliable aircraft such as the Fairchilds and Fokkers ushered in a new era of commercial aviation in Canada. At long last, the HS-2L's and the like could be retired from service. Commercial flying now had the potential of getting onto a sound footing, with safety, fuel economy, mechanical efficiency, load carrying ability and overall performance vastly improved.

De Havilland Aircraft

A major entry into the aviation scene in Canada was that of de Havilland Aircraft Co. Ltd. Canada's association with de Havilland designs began during World War I when many Canadians in Europe flew and fought in de Havilland machines. A single D.H. 6 made by Canadian Aeroplanes Ltd. in 1917 was the first de Havilland design ever built in Canada. More than a decade would pass, though, before the de Havilland connection would be resumed.

Shortly after the war's end, the Canadian Air Force came into being, with its first aircraft being D.H. 4's and D.H. 9's consigned to Canada by Britain as a gift. Twenty-two in all were registered to the Air Board in Ottawa and placed in service primarily on forestry patrol, and survey and aerial photography duties in Western Canada. Two of the D.H. 9's participated in the first trans-Canada flight, Halifax to Vancouver, in October,

1920. Later, a few Moth aircraft were exported to Canada, including the one used on the Hudson Strait Expedition in 1927.

Just about this time the Ontario Provincial Air Service was planning to replace its fleet of aging aircraft. In 1927 Captain Roy Maxwell, Director of the OPAS, visited Britain, where he toured the de Havilland plant at Stag Lane Aerodrome and watched the de Havilland Cirrus Moth fly. The Moth, Sir Geoffrey de Havilland's first civilian design, had made its first flight February 22, 1925, and soon became a favourite among aviators in Britain and as far off as Australia.

Maxwell was impressed by the Moth's performance and requested to see it on floats. This was done and when Maxwell returned home he was able to convince his superiors that the Moth was the ideal replacement for his fleet of aging patrol planes. Four Moths were ordered and were soon in service over Ontario's vast North.

F.E. St. Barbe was sales director with de Havilland in 1927. To him the sale of the four Moths to Canada was a shoe in the door. He sailed for Canada where he became convinced that there was a place for his company's products.

Transportation, or rather the lack of it, had always been the bane of those who, foolhardy as they may have seemed, chose to travel the uninviting Shieldscape. By canoe, on snowshoes, by dog team or trundling tractor train — those were the travel options. Yet people were enticed to the Shield in search of fortune. Furs and timber drew them but so did the ancient lure of gold. In 1925 the dream became reality for two brothers prospecting near Red Lake in Ontario's far Northwest. Here the Howie brothers struck gold and a mad rush was triggered.

Red Lake over night became a busy centre of air travel, and one claim in 1928 was that nearby Sioux Lookout was, next to Chicago, North America's busiest commercial flying centre. A dozen planes were based there — four of Western

Canada Airways, four of NAME, and four of the OPAS. With these aircraft, people were now flying farther and farther north into previously inaccessible country. St. Barbe saw no good reason why his company should not share in the prosperity. Through his efforts de Havilland set up an aircraft sales and service branch in Canada. In March, 1928 this opened for business in the Toronto suburb of Mt. Dennis. The operation was small. The building was a mere 30 feet by 40 feet, and the airfield was 1500 feet of mowed cow pasture known as de Lesseps Field. It had been the site of Toronto's first aerial meet in 1910, and was part of the estate of Frank Trethewey, an enthusiastic member of the newly-formed Toronto Flying Club.

This arrangement was barely adequate for the assembly of Moths shipped from England. Space was always at a premium. On one occasion a fuselage, in for repairs and requiring redoping, had to be finished in the billiard parlor of Trethewey's home.

The Moth was an immediate success in Canada. Sixty-two were sold in the first year and the company had to relocate to more spacious quarters in North Toronto. In late 1929 it was declared an independent operation, de Havilland of Canada. That year, 130 aircraft had been sold and the line extended to include other British designs such as the Puss Moth, Hornet Moth, and Giant Moth.

From its unpretentious beginnings, de Havilland was soon famous across the country. Moths were active in many parts of the country, and, besides normal operations, were chalking up some credible records. In September of 1929, Lt. Kenneth Whyte and his passenger, Harry Campbell, flew the Moth, G-CAUE, to a second-place finish in the air race from Windsor, Ontario, to Los Angeles. Next year, two de Havilland representatives, Sales Manager Geoff O'Brian and George Mickleborough, flew the Puss Moth, CF-AGO, from Toronto to Vancouver and back — 6050 miles, logging 57 hours. Australian aviator Bert Hinkler left Toronto in October of 1931 and 41 days later turned up in London. He and his Puss Moth, CF-APK had traced a course through New York, the Caribbean, Brazil, West Africa and up through Europe. Less than two years later Hinkler was lost when CF-APK disappeared in the Alps while on a flight to Australia.

It was not so much in setting official records that the de Havilland planes excelled. Its reputation was more carved out in the wilds of the Northland. Its ordinary work-a-day achievements were astounding. George Delahaye was one of the early OPAS fliers to get to know the Moth. From June 1 to June 7, 1931, he flew one for 61 hours, 15 minutes while on fire patrol. Fellow pilot George Phillips took his Moth out one day carrying a ranger to a fire site. Routine enough, except that on the same load went the ranger's hose, pump, tent, grub, and other gear. On another emergency, Phillips carried 22 men via Moth, flying just 11 trips! At the dock on another occasion could be counted 13 passengers emerging from his eight-seat DH 61 Giant Moth.

In a world which, at this time, expected the spectacular in aviation, the skill and daring of Canada's bush aviators often went unnoticed. The annual awarding of the McKee Trophy, however, made up for this lack of attention. In 1931 it was presented to George Phillips, but it would be fair to say that this trophy also said something for the planes he flew, notably the little Moth.

Other Famous Names

In 1928 W.T. Reid, former chief engineer at Canadian Vickers, established Reid Aircraft Co. With his partner, Martin Berlyn, he designed a light training and touring aircraft. The prototype was unveiled September 29, 1928, at Cartierville on which occasion it was christened the Rambler. There was great enthusiasm for the Rambler, and shortly afterwards Curtiss in the United States purchased a controlling interest in the company, giving rise to the Curtiss-Reid name. Throughout the years that followed the Rambler became a familiar sight in Canadian skies. Many a novice aviator soloed in the dependable little plane. Eventually 36 Ramblers were constructed.

CF-API, the first de Havilland Fox Moth to fly in Canada. It arrived in Toronto in May 1933 and after serving briefly as a demonstrator was sold to General Airways. Later in its career it flew for such operators as Ginger Coote Airways, United Air Transport, and Leavens Brothers. After being damaged in a storm in 1950 it was rebuilt as CF-EVK and flew for another decade, before being burned out at Amos, Quebec.

Reprinted by permission of the Toronto Sun Ltd.

Curtiss-Reid produced only one other design, an attractive-looking parasol called the Courier. It was originally intended as an economical, fast mailplane, the concept originating with company president, J.A.D. McCurdy. Only a prototype was built, and it was destroyed in a crash in June of 1933 while being test flown at the Fairchild airport near Longueuil. Sad to relate, no Curtiss-Reid aircraft seems to have survived the inconsiderations of time.

Meanwhile on the West Coast, Boeing had set up a plant in Vancouver where it produced flying boats, including its only indigenous Canadian design, the Totem; and Boeing 40-H-4, a combination mail/passenger landplane. In Ottawa Avro Avians were being assembled by Ottawa Car as training craft.

Fleet Aircraft was another busy Canadian operation. Its story began in 1929 when Major Reuben Fleet of Consolidated Aircraft, Buffalo, N.Y., and a Canadian, Jack Sanderson, agreed to build Fleet aircraft at Fort Erie. Fleet trainers were soon in production there and being sold as far off as Vancouver. With this and other aviation activities, it appeared as though Canada was on the way

G-CYXC, an RCAF Curtiss-Reid Rambler, taken on strength in May 1929. It is seen here at Rockcliffe.

Jack McNulty

After the death of J. Dalzell McKee, his Douglas MO-2B was purchased by the RCAF. By that time it had been fitted with a Pratt and Whitney Wasp A of 410 horse power, and a third cockpit. In this form it became the first Canadian-owned aircraft powered by a Pratt and Whitney engine. It served with the RCAF until late 1929.

Aviation and Space Division, National Museum of Science and Technology (6952)

This Fairchild 71C joined the Ontario Provincial Air Service in 1935. It is seen here on Grigg Lake in Northern Ontario in 1947. Fairchild built 21 Model 71's in Canada.

Ontario Ministry of Natural Resources

Developed in Vancouver by Boeing Aircraft of Canada, CF-ARF was the sole Boeing A-213 Totem to be built. The four seat, aluminum-hulled flying boat was powered by a 300 horse power Pratt and Whitney Wasp Jr. Introduced in 1932 it served for a time on fisheries patrols with Canadian Airways but disappeared from the scene in 1942, its fate unknown to this day.

Aviation and Space Division, National Museum of Science and Technology (A 1550)

towards developing a diversified aircraft industry.

Throughout this period, manufacturers in Canada stuck to one or two basic designs. Only de Havilland had a broad range of products. Its first twin appeared in 1933 in the form of the D.H. 84 Dragon. This was followed by the D.H. 89 Rapide. By diversifying, de Havilland was better suited to survive the Depression than was its competitors.

Generally, Canadian manufacturers were producing aircraft designed in Britain or the United States; yet the industry was becoming more Canadian as aircraft turned out were modified to the Canadian environment. At Fairchild, the FC-2 evolved into the 71 which in turn evolved into the 82. The 82 had a gross weight which was 800 pounds greater than the 71 and a 550 horse power Wasp compared to the 71's 420 horse power Wasp. Three Super 71's were also built during this period, one for Canadian Airways and two for the RCAF.

The Norseman

In 1935 the first truly Canadian wheel/-ski/float equipped bushplane appeared. This was the Norseman. It was designed by a native of Holland, Bob Noorduyn, whose interests in aviation dated from before World War I. In 1920 he had gone to the United States to work for Tony Fokker's subsidiary, Atlantic Aircraft. Here he became well known as designer of the Fokker Universal. Sandy MacDonald wrote on Noorduyn's years at Atlantic, "It was the steady invasion of Canadian pilots arriving down at the factory to take delivery of their Fokkers that first aroused Noorduyn's interest in aviation activities north of the forty-ninth parallel." In 1929 Noorduyn moved to the Bellanca plant in Delaware where he again came into contact with Canadian bush pilots. Next he spent some time with the Pitcairn organization.

In 1934 Noorduyn moved to Montreal and began designing a basic aircraft suitable for rigorous Canadian conditions and needs. The Norseman resulted. Its rugged and straightforward features immediately appealed to users, though one shortcoming was apparent. This was its lack of power. From the fifth aircraft onward, the 420 horse power Wright engine was replaced by the 450 horse power

Wasp "C" or 550 horse power Wasp "H." Early customers at Noorduyn's Montreal plant included Dominion Skyways, Mackenzie Air Service, United Air Transport, Wings Ltd., Canadian Airways and the RCMP. Even so, just 23 Norsemans had been built prior to World War II.

Military Procurements

During the mid thirties, the RCAF began looking for more modern designs to update its by-then antiquated inventory. In 1935, two modern types were ordered, the Northrop Delta and the Blackburn Shark. The Delta was a fast monoplane procured mainly as a photo survey machine, and was the RCAF's first all-metal aircraft. Canadian Vickers received orders for three Delta Mark I's. The first one was delivered in August, 1936 and went to No. 8 (GP) Squadron, Rockcliffe. Four Mk II's were delivered within a year and the original three were brought up to their standards with the fitting of extra windows and the provision for armament. In all, twenty Deltas were delivered to the RCAF.

Other activities at Canadian Vickers during these years included the construction of twin-engined Stranraer flying boats, built under licence from Vickers-Supermarine in Britain. This venture began in 1936 with an order for five aircraft worth $780 000. Forty were eventually built, more than double the number of Stranraers built in Britain.

In October, 1936 four Blackburn Shark coastal patrol bombers arrived in Canada for use by No. 6 (TB) Squadron, Trenton. These were joined by three more in 1937 before the type went into

production by Boeing in Vancouver in 1939. Boeing provided the RCAF with a further 19 Sharks primarily for use on the West Coast.

Another modern fighting plane to appear in Canada at the time was the Grumman G-23 Goblin. Manufacturing rights for the tubby-looking fighter were acquired by Canadian Car in 1937, with the first machine flying February 3, 1938. This aircraft was shortly afterwards sold to Nicaragua. The second may have been exported to Japan. The next forty were ordered by Turkey which, it seems, was acting as a middleman. It purchased the Goblins, then resold them to the Loyalist air force in Spain, with deliveries being made through France.

At the tail end of Goblin production, 15 surplus aircraft were taken off Canadian Car hands by the Department of National Defence and turned over to 118 (F) Squadron at Rockcliffe where they served until 1942. The Goblins had been assembled by Canadian Car from components provided by Grumman and Brewster in the United States.

The Gregor FDB-1

For some twenty-five years, the biplane fighter had ruled supreme in the skies. But by the late thirties, its popularity was being challenged by the new breed of fast monoplanes — the Hurricane, the Curtiss P-36, the Bf 109. The rakish Hawker Furies, P-6's and Heinkel 51's were about to be driven from the clouds. In this setting Canada was to make an unusual contribution.

In 1938, Canadian Car and Foundry revealed a new fighter plane, the Gregor

One of 905 Norseman bushplanes built in Canada between 1935-1959. Pictured is a Norseman MK V at Ignace in northwestern Ontario, July 25, 1974.

Larry Milberry

FDB-1. Oddly enough, Michael Gregor's design was a biplane. It seemed late in the day for such a design, yet Gregor was convinced of its importance. He wrote, "It seems to me that the modern biplane fighter, approaching a monoplane in top speed, should be given a chance in actual military operations. It is my belief that the biplane built on similar specifications, having advantage of manoeuvrability, rate of climb and greater ceiling, will outfight the latter."

The FDB-1 was one of the most advanced biplane fighters. It incorporated many of the features standard on the new monoplanes. Its airframe was of all-metal construction with flush rivetting. The shape was aerodynamically clean, and enhanced by a shatter-proof sliding canopy. The main undercarriage was retractable, a novelty for a biplane; but likely owing something to CCF's experience with the Goblin. The pilot, sitting in an adjustable seat, had improved forward vision on account of the gull wing design.

The one and only FDB-1 was powered by a 750 hp Twin Wasp Junior radial engine giving an estimated maximum speed of 275-300 mph, and a cruise of around 250 mph. Landing speed was 57 mph. Armament was to have included two 50 cal. machine guns and two 116 pound bombs. Test pilot George Adye completed the initial test flight, December 17, 1938. During early flights some problems were experienced, including excessive vibration of the canopy at high speed, and a lack of good visibility on takeoff and landing; but in general the plane handled well.

The FDB-1 was evaluated by the RCAF, but the inevitable swing over to the much faster monoplane fighter precluded its production. Canadian Car cancelled all work on the project and the sole machine was slated for export to Mexico. This deal fell through, and the plane was stored at Cartierville. Late in 1945 CF-BMB, the first Canadian-designed fighter plane, was accidentally destroyed by fire.

Theories differ as to why Canadian Car designed the FDB-1. One is that it had been intended for use by the Republicans in the Spanish Civil War; but it seems more likely that it had been an attempt on the company's part to demonstrate its ability as a designer and builder of modern aircraft. For these were the days when Canada was striving to prove its competence as an aircraft manufacturer. War clouds were gathering over Europe and big contracts to build aircraft for Britain were expected. With the exceptional little biplane to its credit, Canadian Car would stand a better chance of winning some of these orders.

While the FBD-1 was being developed,

The sole Gregor FDB-1 fighter, designed and built by Canadian Car in 1938, one of the most advanced biplanes ever built. Left to right in this photo are test pilot George Adye, Canadian Car representative David Boyd and designer Michael Gregor.
Aviation and Space Division, National Museum of Science and Technology (A1406)

One of the original batch of four Blackburn Shark torpedo bombers which came to Canada in 1936. In 1939-1940 17 such aircraft were built for the RCAF by Boeing in Vancouver. This photo was taken at Ottawa, November 7, 1936 just before 503's initial test flight in Canada. It was scrapped in 1944, and no Sharks remain today.
Public Archives of Canada (PA63191)

Canadian Car was also working on a new training aircraft. This was the Maple Leaf Trainer II, a clean-looking little biplane designed by the company's chief aeronautical engineer, Elsie MacGill. The Maple Leaf Trainer II, CF-BPU, flew in November, 1939 but did not go into production.

Other Ventures of the Thirties

Canadian Car was interested in another project at this time — Vincent Burnelli's revolutionary "flying wing" design. Burnelli and the famous trans-Atlantic flier, Clyde Pangborn, brought one of these big transports to Canada for test and demonstration purposes in 1936. At the time, L.A. Peto, Vice President of Canadian Car, announced his firm's intention to produce the Burnelli in quantity but as it turned out, this ambition was a decade premature.

While activity within the industry was fairly brisk and varied at this time, it was clear that the picture was still one of a branch plant operation. Canadian manufacturers depended on Britain and the United States for designs and current know-how. Gradually, though, Canadians were gaining in their ability and confidence in aircraft design and construction. And, as had become standard procedure, imported designs continued to be modified to suit the needs of Canadian operators.

Inevitably, the industry developed its share of exceptional native talent. One such person was Phillip C. Garratt. He had been one of the early graduates of the Curtiss Flying School at Toronto in 1915, and a World War I fighter pilot. He had kept up his interest in flying after the war, and in the thirties worked with de Havilland as a

CF-BDX, the prototype Fleet Freighter, seen in flight over Niagara Falls in 1938.

via J.C. Charleson

redesigned cowling; increased power; and tailwheel.

Soon after this, an order for 200 Tiger Moth fuselages was received from Britain. This reversed the usual flow of aircraft between Canada and Britain.

At Fleet, the production of light trainers continued in the immediate pre-war days, but also included 11 Fleet 21 advanced trainers for export to Mexico and a project begun by Jack Sanderson to produce a twin-engined utility plane for use in the North. This was to be capable of operations from confined lakes, be of sturdy construction and easy to maintain even if dismantling the whole plane were required, and capable of handling the bulky and awkward loads often required in the North. Generally the plane was to be as simple as possible in order to facilitate production, reduce customer cost, and simplify maintenance. What resulted was one of the oddest looking aircraft ever designed in Canada, the Model 50 Freighter.

The Freighter took to the air on its maiden flight on March 1, 1938, from Fort Erie. That summer it flew to Northwestern Ontario on demonstration flights for mining companies. Although there were complaints about the plane's apparent lack of power, its ability to haul oversized items was amply shown and appreciated. Later that summer Grant McConachie leased the first machine and used it on the first direct air mail flight from Vancouver to the Yukon. Unfortunately, this aircraft was wrecked on August 14, 1938, in northern B.C.

Only four other Freighters were built. A few misfortunes, some unflattering rumours, and the advent of World War II seemed to have doomed this interesting bushplane to a foreshortened career. The last two known to have operated were one in Mexico, and one flown by Austin Airways in Northern Ontario. Both ended their flying days in 1946. The only reminders of this unique piece of Canadiana are some bits and pieces in the National Aeronautical Collection. Some of these were salvaged from a wreck north of Nakina, Ontario, by M.L. McIntyre; and the others from a wreck on Sandgirt Lake in Labrador.

Another venture was even less successful. Fairchild designed its own twin-engine bush plane, the Model 45-80 Sekani. By late 1937, seven had been laid down and two completed. The Sekani was an improvement over the Fleet Freighter in looks and early on, seemed a promising

The Fairchild Sekani in the colours of Mackenzie Air Service. Though fine looking, the Sekani was one of the few badly designed aircraft produced in Canada.
Aviation and Space Division, National Museum of Science and Technology (6447)

test pilot, and delivering new aircraft to customers. In 1936 Garratt was appointed

company manager. Through the financially lean thirties he strove to keep de Havilland afloat. A crucial event was a deal he closed with the RCAF in 1937 for 25 D.H.82A Tiger Moths, a milestone, as it was the first time a de Havilland design had been so extensively modified in Canada. Modifications included float and ski fittings; sliding canopy and cockpit heater;

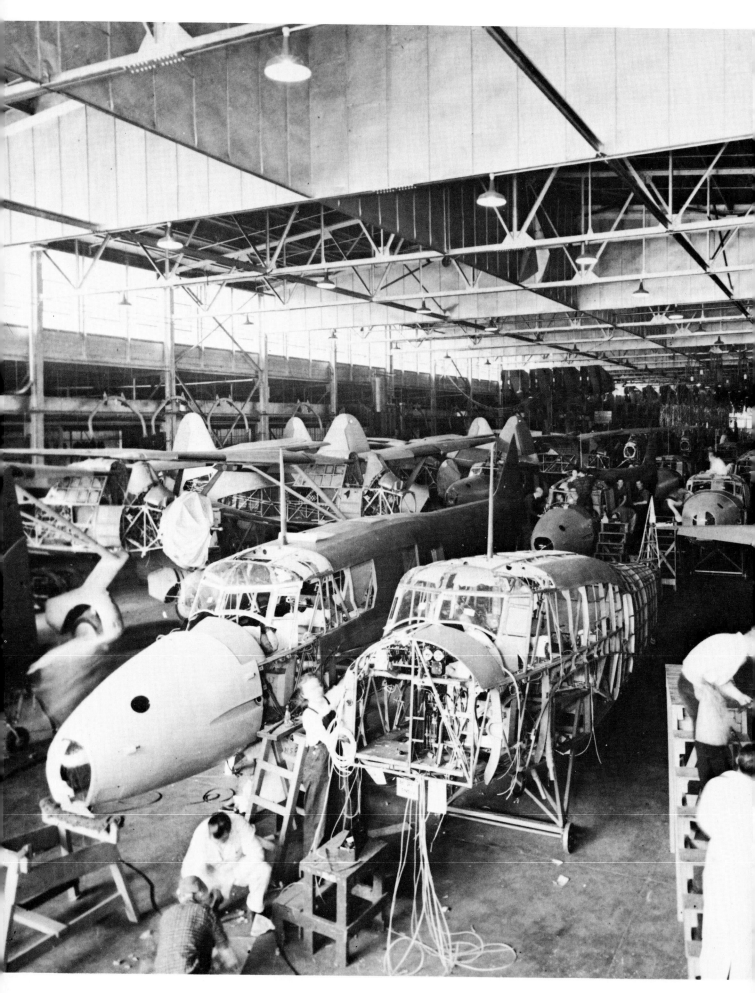

type. Wing Commander A.T. Cowley evaluated it on January 8, 1938, and found it generally acceptable when at gross weight of 10 000 pounds. Unfortunately, further experience showed the Sekani to be unstable in flight. Although one was delivered to Mackenzie Air Service at Cooking Lake near Edmonton, no further production was undertaken. Mackenzie refused to have anything to do with its aircraft and before long, the type faded into history, although it is remembered on a 6-cent air mail stamp of 1938.

Another pre-war venture involved Cub Aircraft Corporation of Canada. In 1936 Russel L. Gibson had received rights to assemble and produce the famous two-seat Cub, and opened a plant at Hamilton airport. At the time, a new Cub could be purchased there for $1895 complete, $795 down. Cub Aircraft operated at Hamilton until shortly after World War II by which time it had delivered over 300 aircraft.

World War II: Organizing for Mass Production

As the thirties drew to a close, the world realized that it was on a collision course with disaster. Democracy and fascism were at hopeless loggerheads, Germany had created a modern war machine and Britain and France were doing their utmost to keep pace. Britain recognized its own vulnerability if ever attacked by Hitler. One real possibility was that its aircraft plants could be knocked out by air raids. This led to a

Taping ribs of Tiger Moth wings at de Havilland. Thousands of Canadian women worked in the aircraft industry during World War II.
Aviation and Space Division, National Museum of Science and Technology (5975)

plan to establish aircraft manufacturing facilities in Canada. Thus in May, 1938 a British Air Mission headed by A/C A.T. Harris visited Canada to explore such possibilities. In July the following year, another mission arrived, this one headed by Sir Hardman Lever. These missions visited Canadian facilities and eventually resulted in a scheme whereby a British-financed consortium of Canadian firms would build the Handley Page Hampden bomber.

The consortium was known as Canadian Associated Aircraft Ltd. It comprised Canadian Vickers, Canadian Car and Foundry, and Fairchild in Quebec; and Fleet, National Steel Car and Ottawa Car in Ontario. Each of these firms received contracts to build components which were then trucked to assembly plants at St. Hubert and Malton. The first Canadian-built Hampden flew at St. Hubert on August 9, 1940, and the type was soon in quantity production. "Red" Lymburner was initially in charge of flight testing at both locations. After being tested, Hampdens bound for Britain were flown to Halifax. Their engines were removed and returned to the CAAL locations; the airframes were shipped overseas.

Hampden contracts were completed in mid 1942 by which time 80 had been assembled at St. Hubert and 80 at Malton. At this point Canadian Associated Aircraft Ltd. ceased operations. Of the 160

The assembly of Avro Anson fuselages at the National Steel Car plant, Malton. Lysanders are to the left.
Aviation and Space Division, National Museum of Science and Technology (A1422)

The Handley Page Hampden was one of the first modern aircraft produced by Canada's aviation industry. This Hampden P5428 was photographed over Vancouver Island while serving with 32 O.T.U., Patricia Bay.

G. Rowe Collection

Hampdens built in Canada, 84 were shipped overseas and 76 were retained in Canada for training and operational purposes.

Other aircraft types built in Canada in the immediate pre-war period and early war years were the Anson, Bolingbroke and Lysander. Of these, the Anson was the key program. Federal Aircraft Ltd., a Crown corporation, was formed to supervise and control Anson production. Plans were made for the manufacture of these trainers from Boeing in Vancouver to Canadian Car in Amherst, Nova Scotia. Nearly 2900 Ansons were eventually produced by this network.

Several production difficulties faced Canadian producers at this time and some of these were briefly outlined by H.M. Pasmore, President of Fairchild: "Recent production of Bristol Bolingbroke bombers has been a difficult task due to extensive changes in design necessary to adapt a modern British warplane to Canadian conditions, and due too, to the fact that most of our men had had no previous experience on this type of construction,

Test pilot Leigh Capreol running up the first Lysander built by National Steel Car, August 1939. In the background is the Malton passenger terminal under construction.

Reprinted by permission of the Toronto Sun Ltd.

with its problems of all-metal structure and stressed-skin covering . . . . ''

National Steel Car/Victory Aircraft

In 1938, National Steel Car, a member of Canadian Associated Aircraft, established a plant at Malton, Ontario. The first National Steel Car contract was for a batch of Westland Lysander army cooperation planes. Test pilot Leigh Capreol flew the first of these on August 17, 1939. Then Ansons went into production for the British Commonwealth Air Training Plan. While this was a major undertaking, the company hoped to get into something more

exciting. When a Short Sterling heavy bomber visited Malton early in the war, the rumour spread that this might indeed be it! The Sterling departed for cold weather tests, but a large wooden crate marked "Sterling" soon arrived to keep the rumour going. Things settled down, however when the crate was found to contain only spares for the visiting bomber.

Finally there was a breakthrough. It was decided that the Martin B-26 Marauder was to be built at Malton. By that time National Steel Car had been renamed Victory Aircraft. A hand-picked group of Victory technicians journeyed to the Martin plant at Baltimore in the summer of

A fine study of CF-BUI, a J3C65 Cub. This aircraft was built at Hamilton in June 1945 and is being flown here by Harold Micheson of the Cub Flying School.

Jack McNulty

One of 431 Fleet Finches built at Fort Erie for the RCAF. No. 1001 was the first delivered, being taken on strength October 27, 1939. It served until September 1947 and was later restored in Edmonton as CF-AAE. It was photographed at the Edmonton Flying Club in July 1976.

Larry Milberry

Over 1500 Tiger Moths were built in Canada by de Havilland Aircraft. CF-BHK is one of many which survived the war and is still flying. It was photographed at the 1975 CAHS fly-in at Brampton, Ontario.

Larry Milberry

KB891, *Fearless Fox,* an Avro Aircraft of Canada Lancaster Mk. 10. It is seen here at Yarmouth, Nova Scotia on June 8, 1945 after completing a trans-Atlantic crossing at war's end. This aircraft was scrapped in 1947.

DND (PMR 71-553)

1941. There, the tightest security reigned as the Canadians were introduced to the still-secret bomber.

Tooling up for the B-26 began at Victory, but before the first aircraft was completed the project was suddenly axed. The early B-26's were turning out to be troublesome, having been involved in a series of accidents. It would have been

tempting fate for Canada to continue work on the project.

What really brought Victory into the mainstream was the decision early in 1942 that it build the Avro Lancaster X. On August 6, 1943, the first Canadian-built Lancaster, the *Ruhr Express,* was handed over to the RCAF. Within a year, the production rate at Victory was hectic with one Lancaster per day rolling off the production line.

Work on the Lancasters was parallelled by other projects. A handful were converted to civilian transports — as trans-Atlantic mailplanes for Trans-Canada Air Lines. These were designated Lancaster X PP (Passenger Plane) and were similar to

the Lancastrians built later in England. In 1944, a sole Avro York transport was hand built at Malton but production was not pursued. Also near war's end production was begun on the Avro Lincoln heavy bomber intended to replace the Lancaster, but only one was flown, and but for a few sets of wings, all Lincoln components were scrapped. Lancaster production by Victory Aircraft totalled 430 by the time the plant was closed.

Fleet-built Cornells of the Norwegian Air Force which operated training schools at Toronto Island Airport and Muskoka, Ontario during World War II. Fleet produced 1642 Cornells in World War II.

Public Archives of Canada (WRF-813)

The Lancaster was the only heavy bomber built in Canada during the Second World War. There were press releases in 1941 indicating that Canadian Car was to build the B-24 Liberator at Fort William but this scheme did not come about.

De Havilland and Other Wartime Manufacturers

The declaration of war had little immediate effect on activities at de Havilland. It had completed current Tiger Moth orders and had to wait through a slow period. For a while it was touch and go as to whether or not payrolls could be met. Finally things picked up. In February, 1940 a large Tiger Moth order was received. By war's end 1549 had been built. At the same time de Havilland produced 375 Ansons and 1134 Mosquitos, the most glamorous of all aircraft built in Canada during World War II. The first of these had been rolled out in 1942 and production reached 120 units per month. The firm which started in 1928 as a one-man operation employed as many as 7200 during the war.

Meanwhile several other plants were busy building aircraft. Canadian Car built over 1000 Hurricanes and over 800 Helldiver bombers. Its first Hurricane was flown by "Shorty" Hatton on January 10, 1940. Hurricane production was the outstanding development in the Canadian aircraft industry in the early war years and engineering-wise was to a large extent in the hands of Elsie MacGill.

Production at Fairchild centred around the Bolingbroke, and Helldiver with Hampden components also being manufactured. Fleet produced Cornells, Fawns, Finches, and Forts. Noorduyn built hundreds of Norsemans for the Americans, as well as Harvards. In 1944 the aircraft division of Canadian Vickers had been reorganized as Canadair and it produced 360 PBY-5A Canso amphibians for the RCAF and U.S. Army Air Corps. Boeing in Vancouver built 362 Cansos and Catalinas for the RCAF, U.S. Navy, RAF, and RAAF, as well as components for the B-29 heavy bomber.

Peacetime Reorganization

Whereas war had created a modern aircraft industry for Canada, peace had the opposite effect. All of a sudden, the industry which had produced 16 400 military aircraft ground to a standstill. At Malton, some 10 000 workers were sent home without notice. Only a skeleton staff of 300 stayed on to clean out the production bays. There followed a time of readjustment within the industry when the fate of huge wartime plants like Victory Aircraft was in question. Although the government wanted to divest itself of these as soon as possible, there were people who believed that Canada had a great future in the aircraft industry. Such a person was Sir Roy Dobson, Managing Director of A.V. Roe, Manchester. During the war he had become familiar with the Canadian industry and felt that something creative could be done with the Malton facilities. Working closely with Fred Smye he concluded a deal with C.D. Howe to take them over.

Avro Aircraft

On December 1, 1945, Avro Aircraft of Canada came into being as part of the Hawker Siddeley Group in Britain. Initially, though, Sir Roy's huge plant had no airplanes to build. To provide employment and to survive readjustment, it turned out such products as plastic hairbrushes, truck and tractor parts, and saucepans.

Even during the war there had been some research going on at Malton into future peacetime projects. A proposal had been made by Sir Roy to Trans-Canada Air Lines to supply it with a new airliner, and in 1946 work began in earnest on that scheme. Jim Floyd came out from A.V. Roe in England to organize it. He worked closely with TCA finalizing specifications, and with his staff set to work on the design of a twin-jet 36-passenger aircraft.

Another early post-war proposal from Avro had been sent to the RCAF for a new navigational trainer as part of an RCAF competition. But given the vast number of war surplus training aircraft, plus scaled-down needs, the idea was put aside by the Air Force. Meanwhile work had started to build the Avro Tudor transport. For these, wings from the discarded Lincolns were to be used. One report at the time claimed that five Tudors had been ordered for the RCAF, but as the RCAF had actually adopted the North Star, work was cancelled on the Tudor.

While the company was working its way through this transitional period, it was to earn its bread and butter doing more routine jobs. This was primarily maintenance and modification work on RCAF and RCN aircraft such as Mitchells, Dakotas, Venturas, and Sea Furies. Maintenance work was even done on LV-ACV, a Lancaster flown up from Argentina. Jim Floyd's project, though, was soon to overshadow all other activities at Avro.

The Avro Jetliner

Seven days a week for two years Floyd and his team had laboured over the new airliner, the C.102 Jetliner. The first aircraft, CF-EJD-X, wasn't exactly as planned, for Rolls-Royce wasn't ready on time with the Avon engines Floyd had hoped to use. Instead, four smaller Derwent engines were installed. At last, in early August, 1949, test pilot Jim Orrell was ready to fly the Jetliner.

At the time, Malton's main runway was undergoing reconstruction, and the shorter one was not ideal for testing the new plane. Besides this, the weather was very hot, complicating takeoff conditions. High speed taxi runs were made as well as some attempted takeoffs. While aborting one of these, all four main tires blew out. Then on August 10, 1949, the Jetliner made its first flight. This event put Canada in the forefront of a major new field ahead of the United States and just behind Britain which had flown the de Havilland Comet just two weeks before.

The Jetliner's flight went off smoothly. "Everything feels wonderful," radioed Orrell as he familiarized himself with things. Floyd summed it up another way, "I've worked on a few airplanes and I've never before seen such an emotional involvement. They were going to make it fly, make it a good one, and they did."

Avro was suddenly in the midst of its most exciting project. Within a few flights the Jetliner exceeded 500 mph. On April 18, 1950, it completed the first international jet transport flight in North America by flying from Toronto to New York. The same trip inaugurated jet transport flight in the United States. On subsequent flights the Toronto-New York distance was covered in just 70 minutes; Winnipeg-Toronto in two hours 33 minutes; and Toronto-Tampa in two hours 58.5 minutes.

The achievements of the Jetliner had a jolting effect on the aviation scene south of the border. Americans were almost as surprised with the Jetliner as they were to be years later when the first Sputnik went up. Wrote the Rochester *Democrat and Chronicle,* "The Canadian plane's feat accelerated a process already begun in this nation — a realization that Uncle Sam has no monopoly on genius."

Avro was soon busy showing off the Jetliner to interested parties all over the continent. Various airlines looked closely at it. It was demonstrated to the RCAF, USAF, and U.S. Navy. Avro's sales approach was simple: "To the airlines, the Avro Jetliner offers increased revenue-earning capacity. By virtue of its speed, airline fleet requirements are reduced and

A striking view of the Avro C.102 Jetliner, showing its simple but pleasing lines. The Jetliner placed Canada in the lead in the design of commercial jet aircraft. The federal government could not appreciate this and failed to support the program after 1950.

Hawker Siddeley Canada Ltd. (35031)

due to its inherent simplicity, maintenance and servicing problems minimized. Although the Jetliner is one of the outstanding technical achievements of the day, its design is straightforward, its construction simple, and a minimum of unconventional features are incorporated.''

Not everyone was ready for commercial jet travel in 1950. After all, while the Jetliner was whizzing along at 500 mph, the Super Constellation and DC-6B, 300 mph airliners, were just coming onto the air transport scene. In fact, the Jetliner preceded both these types. One anecdote illustrates the reluctance of some to accept jet travel. One day the Jetliner was approaching New York; but on calling the tower, the pilot was informed that he might not be allowed to land. The airport manager was concerned about having a "fire spitting" airplane on his airport! When permission was given to land, the Jetliner had to park away from the terminal, and pans were placed under the engines to catch dangerous drippings they were feared to exude.

Only once in its career did the Jetliner cause alarm to its crew. On its second flight, August 17, 1949, its main gear would not deploy and an emergency landing was made with only the nose gear extended. The aircraft was slightly damaged.

Although there was considerable interest in the Jetliner, this great Canadian aircraft never saw production. Even before its first flight, TCA had lost interest. This may have been the result of the airline having second thoughts about being first into the commercial jet age. In early 1948 it rejected Avro's latest specs for the Jetliner, arguing that these were not up to its standards. The TCA specs were themselves unrealistic and apparently have never been imposed on any jet airliner since those days!

The Korean War followed with the result that C.D. Howe ordered Avro to concentrate production on the CF-100 interceptor. USAF interest in the Jetliner as a navigation trainer also disappeared in light of Korea. The RCAF, in the market for a jet transport, ordered two Comets in November, 1951, this being another disappointment for Avro.

The Jetliner flew for several more years, on projects relating to CF-100

development. A curious interlude was its six-month stay in California in 1952 where it had gone to take part in development of the Hughes fire control system. Although this scheme was shelved, Howard Hughes was not deterred from adding the Jetliner to his impressive collection of aircraft at Culver City. Hughes flew it the day after its arrival. Avro test pilot Don Rogers later wrote, "When I checked him out on the Jetliner, which only took a short time, he went around and did, I think, nine landings and takeoffs in a row on his beautiful nine-thousand-foot grass strip. He was a perfectionist on takeoffs and landings, although he tended to come in a little fast in order to make a nice smooth landing. When we taxied in, I mentioned to a Hughes Aircraft pilot we'd done nine landings and takeoffs. He said, 'That's nothing! When he got his Boeing Stratocruiser he did thirty-seven.' I guess he figured the Jetliner was pretty easy to fly, which it was.''

Some of those intimately concerned with the development of the Jetliner. From left to right are: Mario Pesando and Jim Floyd of the Avro design office, flight engineer Bill Baker, test pilots Don Rogers and Michael Cooper-Slipper, Fred Smye, and Gordon McGregor, TCA's president. This photo dates to April 22, 1950.

Reprinted by permission of the Toronto Sun Ltd.

Eventually the Jetliner was grounded as spare parts became scarce and maintenance costly. The aircraft which had brought prestige and glamour to Canada took off for the last time on November 23, 1956. It would be nearly a decade before a comparable 50-passenger interurban airliner would fly. The Jetliner was offered to museums but there were no takers. It was sold for scrap and cut up. Its mainwheels ended up on a farm wagon. Its auto pilot flew on for years in the DC-3, CF-JUV. The nose section is the only sizable piece to have survived and is today part of the National Aeronautical Collection.

The CF-100

Plan view of the prototype CF-100 showing a family resemblance with the Jetliner.
Hawker Siddeley Canada Ltd. (34492)

Only one of Avro's post-war designs ever reached production. This was the CF-100. As with the Jetliner, to which it bears a close resemblance, it passed through a lengthy period of development. It was early in 1945 that the RCAF first set requirements for a two-seat jet fighter: capable of long patrols over Canada's North in any weather conditions, high climb rate, good low speed characteristics, and speeds high enough to enable it to intercept the advanced jet bombers known to be under development in the Soviet Union.

In October, 1946 Avro began a design study to meet these requirements. From three designs worked out, one was selected and a contract awarded for two prototypes and a static test airframe. Then began 40 months of detailed design and tooling up, this under the supervision of John Frost. He had come to Canada from de Havilland in England where he had recently been involved on the advanced D.H.108 swept wing research aircraft.

As Floyd had done with the Jetliner, Frost kept close to traditional ideas with the CF-100. This was to shorten the time needed to get the plane into the air and minimize holdups such as ones that would likely have arisen had a swept wing been adopted.

The CF-100 made its first flight at 2:46 P.M. January 19, 1950, with test pilot Bill Waterton at the controls. The black prototype was powered by Rolls-Royce Avon engines, though work was well advanced on a Canadian engine, the Orenda. It had evolved from research dating to 1943 and conducted by the government organization, Turbo-Research Ltd. Avro later took over this organization and ran the Chinook, the first Canadian jet engine. It later established Orenda Engines Ltd.

Aviation circles were impressed by the CF-100. At over 16 tons it was the world's heaviest fighter; and with a speed of 600 mph, one of the most formidable. The two Mk.I's were soon joined by ten pre-production Mk.II's for use mainly in the flight development phase and in pilot familiarization. No. 18103 became the first

CF-100 fitted with the Orenda engine. The Orenda had been initially flight tested aboard a Lancaster flying test bed. Don Rogers had made the first flight of this aircraft in July, 1950. The following October an Orenda was fitted in a USAF Sabre in California. This Sabre became the first aircraft powered exclusively by the new Canadian engine. Eight months later, June 20, 1951, Don Rogers flew the first Orenda-powered CF-100.

On October 17, 1951, the RCAF took delivery of the CF-100. C.D. Howe was present at Malton for the occasion and in his speech remarked, "The aircraft as it stands before us is a notable achievement . . . a milestone in Canadian industrial development." Soon after, the RCAF formed its first CF-100 unit, No. 3 All Weather Operational Training Unit at North Bay.

On April 1, 1953, the type became operational with 445 Squadron at North Bay. This base was developing into the hub of CF-100 operations. As with any revolutionary new aircraft, the CF-100 was

Early armament test with the CF-100. The prototype aircraft launches 2.75-inch folding fin unguided missiles over Lake Ontario near Picton, Ontario. The CF-100's rocket pods were eventually perfected and became standard armament. The CF-100 Mk. V carried 52 missiles in each of its wing tip pods.

Hawker Siddeley Canada Ltd. (44336)

not problem free. To December, 1953 it had been involved in 37 mishaps, 11 of them serious. One of these was the crash of 18102 near London, Ontario, with the loss of both crewmen. Such difficulties periodically resulted in all CF-100's being grounded pending investigations.

While production focused on the Mk. III, the Mk. IV prototype, hand made, took to the air. Although it resembled its predecessor, 14 000 of its 15 000 or so parts were new. This meant even more rigorous testing. At one time at Avro, there were 18 different CF-100's in the flight test section. This was in addition to aircraft under test with the RCAF's Central Experimental and Proving Establishment at Ottawa and Namao.

One of the many aspects that had to be verified was the CF-100's ability to operate supersonically. This was important in proving the strength of the airframe and in assuring the RCAF that in combat their aircraft would be safe, no matter the circumstances. On December 4, 1954, test pilot Jan Zurakowski dove the Mk. IV prototype through the sound barrier. The CF-100 thus became the first operational straight-winged aircraft in the world to do so. This had not been an officially sanctioned flight, but had been conducted by the test pilot on his own initiative in order to prove out the aircraft's capabilities when exceeding Mach 1. As the CF-100's maximum permissible speed was .85, it was apparent to "Zura" that the CF-100 could

Activity at Avro in the early fifties. This view shows CF-100 Mk. III's, the Jetliner, test bed F-86 on loan from the USAF, and two Lancasters.

Hawker Siddeley Canada Ltd. (38656)

18323, one of the CF-100's that served as test aircraft during development of the CF-100 Mk. VI. When this program was abandoned, tests with the Sparrow missiles shown in this view were continued as part of the CF-105 weapons systems program.
Hawker Siddeley Canada Ltd. (74110)

when found to cause excess buffetting during deployment. Rockets in wing tip pods eventually became standard equipment on a later Mk.IV and the Mk.V. The latter was the ultimate development of the CF-100. Of all versions it had the greatest engine output, and best ceiling and rate of climb. To further increase its effective ceiling from 50 000 to 60 000 feet, Falcon and Sparrow missiles were evaluated on a version designated CF-100 Mk.VI. Two aircraft, Nos. 18638 and 18639, were sent to the U.S. Navy test establishment at Point Mugu, California. These were modified to establish the compatability of the CF-100 and the Sparrow II, but the project was dropped in late 1957 in favour of development at Avro of the CF-105.

By the mid fifties Avro and its subsidiaries counted 22 000 employees, making airplanes, jet engines, specialized metal products, railway rolling stock, and even buses. One CF-100 per day was being produced and Orenda was turning out 100 engines per month. At one time, 75 people were assigned just to the task of preparing technical manuals for the CF-100.

At Avro's tenth anniversary, company President Crawford Gordon commented, "I think that our company has demonstrated that we belong in the realm of exciting prospects. We're going to stay there. We have plans for the future, and we have expansion programs underway to back those plans. We have the design, engineering, and research facilities to keep us up with the pack or stay a bit ahead. We've shown that we can produce as efficiently as anyone. And we have the right kind of people. In the final analysis, that counts more than anything else. To me our future is unlimited."

On December 4, 1958, at Bay 3, Avro, a brief ceremony was held commemorating something special in the CF-100 story. For many of the 13 000 employees at Avro and Orenda it was a nostalgic occasion, for the 692nd and last CF-100 was rolled out.

The aircraft was completed on schedule, to the very day planned four years earlier. Although the event was somewhat overshadowed by other developments at Avro that year, it did represent 11 years of achievement in the Canadian aircraft industry. It had proven Canada's ability to design, develop, and mass produce an outstanding modern jet aircraft.

The full-scale mock-up of the C.103, the proposed Avro follow-on to the CF-100. The swept wings and tail distinguished this design from its predecessor.

Hawker Siddeley Canada Ltd. (38673)

readily approach Mach 1 without a pilot necessarily realizing it. What would happen when this occurred? "Zura's" flight test proved that the CF-100 could break the sound barrier without any trouble.

For his efforts, "Zura" was taken to task by the design office which at the time had been proposing to the RCAF a version of the CF-100 designated C.103 which would be capable of .95. It was now obvious that such an aircraft was unnecessary. The C.103 never developed beyond the wooden mockup stage.

Another test program involved research into icing and its effects on the CF-100. Don Rogers flew on this program and wrote of it, "The Airways Weather-Forecaster looks askance, and the Traffic Controller with something approaching pity at the pilot who requests information regarding the area of worst icing conditions, and then files a flight plan to work right through it. However, like a fireman testing an asbestos fire-protection suit, the only way to really prove an aircraft's ice-protection system is to fly in icing conditions. Which explains why so many Avro Canada flight plans this spring carried the notation, 'Ice Seeking.' Our job was to prove the CF-100's ice-protection system. So we had to go looking for ice!" Both the Jetliner and the "Rockcliffe Ice Wagon", the NRC's North Star, assisted on the program. In such ways the CF-100 was perfected as an all-weather interceptor.

Evaluating aircraft armament was also important. A 50-calibre gun pack was chosen for use in the Mk.III. Machine guns, cannons, and unguided missiles in a ventral pack were options on the Mk.IV. A retractable ventral rocket pack was rejected

This DHC-1 Chipmunk is shown lifting off from Oshawa June 16, 1963. The following year it crashed at Orillia airport after the propeller separated in flight.

Larry Milberry

◄ Development of the CF-100 included JATO (Jet Assist Take Off) experiments. This test was photographed at Malton by Avro photographer Hugh Mackechnie.

Via Helen Bloor

Chipmunk, Beaver, and Otter

With the war over, de Havilland was also faced with a cutback in activity. To reestablish itself, it turned to production of the pre-war Fox Moth, an ideal bush plane suitable to the mining industry which, unlike aircraft manufacturing, was stimulated by peace. This interim project, begun in the summer of 1945, resulted in 52 Fox Moths being produced. Some of these

Aircraft like the Chipmunk, Beaver, and Otter brought fame to Canada's aircraft industry in the early fifties. C-FOSP, Beaver No. 1501, was photographed at Vancouver International Airport as it pulled out of the water August 18, 1976. In all, 1692 Beavers and Turbo Beavers were built.

Larry Milberry

were exported to customers as far away as New Zealand and Pakistan; but most ended up as workhorses in the Canadian North.

Meanwhile, de Havilland designed its first ever indigenous aircraft. This was a small trainer, the DHC-1 Chipmunk. Test pilot Pat Fillingham took it up for the first time on May 22, 1946. The Chipmunk proved a great success and entered into service with the RCAF and the Royal Canadian Flying Clubs Association. De Havilland of Canada completed 217; but 1000 others were built under licence in Britain, and a further 60 in Portugal.

Next year saw de Havilland on the verge of an important development. For two decades it had been catering to the needs of bush operators. The OPAS was in the market for a new design to replace its aging fleet. De Havilland analysed this need and, under the direction of "Punch" Dickins, in charge of sales for the company, went to operators across the country with a questionnaire asking them what they'd like in a new bush plane design.

The questionnaire results verified de Havilland's ideas, and construction of a prototype soon was in progress. On August

One of the Fox Moths built by de Havilland in 1946. Though a design of the early 1930's, the Fox Moth did not come into its own in Canada until after World War II. In this photo Dave Marshall taxis CF-DIW at Kitchener-Waterloo July 9, 1961.

Larry Milberry

16, 1947, it made its first flight piloted by Russ Bannock. The airplane was the DHC-2 Beaver, and the OPAS soon had 27 on order. Before long, international sales began to materialize. The Beaver was off on a career that 30 years later was as active as ever, and even saw the original prototype, C-FFHB, still earning its keep in the Canadian Northland.

While the OPAS was eventually to operate some 40 Beavers, de Havilland's biggest customer became the United States Army. In 1949, Russ Bannock had heard that the U.S. Air Force in Alaska was in the market for a search and rescue aircraft. As the Beaver fitted the requirements, Bannock took one to Alaska and demonstrated it to Bernt Balchen, then commanding USAF search and rescue operations at Anchorage. Balchen was impressed by what he saw and suggested to Bannock that de Havilland send a Beaver to the competition being held by the Army for

this category of aircraft. This was done, and the Beaver was the Army's choice. Twenty-two were immediately ordered; but the order was cancelled under the Buy American Act. The fact was, however, that there was no other aircraft available that could match the Beaver's performance. The Act was rescinded to clear the way for the Beaver to join the ranks of the Army. This marked the first time that a foreign-built aircraft had been purchased in peacetime for the U.S. military. The Beaver went on to a long career in theatres from Korea to Vietnam. Today many of these aircraft have reappeared in Canada and make up a substantial proportion of the 350 Beavers currently operating here.

Success also awaited the Otter, follow-up design to the Beaver. Test pilot George Neal flew it for the first time on December 12, 1951. Throughout Canada's North, in the jungles of the Philippines, in the Australian outback, and in Antarctica, Otters were to provide air transport in places where there had been none before.

The Otter was also ordered by the U.S. Army. The choice had been made during helicopter trials at Fort Bragg. Observers were amazed to see an Otter get airborne

Considerable post-war activity in the aircraft industry is evident in this view of the Noorduyn plant at Cartierville. DC-3's, Cansos, Cranes, Harvards, and Fireflies are some of the aircraft to be seen.

Jack Markow

Three Wardair Otters in flight near Yellowknife.

De Havilland Aircraft of Canada (2956)

faster than a big helicopter with the same power, even though the Otter was carrying twice the helicopter's load. De Havilland's research into Short Takeoff and Landing theory had paid off and by the time the Beaver and Otter production lines closed, 1692 Beavers and 466 Otters had been built.

Canadair

Unlike Avro and de Havilland, Canadair entered the post-war period with lots of work. By mid 1946 it employed over 7500, many of whom were involved converting war surplus C-47's to airline standards. These were total rebuilds and by the time this activity ended in 1947, 225 aircraft had been delivered to 16 customers, including 21 to TCA.

Canadair's big project at this time was

As a result of this, the airline narrowed its interests to the Douglas C-54 and the Lockheed Constellation. These were currently being produced as military transports, and of the two, the C-54 seemed better suited to TCA's needs. It had originated in 1936 as a commercial design but its post-war future in civil aviation was not yet clear. Neither was that of an upcoming design, the DC-6.

After analysing the facts, TCA decided on a compromise. Working with Canadair, it selected the C-54 and developed a program to modify it to its own requirements. For example, the airline wanted more powerful engines, feeling that these would be an asset on high-altitude trans-Atlantic operations. The engine chosen was the Rolls-Royce Merlin 620 of 1760 horse power, compared to the C-54's 1450 horse power Twin Wasps.

Modifications kept Canadair's huge staff busy. Some 9500 C-54, DC-4, and DC-6 drawings were used, many being altered to TCA specifications. The resulting aircraft employed a shortened DC-6 fuselage; DC-6 nose and landing gear; DC-4 tail; DC-4 and C-54 wings; Rolls-Royce engines; and Canadair-designed nacelles. This was the DC-4M, the

to provide TCA and the RCAF with a large modern transport. TCA had pioneered trans-Atlantic operations using its modified Lancasters, and had realized that there was a peacetime need for this kind of service. New equipment was required, though, as the civilianized bombers were never intended for civil use and could accommodate only eight or ten passengers. Canadair was selected to provide the new aircraft. This undertaking was also to symbolize the government's desire to put Canada's post-war aircraft industry on the

One of the North Stars of 107 Search and Rescue Unit, Torbay. This unit operated three SAR North Stars after relinquishing its Lancasters in the early sixties.

DND (PCN-4762)

map in a big way. It was determined to succeed at almost any cost. The driving force behind the project was C.D. Howe.

TCA had actually begun its search for a trans-Atlantic airliner in 1943. That year it sent personnel to tour major U.S. aircraft plants to determine just what types of aircraft might be available after the war.

New Sabres and T-33's prior to delivery from Canadair during the mid fifties. This era was the heyday of aircraft production in Canada in the post World War II years.

Canadair Ltd. (58095-H2)

civilian airline version. There was also a version for the RCAF, the first of which were built from surplus C-54 fuselages and did not reflect the DC-6. The new aircraft was christened the North Star. Test pilot Bob Brush of Douglas Aircraft took the North Star on its first flight on July 20, 1946. Production began almost immediately at Cartierville.

On April 15, 1947, TCA inaugurated trans-Atlantic service using aircraft actually built for the Air Force. These were unpressurized, and soon fostered the North Star's reputation as a very noisy aircraft. Eventually these were replaced by pressurized North Stars built for the airlines. Even these, however, were considered by many, passengers and crew alike, to be too noisy for comfortable passenger travel. A system of cross-over exhausts was later designed to reduce noise levels. This helped but never to the point that the noise level was totally comfortable. Eventually Canadair delivered 71 aircraft in various versions to TCA, the RCAF, CPA and BOAC.

Canadair began another big project after the war. The RCAF needed a fast day fighter to replace its Mustangs and Vampires. The type selected was the North American F-86 Sabre, at the time the fastest fighter plane available. Canadair, by then a subsidiary of General Dynamics Corporation, was chosen to build the Sabres under licence. The contract to build Sabres at Canadair was let in mid 1949; a year later, on August 9, Canadair test pilot Al Lilly flew the first one. Later that month, the RCAF officially accepted the new type.

The Mark I, II, and IV Sabres were essentially similar to the North American F-86A and F-86E Sabres, but the Mark V's and VI's differed by having the Orenda engine. There was only one Mark III, an Orenda-powered aircraft. In total, the RCAF received some 1183 Canadair-built Sabres. Others were sold to West Germany, Britain, Greece, Turkey, Jugoslavia, South Africa, and Colombia. Over eight years of production, 1815 Sabres were built at Canadair.

Canadian Car and Foundry

The post-war years saw a number of smaller scale Canadian aviation projects take wing. At Montreal, Canadian Car was still toying with the idea of Burnelli's odd-looking transport, the Cancargo CBY-3 Loadmaster as it was designated in Canada. It was August, 1945 that the one and only machine made its initial flight over Montreal.

Burnelli himself had begun building airplanes in Connecticut during the early

The Canadian Car and Foundry Ltd. Loadmaster II. This unusual aircraft was designed by Vincent Burnelli and featured an airfoil fuselage. CF-BEL is preserved in the collection of the Connecticut Aeronautical Historical Society.
Aviation and Space Division, National Museum of Science and Technology (A1379)

twenties. His efforts culminated in the CBY-3. With conventional designs, the fuselage was traditionally deadweight, but Burnelli turned it into a sort of flying wing.

Canadian Car saw the plane as a good rugged transport for use in Canada. It was in the same weight category as the DC-3, and had good short field performance. It had convenient side loading doors, and a large rear door that a small truck could back up to. Dual wheels added to its rough-field characteristics. Payload was 2-1/2 tons. It cruised around 200 mph and could land as slowly as 65 mph.

A Northwest Industries Bellanca 31-55B at Ft. McMurray in July 1960. CF-EQQ was built in 1948 and initially operated by Associated Airways. Its days were ended September 6, 1961 when it was destroyed by fire. This view readily illustrates the famous Bellanca flying struts.
Claude Fournier

With its various attributes, the Burnelli looked like a possible alternative to existing transport aircraft. Canadian Pacific evaluated it on an airlift of heavy equipment from Sept Îles to Knob Lake, and it was otherwise widely promoted.

Nonetheless, Canadian Car received no orders for the type. The sole aircraft was exported to the United States in 1952 and re-registered N17N. Later on it did some freighting in Latin America and then returned to the United States where it languished for years at Baltimore. It was finally rescued by the Connecticut Aeronautical Historical Association and trucked to its museum at Bradley Airport.

An important post-war Canadian Car program was the construction of over 200 new Harvard trainers for the RCAF. The first of these was delivered October 27, 1951, in a ceremony presided over by C.D. Howe.

Skyrocket and Husky

Other Canadian firms were pursuing their individual projects to build bush planes for the post-war market. In Edmonton, Leigh Brintnell of Northwest Industries had resurrected an old Bellanca design and modified it to Canadian needs. This was

Three views of the fifth Fairchild F.11 Husky built. CF-EIO was purchased by Sherritt Gordon Air Transport, Sherridon, Manitoba in 1947. It is seen on floats on McKnight Lake, Manitoba, changing over to skis at Sherridon, and after being wrecked on **August 6, 1950. While EIO was picked up by a twister and deposited on its back, a Beaver tied up at the same dock was not touched. The Husky is today a rare type, with only three or four surviving.**

Ralph Shapland

the Bellanca 31-55 Skyrocket. From blueprints to first flight on this project was only five months. The first aircraft, CF-DCH, flew in February, 1946. The 31-55 could be had, fly-away from Edmonton, for $34 000. Only 13 were built.

Meanwhile, Fairchild was developing its F.11 Husky, a modern design with an all-metal fuselage. This was indeed promising, but the company went broke manufacturing prefabricated houses after completing just 11 Huskys. Although accused of being underpowered, the Husky proved a solid dependable bushplane and a few still exist. Some were re-engined in the mid fifties with 550 hp Leonides engines. One of the last Huskys was CF-EIR. It crashed at Campbell River, B.C., March 14, 1977.

During the mid-seventies another

A standard Fleet 80 Canuck with the pilot about to deliver a bundle of newspapers. About 90 Canucks are still flying in Canada.
Kitchener-Waterloo Record

attempt was made to resurrect the Husky. Vancouver interests rebuilt a Husky which appeared as C-GCYV. To date, however, the scheme has not succeeded.

Where the Skyrocket and Husky failed in the marketplace, the Beaver shone and de Havilland prospered. By 1948 Noorduyn, Northwest Industries, and Fairchild were all out of the aircraft manufacturing business.

Fleet Canuck

There were also some light aircraft built in Canada after World War II. Cub Aircraft resumed production and assembly of Piper aircraft; Fleet began turning out the Canuck. Its roots go back to the late thirties, and an aircraft designed by J. Omer "Bob" Noury. This was CF-BPX, the T-65 Series I. It was a small two-seater powered by a 75 hp Continental which first flew January 21, 1940. It was later destroyed in a crash at Hamilton.

Noury carried on with two further designs, one a tandem two-seater and the other with side-by-side seating. Meanwhile, Fleet wanted to get into the light plane field right after the war, and made a deal with Noury to take over his side-by-side design. After some redesign of the tail and cowling, this went into production as the Canuck. It sold for $3750 and by the time production ceased in 1948 over 200 had been built. A few more Canucks were later assembled by Leavens Brothers in Toronto.

The last seems to have been one for the Comox Flying Club that was delivered in 1967.

Found Brothers Aviation

A unique story in Canada's aviation industry is that of Found Brothers Aviation of Malton. From bush flying and technical experience gained with Mackenzie Air Service, and Aircraft Repair in Edmonton, the Found brothers determined that a small, rugged utility type aircraft designed for operation in Canada's northern regions could profitably augment the larger types traditionally used there.

Their concept evolved and towards the end of World War II they built models which were wind tunnel tested at the University of Toronto under the supervision of Professor T.R. Louden. In 1946 Found Brothers Aviation Ltd. was formed and design of the full-scale FBA-1 aircraft was begun. This work was undertaken by Mssrs Frank Disalvo, Fernando Vachon, and others. In 1947 on the Agincourt, Ontario farm of F.M. Staines, construction began. This was supervised by Staines. In 1948 the project was transferred

The Noury T-65 Noranda built in 1945 by Noury Aircraft Ltd. of Stoney Creek, Ontario. This and Noury's two other aircraft were the forerunners of the Fleet Canuck. The T-65 seated two people in tandem.
Jack McNulty

The all-green FBA-1. This was the first aircraft to be built by Found Brothers Aviation. Trials with this aircraft included taxiing on tricycle skis.

Jack McNulty

The prototype FBA-2A taking off from Toronto Harbour with N.K. Found at the controls, May 28, 1961. The aircraft was finished in white and red.

Larry Milberry

to Malton airport and the following year the aircraft, designated FBA-1A, was ready to fly. It had been built as a test vehicle to provide engineering information for use in later production development. Some of its features included a tricycle undercarriage, constant taper cantilever wing with a deep section low drag airfoil, interchangeable tailplanes, and steel tube fuselage. The aircraft was fabric covered.

On June 27, 1949, S.R. (Mickey) Found, at the time a captain with TCA, conducted the first flight of the FBA-1A. The company then engaged a design team under the direction of J.P. Booth to monitor the flight test program and to use the information gathered in the development of a production machine, the FBA-2. By the end of the year, after about 20 hours of flying and taxi trials were concluded, the aircraft was retired.

The FBA-2 incorporated several basic changes including all-metal wings with a slightly modified airfoil and constant chord centre section, metal tail planes, and metal-covered fuselage. The cabin had four doors to facilitate cargo and passenger handling. The square cross section cabin had an unobstructed length of 11-1/2 feet to take cargo normal to bush operations such as drill rods, stretchers and 45 gallon drums. The airframe was designed to accept either tricycle or tail-down undercarriage without major changes. At first it was planned to use the Gipsy Major and Cirrus Major engines in this version. The FBA-2 was to be simply constructed in order to provide easy maintenance and repair with limited facilities in the field. Hinged engine cowls gave easy access to the entire engine compartment, where the battery was readily accessible. These were key assets when servicing a float or ski-equipped bush plane.

The FBA-2's complete main undercarriage could be easily removed as a subassembly. Other easily detached parts were the three wing sections, fin, rudder, stabilizers and elevators. This design was chosen to reduce construction costs and enable an operator to quickly replace damaged sections rather than make repairs to fewer and larger components. The aircraft was readily adaptable to wheels, skis or floats.

In 1950 construction was started on the FBA-2A with tricycle gear. Funds for this activity were provided from a program to scrap and cannibalize Lancasters at Pearce and Penhold in Alberta.

When the RCAF reactivated the Lancaster during the Korean War, these became an important source of spares for de Havilland and Avro which were rejuvenating Lancasters. Over 100 Merlin engines were sold directly by Found to the Canadian Government. D.S. "Dwight" Found was responsible for the Found Brothers Aviation Lancaster disposal program in Alberta; while D.G. "Grey" Found handled sales in Toronto.

In 1952 funds from this source dwindled and attempts to obtain investment capital failed. The FBA-2A program was shelved and the company then concentrated on a diversification program which included aircraft service, subcontracting, and product development.

In 1957 Found Brothers Aviation was able to reactivate its FBA-2A on a limited budget. The prototype was completed in June, 1960. During this period, L.M. Treleman, previously of Avro, joined Found as chief engineer. In the time since its temporary shelving, the Found aircraft had lost much of its market impetus to the Cessna 180 which by the mid fifties was beginning to appear in Canada in large numbers.

Summer of 1960 saw the FBA-2A launched into its test program at Malton. Taxi trials led to short hops. The first of these took place June 13, a 15-second flight 10 feet above the runway. Following this a major turning point for the project occurred when two aircraft were ordered on behalf of Georgian Bay Airways. These were paid for by John David Eaton, who became a major source of support for the program as it developed.

The first official flight took place August 11 when the aircraft was aloft for 20 minutes. Shortly afterwards, the company began demonstrating the aircraft, on August 22 to the Department of National Defence, and on August 25 to the Press. To date all flying was conducted by Stan Haswell who had spent several years flying CF-100's for Avro.

By the time the FBA-2A first flew, 11 years had passed since the original Found plane had been completed, and the concept of British engines had changed to the more practical Lycoming O-540 of 250 hp.

The new plane had a disposable load of 1300 pounds versus the original 950 pounds. During early flights it demonstrated remarkable short field performance, as well as being able to sustain a high rate of climb to 10 000 feet. The following summer it was tested on floats in Toronto Harbour. During this phase of development the value of the plane's rugged structure, strut-free wing, four doors, and excellent takeoff performance became more evident. No unfavourable control, stability, or vibratory characteristics were detected and no major structural or engine installation changes were necessary.

In 1961 the company moved to a 2500-square foot shop in Rexdale near Malton. There construction of three aircraft began, one for certification, and two for Georgian Bay Airways. As Georgian Bay preferred the conventional landing gear, the new aircraft were built with tail wheels and designated FBA-2C's.

The first aircraft built at Rexdale was CF-NWT-X. It incorporated slightly larger tailplanes, approximately 6 inches increased cabin length, and larger rear doors along with hammock-type rear seats which were easily removed or folded upward to accommodate freight.

The FBA-2C used for type certification. It later became an instruction airframe at Centennial College in Scarborough, Ontario, but is now in the National Aeronautical Collection.

Jack McNulty

The last flying Centennial 100 seen at the parachute club near Baldwin, Ontario, in 1975. CF-WFP has since been grounded.

Larry Milberry

On June 26, 1962, NWT was on a local test flight. A refuelling stop was made at Brampton airport but the required octane was not available there. During the ensuing takeoff to return to Malton the engine failed. While attempting to turn back to the field the plane stalled and dove into the ground killing test pilot John Temple. The Department of Transport accident investigation concluded, "The engine failed from fuel starvation caused by a low fuel supply under conditions of steep climb aggravated by a turn."

This mishap delayed certification for the FBA-2C until the following year. CF-OZV-X, serial number 4, was used for this, and on February 2, 1964, the type was certified. During this period the National Research Council provided valuable assistance in the area of major structural and flutter testing. To that time few if any aircraft of the size and category of the FBA-2C had been subjected to such extensive pre-certification tests.

By mid 1964 the company had moved into a neighbouring 10 000-square foot plant and production was in full swing. First deliveries were made to Mahood Logging in Powell River, B.C., and to Georgian Bay Airways. Other early customers included B.C. Airlines, Calm Air, Ocean Air, Pacific Western Airlines, and Northern Mountain Airlines.

Production at Found rose to 2-1/2 aircraft per month during this period. The product coming off the line was very straightforward. No effort was made to dress up the FBA-2C. As the company put it, "As a freighter, every available pound should be used for payload. Spilled cargo or residue from carrying fresh fish can penetrate and accumulate in sound-proofing creating a hazard through corrosion and extra weight."

As production continued, so did ideas for improving the FBA-2C. Certain modifications were planned for 1965. These would reduce production costs, increase payload, and improve appearance and handling characteristics. They would give the aircraft wider market appeal in Canada and abroad where genuine interest was building. At the same time Found was developing a list of changes and refinements to the FBA-2C which would eventually be incorporated in a second generation aircraft.

Although some negative attitudes were expressed about the plane, operators of the FBA-2C were generally satisfied with their new aircraft. Arnold Morberg of Calm Air wrote that after 5-1/2 months of operation, and 400 revenue hours, his Found had flown everything from mining equipment and building materials, to 45-gallon drums of fuel, sled dogs, and medical cases. He closed his remarks saying, "I would like to congratulate you and your company on building an aircraft that has long been needed in the Canadian North."

In spite of a promising beginning, a number of factors were shaping up which would lead to the premature decline of Found Brothers Aviation. In early 1966 the two Found brothers still associated with the company were forced out. At this point the factory was readying aircraft number 22 for delivery to St. Felicien Air Services and the last four aircraft were coming down the line.

After completion of serial number 26 the new management closed the FBA-2C line. At the same time it also set aside Found's concept for a limited modification program for the FBA-2C, and proceeded with extensive modifications which resulted in the development of the second generation aircraft by early 1967. This was the Found Centennial 100. On April 7, 1967, the prototype, CF-1OO-X, made its first flight with George Ayerhart at the controls. Later that year the company relocated to Grand Bend, Ontario.

Design gross weight of the Centennial 100 was 3500 pounds, with a projected disposable load of 1750 pounds. At gross weight, however, the aircraft would not deliver acceptable performance with its 290 hp Lycoming IO-540 engine. Also, due to an unexpected increase in empty weight, the disposable load on floats was only 1000 pounds, just about equal to the FBA-2C!

Type certification for the Centennial 100 was granted in August, 1968 and while three aircraft were nearing completion, one was flown to Western Canada on a sales tour, but customer disinterest resulted in cancellation of the tour at Edmonton.

An immediate reassessment led to the decision that a gross weight of 4000 pounds would be necessary to make it practical. A compatible 400 hp Lycoming engine was available and modifications began on the prototype, but in November, 1968, the firm's financial backing was withdrawn and it was offered for sale. At this time the directors approached N.K. "Bud" Found suggesting that he might consider taking the company back. The offer was declined. On March 4, 1969, the assets of Found Brothers Aviation were disposed of at public auction. With this event, a project nearly 30 years in the making came to an end.

The Found Brothers FBA-2C was the only Canadian-designed light aircraft to reach full production since the Fleet Canuck. Of 26 built, 9 FBA-2C's were still active in mid 1979. Fittingly, they are usually operated in the out-of-the-way places they were intended to serve. Two aircraft, CF-SDC and CF-SOQ, were being flown by their original owners, Starratt Transportation and Air Alma.

Though few in number, the Founds have operated in all parts of Canada, from the West Coast, to the Arctic, to Newfoundland. They've carried such loads as 18 cases of dynamite; 300 loaves of bread; 10 outboard motors; 50 cases of beer; a prospector with his complete outfit, three dogs included; and as bush pilot Bob Grant recalls, a rotund lady and her smelly pet monkey. One FBA-2C still operating has accumulated over 35 000 takeoffs and landings and is still in excellent condition.

The Avro Arrow

Aircraft designers are forever looking to the future. So it was at Avro in the early fifties. At a time when all eyes were on the CF-100, people at Avro were already considering ideas for its successor. The Soviet Union was known at the time to be developing a force of long-range, over-the-Pole strategic bombers that would be ready for deployment around 1958. This being so, in March of 1952, Avro was asked by the RCAF to propose a CF-100 replacement.

Avro submitted two delta-wing designs. One was for a single-engined fighter; the other for a twin. The following summer, Ottawa gave Avro the go-ahead on the twin which soon afterwards was designated CF-105. Under tight security Avro began organizing for this, its most ambitious-ever project. Beyond the plant there were few facts, and not even many rumours to go on concerning the new fighter until it was rolled out on October 4, 1957. Christened the Arrow, it was promptly hailed as a technical masterpiece. Once again Avro could boast the world's most advanced all-weather interceptor. Early performance figures indicated that the Arrow could exceed Mach 2; climb to 60 000 feet in four minutes; and cruise unrefuelled for hundreds of miles. At 34 tons it equalled the weight of its ancient relative, the Lancaster.

Following the tradition of the CF-100, the Arrow was a two place fighter. Armament was to include air-to-air

The No. 1 Avro CF-105 Arrow about to land at Malton. This view shows its tandem main wheels and speed brakes. The weapons bay stands out aft of the engine intakes. The CF-100, 18513, is acting as chase plane.
Hawker Siddeley Canada Ltd.

missiles in a versatile, quick change ventral pack 16 feet in length; interception was to be achieved through a complex onboard system being developed by RCA and known as Astra. This was to complicate the project later on, for even after the Arrow had been rolled out, Astra was still on the drawing boards. Use of an off-the-shelf system like the Hughes M.G.3 would have hastened development without sacrificing aircraft capabilities.

From the onset Avro operated on the production line concept as far as the Arrow was concerned. Thus, aircraft number one was not a prototype but a pre-production machine, and tools to go directly into full production were already on hand by roll-out day. This approach saved time, though was extremely expensive considering the chance that the project might be cancelled by the government as defence projects so often had been. Nonetheless, there were strong indications that the RCAF would be ordering as many as 150 CF-105's.

The Arrow took flight for the first time on March 25, 1958. As thousands of Avro workers cheered, test pilot Jan Zurakowski lifted RL201 off the runway at 9:55 A.M. He took the gleaming white delta to 10 000 feet, then back to Earth after a smooth 35 minutes. Zurakowski's snag list was short for the flight of a proven aircraft, let alone a new one. It consisted of a brief comment about two electrical switches!

Soon the Arrow flight test program was well under way. RL202 flew August 1 and RL203 on September 22. These and the next two Arrows were powered by Pratt and Whitney J75 engines but it was hoped that the sixth would fly with the lighter and more powerful Orenda Iroquois. Mean-

while the Arrow production line began taking shape with 37 aircraft slated for the first run.

Overall, the Arrow performed well during flight tests and actually met RCAF performance requirements with the J75. On just the third flight, it went supersonic and on the seventh exceeded 1000 mph while climbing. Test pilots were Jan Zurakowski, "Spud" Potocki and Peter Cope of Avro, and F/L J.F. Woodman of the RCAF.

Woodman's first flight was April 22, 1958. It lasted one hour ten minutes and was mainly for pilot familiarization. It was limited to Mach 1.4 and 50 000 feet. Pilot's comments later included, "The aircraft at super-sonic speeds was relatively pleasant and easy to fly . . . Relative to the CF-100 or F-102, considerably increased attention was required to fly straight and level or make a turn without side-slip."

On September 28, Woodman again flew the Arrow. Tests conducted included ground handling; takeoff; climb; handling at 50 000 feet at Mach numbers of 1.5, 1.6 and 1.7; descent; handling at 15 000 feet at low indicated air speed; approach and landing.

Woodman's takeoff roll was 3200 feet and he noted, "Acceleration at maximum thrust was very high." Performance was evaluated at 20 000 feet at 350-375 KIAS leading to the observation, "The control system as it exists is too sensitive in these subsonic speed ranges." He also noted that at Mach 1.5 "the aircraft was very stable and the control feel was very good." Final approach was at 180 KIAS and touchdown at 155 KIAS. Six tons of fuel had been burned during the flight.

Parallelling aircraft development at Malton was development of the Orenda Iroquois engine. Avro had decided to design its own Arrow power plant to be free of dependence on foreign products. It had initially considered the Rolls Royce RB.106. When it was cancelled, the American J67 was considered, but it too was cancelled. This led to the decision to build the Iroquois in spite of great added costs to the government. As the Arrow was being flight tested with the J75 engine, the Iroquois was being run on the ground and in the air aboard a modified Boeing B-47 test bed.

Armament was also being developed. The CF-100's previously connected with the CF-100 Mk VI project at Point Mugu became launch vehicles for the Sparrow system being developed for the Arrow by Canadair. Avro pilots flew the CF-100's

RL201, the first pre-production CF-105 Arrow. Its aesthetic lines are clear in this fine view. RL201 was the most extensively tested Arrow. It completed 24 flights for a total of 25 hours 5 minutes aloft.

Avro Aircraft via Helen Bloor

The C.102 Jetliner on the ramp at the Avro plant, Malton, Ontario. The Jetliner, a decade ahead of its time, illustrated the capabilities of Canada's aircraft industry in the post-war years.

Don Rogers

RL202 viewed from rear three-quarter at an angle which emphasizes the Arrow's massive and aesthetic delta wing.

Hawker Siddeley Canada Ltd. (80751)

with up to four Sparrows and in June 1958 made three attempts to conduct actual firings. They were to home on a Grumman Hellcat drone (a pilotless aircraft operated by remote control) on these attempts, but each time snags forced the mission to be aborted. Soon after this funds for the program were cut.

The Arrow had been designed to perform a highly specialized role, that of intercepting and destroying enemy intruders. It certainly looked the plane for the job; but as the program evolved discussion was under way in defence circles concerning NORAD's future requirements for new manned interceptors.

The Russians had recently launched Sputnik I, an event which sent scientific and defence organizations in the Free World into a panic. It seemed that this one event suddenly rendered outdated much existing defence thinking. Experts began to fear a new threat to North American security, the ICBM. Their ability to launch a satellite indicated an advanced state in Soviet missile technology. Now it was a question of defending against missiles. Bombers seemed passé. Thus began the great debate over the Arrow, one in which the government challenged Avro and the RCAF to prove the viability of manned interceptors.

One of the few, if not the only, seven-engined aircraft in the world. This Boeing B-47 was specially modified by Canadair and Orenda as a flying test bed for the Orenda Iroquois turbojet engine. XO59 was flown exclusively by test pilot Michael Cooper-Slipper. The aircraft is seen flying over Malton airport.

Hawker Siddeley Canada Ltd.

It was to be rough for those who favoured the Arrow. As if to deliberately make matters worse, that tiny Sputnik had gone into orbit the same day the Arrow was unveiled. But there were good reasons for proceeding with the Arrow. At the time there was no aircraft in the world that was in the Arrow's class. As well, the Arrow meant jobs for thousands of workers at Avro and about 2500 subcontractors. As long as the Arrow continued, an important

sector of Canada's scientific and technological community remained intact, and Canada retained a prestigious place on the global aviation scene.

On September 23, 1958, Prime Minister John Diefenbaker announced that Canada was placing an order for Boeing Bomarc B antiaircraft missiles. There was little doubt what this meant for Avro. The Arrow was not likely to be ordered into full production. At this point Astra and the Sparrow missile development projects were terminated. A limited flight test program on existing Arrows was approved as was completion of the remaining Arrows on the production line. As Diefenbaker later explained, this was to allow Avro time to readjust given the assumed fact that the total program was to be dropped.

During these final months both Avro

and the RCAF continued to press their arguments. Several propositions were made. A strong one was the airplane-versus-missile theory. An Arrow could be

RL202 after a landing gear failure. This incident occurred Nov. 11, 1958.

Paul J. Regan

scrambled to intercept and identify a target. If required, it could then attack and return to base. There was no such option for the Bomarc once it was fired. It lacked the "identify" function. It was on a one way trip.

Also, the Bomarc could not fly far. Its intercept range was just 400 miles. It was

also becoming apparent at the time just how vulnerable such missiles could be to jamming by electronic countermeasures emitted by intruders. Added to this was the fact that the Bomarc B had suffered a series of unsuccessful launches, had been dropped by the USAF, and no decision had been made in Canada as to how it might be armed. As time revealed, procurement of the Bomarc became one of Canada's great military blunders.

By early 1959 the Arrow program had run up bills of over $400 million. What had begun as a $1.5 million aircraft had become a $2.6 million one by 1955, and a $7.8 million one by 1958, with $9 million anticipated for production aircraft.

Because of accelerating costs, the

A view down the Arrow production line. In the foreground is RL206, slated to fly with Iroquois engines. This aircraft was almost ready to fly at the time of cancellation, although development of the Iroquois had not kept pace with that of the Arrow. By early 1959, the Iroquois was still a long way from being accepted as an operational engine.

Hawker Siddeley Canada Ltd. (1424)

Seven of Avro's veteran test pilots. From the left are Chris Pike, Jan Zurakowski, Peter Cope, Stan Haswell, Glen Lyons, Mike Cooper-Slipper, and Don Rogers.

Hawker Siddeley Canada Ltd.

government had never given Avro carte blanche to develop and produce the Arrow. Rather, it pursued the venture strictly on a year-by-year basis. As early as June 28, 1955, C.D. Howe spoke of the expense of the Arrow when he said in Parliament, ''I can say that now we have started on a program of development that gives me the shudders, a supersonic plane and a supersonic engine.'' It was costs that gave Howe the ''shudders.''

The arguments went on. Avro and the RCAF tried to show how the Bomarc and its costly SAGE control system, plus off-

One of the great tragedies in Canadian technological history. Four Arrows under the cutters' torches at Avro. In total, five Arrows logged 64 flights and 68.45 hours. High time plane was RL201 which flew 25.05 hours. RL205, seen at the left in shambles, flew just once for a total of 40 minutes. RL202 is not shown in this view.

Herb Nott

the-shelf fighters purchased from the United States would equal the cost of carrying on with the Arrow. Avro also warned the government that it could not afford to cancel the Arrow on account of the unemployment that would result.

Last minute measures pushed for the completion of the 37 aircraft initially ordered. These could be used for on-going development and to equip two operational squadrons. Expenses could be pared by substituting a Hughes fire control system for the Astra. Possibilities of foreign buyers were investigated. There was even a suggestion that the Arrow be adapted as a future launch vehicle for an anti-ICBM missile. It was all futile.

On February 20, 1959, the government announced total cancellation of the Arrow program. Over 13 000 workers, who had for months been fearful of just such a decision, stopped what they were doing and went home. For them it was Black Friday. Thousands of jobs among subcontractors also dissolved overnight.

The decision had been a difficult one for the government. The pros and cons had been carefully weighed. In explaining his

government's decision, Prime Minister Diefenbaker said in the Commons, ''These outstanding achievements have been overtaken by events . . . Potential aggressors now seem more likely to put their effort into missile development than into increasing their bomber force.'' Otherwise, the Commons Debates following the cancellation are full of last minute arguments, explanations, and recrimination, but the government stood its ground.

In the post cancellation clean up, Ottawa inexplicably ordered the destruction of all Arrows, either completed or on the production line. Most other reminders that there had ever been an Arrow were also swept away.

Overnight, one of the world's most advanced technological organizations disintegrated. This was at first a trying situation for the thousands of families affected. Most Ex-Avro workers, though, were to find employment in other areas of the industry. Many migrated to the United States where jobs in the aerospace industry were plentiful. Some of these went on to make important contributions in the space program.

Over the years since its demise there has been much reminiscing about the Arrow. Canadian fighter pilots still muse about what it would have been like to fly it. And as time has shown, the manned bomber has not yet disappeared. The Soviets operate Mach 2 bombers like the Backfire and although deprived of the B-1, Strategic Air Command is still very much committed to bombers like the B-52 and FB-111. This keeps the old bomber-vs-missile argument alive. Meanwhile, the marketing of $20 million fighters like the F-15 and the dropping of the B-1 perpetuate the conundrum that defence thinking has often been.

The Avrocar

While the Arrow was awaiting the cutting torches, Avro was continuing work on a novel project, the VZ-9Z Avrocar. This was a flying saucer-like aircraft, the result of research Avro had been doing into VTOL since 1951. Ottawa had at first backed the research, then both the USAF and U.S. Army came in to provide support.

Two Avrocars were built to research near-the-ground air cushion flight, level flight using the aerodynamics of the circular wing, and hovering at higher altitudes.

The machine accommodated pilot and observer. It was 18 feet in diameter and had an all up weight of 6000 pounds. Three small 1000 shaft horse power jet engines provided power. Gas from these propelled a large fan at the vehicle's hub.

First flight of the Avrocar was made December 5, 1959, by test pilot "Spud" Potocki. All flights were initially tethered ones. It was over a year later before actual forward flight was attained. It was soon apparent, however, that in flight above four feet the Avrocar became dangerously unstable. In December of 1961 the Avrocar development contract was concluded and the project abandoned. One of the Avrocars is now on display at the U.S. Army Transportation Museum, Fort Eustis, Virginia.

Avro Folds

During these post-Arrow times, Avro continued bidding on government tenders. It manufactured 300 wing-tip and pylon fuel tanks for the CF-104, but received no substantial orders. This forced the company to turn to other means of survival. It formed a partnership with the Richardson boatbuilding firm to produce aluminum hulls for cabin cruisers and even began turning out vending machines. This was forestalling the inevitable, and in 1964 the name Avro disappeared from the Canadian aviation scene.

The Avro plant was sold to de Havilland Aircraft, at the time in the midst of a boom. De Havilland contracted with Douglas Aircraft in California to manufacture major components for its new airliners: floors, wings, and tails for DC-8's and DC-9's. These were then shipped by rail to Long Beach for final assembly.

This project revitalized the Malton operation, but didn't turn out for the best for de Havilland. World airlines were rushing to update their fleets and so many orders were received that it was hard for Malton to keep up. A solution was worked out in 1965 when Douglas Aircraft took over manufacturing there. Today the name McDonnell Douglas greets the passer-by at Malton, the sixth name to hang over the big plant since 1938.

De Havilland in the Mid Fifties

While Avro had specialized in costly sophisticated military ventures, de Havilland devoted its attention to more practical and marketable concepts. Beavers and Otters could be afforded by the least significant nation; not so the Arrow.

In the mid fifties de Havilland entered a new phase in STOL design with the DHC-4 Caribou, a large twin-engined transport. On July 30, 1958, test pilots George Neal

An aerodynamic model of a Caribou mounted on a test rig atop an Otter. This model was used to evaluate various tail configurations before the Caribou design was finalized.

De Havilland Aircraft of Canada Ltd. (7283)

and D.C. (Dave) Fairbanks took the new plane into the air for the first time.

The Caribou was in the weight category of the DC-3, but fully loaded could become airborne in as little as 200 feet. Five were evaluated by the U.S. Army which was so impressed by their performance that it argued successfully for an increase in the gross weight of fixed wing aircraft it was permitted to operate. Over 200 Caribous eventually flew in U.S. Army colours.

Other Caribous were delivered to the air arms of Australia, India, Indonesia, Spain, Kuwait, Abu Dabi, Kenya, and Ghana. A few were sold to civil operators abroad and the RCAF received nine mainly for use with Canada's Middle East, Yemen, and Kashmir peace-keeping operations.

The Caribou has been proving its ruggedness and dependability around the world for nearly 20 years. One early operation of interest took place between February 2 and February 15, 1961, when Nordair chartered CF-LAN, the second

One of the Avrocars being readied for tethered flight. This photo was taken by *Toronto Telegram* photographer Les Baxter. *Reprinted by permission of the* Toronto Sun Ltd.

The prototype DHC-4 Caribou at the de Havilland plant in 1958. Results of early flight testing led to its nose being extended about two feet. In the background are newly completed Otters and a U.S. Army Beaver.

De Havilland Aircraft of Canada Ltd. (8635)

Caribou built. The object was to lift 25 000 pounds of cargo from Frobisher to the BMEWS radar station on inhospitable Resolution Island, 195 miles to the south. This was the first commercial contract involving the Caribou.

Resolution had little to offer in the way of airport facilities: 1300 feet of east-west runway, with a prevailing north-south wind. One end of the strip sloped into a rocky valley; the other ended in an 800-foot drop into the sea! On final approach, a pilot was sure to be greeted by severe turbulence and cross-winds.

On the initial flight from Frobisher, with de Havilland's Bob Fowler in command, CF-LAN carried in a 2500 pound load without incident. From then on, 4000 pound loads were carried. Because of limited daylight, unpredictable weather reports from Resolution, rapidly changing weather en route, and grim surface wind conditions, only one flight per day was operated.

The most challenging aspect of the operation from a pilot's point of view was getting the Caribou onto the Resolution strip. The sides of the strip were banked with snow above the Caribou's wing height, and there was no overrun at either end. The Caribou, though, could approach at just 70 mph. Once down, however, the pilot did not have such luxuries as spoilers or reverse pitch to help stop the plane. The airlift was successfully completed, but it is of interest that during its two weeks, the average crosswinds were 30-40 mph.

Later in its career, CF-LAN flew extensively for Imperial Oil during the busy exploration period in the Rainbow Lake region of Alberta.

Also during the mid fifties de Havilland began production of the Grumman Tracker. This modern ASW aircraft was required by the Royal Canadian Navy as a replacement for its aging Avengers. The first of 100 Trackers came off the de Havilland production line in August, 1956. These aircraft were extensively Canadianized for use aboard HMCS *Bonaventure.*

Argus, Cosmopolitan and Yukon

Canadair was still producing Sabres and T-33's in the mid fifties but was also beginning several new ventures. Of these the most significant was the CL-28 Argus, a long-range maritime patrol plane. The

One hundred Grumman Tracker ASW aircraft were built by de Havilland in the late fifties. This Tracker of VU-32 was photographed with its wings folding down at Oshawa, June 15, 1962.

Larry Milberry

concept for this aircraft dated back to 1945 with a proposal for a North Star maritime patrol conversion. This went by the board. Then, in 1952, the RCAF approached Canadair on the topic. At that time it was using refurbished Lancasters on maritime

patrol. Lockheed Neptunes were acquired in 1955, but to meet overall requirements a larger aircraft was needed.

The Argus was Canadair's proposal for such an aircraft, with design based on the Bristol Britannia. The basic wing, tail, control surfaces, and undercarriage of the Britannia were to be used, but otherwise the Argus was a new airplane. Engines selected were Wright R-3350 turbo-compounds of up to 3700 hp each. The fuselage was designed to accommodate two large weapons bays and tons of electronics, including the big chin radar, and 18-foot-long MAD boom in the tail. Sixteen crew were required to fully man the new plane.

The first Argus was rolled out at Cartierville December 21, 1956, with the maiden flight occurring March 27. A year later the first one was delivered to Maritime Air Command. First squadron to receive the potent new weapon was No. 405 at Greenwood, Nova Scotia.

Production of the Argus continued to July 1960 when the thirty-third and last was completed. Two basic versions had been produced: 13 Mark I's with their bulbous chin radomes housing American search radar; and 20 Mark II's with their more compact radomes housing British radar. The Argus has since served with six RCAF units at Greenwood, Summerside, P.E.I., and Comox, B.C.

Another Canadair project was a conversion of the Convair Liner. Two airframes were converted to take Napier Eland turboprop engines. The first of the modified Convairs, designated CL-66, flew February 2, 1959. Ten new aircraft

followed and were delivered to the RCAF as the Cosmopolitan. While Quebecair evaluated the CL-66 no commercial sales were made.

Late the same year, Canadair introduced another major design, the CL-44. Like the Argus, it was based on the Britannia, and became the largest aircraft ever built in Canada. One version was 151 feet long and seated 214 passengers. Twelve side-loading aircraft designated CL-44-6 Yukons were sold to the RCAF. Ten of these served with 437 Squadron, while two became VIP aircraft with 412 Squadron. Twenty-seven other aircraft were sold to such civilian operators as the Flying Tiger Line, Seaboard and Western, and Slick. These were all CL-44D-4's with the exception of the lone stretched CL-44J. When it flew away from Cartierville in November of 1965 another era in Canadian aviation history came to an end. Today CL-44's are operated by lesser known airlines in far corners of the world, where they are still in demand as reliable freighters.

The Beech Mentor

The only Canadian Car project in the mid fifties, after it had completed a run of new Harvards, was the production of Beech T-34 Mentor trainers. Twenty-five were acquired by the RCAF, and a further 100 by the U.S. government's Mutual Aid Plan. The RCAF ran one course using Mentors. This was held at Penhold, Alberta, in 1954-1955. The plan to replace the Harvard with this new type was dropped, and the RCAF Mentors were presented to Turkey.

Canadair in the Sixties

No sooner had the Arrow been dropped than the RCAF was in the market for a new fighter to replace its Sabres in Europe. The aircraft chosen was to fit the new RCAF NATO role of strike/reconnaissance.

A variety of current designs was evaluated, and in the end the Lockheed F-104 won out. Canadair was selected to modify and build the plane to RCAF specifications. By 1961 production was under way and soon afterwards Sabre

An Argus Mk.II at RCAF Station Trenton during the airshow held on July 1, 1961.
Larry Milberry

The Canadair 540 (CL-66) demonstrator seen at Dorval September 5, 1960 in Quebecair colours. CF-LMN was later sold to the RCAF as 11161 then joined North Central Airlines as N969N.
Larry Milberry

One of the 160-passenger CL-44 400's purchased by Iceland's Loftleidir, and used on economy-priced trans-Atlantic operations.

Canadair Ltd. (38228)

Later in their development, two CL-84's were used on test programs from Patuxent River Naval Air Station, Maryland. One was used evaluating the shipboard use of V/STOL aircraft. This one operated in a tri-nation program evaluating V/STOL landing and approach aids and procedures. Canada, Britain, and the United States took part in this program. This photo was taken at Patuxent River in August, 1974.

Rae R. Simpson

pilots were exchanging their mounts for the new fighter. Eventually Canadair turned out some 200 CF-104's for the RCAF, and 140 F-104G's for the U.S. Government. These were provided to NATO allies, and were part of a deal struck between Ottawa and Washington, whereby if Canada would purchase F-101B Voodoo interceptors from the U.S., and assume the costs of operating the Pinetree Line, the U.S. would help support the Canadian aircraft industry by placing orders with Canadair. This was in lieu of a deal preferred by Ottawa whereby Washington would order CL-44's for the USAF if Canada would buy the Voodoos and finance the Pinetree Line.

On January 13, 1960, the first Canadair CL-41 jet trainer took to the air. Known as the Tutor, it had been designed to RCAF specifications for an ab initio trainer to replace the Chipmunks and Harvards.

Over 200 Tutors were completed, including 20 ordered in 1965 by Malaysia as counter insurgency aircraft. These were known as the CL-41G Tebuan. The CL-41

A trio of famous Canadair aircraft: an F-86 Sabre, a CL-41 with the CF-104 nose fitted for navigation training, and a CF-104.

Canadair Ltd. (32581)

CF-YXG, one of fifteen CL-215's owned by the Quebec Government. It and the photo plane are fitted with spray booms. These aircraft are finished in a yellow and red paint job.

Canadair Ltd.

became the first all-Canadair design to reach production status.

Canadair's next military jet program got under way in the mid sixties. This was for the manufacture of the Northrop F-5 ground support fighter. A large order was received from the RCAF for CF-5's to equip home squadrons, and by the end of production 240 had been built, including 105 for the Netherlands. In 1972, 20 were declared surplus to Canadian Forces needs and sold to Venezuela. The CF-104's Tutors and CF-5's were all powered by engines built under licence by Orenda.

A unique Canadair undertaking in the mid sixties was the CL-84 Dynavert, a VTOL aircraft. It was rolled out in late 1964 and flown initially the following May 7. The Dynavert was basically a research aircraft. It incorporated a tilt wing and was intended to develop as a troop transport, ground support, reconnaissance, and search and rescue aircraft. Its unique characteristic was the ability to take off and hover like a helicopter, or operate in level flight like a conventional aircraft at speeds up to 350 mph.

Development of the CL-84 continued

for several years. It was evaluated by the Canadian Forces and the United States Navy. The Navy evaluated its shipboard landing capabilities. While at Patuxent Naval Air Station, one of two CL-84's on test and evaluation crashed. The prototype, CF-VTO-X, had crashed earlier, on September 12, 1967. Eventually the program was shelved and the remaining two aircraft were stored at Cartierville.

Canadair's other big undertaking in the sixties was the development of a water bomber, the CL-215. This aircraft, first flown in October of 1967, was designed for ruggedness and easy handling at low speed and low altitude.

Two STOL Classics

At de Havilland this era was notable for the introduction of the DHC-5 Buffalo in 1964 and the DHC-6 Twin Otter the following year. The Buffalo had been developed for the U.S. Army which took delivery of the first four aircraft. During this period, however, the Pentagon revised the gross weight figures for aircraft the Army could operate. These were adjusted downward to a point where the Buffalo was too heavy, and no more could be sold to this traditional de Havilland customer. Other markets were eventually developed for the Buffalo. It joined the Canadian Forces, as well as the air arms of numerous Third World countries, where its inherent STOL

One of the six Beechcraft Bonanzas converted at Fort Erie to Super V's. N4530V was photographed at Toronto Island Airport.

Larry Milberry

qualities could be put to best use.

The Twin Otter was designed as a rugged feeder liner and bush plane. After a slow start, similar to the Buffalo, it duplicated the international sales success of its famous predecessors, the Beaver and Otter. Orders began rolling in from operators in such far flung parts of the globe as Nepal, Afghanistan, Australia, Norway, Surinam—wherever there was a need.

Short Lived Designs

During the sixties, Fleet was considering re-entering the personal plane market. Interests in the United States had been developing a modified Beech Bonanza, fitted with two 4-cylinder 180 hp Lycoming

Dave Saunders' four-seat design, the Cheetah.

Via Canadian Aviation Magazine

One of the Avian 2/180 development aircraft.

York University, Scott Archives

O-360 engines. This project eventually ran aground due to lack of funds.

The Super V, as the plane was called looked like a good idea to Fleet. A deal was completed which brought the whole project to Canada from San Francisco. A Fleet subsidiary, Pine Air, was set up to handle the program. A Super V was flown to Fort Erie and spent the next eight months in the shops undergoing numerous modifications. The result was a very refined light twin. The first Fleet-modified machine flew on June 1, 1962.

While the Super V was a sound and attractive aircraft, sales did not meet expectations. It was felt that sales of 50 aircraft were needed, but only six Super V's were ever converted at Fort Erie. Sales were probably hampered by competing American types like the Travel Air and the newly introduced Twin Commanche. Besides this, the Super V could not be marketed in Canada as it was not certified here. In 1964 the manufacturing and sales rights for the Super V were sold back into the United States.

Also during the sixties, Northwest Industries showed interest in two aircraft types. One of these was the Lockheed-Macchi AL 60 promoted in Canada as the Northwest Industries Ranger. This was a light aircraft for operation in the bush, but other than the demonstrator, CF-NWI, no other AL 60's appeared in Canada. The other aircraft was the Handley Page Jetstream, a twin turboprop for corporate and airline use. Northwest Industries was a major subcontractor for the Jetstream, but this project also fell through when sales failed to materialize and the parent company closed its doors. As recently as 1978 there were hopes on the part of Scottish Aviation of the U.K. to resume Jetstream production with Northwest Industries again to be a subcontracting partner.

Another venture into light aircraft during this period resulted in a sole four-seater called the Cheetah. It had been designed and built by Dave Saunders, an ex-Avro engineer. The aircraft operated for a time in 1964, but soon faded from the scene.

Another offshoot of the Arrow program was headed by Peter R. Payne, an engineer who had worked at Avro on a rotating wing project. For a year-and-a-half prior to the company folding, two dozen engineers had been engaged in this study. After February, 1959, he and a handful of others decided to pursue the practical application of their theory. Finances were arranged and the new firm, Avian Industries, was formed.

Work immediately went ahead to design and build a small gyroplane, the Avian 2/180. As a relatively inexpensive two-to-three-seat aircraft, it was aimed at the personal plane market. It was to be easy to fly, and have a speed of 150 mph.

Within seven months of start up, the prototype was ready for testing. Through 1959-1960 many hours were spent evaluating various rotor and propeller designs. During this phase, numerous short hops were made. On one of these, CF-LKF-X, the prototype, was involved in a mishap which seriously injured the test pilot.

In October, the following year, the first sustained flight was logged at Kitchener airport. Eventually, six Avians were built, the last of which, CF-JTO, represented the refined production model. In November 1968, the Avian received its certification from the Department of Transport. The following June, after tests at Hot Springs, Virginia, it was certified by the FAA in the United States. Coinciding with this event, unfortunately, were financial difficulties. These led to the demise of Avian in December, 1969. Avian's rights and assets were taken over by a party in Listowel, Ontario, with hopes of someday reviving the project.

The Industry Today: Twin Otter and Buffalo

Canada's aircraft industry is today at its technological peak, with products like the Challenger, Dash 7, reconnaissance drones, flight simulators, advanced avionics and even satellites being manufactured.

At de Havilland production continues of two well-known types. The Twin Otter has been a perennial seller around the world since 1966. To date over 680 have been sold to customers in over 70 countries. Several original customers have reordered the Twin Otter, probably the best indication of its success.

Widerøe's, Norway's oldest commercial flying operation, purchased Otters in the fifties, and was an early Twin Otter customer. In 1978 it ordered its sixteenth Twin Otter for use on its system of 33 stops. Stages along the system range from 23-130 miles. Widerøe's fleet connects Norway's remote Arctic communities and provides them with access to the rest of the country. In 1977 Widerøe achieved a 97 per cent dispatch reliability for 60 561 Twin Otter flights.

Elsewhere the Twin Otter operates as a feederliner and air taxi. In the U.S. it serves with commuter airlines like AeroMech, Metro, Pilgrim, Rocky Mountain, Seaplane Shuttle, and Suburban. Other such operators range from Norontair in Ontario to Southwest Air Lines in Japan and Air Volta in West Africa. Air Volta uses a Twin Otter to link Ouagadougou and Bobo-Diaulasso. In Venezuela Aeropostal's six Twin Otters fly throughout the isolated southern interior where terrain ranges from floodplain to mountains. Nine Twin Otters fly with Burma Airways, having replaced DC-3s on domestic routes; and in Nepal, they have helped solve air transportation problems in that remote and rugged country.

The Twin Otter is also at home in the Canadian Arctic, Greenland, and Antarctica. Canadian operators in the far north include Wardair, Bradley Air Services, Lambair, Ken Borek Air, Austin Airways, the RCMP and the Canadian Forces. In Antarctica, Twin Otters fly with the British Antarctic Survey. Of this operation, Chief Pilot Giles Kershaw has noted, "The whole

CF-PSM, the prototype de Havilland Turbo Beaver. This update on the standard Beaver first flew December 30, 1963 and was de Havilland's first production type fitted with the famous PT6 engine. PSM is seen fitted with amphibious floats taxiing at Toronto International Airport in its white and red livery. Sixty Turbo Beavers were built, with the major customer being the Ontario Provincial Air Service.

Larry Milberry

operation depends on the ability of the Twin Otters to fly into very small areas—often landing uphill and taking off downhill. Landing and takeoff runs are highly variable on skis, depending on the condition of the snow surface, but with headwinds of 40 knots, my experience is that the Twin Otter's STOL performance will produce a landing roll of no more than 15 yards — virtually no forward progress at all!''

In 1978 a breakthrough was made when three Twin Otters were delivered to the Peoples Republic of China. These aircraft were purchased for use by the China Geological Survey Co. Prior to this, the Twin Otter had proven itself as a viable aero survey aircraft with operators such as INCO. Another specially equipped Twin Otter was delivered to Greenlandair in 1978. This aircraft is fitted with Canadian manufactured search and navigation systems plus long range fuel tanks that permit maritime reconnaissance missions as long as 10 hours.

Having been around for so many years the Twin Otter by now has produced many a veteran in the cockpit. One Canadian expert is Paul Regan, a Captain with Norontair. Paul has over 8000 hours on Twin Otters!

Although its first flight dates to April 9, 1964, the de Havilland Buffalo continues in production. Ninety-four were completed or on order to mid 1978, at which time de Havilland was committed to build up to aircraft number 126 by the end of 1981. Primarily a military transport, the Buffalo operates in Canada, Peru, Brazil, Ecuador, and such African states as Zaire, Kenya, Tanzania, and Togo. It is also found in the Middle East where it is in service with the air arms of Sudan, Abu Dhabi, and Oman.

Even though it dates to the early sixties, the Twin Otter is still much in demand by operators around the world. Over 680 have been sold to date. The production rate through 1979 was five aircraft per month. The Twin Otters of the Canadian Forces, three of which are seen here, serve mainly in the search and rescue role. De Havilland's seven post-war designs have all become internationally famous, including the new Dash 7.

De Havilland Aircraft of Canada (35343)

The Dash 7

Thirty years of specializing in STOL designs has resulted in de Havilland's ultimate achievement, the Dash 7. This is a four-engine, 50 passenger interurban and general purpose STOL airliner. It has been designed to particular environmental and market specifications and features the most current STOL technology. This includes a wing trailing edge 80 per cent covered by flap, spoilers, and a high T-tail that leaves the elevator clear of flap downwash.

The factor of four engines increases safety in event of engine failure at a critical point. It also means that power is moved down the wing, away from the cabin, thus increasing passenger comfort. The low RPM's required in the combination PT6A-50 engines/Hamilton Standard propellers is also a key noise abatement factor, as the propeller tip speed is low. Also contributing to quiet is the position of exhaust stacks which duct exhaust over the wing. The result of such technology is the world's quietest commercial airliner.

Besides contributing to a quieter environment, the Dash 7 by its STOL nature points the way towards smaller airports, hence to land conservation. It can land to a full stop from 35 feet in a distance of 1300 feet. A medium-sized commercial jetliner requires at least 5000 feet. Besides being inherently quiet, the Canadian designed and built PT6A-50 engine is known for its fuel economy, and low level of pollution emission.

The Dash 7 first flew on March 27, 1975, with test pilots R.H. (Bob) Fowler and A.W. (Mick) Saunders at the controls. Between that point and Canadian/U.S. certification on April 15, 1977, two Dash 7's logged some 1700 hours of test flight. In late 1977 Rocky Mountain Airlines of Denver became the first customer to accept the new type. It acquired the Dash 7 mainly to serve the ski trade. Its first Dash 7 began flying to resorts like Vail, Aspen, and Steamboat Springs, and in January 1978, it joined the company's busy fleet of Twin Otters. For its first year of service Rocky Mountain's first Dash 7 completed 4250 flights and logged 3100 hours for a 98.5 per cent dispatch reliability rate.

Other early sales of the new STOL airliner were to Grønlandsfly, Emirates Air Service of Abu Dhabi, Spantax of Spain, Wardair, the Canadian Forces, and Canadian Coast Guard. The Emirates' Dash 7 is for use resupplying petroleum operations on Das Island in the Arabian Gulf. Spantax now operates between Malaga on Spain's south shore and Melilla, Morocco.

Wardair's two aircraft are a convertable passenger/freight version equipped

De Havilland's two well-known test pilots, **Bob Fowler (left) and Mick Saunders.**
R.H. Fowler and A.W. Saunders

with a large cargo door. The first of these was handed over to Wardair May 23, 1978. The Air Transport Committee has approved the operation of this aircraft from Yellowknife as a direct replacement for the Bristol Freighter type which Wardair had operated for many years until the crash of the last one at Hay River in November, 1977. The conclusion of the ATC concerning Wardair's application to operate the Dash 7 read, "The Committee is satisfied that the Dash 7 as a replacement for the Bristol Freighter can provide adequate freight carrying capability and much improved passenger service and would represent the first use by a Canadian air carrier of this innovative Canadian aircraft type."

The Canadian Forces Dash 7's are for use with NATO in Europe, while the Coast Guard ones are for such tasks as offshore pollution monitoring and enforcement of the 200 mile economic limit along Canada's shores.

By early 1979 further Dash 7 orders had been announced. Time Air of Lethbridge, Alberta ordered two for use on its Alberta feederline system. Other customers included Ransome of Philadelphia, Air Wisconsin of Appleton, Wis., Golden West of Los Angeles and Air Pacific of San Francisco. Break even point for the Dash 7 is 200 aircraft. De Havilland anticipates a market for at least 250.

Canadair: Water Bomber to Challenger

At Canadair, activities slowed to a minimum after the CF-104 and CF-5 production contracts had run out. For several years the only aircraft being built there was the CL-215 water bomber, though other projects were under way nonetheless. As a contractor for the Avro Arrow weapons system, Canadair had

developed considerable missile expertise. After the Arrow fell through, Canadair set about developing a unique missile system. The result was the CL-89 Surveillance Drone System, the world's first such system to become operational. This recoverable missile performs the same role as the traditional reconnaissance aircraft, and now serves with the military forces of Canada, Britain, France, and West Germany. The CL-89 flies at up to 470 mph between 1000-4000 feet with a 75-mile range. It is recovered by parachute and upon touchdown is protected by air bags. The CL-227, a peanut-shaped drone with counter rotating propellers, is the latest reconnaissance vehicle produced by Canadair.

Canadair has also participated as a subcontractor manufacturing components for such aircraft as the Boeing 747 SP, F-15 Eagle, F-111 and P-3C/CP-140 Aurora maritime patrol aircraft. But its major current activity centres on the CL-600 Challenger. This aircraft evolved from a concept developed by William Lear. Announcement of the go-ahead by Canadair to build the Challenger was made in April, 1976 and roll out of the first machine occurred May 28, 1978 — from concept to reality in a brief two years!

The Challenger embodies the latest in aeronautical engineering and many customer-appealing features. These range from a revolutionary airfoil which reduces drag and increases lift to a wide-body format to a new generation of turbofan engines. The Challenger has intercontinental range and will cruise at Mach .8 at up to 49 000 feet. It meets all United States FAA requirements for design, safety, and noise limits.

The Challenger is primarily intended as a corporate/executive aircraft, but may be configured for high density for up to 30 passengers. Federal Express of Memphis has shown interest in 25 stretched Challengers as package freighters to replace its fleet of Falcons. First flight of the Challenger occurred from Cartierville

Wheels down, the first Dash 7 overflies Toronto Island Airport. The 50-passenger STOL aircraft is equally at home here, at more complex airports, or on ice strips in the Arctic. In the de Havilland tradition, the Dash 7 has already found buyers in the North—Wardair in Canada, Grønlandsfly in Greenland, and Widerøe's in Norway.

De Havilland Aircraft of Canada Ltd.

Launching a CL-89 Airborne Surveillance Drone. This missile has been operational since 1972 and to mid-1978 over 500 had been delivered to five nations.

Canadair Ltd.

November 8, 1978, with test pilots Doug Adkins and Norm Ronaasen aboard. On this occasion the aircraft flew to 9500 feet and landed after 50 minutes aloft. The second flight followed that afternoon and lasted 45 minutes. After 36 hours of flying, the Challenger flight test program was moved to Canadair's facility in the Mojave desert in California. To late 1978 five developmental Challengers had been completed including two non-flying ones for static and fatigue testing. Aircraft No. 6 will be the first Challenger to be delivered to a customer and a production rate of

◀ Mating of the wing and fuselage of the first Canadair Challenger. This took place on May 8, 1978. The person in the wheelchair is Harry Halton, who heads the Challenger program.

Canadair Ltd.

CF-LOL, the sixth ST-27 conversion, photographed at St. Andrews, Manitoba, departing for Island Lake in the northern part of the province. During its career as a Heron, LOL served in Norway, Denmark, and Britain.

Larry Milberry

seven units per month is anticipated for 1980. To early 1979, over 100 Challengers had been sold including 63 to the United States and 32 to Saudi Arabia.

Meanwhile, production of the CL-215 continued at Canadair to mid 1978. By that time 65 aircraft had been built and 52 sold. The most recent deliveries had been two aircraft to the Royal Thai Navy for transport and SAR duties, and two to Venezuela.

Saunders Aircraft

There have also been recent attempts by smaller manufacturers to launch their ideas in Canada. Saunders Aircraft came into being in May, 1968 with its proposal for a commuter aircraft. The intention was to redesign the de Havilland Heron and reengine it with two PT6A-34 engines.

At first Saunders operated from Dorval. From there the prototype made its first flight on May 29, 1969. This aircraft was the ST-27. Soon afterwards, the Saunders operation relocated at Gimli, Manitoba. New financing was arranged through the Manitoba Development Corporation.

Canadian type approval for the ST-27 was granted on June 28, 1971. Aerolineas Centrales de Colombia became the first customer, receiving three aircraft on lease. Sales, however, were slow to materialize. Token aircraft were acquired in Canada by St. Andrews Airways, Otonabee Airways, Bayview Air Service, and On Air.

With experience gained converting Herons and cash provided from initial sales and government grants, Saunders began developing an improved aircraft, the ST-27B. In late 1973 the Federal government invested almost a million dollars in this project. The new aircraft, redesignated the ST-28, flew on July 17, 1974, but before it could be certified, time ran out. With several ST-27's still unsold and sales prospects not brightening, the Manitoba

◀ The first Canadair Challenger during one of its early test flights. Trailing behind is the ever-present chase plane, a CL-41. The Challenger flight test program was conducted through 1979 at Canadair's test facility at Mojave, California.

Canadair Ltd.

The prototype Trident Trigull at the 1976 Abbotsford International Air Show where it was demonstrated by test pilot Norm Ronaasen.

Larry Milberry

government pulled out of the venture. It had lost $37 million on the gamble. Coinciding with its takeover of de Havilland, the federal government also lost interest in Saunders, and the plant closed its doors on December 31, 1975. In all, Saunders had converted 13 Herons as ST-27's and built three ST-28 airframes, one for destructive testing and two for flight test.

The Saunders operation was offered for sale but interest was limited. Finally, in the spring of 1979 most remaining aircraft, stores, and tools were acquired by Otonabee Airways of Peterborough, Ontario.

The Trident Trigull

The Trident Trigull is the dream of David Hazelwood of Vancouver. It is an attractive high performance amphibian reminiscent of the Republic Seabee in appearance. In the early seventies, Hazelwood was able to arrange financing to build a prototype. This aircraft, CF-TRI-X, was first flown by Paul Hartman on August 5, 1973. It was found to be a good performer, and on one flight, Hartman inadvertently exceeded a world altitude record for light single-engine amphibians. During flutter tests he edged the Trigull past 25 000 feet.

The Trigull was certified in 1977 but the company faced increasing financial woes. Venture capital and government support were scarce and in late 1977 most staff were laid off. Six months later, however, the picture was bright again. The federal government agreed to make $6 million available to Trident and Hazelwood, with $10 000 deposits on 43 aircraft, was able to announce that his Sidney, B.C., plant would go into production with first delivery slated for early 1980. The Trigull was initially offered at $105 000 per unit, with 250 sales required to break even. Other support for the Trigull has come from the B.C. government, as well as from Grumman in the United States.

Another attempt to produce light aircraft in Canada during the seventies was one by a group of businessmen interested in

One of the world famous Zenith homebuilts, in this case a Tri-Z CH300 piloted by Red Morris. This is the aircraft in which Red flew across Canada non-stop on July 1-2, 1978.

Larry Milberry

manufacturing the Teal amphibian. A lack of financing doomed the venture and the Teal eventually entered production at a plant in Florida.

The Zenith: Trans-Canada Winner

The first Canadian-designed sport plane to succeed in the post World War II market is the Zenith homebuilt developed by Chris Heintz, who had worked in France on the Robin light plane then come to Canada. His first Canadian aircraft, C-FEYC, flew in June, 1973 and since then the Zenith has become very popular. Within five years, over 500 Zenith kits and sets of plans had been sold to homebuilders in 15 countries. The Zenith comes as a one- or two-place aircraft powered by engines ranging from 55 hp to 180 hp. A four-seat production model is planned by Heintz who operates from Richmond Hill, Ontario.

On July 1-2, 1978, pilot Red Morris flew non-stop from Vancouver to Halifax in a Zenith. This was the first official non-stop, non-refuelled flight across Canada and the first non-stop flight since a North Star flew between the same points in 1949. Time for the Zenith's flight was 22 hours, 43 minutes, 40 seconds.

The Cox Turbo Otter

A recent entry on the air industries scene is the Cox Turbo Otter. Ray Cox of Edmonton has developed this aircraft, a turboprop version of the DHC-3 Otter. Ray has a long history in Canadian aviation, primarily as an expert in the recovery of downed aircraft in particularly inaccessible areas. His recoveries have included such large aircraft as the DC-3, DC-4, and Hercules. His latest venture is his conversion of the Otter to take the PT6A-27, the same engine as powers the Twin Otter. Ray foresees a market for 100 of these conversions. Compared to the standard Otter, the $250 000 Turbo Otter offers increased speed, range, payload, and aircraft life as well as updated systems. The prototype made its first flight September 26, 1978, piloted by Jerry Westphal.

Diversification

Canada's aerospace industry produces a wide range of aircraft and space technology support products. These vary from engines to flight data recorders, ELT's, flight simulators, space vehicle components, and floats such as those used on the Twin Otter.

McDonnell Douglas continues work

The ex-Air Canada Viscount used as a flying test bed in development of the PT6A-50 engine which powers the de Havilland Dash 7.

Pratt and Whitney Aircraft of Canada Ltd.

on DC-9 and DC-10 wing and tail sections. Other major contractors include Boeing of Canada in Arnprior making components for Boeing jetliners and helicopters, and Fleet Industries in Fort Erie working on 707, 747, Buffalo, Twin Otter, DC-9, L-1011, A-4, and A-6 components. Fleet also operates a hovercraft and a sonar division. Northwest Industries in Edmonton builds L-1011 components and provides a major overhaul facility for large civil and military aircraft. The industry is beginning to benefit from orders for components to be used in building the Lockheed CP-140 Aurora maritime patrol aircraft and will also participate in contracts associated with the Canadian Forces' NFA (New Fighter Aircraft). In early 1979, Canadair announced a big contract to build the rear fuselage section for the Boeing 767 airliner.

The Orenda Division of Hawker Siddeley Canada Ltd. and Pratt and Whitney Aircraft of Canada Ltd. continue the manufacture, development, and overhaul of turbine engines. Orenda dates to the late forties since which time it has produced thousands of turbine engines

primarily for the CF-100, CF-105, F-86, CF-104, CL-41, and CF-5.

Pratt and Whitney's most famous product is the PT6A engine series, developed in the late fifties when it became apparent that the piston engine would soon be surpassed technologically. The first PT6A was run in February, 1960. Certificate approval was granted December 31, 1963; the engine's break into the marketplace came when Beech Aircraft selected it to power the King Air. The King Air is the turbine-powered evolution of the Queen Air, but in its conceptual stage it was the subject of controversy within Beech. This was settled by Mrs. Beech who intuitively ordered the go-ahead for the King Air. It was a momentous decision both for Beech and Pratt and Whitney, the latter was at the time quite desperate to find an airplane to hang its new engine on.

Today the PT6A is the world's most popular and thoroughly proven aircraft powerplant in its class. It has found over 120 applications in aircraft, ships, trains, hovercraft, and other vehicles. To 1977 it has accumulated over 25 000 000 flying hours. These have been logged by 12 000 engines in 4000 aircraft in some 100 countries. The basic engine is currently available in 26 versions with power outputs ranging from 550 shp to 1970 shp.

Some of the inherent features of the PT6A series include its ease of installation and maintenance, low noise output, relative light weight, anti-icing certification, built-in protection from foreign object damage, and low infrared signature. The latter is an important factor in military aircraft as it reduces their vulnerability to heat-seeking missiles. Engine reliability is very high, with an in-flight shut down ratio of 1:100 000 flying hours. Time between overhauls is also high, currently at 3500 hours for several versions.

Today the PT6A powers such aircraft as the Turbo Beaver, Twin Otter, Dash 7, Beech 99, Short SD3-30, Pilatus Turbo Porter, Bell 212, and S-58T. Two unique new PT6A-powered aircraft are the Hustler 400 executive plane and the three-engine DC-3 conversion built by Jack Conroy of California. As to the King Air, there are currently some 2000 in service around the world.

Another important engine designed and built by Pratt and Whitney is the JT15D turbofan. The first of these ran in September, 1967 and the first ones were delivered to Cessna in August, 1969 for use

in the Cessna Citation bizjet. The JT15D now powers some 400 Citations, and has been chosen to power the Aerospatiale Corvette. Research, development, and production of turbine engines employ over 5000 people at Pratt and Whitney's Longueuil and St. Hubert facilities. Engine development alone has resulted in over 160 000 hours of running time.

Another specialized product of Canada's aerospace industry is the flight simulator. CAE Electronics in Montreal is a world leader in this sophisticated form of technology. By now, the world's major airlines are committed to programs wherein 100 per cent of pilot training will be done on simulators. The rationale behind this philosophy is straightforward: simulators cost much less than real aircraft. They enable realistic training without tying up aircraft which in pre-simulator days meant lost revenue. Training is completely safe. Dangerous manoeuvres and emergency procedures may be executed in total realism. The simulator helps to decrease air traffic, and air and noise pollution. As well, utilization up to 20 hours daily is possible.

The simulator is a computer complex capable of processing a million instructions per second. It simulates such factors as atmospheric conditions with a full range of normal and abnormal factors; the ground

environment; navigation and radio aids. It has a fully instrumented and operational flight deck, and simulates motion; out-of-the-window visual cues; aircraft pressurization; and normal cockpit sounds. As the trainee "flies" as assigned program, his/her proficiency may be assessed through the system's complex instructor's station.

CAE Industries has produced simulators for civil and military customers. Included are many Canadian and foreign airlines. KLM has CAE simulators for the DC-8, DC-9, DC-10, 747, and F.28. Recent Canadian simulators have been for the Chinook helicopter, Aurora patrol plane, and Challenger executive jet.

Another type of specialized aviation service is provided by Innotech Aviation Ltd., formerly Timmins Aviation. Innotech operates a trans-Canada network of aircraft service centres which cater to general aviation; but it also runs an operation in Montreal which specializes in installing avionics and aircraft interiors. The first Timmins executive aircraft conversion was done in 1957 when the Lockheed 18, CF-TCV, was completed. It was delivered as a seven-passenger VIP plane to Noranda Mines at Malton. Since then hundreds of corporate aircraft have passed through the Timmins/Innotech facility, including over 50 H.S. 125's.

Boeing 747 and 727 flight simulators manufactured for CP Air by CAE Electronics Ltd., Montreal.

CAE Industries Ltd. (1090)

Corporate and Government Aviation

The airplane is today recognized as an efficient and economical means of expediting business. In Canada, all sorts of aircraft are used for this, from the 1946 Aeronca used by Al's Water Wells of Lacombe, Alberta, to the Gulfstream II's flown by big oil and mining companies. Aircraft price tags range from $6000 to $6 000 000.

The First Corporate Aircraft

Canada's first corporate-owned aircraft date back to the immediate post World War I years, when forestry interests in Quebec procured aircraft for experimental patrol work. The first to enter service were two war surplus HS-2L's. In June 1919,

Stuart Graham and his engineer, William Kahre with Mrs. Graham as passenger, ferried these aircraft from Dartmouth to Lac à la Tortue in Quebec. The following season they were placed in service on forestry duties. Other firms in the region soon realized the effectiveness of airplanes and established their own aerial services. Price Brothers purchased a Martinsyde for patrol work out of Chicoutimi; the Ontario Paper Co. based an HS-2L at Franquelin Bay on the Lower St. Lawrence. These pioneer efforts launched the airplane on a career in forestry work that was to continue and develop without interruption to the present.

Of the early examples of the airplane

used in a corporate role, that of Imperial Oil, and *Vic* and *Rene* is the best known. From such adventuresome experiments, the airplane gained in popularity, especially in natural resource development. It gave wings to prospectors, forever transforming the approach to prospecting and mining. Men, equipment, and supplies could now be moved about faster and farther than ever before. Previously inaccessible regions of the Canadian Shield were suddenly opened up. Famous names such as Colonel McAlpine, Harry Oakes, Lord Beaverbrook, W.M. Archibald, and Gilbert Labine became associated with this new approach to mineral development in Canada. Archibald, manager of Consolidated Mining and Smelting, was awarded the 1935 McKee Trophy for his contributions in this field.

Throughout the thirties, other businesses began to make use of the airplane in day to day affairs. People such as construction and mining magnate Harry

One of Canada's earliest corporate aircraft was this ex-U.S. Navy HS-2L, seen here being launched at Dartmouth late in World War I. It was later acquired by the St. Maurice Forestry Protective Association, a consortium of forestry companies in Quebec. This and a similar aircraft were ferried from Dartmouth to Lac à la Tortue near Grand 'Mère in June 1919 and initially operated on patrols still in military markings. 1876 was registered as G-CAAC in June 1920. It crashed in Northern Ontario in September 1922. Forty-seven years later its remains were salvaged for the National Aeronautical Collection and are now on display at Rockcliffe.
Aviation and Space Division, National Museum of Science and Technology (2703)

CF-BBG, the de Havilland Rapide purchased by the *Globe and Mail* in June 1937, and intended to keep the paper in touch with fast moving changes in the mining industry. After a northern tour, BBG returned to Toronto where on August 21 it was burned out in a fire during refuelling.

Via F. W. Hotson

McLean, newspaper publisher George McCullough, and John David Eaton of retail merchandising fame became associated with aviation.

World War II curtailed business flying to a degree. Some aircraft, such as J.P. Bickell's Goose, and the Eatons' Beech 18 were impressed by or donated to the RCAF. After the war, business flying resumed and was encouraged by the availability of war surplus aircraft, some of which were suitable for corporate service. Thus did aircraft like the Anson V find work with companies like Goodyear Tire and Rubber. These ex-military aircraft filled an important gap during a period when the aircraft industry was not yet producing aircraft for the express needs of business.

Expansion After World War II

Another important source of corporate aircraft after the war was TCA and CPA. In 1946 these airlines began to modernize. Their fleets of older Lockheeds came onto the used plane market. Of these, the Lockheed 18 Lodestar was to become the first of Canada's popularly used executive planes. By the early fifties the Lodestar was being flown by such companies as B.A. Oil, Canada Packers, Imperial Oil, Mannix, Massey-Harris, and Noranda Mines.

Typical of these was CF-TDG. After logging 11 000 hours with TCA, it was acquired by Massey-Harris in 1947. It was converted to a nine-passenger executive plane and, as the years went by, was progressively updated by companies that specialized in executive conversions. CF-TDG served its owners until 1965, flying 8000 hours on top of its original airline time.

During this same period, the DC-3 became Canada's most popular large executive aircraft. Abitibi Paper, Algoma Steel, Avro Aircraft, the T. Eaton Co., Ford Motor Co., Imperial Oil, K.C. Irving and Shell Oil were some of the many firms that operated it. Also during this time, the Beech E18, de Havilland Dove and Grumman Mallard were introduced. The Convair 240/440, de Havilland Heron and Lockheed Ventura were other types operated by Canadian firms during the fifties. For lighter requirements, the Aero Commander, Beech Travel Air, Cessna 310, and Piper Apache became popular business aircraft.

Corporate Flying Today

An important development in business aviation came in 1958 with the introduction of the Grumman Gulfstream, a fast modern turboprop designed expressly for corporate use. The first of these to come to Canada was Home Oil's CF-L00 in 1960. The Gulfstream was both the herald of things to come and of things to go; for it signalled the beginning of the end of the older generation of aircraft. Massey-Ferguson, J.F. Crothers, Imperial Oil and Algoma Steel were soon phasing out older types in favour of the Gulfstream.

Another milestone occurred in 1962 when the first corporate jet came to Canada. This was a Lockheed Jetstar owned by the T. Eaton Co. Two years later, Canada Packers became Canada's first owner of the H.S. 125. Before long, a whole range of bizjets was on the market — Lears, Falcons, Sabreliners, Jet Commanders, Gulfstream II's and Citations.

The new generation of aircraft introduced by the Gulfstream better suited the growing needs of Canadian business. Personnel could now be transported twice as fast as they had been in the zippiest of the older planes. With their speed, range, sophisticated avionics, and comfort, the jets could keep pace with commercial airliners and overfly bad weather which would normally ground the DC-3's and

Lodestars. Such capability became increasingly important as corporations expanded their interests nationally and internationally. Convenience and time saved through the use of private jets today seems to justify the high costs they incur.

There are now over 100 corporate jets in Canada. Over 30 are H.S. 125's. Even in their heyday as corporate aircraft the DC-3 or Lodestar never numbered so many. Meanwhile, general aviation awaits the first delivery of a Canadair Challenger to a Canadian corporation. This will usher in the latest era in executive jet travel.

Transport Canada

Government aviation has been important in Canada since the early twenties. At the federal government level today a large fleet of fixed and rotary wing aircraft is operated. Most belong to Transport Canada and include the Beaver, Baron, Queen Air, King Air, Twin Otter, DC-3, Jetstar, Viscount, and Gulfstream II. These are used on a variety of tasks — calibration of airport approach aids, airways development, evaluation of avionics, transportation of Ministry personnel and of VIP's, training of Ministry flight crew, etc.

An important service provided by Transport Canada is accident investigation. Through 1977 its teams investigated 718 accidents. These included minor incidents, but also numerous serious ones and involved many civil types from homebuilts, to a DC-8 which overshot the runway at Gander on October 3.

Investigations are sometimes quick and straight forward, but in the case of serious accidents, often take months of work to finalize. Accident causes vary widely and include many human, natural, and technical factors as shown by this sampling taken from accident reports over a period of years:

"Fuel which was leaking from a fitting in the carburetor became ignited." (Stinson Reliant, CF-BGJ)

"Fatigue failure of the front eyebolt on the left wing strut." (Norseman, CF-BHW)

"The pilot encountered radio navigation and weather difficulties and became lost. Unable to obtain emergency

assistance he ran out of fuel after four hours but successfully ditched the aircraft on a large lake." (DC-3, C-GLUC)

"Pilot bailed out when controls failed." (Duster, C-GSPD)

"Downdraft during flight over hazardous terrain at a low altitude and airspeed." (Helio Courier, CF-CFL)

"Attempted flight by an unqualified pilot." (Anson, CF-GML)

"The pilot did not ensure that the undercarriage was in the fully down and locked position prior to landing." (C-46E, CF-HTI)

"The pilot failed to observe power lines in time to avoid collision with them." (Avenger, CF-MSX)

"Failed to compensate for wind and to abandon takeoff." (Canso, CF-OFJ)

The Northland being a vast region of lakes and rivers, Canadian corporations have historically favoured amphibious aircraft. Here is the first Grumman Widgeon brought to Canada. It was purchased in 1942 by J.P. Bickell of McIntyre Mines. A light six-passenger aircraft, it was ideal for business and pleasure trips in the North. Posing beside BVN are pilot Don Murray and engineer Walter Duncan. After 25 years in Canada and nine different owners, BVN was exported to the U.S. in 1967.

Via Don Murray

Canada Packers' Lodestar running up at Malton, February 5, 1961. The company later used a Learstar, then a H.S.125 in its aviation operation. CF-CPK was originally a CPA airliner.

Larry Milberry

Since the fifties, Canadian Comstock has operated this de Havilland Heron, a Douglas A-26 and a Jet Commander for executive air transportation. The Heron and its smaller relative, the Dove, were well known on the corporate aviation scene, but had all been replaced by the mid sixties. CF-HLI was photographed at Malton in 1959.

Larry Milberry

One of the world's most famous light twins, the Beech 18. Since the first of these came to Canada in 1937, hundreds have operated here as airliners, bush planes, corporate aircraft, and military trainers and transports. The Beech E18 became one of the popular corporate types of the fifties and sixties, this example belonging to the Ford Motor Co.

Larry Milberry

In 1962 Eaton's of Canada purchased this Lockheed Jet Star to replace its DC-3. This was the first corporate jet to be owned in Canada, and is still in service today with the Transport Canada fleet.

Jack McNulty

The Ontario Paper Company's H.S. 125. This type is the most widely used corporate jet in Canada.

Larry Milberry

The Department of Transport's Viscount 737 at Malton, August 16, 1960. After 23 years of service, it was still in use in 1978. When formed in the late thirties, the Department of Transport used such aircraft as the Stearman 4C, Beech D-17S and Lockheed 10. Currently it operates the Beaver, Baron, Queen Air, King Air, Twin Otter, DC-3, Viscount, Jet Star and Gulf-Stream II.

Larry Milberry

C-GTWO, a Grumman Gulfstream II operated by INCO and based at Toronto. The Gulfstream II represents the most exotic class of corporate aircraft currently operated in Canada.

Larry Milberry

"While the pilot was practicing forced landing approaches in a mountain valley, the aircraft could not out-climb the rising terrain and was intentionally stalled into trees." (Cessna 150, CF-BIJ)

"Explosion of a device which resulted in aerial disintegration." (DC-6B, CF-CUQ)

"The pilot flew into adverse weather conditions and was unable to maintain flight due to ice accretion from freezing rain." (S-55, CF-JTA)

"The cargo net fouled the tail rotor drive shaft in flight breaking the shaft and causing loss of directional control." (Hiller 12E, CF-OKC)

"While air taxiing over glassy water, the pilot allowed a float to touch the water, rolling the helicopter over." (Bell 206, CF-GEM)

"The helicopter was parked on a railroad line parallel to the tracks and was struck by a train." (Bell 206B, CF-QOI)

Other Federal Activities

Other federal agencies also use aircraft. The Royal Canadian Mounted Police Air Division was formed in 1937 with the acquisition of four Rapides. Since then it has used such types as the Cornell, Beaver, Otter, Beech 18, Turbo Beaver, and King Air. The Twin Otter is the basis of the current fleet. The RCMP also operates helicopters, with Bell Jet Rangers and a 212 having been added in the seventies. In 1977 its fleet numbered 27 aircraft which through that fiscal year logged 19 631 hours.

Since the early fifties the Canadian Coast Guard has maintained a fleet of helicopters. These are today used aboard icebreakers and in maintaining coastal navigation aids and resupplying lighthouses. Presently, Bell 47G-2's, Jet Rangers, Bell 212's, Alouette III's and an S-61N are in service coast-wise and along the Great Lakes-St. Lawrence Seaway.

The Canada Centre for Remote Sensing flies Dakotas, a Convair 580, and a Falcon. It is a branch of Energy, Mines, and Resources which has operated its own Skyvan on geophysical research since 1968. Another Ottawa-based federal government organization is the National Aeronautical Establishment, a division of the National Research Council. The NAE uses aircraft like the T-33, Convair 580 and Bell 205A on research projects. Environment Canada has two Electras on contract from Nordair and used in ice reconnaissance.

Provincial Aviation

The provinces became interested in aviation in the post World War I era mainly for forest management purposes. In 1924 the first provincial air service was formed by Ontario. Manitoba followed in 1932. HS-2L's, Gipsy Moths and Vedettes were the early workhorses used by these two provinces. Today most provinces operate their own aircraft. In Ontario, the Ministry of Natural Resources flies mainly

Giff Swartman, an early flier with the Ontario Provincial Air Service, stands by an HS-2L equipped with a large aerial camera. This type of camera was used in oblique photography. Early use of aircraft by the Ontario and Manitoba governments quickly proved their value in natural resource-oriented tasks.

Ontario Ministry of Natural Resources

During the early fifties, the Beaver and Otter became the backbone of the OPAS, replacing a fleet of pre World War II aircraft. Other provinces also purchased Beavers, though in Manitoba and Saskatchewan, the Fairchild 82, Husky, and Norseman persisted for some years longer. CF-ODL, the fifteenth production Otter, is shown here at Swastika, Ontario, with an OPAS Beaver landing in the background. Float-mounted water bombing tanks lie on the dock. ODL was still with the OPAS in 1979, though all but one Beaver have been sold off. In 1977 the OPAS purchased and rebuilt seven additional Otters for work in the North.

Ontario Ministry of Natural Resources

Turbo Beavers, Otters, Twin Otters and Trackers on such tasks as fire-fighting, wildlife counting, fish stocking, and fish and game regulation.

Ontario uses aircraft in other roles. Ontario Hydro has a fleet of helicopters. It pioneered in the early fifties using Bell 47's in line patrol and later acquired an S-55 to use in erecting power transmission lines. This was replaced by an S-58, which in turn was updated to S-58T standards. The 1978 fleet included Bell 47's, Jet Rangers, a Hughes 369, and two S-58T's.

The Ontario Centre of Remote Sensing has used a Piper Aztec on a variety of research projects. These have included the detection of forest tracts affected by fungus disease, bud worm infestation and industrial pollution; shoreline erosion studies; and the infrared mapping of wildlife. Otherwise in 1978, the Ontario Provincial Police was operating two Bell Jet Rangers, a Turbo Beaver and an Otter; while a Bell 212 was flying as an air ambulance for the Ontario Ministry of Health.

A medical evacuation being conducted by a Norseman of Saskatchewan Government Airways, July 1946.
Aviation and Space Division, National Museum of Science and Technology (5604)

Quebec maintains Canada's largest fleet of provincially-owned water bombers — 15 Canadair CL-215's and six Cansos. To 1977 it also owned a Beaver, two F-27's, a DC-3, several helicopters, and an H.S. 125 for VIP requirements. The Quebec Provincial Police also operates Jet Rangers.

In the West, Manitoba operates such types as the Beaver, Turbo Beaver, and CL-215. Saskatchewan's fleet includes six Trackers, and Alberta's a DC-3, five light twins, and six light helicopters. Two King Airs in service are primarily for personnel transport; a Queen Air for photo work; a Baron and Skymaster for fire patrol and miscellaneous duties; and the helicopters for fire suppression, game control, servicing look-out towers, and survey work. The DC-3 was initially acquired to transport fire-fighting crews and to supply their camps.

British Columbia to date operates Beech 18's, Beech Super King Air's, and Cessna Citations. Ambulance service is their prime function.

The Alberta Hail Project is an example of specialized use of aircraft by provincial governments. Begun in 1974 as a five-year study, it is run by the Alberta Weather Modification Board. Its main objectives are hailstorm research and cloud seeding to develop hailstorm damage control technology for Alberta farmers. During 1978 a fleet of seven aircraft based at Red Deer was used in seeding certain townships while others were not seeded for comparative purposes. Aircraft employed were two Cessna 310's, three Cessna 320's, one Cessna 411 and one Aztec, these being capable of attaining 25 000 feet. The aircraft carry batteries of flares which upon ignition emit silver iodide particles which nucleate the hail-forming process. Ideally, this infusion of artificial nuclei will lead to the formation of countless small hailstones which may melt during their fall-time, or cause minimal damage even if they do reach the gound.

Saskatchewan has operated an air ambulance service since 1947. This provides patients in outlying areas with rapid transportation to urban medical centres when emergencies arise. For the year beginning March 31, 1976, the service operated 420 flights, and carried 447 patients, for a round trip average of 401.2 miles. A Piper Navajo was the primary aircraft used, but two Beech Barons also served as required. Since it was established, this unique Saskatchewan service has carried some 25 000 patients.

Flying for Fun

The Lohner No. 1 built in Ottawa by George Lohner in 1909-1910. The project was supported by a group of local people. In this view, the aircraft was being readied for gliding tests at Lansdowne Park on March 14, 1910. But the wind came up and blew over the Lohner before a flight could be attempted. Lohner's backers insisted on seeing the plane fly before providing money for an engine. He thus repaired it and on July 22 got airborne by being towed behind a car. Even so, no more money was forthcoming and Lohner and his airplane faded into obscurity. So ended one of Canada's early homebuilding efforts.

DND (RE 15360)

Today small single-engined aircraft make up 80 per cent of the over 22 000 civil aircraft flying in Canada. Of these the majority are either privately owned, or owned by clubs and flying schools. Otherwise, there are some 500 gliders, 100 gyroplanes, and 50 balloons on the Canadian Civil Aircraft Register. The numbers continue to climb. For 1978, 407 of the 503 new aircraft imported into Canada were single engined, further indicating the popularity of recreational flying in Canada.

How It All Began

Recreation was the original role of aviation in Canada, for entertainment was the object of the balloon artists of over a century ago. Later when people experimented with other forms of flight it was often for personal enjoyment. Thus did 14-year-old Larry Lesh build himself a glider in 1907. Towed behind a boat, he flew it over the St. Lawrence to become Canada's first glider pilot.

The same year, the Underwood brothers, John, George, and Elmer built and flew a series of kites on their farm near Stettler, Alberta. These were unmanned until they produced their ultimate design — a 42-foot elliptical wing, a sort of flying saucer. It had a 900-square foot wing area and weighed 450 pounds. The Underwoods exhibited their kite at the 1907 Stettler exhibition where it became a popular attraction.

The big kite was first flown on August 10, 1907. It went aloft, as Frank H. Ellis relates, attached to a 700-foot tether anchored to a fencepost. In what would have passed for the cockpit, the brothers placed sacks of wheat, no doubt to simulate a passenger. Manned flight was the next phase in development; one day John Underwood took off for a 15-minute flight, hovering above the ground at about 10 feet.

For their next experiments, the Underwoods rigged to their kite a 7-hp motorcycle engine, turning a four-bladed bamboo and canvas propeller. This provided enough power for taxiing about on the ground, but no more. These tests were conducted on what Ellis has designated Canada's first airstrip. This was 80 rods by 20 rods and had been expressly laid out for the flying machine.

During these pre-Silver Dart times, there were no suitable aero-engines available in Canada, indeed, in most other countries. Without such an engine, the Underwoods knew there was no chance of ever getting their machine airborne in free flight. They wrote to Glenn Curtiss in the United States for a quote on one of his engines. Curtiss obliged asking $1300 for the engine, enough to discourage the Underwoods. They decided to stick to kite

In 1917 Vancouver boat-builders James and Henry Hoffar produced this seaplane. The aircraft flew successfully but later sank when the float struck a log. The Hoffars also built a flying boat. It met an untimely end when it crashed through the roof of a Vancouver home on 1918. The seaplane pictured above had no bracing wires supporting the wings, though some have been mistakenly pencilled in!
Aviation and Space Division, National Museum of Science and Technology (2631)

flying and carried on with many more flights. On one of these, the kite accidentally crashed, ending the flying experiments of the Underwoods.

William Wallace Gibson was another aviation pioneer in Western Canada. Since he was a boy in Regina, he had been fascinated by flight. He constructed a series of flying models, including one he powered with the modified spring-loaded end of a window blind roller. This model Gibson successfully flew from a roof top in June, 1904.

In 1906, Gibson moved to British Columbia, having gone broke on a railroad building venture on the Prairies. By this time he had begun designing an aero-engine. His chief qualification on this undertaking seems to have been his earlier experience as a blacksmith. On the Coast, Gibson raised some money in a gold-mining venture and proceeded to hand-make a 4-cylinder engine, which he had

Another pre-World War I homebuilt, the Mackenzie monoplane built at Red Deer, Alberta. Due to engine problems the aircraft probably never flew. Standing by the propeller is Mr. MacKenzie. Frank Ellis, Canada's famous aviation historian, is to the right, while his friend Tom Blakely is above.

Aviation and Space Division, National Museum of Science and Technology (4976)

completed by 1908. The engine was a failure on account of excessive vibration when running. He immediately began work on a 6-cylinder engine. When completed in 1910, it was found to run well, and produce up to 60 hp. Gibson had designed and built Canada's first successful aero engine.

Now that he had an engine, Gibson began building an airplane to go with it. This was the opposite of what most pioneer aviators had done. They had generally started with a flying machine, and later worried about an engine. Before long, Gibson had come up with a design he called the Twin-Plane, which featured two 20-foot silk-covered wings, one behind the other. The position of the wings could be varied using adjustable fittings. On September 8, 1910, the Twin-Plane flew successfully from a farm near Victoria, becoming the first free flight of a Canadian-designed aircraft.

Gibson now redesigned his machine,

William W. Gibson seated in his Multiplane.

Glenbow-Alberta Institute (NA-1258-62)

using a series of long narrow wings made of solid spruce. By this time, he was running short of funds and had to sell his house in order to continue his work. A prolonged spell of wet weather had plagued the Victoria area, having an adverse effect on the glue used on the plane, so Gibson moved to the dry interior of B.C. at Kamloops.

Ever seeking to avoid publicity, Gibson didn't stay long at Kamloops, where a bothersome promoter kept trying to convince him of how the test flights could be turned into a money-making proposition. Gibson moved to a ranch near Calgary where, in August, 1911, several successful flights of his Multi-Plane were made by his assistant, Alex Jaap. On August 12, after a flight of about a mile, Jaap cracked up and wrecked the machine. By this time Gibson had spent a small fortune on his experiments and was unable to carry on designing airplanes.

A get-together of flying enthusiasts after World War I. This trio of JN-4's was seen at Comox on Vancouver Island, June 11, 1919.

Provincial Archives, Victoria, B.C. (18868)

The Underwoods, Gibson, and other aviation pioneers in pre World War I Canada were special individuals. They were the country's first aeronautical engineers, first test pilots, first home-builders, and they did it for the challenge and enjoyment it provided. They were the forerunners of those thousands of Canadians who today hold private pilot licences.

World War I curtailed the efforts of the pioneers, but by 1919 "private" flying had returned with greater vigour than ever. Now there were thousands of trained airmen in Canada, and surplus military aircraft were available at low prices. Many of these were purchased for private use. In 1919 under the auspices of the Aerial League of Canada there were occasional gatherings of two or more such aircraft, usually at some community celebration. Such were the roots of the flying club movement of later years.

The Aerial League was especially active in British Columbia in 1919. A report in the Victoria *Daily Colonist* refers to the flight taken June 6 that year by Mr. T. Temple aboard the JN-4 "Pathfinder":

"Arriving back over the aerodrome, Mr. Temple asked to be stunted, and his request was complied with. As usual, someone phoned the *Colonist* office to know if it was true the Pathfinder crashed over Fairfield, because it had been seen coming down very fast over that part of the country."

In its June 12 edition, the *Daily Colonist* reported that Miss Gwendolyn Richards and Miss Sweeney had been passengers in the Pathfinder, flown by Captains George Dixon and Ernest Hoy and that Miss Richards was the first woman to fly over Victoria. The comment is made, "At the request of Mrs. Richards [her mother], no stunting was done."

Other news reported the 52-minute flight by Lt. Robert Ridout on June 10 from Victoria to Vancouver. He crashed on landing at Vancouver but neither he nor his passenger were injured. Later that day, Ridout returned to Victoria in a borrowed aircraft and in formation with two other machines. The flight lasted one hour 14 minutes. These flights were noteworthy for their daring, as they were over open water, in wheel-equipped aircraft.

The New York-Toronto Air Race

North America's first post-war aerial extravaganza was staged in 1919. This was the New York-Toronto air race, an event conceived by Chance Vought, and co-sponsored by the American Flying Club, the Aero Club of Canada and the Canadian National Exhibition. Ten thousand dollars in cash prizes plus trophies were offered to entrants, though military fliers were ineligible for cash prizes.

The course laid out was Toronto-Buffalo-Syracuse-Albany-New York. Contestants could start at either end, but had to make the return trip in order to complete the race. Total distance was 1044 miles. The event got under way August 25 with poor weather prevailing at both Toronto and New York. Twenty-seven aircraft took off from New York, but because of a late start none got past Syracuse. The race was to continue until the deadline of August 29 by which time 65 aircraft had participated, with many completing the prescribed course. The five days of flying saw numerous crashes and forced landings, but fortunately no fatalities. Aircraft represented included such types as the D.H.4, S.E.5A, Fokker D VII, Curtiss Oriole, various models of the JN-4, and one Caproni bomber, the largest type entered. Several categories of prizes and trophies were awarded including the CNE Trophy, won by Lt. B.W. Maynard for the fastest time New York-Toronto. Maynard completed the trip in a D.H. 4 in 465-1/2 minutes. Two Canadians, C.A. "Duke" Schiller and W.G. Barker, won cash prizes in the handicap contest. Schiller had flown a JN-4 and Barker a Fokker D VII.

Two famous American airwomen performed in Canada in 1918. These were Katherine Stinson and Ruth Law. This photo shows Ruth Law racing an automobile at the Canadian National Exhibition grounds in Toronto.

Via Walter Hurst

The Flying Club Movement

As aviation grew through the twenties, the demand for pilots increased while the pool of wartime pilots decreased. Realizing this, the federal government, encouraged by men such as Col. J.L. Ralston and James MacBrien, devised a pilot training scheme. To any community in Canada that would provide an approved flying instructor, mechanic, and airstrip it would donate two training aircraft, and subsidize student pilots' tuition. This was a great incentive to communities everywhere to become involved in aviation, and in 1927 and 1928 flying clubs sprang into existence from coast to coast. Typical was the Montreal Light Aeroplane Club, established in September, 1927. In its first week of operations it logged 54 hours of instruction. Its initial 128 members had soared to 175 flying and 1700 non-flying members by year's end. Twelve thousand people attended the opening of the Winnipeg Flying Club and dedication of Stevenson Field in 1928. The same year Toronto hosted the first National Aircraft Show. The Canadian Flying Clubs Association was established to coordinate club activities. The Aviation League began publishing its own journal, *Canadian Aviation*. Flying was in the headlines everywhere.

Quebec to the Maritimes, where, by late August, the fleet of aircraft was hosted by centres like Charlottetown, Sydney, Halifax, Moncton, and Saint John. The entire cavalcade came to a finish at London, September 12. In all, 26 flying displays had been put on. Over 300 000 spectators had seen these shows, and receipts of $16 996.27 were realized, a surplus of $585.02. Each aircraft that completed the tour flew over 10 000 miles.

Flights of Fancy

Private flying was widely accepted by the mid thirties. More and more Canadians were flying for the fun of it. A historic, if

The U.S. Air Service Caproni trimotor bomber *Ca Giulio Cesare* seen at Leaside during the New York-Toronto air race of 1919. It was crewed by four, with Col. Phillips Melville commanding. Largest entry, *Giulio* began the race August 26 and made the New York-Toronto-New York circuit, but was so delayed by mechanical snags and other problems that it arrived home August 31, two days after the race ended.

K.M. Molson Collection

An important event during this era was the Trans Canada Air Pageant of 1931. Intended to increase airmindedness among Canadians, it was a parade of aircraft across Canada and back that included the RCAF's Siskin flight demonstration team, and many other civil and military aircraft. Things got under way at Hamilton, July 1. The day was marred by the fatal crash of a Travelair, but the Pageant continued regardless — to Windsor, across the midwestern states, to Winnipeg by July 10; over the Prairies and mountains to Vancouver ten days later; then all the way back east, across southern

not somewhat extreme example of this was the flight from Ottawa to Jamaica in 1935 by Jack Charleson and Yvan LeMoine. The adventure began in the midst of winter in Ottawa. Jack and Yvan, tiring of frigid temperatures and snowdrifts, gathered together the grand total of $90 and headed south in their Avian, CF-AIE. First stop was Montreal where the Avian's skis were exchanged for wheels, then off for New York. On arrival there the Ottawa boys were greeted by more wintery weather. There was so much snow that they were grounded, wishing, for more reasons than one, that they had their skis back. There was money to be made by anyone with a ski-equipped plane as photographers were clambering to get aloft to photograph the snow-covered cityscape.

After three days, the Avian was off again. Somewhere south of Raleigh, a forced landing was made on account of carburetor icing. This resulted in a bent prop which was duly hammered straight and the journey continued. In Jacksonville, both prop tips were sawn off, roughly

The de Havilland Moth was the most widely used training and pleasure airplane in Canada during the years following 1928. This one was the subject of attention at Toronto's Leaside field during an open house there.

James Collection, City of Toronto Archives

Aircraft participating in the Trans Canada Air Pageant while at Edmonton. To the left are the Siskin flight demonstration team and an RCAF Fairchild and Ford. The large aircraft on the flight line is CF-ARB, the Montreal-owned Saro Cloud.

Provincial Archives of Alberta, Alfred Blyth Collection (BL.87/6)

equal, and the propeller was found to perform quite normally.

A week was spent in and around Miami, enjoying the "good life" and doing some impromptu flying instruction and joy riding in order to restore funds. From here, the fliers headed for Key West, where arrangements were made with Cuban officials to clear CF-AIE to land at Havana. This included a declaration of funds on hand. Turning out their pockets, the lads came up with the grand total of $41.30.

The hop across the Florida Strait was made, leaving plenty of time to arrive in Havana before Customs closed for the day. This was to avoid a penalty fee for late arrival. The plane set down well before Customs' 5 o'clock closing time, but there was no sign of any officials. Finally, at 5:30, the Customs people showed up and made no bones about charging the penalty fee. After all, Customs was closed! The officials proceeded to make out a wad of documentation. This completed, and everything appearing to be in order, the Canadians were presented with a Customs' invoice for $41.30!

This episode so infuriated Yvan that he insisted on seeing the President. He was informed that this was a certain Fulgencia Batista. Off went the two Canadians, one closer inspection were found to be overgrown with sugar cane. As a result, the lads set down on the Kingston polo field, much to the dismay of the grounds keeper!

There followed a two-month period during which Jack and Yvan sold rides at £5 each; took up photographers; gave flying lessons; contemplated forming an airline to fly a Kingston-Montego Bay service; and airdropped leaflets to incoming cruise ships — to entice tourists into Edwin Charley's bar with the promise of a free drink!

Eventually, it seems that local officials became a bit suspicious of the busy comings and goings of CF-AIE. Besides

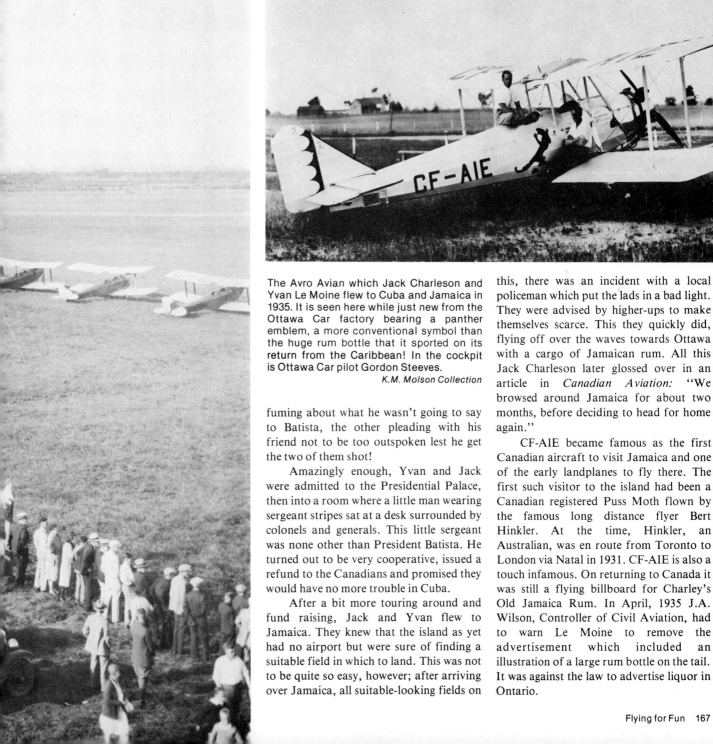

The Avro Avian which Jack Charleson and Yvan Le Moine flew to Cuba and Jamaica in 1935. It is seen here while just new from the Ottawa Car factory bearing a panther emblem, a more conventional symbol than the huge rum bottle that it sported on its return from the Caribbean! In the cockpit is Ottawa Car pilot Gordon Steeves.
K.M. Molson Collection

fuming about what he wasn't going to say to Batista, the other pleading with his friend not to be too outspoken lest he get the two of them shot!

Amazingly enough, Yvan and Jack were admitted to the Presidential Palace, then into a room where a little man wearing sergeant stripes sat at a desk surrounded by colonels and generals. This little sergeant was none other than President Batista. He turned out to be very cooperative, issued a refund to the Canadians and promised they would have no more trouble in Cuba.

After a bit more touring around and fund raising, Jack and Yvan flew to Jamaica. They knew that the island as yet had no airport but were sure of finding a suitable field in which to land. This was not to be quite so easy, however; after arriving over Jamaica, all suitable-looking fields on this, there was an incident with a local policeman which put the lads in a bad light. They were advised by higher-ups to make themselves scarce. This they quickly did, flying off over the waves towards Ottawa with a cargo of Jamaican rum. All this Jack Charleson later glossed over in an article in *Canadian Aviation:* "We browsed around Jamaica for about two months, before deciding to head for home again."

CF-AIE became famous as the first Canadian aircraft to visit Jamaica and one of the early landplanes to fly there. The first such visitor to the island had been a Canadian registered Puss Moth flown by the famous long distance flyer Bert Hinkler. At the time, Hinkler, an Australian, was en route from Toronto to London via Natal in 1931. CF-AIE is also a touch infamous. On returning to Canada it was still a flying billboard for Charley's Old Jamaica Rum. In April, 1935 J.A. Wilson, Controller of Civil Aviation, had to warn Le Moine to remove the advertisement which included an illustration of a large rum bottle on the tail. It was against the law to advertise liquor in Ontario.

Elsewhere in the file on CF-AIE is a complaint about its having flown very low in the vicinity of the Chateau Laurier in Ottawa. Another complaint originated from the Boy Scouts Association of Ste. Anne de Bellevue on March 9, 1936, to the effect that it was "creating an intense nuisance by taking up passengers every three or four minutes for money." This caused Stuart Graham to write the owner, "We have received a complaint . . . that aircraft CF-AIE has been flying low over the town to the consternation of the populace." After its unique career, CF-AIE was wrecked in a crash at Cartierville in November, 1939.

Over 40 years have passed since the Caribbean adventure with CF-AIE, and today Canadians take their private aircraft to such distant places as a matter of

The Pou-de-Ciel, CF-AYM on skis at St. Hubert, 1936. The airship mooring tower was still standing at the time.

Public Archives of Canada (C14970)

routine. July 18-August 28, 1973 represents a case in point. During that period, the Piper PA-28R Arrow, CF-YZQ, flew from Toronto on a vacation trip to touch at such centres as Winnipeg, Churchill, Chesterfield Inlet in the Northwest Territories, Regina, Calgary, and Victoria. Subsequently, CF-YZQ has made several Caribbean trips, reaching as far south as Port-au-Prince, Haiti.

Homebuilding

As Canadians took to flying, more and more of them got the urge to own airplanes. But few could afford such a luxury. A new Gipsy Moth cost $3500 at the height of the Depression, and surplus aircraft of World War I vintage had all but disappeared. One practical solution to this predicament did exist, however. A person could build his own airplane. Thus, in the twenties and thirties, Canadians took up the pastime of homebuilding planes. An enthusiast could purchase plans and

Two Harvard IV's of the Canadian Warplane Heritage seen in formation over the countryside near Hamilton, Ontario in May 1974. The aircraft in the foreground is in the colours of the CWH's Harvard demonstration team which has performed at airshows across Canada and the United States. The CWH is Canada's most enthusiastic association dedicated to the preservation of flyable historic aircraft.

Larry Milberry

components for a variety of simple designs — Corbens, Heaths, Pietenpols, and so on. A few actually created original designs. A choice of engines could be fitted, including the Ford motor car type. Many odd parts were available from World War I leftovers. Homebuilding caught on and by World War II over a hundred homebuilts had been registered in Canada, not to mention many others never registered but nonetheless flown. Some of these flew for years without officialdom being any the wiser.

Typical of the homebuilt of this period was CF-AYM, a Pou-de-Ciel. Translated, CF-AYM was a Sky Flea, and a more apt name couldn't be found. It was all of 10 feet 8 inches long, with a wing span of 19 feet 8 inches and was powered by a 35 hp engine. All up weight was 495 pounds. It was built by Dr. George E. Milette of Montreal.

On March 2, 1935, District Inspector,

R.D. Robinson flying his Schreder HP 14T glider near the Rockton Gliderport in Southern Ontario. The aircraft was built by Steve Burany in the early seventies. Like other forms of sport flying in Canada, gliding is steadily gaining in popularity.

S. Burany

A primary glider built by the McGill University Gliding Club and photographed in November 1933.

Public Archives of Canada (PA 70830)

A typical light plane of the late thirties. This Aeronca K was owned by the Toronto Flying Club. At the time of this photo it was marooned in a field near Prescott, Ontario after running out of gas flying from Montreal to Toronto. Two young pilots, Don Murray and F.W. Hotson, were aboard. Don is in the suit while Fred was behind the camera.

Air Regulations, Stuart Graham flight tested CF-AYM. He was fully satisfied with its construction and airworthiness. On July 2, 1936, however, CF-AYM suffered an engine failure on takeoff from St. Hubert, dove into the ground and was wrecked. Fortunately, pilot E.T. Webster, was uninjured. In the following investigation, Mr. Graham summarized his feelings regarding the airplane: "Aircraft CF-AYM was meticulously constructed entirely of the best aircraft material and rigged exactly in accordance with the designer's recommendations." This was a fine testimony to the quality of workmanship that went into many early Canadian homebuilts.

Wartime Slowdown, Post-War Revival

World War II curtailed general aviation in Canada. Private flying almost ceased as pilots and the country's flying clubs made a sudden transition to the war effort. Civil aircraft were requisitioned by the RCAF; gasoline and parts became almost impossible to acquire for private use. The flying clubs ceased operations and became incorporated companies running 22 flying training schools, paid on the basis of a dollar for every hour of flying instruction. This had amounted to six million dollars by war's end.

Immediately after the war, civil aviation began returning to normal. The flying clubs reformed and handed over their wartime profits to the government in exchange for an arrangement to get civil aviation moving again. On January 28, 1946, the newly formed Royal Canadian Flying Clubs Association held its first meeting at Winnipeg. Meanwhile general aviation benefited from the availability of thousands of surplus aircraft. Tiger Moths, Cornells, Ansons, and Cranes seemed to be everywhere, but now wearing "CF"

registrations and colourful paint jobs over their old RCAF yellow.

Beginning in 1949 the RCFCA instituted a scheme to subsidize flying training at the rate of $100 per student and $100 for his club. There was also a scheme to train Air Cadets, and one to provide refresher flying for RCAF reserve pilots. For these plans the flying clubs received new Chipmunks to replace their Tiger Moths and other surplus trainers.

The Warbirds

Of the aircraft disposed of after the war there was hardly any place on the civil market for bombers and fighters and most were destroyed. The exceptions were a few aircraft converted to aerosurvey standards, other commercial uses, and in two cases to racing planes.

World Wide Airways of Montreal purchased a Mosquito to enter in the 1948 Thompson Trophy race in the United States. This aircraft, CF-FZG, was flown by Don McVicar but ran into engine trouble near Kansas City while en route to Los Angeles for the start of the race. The other aircraft was the Spitfire, CF-GMZ. It placed third in the 1949 Tinnerman Trophy race. Pilot J.H. McArthur took the Spitfire seven times around the 15 mile course averaging 359.5 mph. Neither aircraft ever returned to Canada, yet they are historical as the first examples of high performance fighter planes registered in Canada for sport flying.

In the years that followed few people

The Canadian Spitfire flown in the 1949 Tinnerman Trophy race. This aircraft is now in the collection of Len Tanner of Connecticut.

Jack McNulty

thought much about this exotic kind of flying. Considering the costs, it just wasn't practical. Meanwhile the barnyard bombers purchased by farmers across the country from War Assets lay rotting and rusting.

In the early sixties, though, an awareness began to develop that something should be done about these sad remains. People began scouring the countryside for what might still remain of the warplanes of the previous generation. Gradually a small but enthusiastic group of latter day archaeologists began turning up a few examples of Ansons, Bolingbrokes, Lysanders, and Hurricanes. These were usually in grim condition, sometimes hardly recognizable as aircraft.

Going along with this renewed sense of history was a period of affluence which enabled a handful of Canadians to again experience the thrill of flying fighter aircraft. On and off, the Canadian Civil Aircraft Register showed a Mustang, a P-40, a Spitfire, even a Vampire. But for financial, technical or historic reasons, these aircraft again disappeared from Canadian skies. Some were sold south of the border where high interest in warbirds and seemingly unlimited finances created an eager market. Others went to museums as did John N. Paterson's Spitfire, CF-NUS.

The seventies brought a real upsurge in general aviation. From homebuilts to executive jets, business boomed. History was bound to profit from such good times. That was evident in the work being done by the Confederate Air Force in the United States. Its aim was to preserve in flying condition as many types of World War II aircraft as possible. Added to this, unlimited air racing had made a popular comeback at Reno, with Mustangs, Bearcats, and Lightnings again jockeying for position around the pylons. The enthusiasm inevitably reached into Canada.

In 1971 a small history-minded group came together and formed the Canadian Warplane Heritage. Its members were motivated by a desire to collect and restore

Ormond Haydon-Baillie's Hawker Sea Fury Mk. XI, CF-CHB. This ex-Australian navy fighter was restored by Haydon-Baillie in 1970 while he was a test pilot with the Canadian Forces at Cold Lake, Alberta. Here it is in formation with a CF-104 and a CF-5. Haydon-Baillie returned later to the U.K. taking along the Sea Fury and his other war birds. He died in the crash of a Mustang in Germany in 1977.

Via Canadian Aviation Magazine

examples of the aircraft Canadians had flown during and just after World War II — a worthy cause, but what could be done at this late date? And who was going to finance such a costly enterprise?

These were really just academic questions, for with its determination, the CWH was confident of finding solutions. At first it didn't even have an airplane. Someone had the idea that it would be nice to have a Spitfire, but that was a pipe dream. Then a rumour was heard of a warbird available in Georgia. The rumour was checked out, and, sure enough, there was the airplane — a big Fairey Firefly. The aircraft, still in its Royal Australian Navy markings, had been shipped to the United States for a career in crop spraying which had never materialized; now the aircraft was lying in a corn field.

The Firefly was available, and, as the type had served in the Canadian Navy in post-war years, it met CWH requirements.

The aircraft which put the warbirds movement in Canada on a solid footing. The Firefly Mk.VI of the Canadian Warplane Heritage at Mount Hope during the 1975 CWH airshow, when it was flown by George Stewart.

Larry Milberry

C-GCWM, the B-25J which was added to the CWH collection in 1976.

Larry Milberry

Keith Hopkinson of Goderich in his Stits Playboy, taken at Kitchener-Waterloo on July 9, 1961. Largely through Hopkinson's efforts, homebuilt aircraft gained acceptance by the Department of Transport. In 1979 the aircraft went to the National Aeronautical Collection in Ottawa.

Larry Milberry

A deal was made on the spot, and the Firefly was flown to Toronto for restoration. This was done to perfection, and the next year 1972, the aircraft, registered CF-BDH, visited the great warbird gathering at Oshkosh. There, from among dozens of warbirds present, it was chosen as the best restoration, and awarded the Grand Champion Warbird Trophy.

The Canadian Warplane Heritage has flourished since then. Its hangar at Hamilton Municipal Airport is now crowded with historic aircraft. Some, like the Avenger, Corsair, Crane, Harvards, and Mitchell are regular performers at airshows in Canada and the United States. Others are being painstakingly restored and will gradually become operational and join in the flypasts. These include such famous names as Anson, Lancaster, Lysander, Seafire, and Yale.

Tragically, the Firefly crashed into

Homebuilts take many forms. There are low, mid, and high wing designs; one- and two-seaters; land and sea planes. This Volmer is a popular two-seat amphibian and was snapped just as it touched down at Orillia airport during the 1971 EAA fly-in there.

Larry Milberry

Lake Ontario while performing at the 1977 Canadian International Air Show. Alan Ness, pilot and co-founder of the CWH, lost his life in the accident. This was the first mishap experienced by the CWH after hundreds of performances all over North America.

The search goes on in Canada for warbirds that may have survived even to this late date, in field, woodlot or barnyard. A P-40 was actually unearthed in a prairie farmyard, after 30 years of interment, and was shipped to the United States for restoration! In Assiniboia, Saskatchewan, Harry Whereatt began salvaging aviation relics in the early sixties. His barns and sheds have come to house Lysanders, a Hurricane, a Bolingbroke, a Crane, a Fleet Fawn, and other historic types.

In Kapuskasing, far to the north in Ontario, one of the old Spartan Air Services Mosquitos is being gradually restored; while in Victoria, B.C., George Maude has restored a P-40E. This story goes back to the post-war forties when George purchased two War Assets Bolingbrokes at Patricia Bay near Victoria. Next year he acquired a P-40E Kittyhawk. Total expenditure for the three aircraft was $135. All three were moved by raft to Salt Spring Island where George lived.

One of the Bolingbrokes was later sold to a neighbour who used it as a storage shed, while the other two aircraft were simply left to the elements. The wings were cut off the Kittyhawk. Eventually, the second Bolingbroke was donated to the

Flown by its builder, Hugh Ellis, this Corben Baby Ace "C" is another fine example of homebuilding in the fifties.

Jack McNulty

National Aeronautical Collection.

In 1974, after having watched it languish for so long, George decided to restore his Kittyhawk. He researched its history and found that it had been taken on strength by the RCAF at Sydney, Nova Scotia, in 1940. In 1942 it was transferred to the West Coast where it served in Alaska with 118 Squadron. Next it was transferred to Patricia Bay where it finished out the war with 133 Squadron.

After a new set of wings was located in Alberta, restoration work began at Victoria. By 1978, George's P-40E was again airworthy, after over 30 years in limbo.

Growth of the Homebuilding Movement

Homebuilding experienced a renaissance after the Second World War. For a decade, however, the Department of Transport enforced tight airworthiness restrictions which amounted to an effective ban against homebuilts, or ultralights, as these aircraft were classified. Even so, those interested in modifying existing light aircraft, building from readily available plans, or even

Most pilots in Canada fly for the fun of it. Their wings come in a hundred and one varieties. Here a Luscome 8A touches down at Toronto Markham Airport.

Larry Milberry

For some enthusiasts, nothing but the wind in the wires will do. Hundreds of vintage aircraft have come back to life since 1960. In this case the subject is a Waco 10 especially restored for the fiftieth anniversary of Leavens Brothers.

Jack McNulty

By far the most popular training and recreational aircraft in Canada since World War II have been Cessnas. From 1946, Ce.120's up to the latest such as the Ce.177RG's, there are today some 7000 single-engined Cessnas in Canada, or about one of every three civilian aircraft. CF-MTT, a 172B, was photographed over west Toronto on February 22, 1961. Some time later it disappeared without a trace while on a local flight from the Island Airport.

Larry Milberry

creating original designs were determined to fight for the homebuilding cause.

Perhaps the first post-war venture in the do-it-yourself category of airplane building was A. McKimmon's conversion of a 1935 Taylor Cub, CF-ANT-X. It was modified at Guelph in 1946 when the owner replaced its 40 hp Continental engine with a 65 hp Lycoming. Otherwise, it had its tail replaced with one from an Aeronca and it had a self-designed engine cowling. These modifications had been done after the aircraft had been damaged in a forced landing.

Leading the movement for home-building in Canada was Keith Hopkinson of Sky Harbour Air Services, Goderich. He and a handful of other enthusiasts in the Goderich and Hamilton area worked diligently to convince the DOT that their standards of engineering and workmanship were as good and their aircraft as safe as those of any manufacturer. Their efforts paid off, for in September of 1956 the DOT introduced a new system for licencing

ultra-light aircraft. The first aircraft to fly registered under the ultra-light category was Hopkinson's Stits Playboy, CF-RAD.

The homebuilders formed the Ultra-Light Aircraft Association of Canada and within five years there were some 40 ultra-lights flying in Canada. These included everything from modified Cubs to traditional homebuilt designs like the Corben, Stits and Jodel, to original efforts like the McKimmon Amphibian.

In general, the ultra-light fans were getting into the air at bargain prices. Ben Keillor estimated that his Jodel, CF-RAM, built in the late fifties, cost $750 complete. This figure represented materials and an engine, but hardly the thousands of hours of planning, cogitating, and labouring in seeing the project through. By now, $4000 is a more likely amount required for a similar airplane:

In 1967 homebuilding in Canada came under the auspices of the Experimental Aircraft Association. The first Canadian chapter of this international organization was established in Edmonton. Today there are some 40 chapters in Canada, with over 3000 members. At present, the homebuilt scene in Canada counts over 1000 aircraft. The many types currently active include Emeraudes, Fly Babies, Jodels, Pietenpols, Pitts, Stits, Volksplanes, and Zeniths. In 1978 the busiest EAA operation in Canada was Chapter 41 of Brampton, Ontario. That year it counted about 50 homebuilts airworthy with several under construction.

The Sky's the Limit

The extent of recreational flying in Canada is also illustrated by the variety of clubs and associations to which fliers belong.

A long-time favourite of sport aviators, the Globe GC1B Swift. First introduced in Canada in 1946, there are still about 30 Swifts flying here. CF-JMR has been modified to take wingtip tanks. It was photographed over Hamilton in October, 1963.

Jack McNulty

These provide members with the benefits of fellowship, assistance in locating, construction, restoration, and maintenance of aircraft as well as flight safety, travel, and insurance information. One of the major organizations is the Royal Canadian Flying Clubs Association.

The vitality of the RCFCA member clubs is reflected in total hours logged for 1960 — 120 000 hours. For a few years hereafter, hours dropped with changes in DND training requirements and the subsidy arrangement, but figures again soared, reaching 158 030 hours in 1967. That year the RCFCA introduced its Certificate of Proficiency pilot training scheme. This was hailed by the Fédération Aéronautique Internationale as the best

A giant flying billboard! This hot air balloon made several ascents during the World Ploughing Match held in Ontario County in September 1975. Ballooning is gaining in popularity as a form of sport aviation, making a comeback after a century in the doldrums.

Larry Milberry

incentive for improvement of pilot skills to appear on the aviation scene to date; it was later adopted by other nations.

Since 1975 RCFCA members have been logging over 200 000 hours a year; up to 1977 the Association counted 39 Participating, 21 Affiliated and 17 Associate members operating in 10 provinces.

One of Canada's most active flying clubs in recent years has been the Moncton Flying Club, with some 450 members. As a flying training operation it has one of the highest ratings in Canada, and regularly attracts foreign students. To accommodate its many students from afar, the Moncton Flying Club has erected a dormitory at the airport, and houses others in town. At one point in mid 1978 the club had on its role six students from Pakistan, two from the West Indies, one from Britain and one from Syria, plus many Canadians. At the same time it was operating 10 single-engined aircraft and a Seneca used in IFR training. There were nine full-time instructors and some 18 000 hours were expected to be logged for the year.

The Edmonton Flying Club is the largest flying club in Canada. Founded by "Wop" May and others in August 1927 as the Edmonton and Northern Alberta Aero Club, it counted over 2500 members in 1978. Its fleet of 35 aircraft logged some 26 000 hours for the year.

Statistics further indicate the vitality of general aviation in Canada. As of October, 1978, there were 62 835 Canadians holding pilot licences of all kinds, and at the same time, 20 696 student pilot permits in force.

Other fliers' organizations in Canada include the Canadian Owners and Pilots Association (COPA) with 15 000 members; The 99's, a women fliers association; the Flying Farmers; the Flying Physicians; provincial groups like the Alberta Aviation Council; the Soaring Association of Canada; and specialists' groups like the International Cessna 170 Association. Each year pilots' calendars note such highlights as EAA and antique aircraft gatherings; breakfast fly-ins sponsored by flying clubs; seminars; poker runs; and air rallies such as the one for the Governor General's Cup.

The latest generation of light aircraft in Canada is represented by this Piper PA-38 Tomahawk.

Larry Milberry

The intensity of pleasure flying and general aviation in Canada may also be gauged by airport movement statistics. Five airports where the majority of aircraft movements are classified as "local" are Pitt Meadows, B.C.; Springbank, Alberta; St. Andrews, Manitoba; Buttonville, Ontario; and St. Hubert, Quebec. For 1977 each of these exceeded 200 000 aircraft movements, with the busiest being St. Hubert with 272 506 movements. Activity at these five airports accounted for approximately 20 percent of all aircraft movements at civil airports in Canada for 1977.

With their intense interest in aviation, Canadians inevitably distinguish themselves with outstanding achievements. There are annual awards for excellence made by various clubs and associations. The EAA, for example, annually makes its Keith Hopkinson award for the best Canadian homebuilt. Individual efforts in the air have included the world's light aircraft altitude record set April 10, 1972. At that time, Lt. Col. Roy W. Windover piloted an Interstate Cadet over Pikes Peak, Colorado, to a height of 30 800 feet, verified by the Fédération Aéronautique Internationale. Windover had set a Canadian record the previous February 29 by piloting a Cessna 140 to 27 050 feet.

Another altitude record was set January 9, 1977, this time a Canadian gliding record. Also flying over Colorado Springs, Walter Chmela of Toronto flew a Slingsby Kestrel 19, CF-FEI, to 40 843 feet. The gain in height after release from the Super Cub tow plane was 27 300 feet.

Also in 1977, Canada's national parachute team, sponsored by the Canadian Sport Parachuting Association, won three gold medals at the World Parachuting Championships at Gatton, Australia. This was Canada's best showing in 13 world competitions since 1958. Included among the 1977 team laurels was a world record in the four-man event during which the team completed 13 manoeuvres in one jump.

Military Aviation

McCurdy and Baldwin, 1909

Military aviation in Canada dates to 1909. At that time, shortly after the successful flight of the *Silver Dart* at Baddeck, Alexander Graham Bell attempted to interest government officials in aviation. On March 27, 1909, he spoke to the Canadian Club in Ottawa urging that, "control of the air, as far as a nation was concerned, was as important for tomorrow as the control of the sea is today." He strongly recommended the service of his two protégés, McCurdy and Baldwin.

Bell was supported that evening by the Governor General, Earl Grey, who commented, "It only remains for Canada, which gave to the world the telephone and wireless telegraphy, to complete her services to the British Empire and to civilization by giving to the world the best aerodrome, the possession of which will make the nation that is fortunate enough to own it . . . the foremost nation of the world."

Some weeks later, on May 4, the Militia Council met to discuss Bell's proposal. The Council suggested that McCurdy and Baldwin "might also be asked what aerodrome and other appliances they had at present on trial or in use, and whether they would be prepared to carry out any demonstrations or experiments at, say, Petawawa." A letter was sent to Bell informing him that McCurdy and Baldwin were welcome to demonstrate their "aerodromes" at Petawawa, but that the Department of Militia and Defence was in no position to help financially.

In early June the *Silver Dart* was freighted from Baddeck to Petawawa. A shed was erected to house the machine, and a new engine shipped in. This was a 40 hp Kirkham automobile engine. By late July, the *Silver Dart* was ready to be test flown, and on August 2, was rolled out and flown briefly by McCurdy. After this hop, Baldwin joined McCurdy for a ride. Two more short hops followed, these being flown at up to 50 feet, and between 40-50 mph, the machine's highest speeds to date.

On the fourth flight that morning, McCurdy misjudged his landing and crashed. He and Baldwin were shaken up and cut, and the machine badly damaged. This was the *Silver Dart's* first accident after some 300 flights.

This misfortune was covered widely in the Toronto press. On August 3 *The Globe* headlined a story, "Aerodrome Silver Dart Smashed at Petawawa, Remarkable Escape of Messrs Baldwin and McCurdy, Struck A Hill While Landing, Mr. Baldwin Takes a Philosophic View of the Accident." *The Globe* described the successful flights of the *Silver Dart* at Petawawa, how the new engine worked very well, and how the "drome" was quite capable of carrying two men in flight. It went on about the two aviators, "They will have the sympathy of a host of well-wishers who will eagerly await their recovery and their further attempts to keep Canada abreast of the times in aviation. . . . It is of interest to note that, as with many other flying machines, the Silver Dart came to grief while making a landing and not through any error of construction or handling while in the air. Canada hopes that complete

success will attend her own aviators in their future experiments."

The Toronto Star also offered detailed coverage of the events at Petawawa. Its August 3 edition carried the story of the crash under the headline, "Undaunted Aeroplanists Will Fly Again This Week, McCurdy's Nose Still Bleeds from Cut and Baldwin Is Limping, But They Will Fly on Friday or Saturday, New Machine Being Rushed."

The aviators had a back-up machine, *Baddeck No. 1,* soon erected and fitted with the *Silver Dart's* Kirkham engine. On the evening of August 12, the aircraft was ready for its official demonstration flight. This was also to be its first flight, a fact which caused McCurdy and Baldwin some concern. They would have preferred to try the new machine out in privacy. Circumstances precluded this luxury.

A party of top-ranking Militia officials arrived from Ottawa to observe the flights. The first attempt was not spectacular as the *Baddeck No. 1* struggled along the ground for a long distance before getting airborne for a few seconds, at no more than 15 feet. Even so, one of the observers noted that "for the first trial with a new machine it was very good."

Colonel E. Fiset, however, was not very optimistic about the military future of aviation in Canada. He was quoted in *The Star,* August 12 as saying of the airplane, "I don't think it can ever be an offensive weapon . . . You cannot expect a young country like Canada to strike out and adopt an airship policy. It is too expensive." He also wondered, "Who knows what these aeroplanes can do? Can they lift a great weight? What protection would the canvas planes offer? I think they must find something of a more suitable nature than canvas to cover the great wings with. We must wait a great many years and experiment much before the true use of these machines can be demonstrated.''

Next evening, after some adjustments had been made to the machine, McCurdy conducted another test flight. This, sadly, ended in another crack up. McCurdy again escaped with a shaking up, but the *Baddeck No. 1* was a total wreck. Soon after, he and Baldwin packed up the ruins of their two machines and returned to Baddeck.

Debate continued at an official level regarding the feasibility of the Canadian

Canada's first military involvement with aviation came in the summer of 1909, when McCurdy and Baldwin demonstrated two of their flying machines to the Militia at Camp Petawawa. This photo shows the Baddeck 1 being readied there. The figure second from the left appears to be Baldwin.

Militia employing aircraft. A quote from Hansard, December 13, 1909, reads that it was not yet "desirable for the Dominion Government to spend money in assisting inventors, but all reasonable facilities will be afforded to persons, possessing satisfactory credentials, in the way of giving the use of Government land for purposes of experiment.''

Meanwhile, in Baddeck, McCurdy and Baldwin had established the Canadian Aerodrome Company. On September 25 they flew *Baddeck No. 2* and within a month had completed some 50 flights with it. On November 11, a flight of 15 miles was completed in 21 minutes. After thoroughly proving the machine, they invited the Militia to again observe their progress. Major G.S. Maunsell arrived at Baddeck and spent four days observing flights and activities at the Canadian Aerodrome Company. Maunsell went up for two short hops in *Baddeck No. 2* over frozen Bras d'Or Lake, and was favourably impressed with the overall operation.

While Maunsell was still at Baddeck,

McCurdy and Baldwin wrote to the Militia Council offering them both *Baddeck No. 1,* now rebuilt, and *Baddeck No. 2* for $10 000, including the training of one or two pilots. Then Maunsell made his recommendations to his superiors. These included establishing the Militia's own flight research and development section to duplicate what McCurdy and Baldwin had already done, accept the offer from the Canadian Aerodrome Company, or provide the Company with financial aid in the form of a grant in return for one machine.

On April 7, 1910, the Militia submitted a proposal to the Governor General recommending the third option, the amount to be granted to be $10 000. This was turned down by the Privy Council. On May 10 it was proposed in modified form, requesting $5000. This too was denied, and Maunsell had to cable McCurdy and Baldwin, "Very sorry Department is unable to make your grant towards aviation this year.''

Maunsell tried to reopen the case for

McCurdy and Baldwin in August 1910, but without success. Two years later he was still pressing the matter, urging the training of a few Canadian militiamen in flying, in order to lay a basis for future developments in aviation. The Chief of the General Staff agreed, noting that, ". . . A military organization which does not keep pace with the latest scientific developments must be hopelessly left behind by organizations which are alive to that necessity." Nonetheless, the proposal was vetoed by the new Minister of Militia and Defence, Colonel Sam Hughes. This decision was delivered on March 12, 1912, and was to hold for over two years.

World War I — The Canadian Aviation Corps

In August, 1914, two months after the outbreak of World War I, McCurdy was again promoting military aviation. At that time he met with Colonel Hughes, again stressing the usefulness of aircraft in the military. Hughes seemed uninterested, and reportedly told McCurdy, "Aviation is of

no value in war, and I do not propose to tie the government up financially to such a ridiculous scheme."

Then, on August 25, Hughes cabled Lord Kitchener, offering six "expert" Canadian airmen for the war effort. This, in spite of the fact that Canada did not even have one expert military aviator! The reply was affirmative and on September 16, Hughes approved the formation of the Canadian Aviation Corps. E.L. Janney was appointed commander of the new organization, even though he had very little knowledge of aviation.

Janney was given approval to purchase Canada's first military aircraft, but instructed to stay within a $5000 budget. As no aircraft was at the time available in Canada, he journeyed to Massachusetts to visit the Burgess-Dunne aircraft concern. One of its designs was a tailless, swept-wing, float-equipped pusher-type biplane. It had a 46-foot wing span; could accommodate two people; and, with its 100 hp Curtiss engine, could cruise at 60 mph.

Janney immediately closed a deal for the Burgess-Dunne, with his only stipulation being that the aircraft be immediately turned over to him. This was agreed, even though it had already been contracted to fly a local political candidate on a whirlwind tour of his constituency. To the politician's dismay, the airplane suddenly disappeared! It was shipped to Lake Champlain where an American pilot, Clifford Webster, was ready to ferry it to Canada. This was required as Janney was not a qualified pilot. On September 21,

Webster and Janney took off for Canada, headed for Quebec City. On this leg of the trip, Janney received his first flying lesson.

The Burgess-Dunne arrived at Sorel at the mouth of the Richelieu River after almost two hours aloft. The distance covered was about 80 miles. At Sorel the rumour spread that the two mysterious aviators were actually German spies! It took a bit of explaining before Webster and Janney were allowed to continue on their way.

A news story described this strange episode: "The Minister of the Militia received word that E.L. Janney, of Galt, Ont., the aviator who was flying from Massachusetts to Valcartier Camp, was arrested by Canadian customs officers this morning at Sorel, Quebec. The aviator made a descent at Sorel for gasoline and was promptly marched to the lockup. Later he was permitted to telephone Col. Sam Hughes and orders were at once given for his release."

The trip from Sorel to Quebec was plagued by mechanical difficulties. These were the result of Janney's haste to get hold of the machine. At the Burgess-Dunne factory, he had been warned that his engine needed extensive overhaul, but had ignored the warning. It was September 30 before the aircraft arrived at Quebec, just in time to board the *Athenia*. Also aboard ship

The Burgess-Dunne tailless sweptwing biplane aboard ship. Canada's first military aircraft.
Aviation and Space Division, National Museum of Science and Technology (001535)

Prior to the RFC coming to Canada, flying training was available in Toronto from the Curtiss flying boat and land plane schools. Most graduates went overseas to fight in World War I. Seen in this photo is the class of July 1916. The airplane is a Curtiss JN-3 Jenny.

Metropolitan Toronto Library Board

were Lt. W.F. Sharpe, and Lt. Harry Farr, both of whom had had experience with aircraft in the United States, but apparently not as pilots. Nonetheless, they were now members of the Canadian Aviation Corps. Webster returned home, his contract fulfilled.

The *Athenia* reached England on October 17, and the Burgess-Dunne was transshipped to a military camp. Three weeks later, Janney submitted his budget for the coming year's operations for his one-plane air force. The total came to $116 679.25! A few days later he set off to inspect RFC facilities. When he failed to reappear for several weeks, he was listed as AWOL. He finally surfaced, promoting a scheme to raise money in Canada by private barnstorming. At this, Ottawa decided to sever its association with Janney. He resigned January 1, 1915.

During this period, the Burgess-Dunne was faring badly. The RFC had apparently declared it useless, and destroyed its wings. Only the motor, radiator, and propeller remained. In time, the remains were picked apart, and scattered here and there. An investigation was begun to locate what remained, but all that turned up were two new inner tubes which had been left at an

inn at Bustard on the Salisbury Plain and some rusted components that had lain outside all winter and were described as "absolutely worthless, even for scrap iron."

Both Sharpe and Farr transferred to the Royal Flying Corps. In February, 1915 Sharpe died in the crash of the Maurice Farman he was flying at the RFC aerodrome near Shoreham. He thus became Canada's first military flying casualty. In May of that year, the ill-conceived Canadian Aviation Corps was disbanded.

Military Aviation on the Home Front

From 1915 onward, the pace of aerial warfare began rapidly accelerating. Mass producing aircraft and crews to fly them became a major concern. In 1915 this led the War Office and the Admiralty to request Canada to begin enrolling men for the Royal Flying Corps and the Royal Naval Air Service. Interested candidates were expected to pay for their own flying tuition, though if successful, they would receive most of it back as a rebate.

Parallelling this, the Curtiss Aviation School began operations in Toronto in the spring of 1915. The school offered two types of training. At Long Branch, a western suburb, training was given on the JN-3 Jenny. At Hanlan's Point on Toronto Bay, a flying boat school was operated using Curtiss F-boats.

In support of these operations, Curtiss

also established aircraft manufacturing facilities in Toronto.

By the end of 1915, when winter conditions put a halt to flying, the Curtiss Aviation School had graduated 66 pilots, and partially trained many others — this in spite of the considerable tariff of $1 per minute of flying. The complete course involved about 400 minutes in the air. The following year, 63 more pilots graduated, for a total of 129 by the time the operation ceased.

The first two Curtiss graduates had been A.S. Ince and F.H. Smith of Toronto. Other graduates later to become well known included W.A. Curtis, A.T. Cowley, and Bert Wemp. Of the 129 graduates, 35 were later to die in action or in flying accidents, including all five men who had graduated November 11, 1915. Meanwhile other Canadians had learned to fly at schools in San Diego, Norfolk, Dayton, and Ithaca, N.Y. The Wright school at Dayton apparently graduated 42 Canadians.

It was soon realized that Britain would require a more elaborate training scheme in Canada; in late 1916 plans were made for such a scheme to train aircrew and technical personnel and also for the mass production of training aircraft. Canada was considered the ideal place for such a scheme: it was safe from enemy attack, had the necessary natural and human resources, and good overall flying conditions.

In January 1917 the advance party of the Royal Flying Corps, Canada arrived in Toronto. Within a week, work had begun

to establish its first aerodrome — Camp Borden. Within six weeks most of its 15 large hangars had been erected. At the same time, the Curtiss operation at Long Branch was taken over and the first unit of the RFC Canada posted there. Long Branch became a ground school operation and flying was established at new fields at Leaside and Armour Heights (Toronto suburbs), Rathburn and Mohawk along the Bay of Quinte shore of Lake Ontario, and at Beamsville in the Niagara region.

Cadets received basic training at Long Branch and studied at the School of Military Aeronautics at the University of Toronto, with some in-service training at the Canadian Aeroplanes facility where JN-4 training planes were being mass produced. The Cadets' curriculum included such topics as meteorology, especially as it applied to northern France; target interpretation; photography; air-to-ground signalling; bombing; aero engine and aircraft rigging; military law; and procedure and organization. After all this, cadets were ready for their introduction to flying.

With such a hectic pace being set, there were many training accidents, so many that on certain days planes must seemed to have wrecked as quickly as Canadian Aeroplanes could turn them out. The accident rate continued high until the School of Special Flying was established at Armour Heights. There, cadets had their flying techniques polished, learning such skills as spin recovery. In June, 1918 just before the School of Special Flying was established,

the RFC Canada recorded 204 flying accidents. By November, after it had opened, accidents had been reduced to 47.

In the summer of 1917, a reciprocal arrangement was made between the RFC Canada and the U.S. Army, whereby U.S. cadets would be trained in Canada, and British pilots in Texas. The rationale for this was to bypass severe winter flying conditions in Canada which often interfered with flying. Originally, the RFC Canada had considered operating in the Vancouver area. This concept was dropped when weather conditions there were considered. While there was no intense cold, there would have been too much flying lost to foggy and overcast days.

That July, the first American cadets arrived in Toronto, while the RFC made its move south in October. Five thousand men with their gear entrained 375 railway cars, and within five days, RFC aircraft were flying over Texas.

Between November 17, 1917, and April 12, 1918, the RFC in Texas accumulated 67 000 hours in the air, training a total of 1960 RFC and American pilots. As well, 4000 non-flying personnel were trained. Flying fatalities were 1.8 percent of pilots trained. By the time the RFC training scheme was phased out in late 1918, 16 663 cadets and mechanics had been trained. Of these, 3135 pilots and 137 observers had graduated, most of whom served overseas. Between May 1917 and October 1918 some 125 flight cadets and instructors had been killed in flying accidents.

One of the thousands who served with the RFC Canada was Walter Hurst of Toronto. When the war started he was a mechanic with McLaughlin Motors, and as such, a natural candidate for a mechanic in the RFC when he enlisted in 1917. His first posting was to Camp Mohawk. As he recalled, 60 years later, the Mohawk operation consisted of four flights of 16 JN-4's each. Preparations for the day's flying began at 3:30 a.m. Flying began at first light, and by 8:00 a.m. it was not unusual to find half a dozen aircraft already up on their noses on account of takeoff and landing mishaps.

Mr. Hurst's many recollections include endless cracked up JN-4's. One which crashed into a hangar at Mohawk ignited, and within minutes the hangar was razed. Another memory is of his many test flights, and occasional joy riding, when a pilot would hedge-hop across the countryside to his mechanic's delight. He also recalls the angry instructor who brought his slow-learning student in from a flight, jumped from the cockpit and told the cadet to go ahead and break his neck. The cadet took off again, and proceeded to make three perfect landings. Asked later why he couldn't do it with the instructor along, the cadet replied, "How could I with him shouting at me all the time!"

In late 1917, Mr. Hurst moved with the RFC to Texas. Even though they were now operating well to the south, he still remembers many a cold night, and having to drain the water from the rads of the JN-4's to prevent freeze-up. There was also the

JN-4 Canucks of the Royal Flying Corps, Canada. Many Canadians learned to fly in these aircraft from training bases in Southern Ontario and Texas during 1917-1918. The names of sponsoring communities are inscribed on the fuselage.
Aviation and Space Division, National Museum of Science and Technology (A1050)

A short-lived training operation at Toronto was that run by W.A. Dean. The Curtiss flying boat shown is the Sunfish and was piloted in this case by T.C. Macaulay. The Sunfish was Canada's first flying boat, the first aircraft to carry a passenger between Canadian cities (Toronto-Hamilton), and the first aircraft known to have been used in aerial photography in Canada. It was wrecked in Toronto Bay by E.L. Janney.
Ontario Archives, Toronto (S15751)

FLYING IS THE MOST ATTRACTIVE SPORT OF THIS AGE

TORONTO AVIATION SCHOOL

WE TEACH you to be a Pilot or an Aviation Mechanic, positions which command excellent salaries. FLYING BOATS, SEAPLANES and AEROPLANES—everything pertaining to the skilful operation of these wonderful craft, fast coming into general use—will be taught by our school by men of wide experience in aviation. All those desiring to enter the school should make application at once. Call, or write for particulars to

W. A. DEAN, Room 21, Bank of Toronto Building, 205 Yonge Street, Toronto

A good view of the RFC School of Special Flying at Armour Heights. It was located near where what is today the intersection of Avenue Rd. and Hwy. 401 in Toronto.

Crashes abounded during flight training, with the RFC, Canada. Here two JN-4's have been involved in a serious confrontation.
Three photos from the album of Walter Hurst

problem of changeable winds over the vast Texas expanses, and the gumbo-like mud which on one day's flying alone accounted for 40 broken propellers.

Canadians Fight Overseas

Overseas Canadians were distinguishing themselves early in the war. On December 14, 1915, A.S. Ince became the first Canadian airman to shoot down an enemy aircraft. Flying as an RNAS observer he downed a German seaplane off Belgium. Five days later M.M. Bell became the first Canadian member of the RFC to score a victory in the air. The next three years were to produce dozens of Canadians famous for their expertise in aerial warfare. Three were to be awarded the Victoria Cross. Of these the first was W.A. "Billy" Bishop.

On June 2, 1917, while patrolling alone, Bishop attacked a German airfield, downing three of the enemy as they took off. For this action he won the V.C. By late August that year, Bishop had counted 47 enemy aircraft shot down. The following spring he added 25 victories in 24 days, including five downed on June 19. Bishop finished the war with 72 victories.

Canada's second V.C. resulted from an action fought March 27, 1918. On that day eighteen-year-old Manitoban Alan McLeod was piloting an Armstrong Whitworth bomber on a raid over France. His gunner was A.W. Hammond. En route to target, McLeod diverted slightly to allow Hammond to down an enemy triplane. This immediately brought seven more of the nimble fighters down upon them. Hammond downed another, but then the bomber was badly hit from below. Both crewmen were shot up and their plane burst into flames.

McLeod was forced out onto the port wing. Hammond had to climb onto his gunring, from where he downed a third German. By this time the bomber was a blazing torch, and the triplanes left it. McLeod, however, managed a crash landing in No-Man's Land. Both crewmen were thrown clear, but the bombs and ammunition in the wreckage began exploding. McLeod immediately began dragging Hammond towards the British lines. At this point he was hit by German

WE CALLED THIS AMBULANCE "HUNGRY LIZZIE"

A JN-4 hung up in overhead wires in downtown Oshawa. On September 22, 1918, Cadet Weiss of 91 CTS made this embarassing landing!

K.M. Molson Collection

Forced landing in a cow pasture. One cow and one airplane a lot the worse for wear!
Aviation and Space Division, National Museum of Science and Technology (4809)

infantry fire, receiving his sixth wound of the day. British soldiers then made a sortie from the trenches to rescue the hard-pressed fliers. For his part in the day's action, Hammond received a bar for his Military Cross.

W.G. Barker, also of Manitoba, was the third Canadian air man to be awarded the V.C. The official citation reads: "On the morning of October 27, 1918, this officer observed an enemy two-seater over the Forêt de Mormal. He attacked this machine, and after a short burst it broke up in the air. At the same time a Fokker biplane attacked him and he was wounded in the right thigh, but managed, despite this, to shoot down the enemy aeroplane in flames. He then found himself in a large formation of Fokkers, which attacked him from all directions, and he was again severely wounded in the left thigh, but succeeded in driving down two of the enemy in a spin.

"He lost consciousness after this and his machine fell out of control. On recovery he found himself being again attacked heavily by a large formation, and, singling out one machine, he deliberately charged and drove it down in flames.

"During this flight his left elbow was shattered and he again fainted, and on regaining consciousness he found himself still being attacked; but, notwithstanding that he was now severely wounded in both legs and his left arm shattered, he dived on the nearest machine and shot it down in flames.

"Being gravely exhausted, he dived out of the fight to regain our lines, but was met by another formation which attacked and endeavoured to cut him off, but after a hard fight, he succeeded in breaking up this formation and reached our lines where he crashed on landing." Barker survived the war with 50 enemy aircraft to his credit.

Many other Canadians became famous in the air war over Europe. A partial list includes Nanaimo-born Ray Collishaw, veteran of some 2000 combat missions who downed 59 enemy aircraft. As commander of No. 10 Squadron RNAS, he and four other Canadians in his squadron accounted for 87 of the enemy in the spring and summer of 1917.

As the cowls and metal side plates of his flight's Sopwith triplanes were painted black, Collishaw's outfit was dubbed the Black Flight. Its aircraft were duly named Black Roger, Black Death, Black Prince, Black Sheep, and Collishaw's own, Black Maria.

Collishaw was later to write extensively of his flying career. At one point he describes World War I fighter tactics: "It was commonplace for contending antagonists to meet 'head-on.' This introduced the most hair-raising experience for fighter pilots. At a distance of about 1200 feet both opponents would open fire. Each pilot could see his own and his opponent's tracer bullet intermingling and he could feel his aircraft shudder from the impact of bullets, while the near misses reacted harshly upon his ears. In about 3 1/2 seconds of fire, the intervening 1200 feet interval was covered and the contending pilots tried to dodge collision, over or under . . . A so-called 'air dog-fight' was the most exciting experience possible to the contestants. Dozens of waltzing couples could be seen in all directions. If one contender became disengaged and saw a likely opponent, it was highly likely that still another intervener would assault him from the rear . . . ."

Donald R. MacLaren of Vancouver became another of Canada's top scoring ace of World War I, having destroyed 48 enemy aircraft plus 6 balloons. He too has described the mayhem of the dog-fight. One of these took place over France and included Camels, S.E.5's, Bristol Fighters,

Canadian ace W.G. Barker in his Sopwith Camel while he was serving with No. 28 Sqdn, RFC in Italy, 1917.

Public Archives of Canada (C 59854)

Victoria Cross winners Bishop and Barker at Leaside in August 1919. At the time, Barker was performing for the crowds at the Canadian National Exhibition, flying a Fokker D.VII.

DND (RE68-5450)

Pfalz's and Albatrosses: "... In the meantime the Bristols and the S.E.5's were having the time of their lives. One S.E. which had shot down a Hun was being given a ride by three others, but by a quick climbing turn he managed to get the advantage over one of the trio. The Hun, in trying to avoid him, turned slowly and rammed one of his fellows. Both machines were badly smashed, and went down leaving bits of fabric floating behind them.

"The Bristols had managed to split up the German formation, and the enemy, thinking he had had enough, drew off and made for home as fast as he could. Our ammunition had been pretty well used up, so we decided to call it a day. We concluded that at the end of the mix-up there must have been nearly 100 machines taking part."

Other famous Canadian names in the air war were Fred McCall, W.G. Claxton, F.G. Quigley, A.D. Carter, A.E. McKeever, and A. Roy Brown. The latter became famous as the pilot who downed the German ace, Baron Manfred von Richthofen. This action occurred April 21, 1918.

The day had started off with von Richthofen leading a flight of 15 triplanes and Albatros fighters on a patrol. The day before he had added victims 79 and 80 to his list of aerial victories. At the same time, Brown was leading his flight of eight

Camels on a patrol. Brown noticed action in the distance and headed for it. The action took the form of the German flight attacking two Australian reconnaissance aircraft. As the odds were in the Germans' favour, things were hot for the Camels once the dog fight began. Following orders, W.R. May, a novice in Brown's flight, headed for his lines as soon as he got the chance. Von Richthofen spotted him exiting, and dove for the kill. Too eager, the 25-year-old German failed to watch his own tail. Brown moved in on him and fired. At the same time, machine gunners below had trained their sights on von

Richthofen's red triplane.

Suddenly the triplane faltered, and made a bumpy landing behind Australian lines. The first soldiers on the scene found von Richthofen dead, a bullet through his chest. After an investigation of the action, it was decided that the fatal bullet must have come from Brown's fire.

Several German Zeppelins also fell to Canadian guns. In October, 1916 W.J. Tempest downed the Zeppelin L.31 over southern England. The following year L.22 and L.43 fell to flying boats piloted by Robert Leckie and Basil Hobbs; while L.P. Watkins, flying a B.E. 12 destroyed L.48.

Leckie's H.12 flying boat at the time he and the others aboard were rescued from their ordeal adrift.

National Museums of Canada (10382)

Later in the war, flying as observer in a D.H. 4, Leckie was to personally shoot down L.70. On board had been the commander of the German Zeppelin Service. These Zeppelin losses did much to demoralize the enemy and bring their night bombing raids over England to a halt.

On September 5, 1917, one of the most famous Zeppelin patrols of the war headed out to sea from the RNAS at Great Yarmouth. At the controls of the Curtiss H.12 flying boat was Robert Leckie. A D.H.4 accompanied the boat. Near Terschelling Island off the Dutch coast, two Zeppelins were encountered. Leckie's gunners opened fire on one of the airships. It answered in kind, then dropped ballast and climbed quickly away. At the same time, enemy vessels fired on the British planes. Leckie's was damaged, and then the D.H.4 suffered engine failure and had to ditch.

Though the H.12 was damaged, Leckie set down and rescued the two downed airmen. Unable to get airborne, he began taxiing towards England on one good engine. The H.12 leaked badly and was in danger of being swamped. Eventually it ran out of gas and was left to drift helplessly. While some men bailed, others had to position themselves on the port wingtip as its opposite float had been torn away, unbalancing the craft.

The flying boat had four homing pigeons on board for just such an emergency. These were released at intervals. One reached a coast guard station in Norfolk with news of Leckie's predicament. A search ship was dis-

patched, and on September 8, he and his five companions were rescued. For this exploit, Leckie was awarded the DFC.

Of all Canadian aviators of the World War I era, none engaged in such a variety of activities as R.H. Mulock. Mulock went to war as a soldier and was a member of the Canadian Field Artillery. Once in England, he arranged for a transfer to the RNAS, received his flying training, and on May 17, 1915, went out on his first recorded patrol.

At 1:40 A.M. that day Mulock took off in an Avro 504B on a mission to intercept the Zeppelin L.38. The German intruder had been sighted over Westgate-on-Sea at 2000 feet. By the time he intercepted it, Mulock was near Ramsgate. He found the Zeppelin floating free, probably having shut down to effect its bombing.

Mulock was ready for action. He had on board two incendiary bombs, two hand grenades, and his revolver — a fair arsenal for those early days of aerial warfare. As he prepared to attack, however, the L.38 restarted its engines and climbed rapidly from the scene. Mulock did his best to pursue the Zeppelin, but its ascent out over the sea was too rapid and he lost sight of it at 7000 feet. At 3:25 A.M. Mulock was back on the ground.

On August 26, 1915, Mulock was on patrol off Ostend when he spotted a German submarine on the surface. He immediately returned to his base near Dunkirk where his aircraft was armed with five 20 pound bombs. He took off again, located the target, and bombed it from 400 feet. Two bombs struck the ship as it dove, but these apparently caused little damage.

Another of Mulock's noteworthy actions was a solo raid he conducted September 28, 1915. This consisted of a long cross-country flight to bomb the Zeppelin storage sheds near Brussels. The

raid was a success, the sheds being set ablaze. Black smoke which poured from them indicated that a Zeppelin had likely been inside. On January 24, Mulock registered his first confirmed enemy aircraft destroyed.

Mulock participated in many special flying operations in addition to his routine activities. He conducted experimental flying involving work with wireless and photographic equipment and with parachute and landing flares. On April 4, 1916, he flew what appears to have been the first night-time artillery spotting mission.

Early the same year, on February 1, he had been on a patrol of 11 Nieuports from Dunkirk, watching for Zeppelins returning from raids on England. Conditions deteriorated, and most of the fighters became lost. Only Mulock and one other pilot were able to find their base. As soon as possible, Mulock was back in the air, accompanied by a mechanic and his tool kit. Before long, he had located five Nieuports which had force landed on beaches and sand bars. In each case, Mulock landed, made certain that the Nieuports were airworthy, and pointed the errant pilots towards home.

In March, 1918, Mulock was appointed commander of No. 82 Wing, comprising three squadrons of bombers: No. 38 with F.E. 2b's, No. 214 with Handley Pages, and No. 218 with D.H. 9's. The following July he returned to England on another special task, that of forming No. 27 Group, a proposed bombing unit to be equipped with the Handley Page V/1500 four-engined heavy bomber. This unit was to train for long-range raids on Germany. The war ended before No. 27 became operational and Mulock returned to Canada where he became active in civil aviation.

Christian Burgener: Diary of an Airman

Many Canadians and Americans served with Mulock's bombing wing. These men were pioneers in night-bombing. They flew bombers on long cross-country raids with only rudimentary navigation aids. One of the Canadians on these historic operations was Lt. Christian Burgener. He had gone overseas with the Eastern Ontario Regiment, Canadian Infantry, then transferred to the Royal Flying Corps. His introduction to flight occurred October 12, 1917, when he went up in a Maurice Farman for 15 minutes. By November 26, he had logged 7:50 hours.

In December he moved to Narborough in Norfolk where he and his friend W.J. Dalziel from Saskatchewan began advanced training on B.E.2 E.'s. On December 11, with a total of 11:55 hours in the air, Burgener soloed. The five-minute flight was not too auspicious for Burgener made a bad takeoff, stalled, and nearly came to grief. He crashed into a tree on landing and later notes in his diary: "Smashed my nose and spent a few days in hospital. Had a beautiful black eye for about two weeks . . . Dalziel also crashed on Dec. 17th."

Norfolk winters brought poor flying weather, assuring the student aviators their share of boredom. Mail was especially important during such spells. On January 18 Burgener wrote: "At last mail from Canada. Got five letters. Raining practically all day so had good chance to read them."

On January 21 Burgener took some instruction on the D.H. 6 and soloed on it the same day. January 25 he remarked: "Fly my old D.H.6. Like them very much. Also have a ride in an R.E.8. Think I will like them as well."

Training carried on and became intense during the following months:

February 21: "Very windy but put in one hour and 15 min. in the air . . . very bumpy. Have developed a wonderful confidence in the air now, and simply love flying. What a contrast to about six weeks ago. Passed all tests now and expect to graduate soon. Poor Shaw and Low are getting buried today." They had died two days earlier in the crash of their D.H.4.

February 23: "The third fatal accident occurred today. One of our best pilots, Lt. Laws, a Canadian who had done a lot of flying, crashed a D.H.4 . . ."

March 21: "Fine trip today on photographic work. Remained in air for two hours. Stayed over the water over 1/2 hour taking pictures of English Zeppelin."

March 22: "Put in some more time in

R.E.8, 'graduate' and get permission to take up passenger . . . Anderson of 121 Sqd as first passenger. Am now supposed to be a full-fledged pilot but do not feel like it although have done 48 hours solo flying."

March 28: "Received my pilot's certificate today. Needless to say, very proud of it."

May 6: "What a different life. Was told today that I needn't attend any more lectures and can fly whenever I like . . ."

May 30: " . . . a real good game of baseball between our American boys . . . it gives us Canadians all a feeling of home again to hear their typical expressions."

On June 15 Burgener was posted to the No. 1 School of Navigation and Bomb Dropping at Stonehenge. He arrived there two days later, but had had to report the sixteenth: "A black day for the squadron. My friend Lt. Aldertin with whom I was in Lynn last evening and had dinner with, cracked up in a 4 today and paid the price."

"Got a new Bus today, little A.W. (Armstrong Whitworth) Russell takes me up and loops eight times. Do not like the sensation after the third or fourth attempt, but on the whole think they are a fine Bus." This entry appears in Lt. Burgener's diary for February 28, 1918. His log shows that he flew B9620 on May 2, 1918. In all, he flew 26 hours 35 minutes on this type.

Public Archives of Canada (C 28065)

At Stonehenge Burgener was soon busy checking out on new types and learning night flying. His notebooks cover many details of the F.E.2 B: "Running on the ground: Run the engine at about 600 revs until thermometer needle commences to move. Then run it up to 1000 revs and test both mags separately. Open throttle fully and note revs . . . . Do not run engine full out for more than 1/4 min. on ground

. . . engine should be looked over for water leaks while it is running on the ground. Never let a mechanic climb about on the machine while the engine is running, with his cap on, as he may knock it against a wire, in which case it goes through the prop and may break same causing a lot of damage . . . .

"Fire: If the machine catches fire in the air, turn off petrol at once. Close throttle. Switch off. Land.

"Draining water: In frosty weather care must be taken to drain off all water. To do this, the tail of the machine must be raised just above flying position and the prop rotated . . . .

"Cross Country: White rockets are sent up when a machine is due back and it is in sight 18-20 miles away . . . . Permission to land must be asked for by firing the colour of the day. This must be replied to by a like colour . . . .

"Engine trouble: . . . If you have to have a forced landing and you have fired Michlin Flares and found no suitable

landing space, fly over and fire 'Very's lights.' They give considerable light and a landing place may then be discovered."

Lt. Burgener had not been excited about becoming a bomber pilot. On June 21 he entered: "Saw 'Windy' and he kind of got me to console myself with the idea of becoming a night pilot." But he soon adjusted. After a few nights on the Maurice Farman and F.E.2.B he went straight on to Handley Pages.

June 27: "Go on H.P.'s for my first time and this makes my 8th Bus . . . . . Am not very struck on H.P.'s but will try and stick them."

June 28: "Since I did all my H.P. flying required to pass my day tests I won't have anything to do for about a week."

June 29: " . . . Take a walk to the

Stones which make Stonehenge famous. The weather is very hot now and it is none too pleasant hanging around aerodrome and attending lectures."

July 5: " . . . from now on am a night bird. Had to put in my first three hours during the night. All went off successfully. At the same time do not find any great fascination in the work and so far would prefer day flying."

July 11: "Finished all tests on F.E.2.B. so didn't have to fly last night . . . ."

July 13: "Moved to H.P. today, and even after staying up all night didn't get a chance to make a good start. First a heavy ground mist came up and then when we did get a start, burst two tyres."

squadron and consider myself very lucky."

August 8: "My first start today. Go up as rear gunner on raid to Bruges . . . do not reach objective on account of dud weather."

August 10: "Another raid as rear gunner with Russell, and this time a real one. Raided Bruges with 1660 lb bombs. Found it quite exciting and saw there a sight which I will for a long time remember. Everything turned out O.K. Arrived back at Dunkirk. Land on beach and return from here in the morning."

August 12: "Am now quite sure of getting a Bus of my own almost any day. Would, however, rather put in more time as passenger, but am afraid will not get the chance."

August 24: "Raid Zeebrugge . . . got attacked by three E.A. off Ostend. Also port engine went dud on return. Again afraid I might have to come down in Holland but managed to get back."

August 25: "A great surprise today. Old Dalziel came over in his Bus before I was out of bed this morning."

September 13: "Raining again and the inactivity nearly driving us crazy . . . ."

September 23: "Go to Calais to do some shopping. At night getting settled down nicely writing letters when orders come to turn out for raid. It had been dud all day but suddenly cleared and off we went. On my return had the misfortune to come down without warning . . . landed O.K. in water off beach at Clipon. Have to

Lt. Burgener leans an arm on the cockpit edge of a Handley Page bomber. Beside him is his friend Lt. Dalziel.
Public Archives of Canada (C 28035)

On July 18 Lt. Burgener went to London where he saw the plays, "Man from Toronto" and "The Naughty Wife."

July 19: "After arriving back from London last night found that the severe rain here had blown my tent over. Luckily however my batman moved everything into a new tent and no damage was done. Had to stay up all night and finish my time on H.P. Got along fine. Did my bombing, cross country and landings O.K." The night's work had included six flights in aircraft No. 9671 for a total of 3.8 hours.

On July 24 came orders to report to 214 Sqdn. near Dunkirk. Lt. Burgener arrived there the same evening and noted: "Find out here that this is a famous

August 13: " . . . am on the raiding list for tonight . . . . Reach my objective O.K. . . . attacked by E.A. . . . but nothing serious. On the whole took the whole procedure very coolly and after meeting no further troubles managed to drop bombs and return to Dunkirk . . . followed by a Hun but he did not attack . . . had the misfortune to run into my hangar and damage Bus so it will be out of action for a few days . . . ."

August 21: " . . . A very long and tiresome raid. In the air five hours. Got it very hot over Bruges and Zeebrugge. Came back with one engine dud. The night was as light as day and we could see everything below. Thought once or twice that we would not survive the barrage and made for Holland, but we were safe once out to sea again." On this raid aircraft No. 3489 was used and 16 112 pound bombs were dropped from 5000 feet on a canal.

wait an hour before tide goes down and go ashore. Took us two hours of walking around in night to find a telephone. Found one at Casino at Clipon 10 km from Dunkirk. Found out at daybreak that machine was O.K. Engines cut out from lack of petrol . . . . Relief came at 9 o'clock. Got her filled up again, left for home at 10:15. Arrived 30 minutes later. Spent the rest of the day in bed having a well-earned rest. The only thing I had to eat or drink since the night before was a cup of coffee at a French farmhouse. Fortunately for me my observers could both speak French nicely." As a result of the forced landing in the water, Burgener's observer, a Cpl. Thomas, contracted pneumonia and died soon after.

October 4: "And another raid tonight . . . weather very bad and had a hard time finding our way. However, succeeded in bombing obj. On return surprised both engines cut out over aerodrome and unable to land on account of another Bus ahead of us getting the right away signal. On trying to land on upper end of drome the machine became unmanageable and crashed into woods just above aerodrome. The Bus is a total wreck and we all narrowly escaped injury and again must consider myself exceedingly lucky. Stay in bed all day trying to recuperate from shock.''

October 6: ''Big doings today. Have our RAF band from England, on tour in France. Here for a concert in the afternoon. Got a bunch of the doctors and nurses from the Canadian hospital up.''

October 11: '' . . . War news is continuing good. Everybody begins to think that we won't have to do so very many more raids.''

October 14: ''Another raid tonight. All goes well again except that the weather is very bad . . . saw tonight the greatest sight I have ever experienced in war flying. Almost the whole of the Belgium front seems to be on fire.''

October 18: '' . . . signs of us having to move up soon as the Huns are evacuating the Belgium coast and we will soon be able to go and see our own bomb holes. Our C.O. has the honour today of taking the King and Queen of Belgium over to Ostend in a Handley. Some honour.''

October 20: ''Another day which I will not forget so soon. A bunch of us decided to take a run up to the lines . . . . Never had even the remotest idea of the devastation and state of the country and the largeness of the whole battle front. I have flown over the district before but at night and consequently not seen it the same as I have today . . . .''

October 30: ''A perfect day for our moving. Start off at 10 o'clock and after 1:20 hours of very interesting trip arrived at the new place . . . . What a sight we saw when crossing No Man's Land. Have fairly good quarters in a chateau where the Huns had been 10 days ago.''

November 10: '' . . . Hate to go tonight as every hour we expect an armistice and would hate to meet with a mishap . . . . Have engine trouble at first, therefore a long time behind the rest . . . . Raid Louvain siding which we find all ablaze from previous bombing . . . . The greatest news when I open my eyes in the morning. The armistice has been signed and our work is over so expect to have done my last raid last night. A fine finish and completely satisfied to pack up. Everybody almost wild with joy and celebrate all day . . .''

November 12: ''All have thick heads today . . . it hardly seems possible that the show is over.''

After the Armistice: The Canadian Air Force

Of the over 22 000 Canadians who served with the RFC, the RNAS, and the RAF nearly all returned home. About 1500 had given their lives, mostly pilots and observers who died in training or in action. There were a few fatalities just after the war in the original Canadian Air Force. This was the fate of fighter ace A.D. Carter who died in the crash of a No. 2 Squadron Fokker D. VII in 1919. McKeever died the same year in an auto accident in Ontario. Alan McLeod and F.G. Quigley succumbed to the global flu epidemic of late 1918 which killed more people in a few months than had the preceding five years of war. Most of the flying veterans, however, returned eagerly to civilian life, hanging up their goggles forever. A few, like Christian Burgener, retained an interest in flying, especially after the flying club movement began developing. Otherwise, a relatively few veterans stayed close to flying, either as members of the post-war Canadian Air Force, or as Canada's first commercial aviators. Wartime names such as Ashton, Berry, Brintnell, Dickins, Gilbert, May, Oaks, and Stevenson were eventually to go down in history as Canada's great pioneer bush pilots.

Ironically the war ended just as Canada was establishing its own military flying organization. Part of this was in response to the need for anti-submarine patrols to protect convoys using Halifax. As many of the convoys were American, the U.S. provided aircraft and crews while Canadian recruits were being trained for the Royal Canadian Naval Air Service. Several U.S. Navy HS-2L's arrived at Dartmouth and on August 25 two of these flew the first patrol. It was initially planned to cover convoys out to a distance of 80 miles.

At this time the name E.L. Janney again crops up. This time he was a Sub-Lieutenant in the RCNVR recruiting western applicants in Regina. The war ended, however, before the RCNAS could take over the flying boat patrols from the U.S. Navy and on December 5, 1918, the service was disbanded. The H-boats with their support equipment were then donated to Canada.

On September 19, 1918, the Privy Council approved the formation of two squadrons of the Canadian Air Force in England. These were No. 1, a fighter squadron, and No. 2, a day bomber squadron. These formed in late November, under command of W.A. Bishop. The following March No. 1 Wing formed to administer the two squadrons with R.

Leckie commanding.

No. 1 Squadron began operations November 20, 1918, at Upper Heyford, Oxfordshire, flying Avro 504K's, Bristol Fighters, Fokker D. VII's, S.E. 5a's, Sopwith Dolphins and Sopwith Pups. No. 2 flew from the same base using D.H. 9a's. Many well-known Canadian fliers served with these squadrons including such aces as D.R. MacLaren, A.E. McKeevor, C.M. McEwen, C.F. Falkenburg, G.O. Johnson, and G.R. Howsan.

Early in 1920 Canada decided against a permanent air force and disbanded its two overseas squadrons. The Canadian Air Force ceased to exist on August 9, 1920.

Early Post-War Flying

In June, 1919, Britain made a gift to Canada of over 100 aircraft, 12 airships, and a vast quantity of other material including hangars and vehicles. This equipment was to form the nucleus of Canada's new home-based air force. The same year the Air Board came into being in Canada, with R. Leckie as Superintendent of Flying Operations. In December, 1919, the Air Board submitted to the government its recommendations for the organization of a Canadian Air Force. Authorization for its formation was given on February 18, 1920. This was to be a non-permanent organization, with former officers and men of the RAF and the CAF in England being invited to serve for up to five weeks a year. The authorization given allowed for a force of just over 5000 personnel. Operations were initially centred at Camp Borden, and by the end of 1920, 197 officers and men had undergone refresher courses there, and logged 733 hours.

Other activities that year included forest fire patrols, aerial photography, and a survey of pest-ridden forest tracts to determine the extent of damage.

By year's end the Air Board had established stations at Jericho Beach, Vancouver; Morley, Alberta; Rockcliffe; and Roberval on Lac St. Jean. Aircraft in service included the Avro 504, Bristol Fighter, D.H.9a, Felixstowe F.3 and HS-2L. This was also the year of the Air Board's famous trans-Canada flight from Halifax to Vancouver using a Fairey Transatlantic, HS-2L, F.3, and three D.H. 9a's.

In 1921 the Air Board conducted operations for nine federal government departments and three provinces, and flew from seven stations at Jericho Beach, High River, Victoria Beach on Lake Winnipeg, Sioux Lookout, Rockcliffe, Roberval, and Halifax. Avro 504's, D.H.4's, F.3's and HS-2L's were employed. Additional operations included army cooperation and coastal patrols to help control smuggling.

An important step towards strengthening aviation in Canada occurred on June 28, 1922, with the passing of the National Defence Act. This Act brought under one scheme the Department of the Naval Service, the Department of Militia and Defence, and the Air Board. This led to an amalgamation within the Air Board of its civil and military jurisdiction into one organization and to the institution of a plan to grant temporary commissions or enlistments in the CAF. At year's end, the Air Board air stations were handed over to the CAF. A new type of operation that year was a series of 21 flights made in Northern Manitoba for the Department of Indian Affairs. These were for the purposes of delivering treaty money to Indians, an operation that usually took months of travel by canoe. These treaty-money flights

One of the National Aeronautical Collections three Avro 504K trainers. The 504 was one of the most widely used training aircraft of WWI and earlier in the war was also used in combat roles. Many Canadian airmen flew the 504 overseas, and back in Canada after the war. This 504 was restored as a Centennial Year project and flew at airshows across Canada as part of the RCAF's Golden Centennaires aerobatic team.

Bill Ewing

were to become annual undertakings from here on. Sometimes double duty was performed, with the Indian Affairs agent delivering money, while a doctor, aided by pilot and mechanic would administer vaccinations.

For the most part, the tribes of northern Manitoba had never seen aircraft. The arrival of an H-boat often meant much ceremony for the inhabitants of a settlement. Sometimes fliers were given colourful titles by the Indians. Air Commodore A.D. Ross recalled years later that his was "Chief of the flying gasoline canoe."

Another notable event of 1922 occurred when Major F.S. Cotton flew to Labrador. On March 3 he left Botwood, Newfoundland. He flew his Martinsyde northwest towards the bleak Labrador coast, navigating with nothing more sophisticated than a map drawn by hand by a Dr. John Grieve.

After a stop at St. Anthony, Cotton pushed on for Cartwright where he landed safely on the fourth. After a stay of several days, he departed March 12 with a load of mail and furs and reached St. John's safely. Cotton's flight was significant in that it was the first time the winter isolation of the remote Labrador coast had been broken. This must indeed have warmed the hearts of the coastal settlers.

On February 15, 1923, King George V approved the redesignation of the CAF to Royal Canadian Air Force. Reorganization for this new administration was completed April 1, 1924, the official birthday of the RCAF which now assumed control over all Civil Government flying and that year logged 2472 hours in the air. Its most notable operation of the year was an aerial survey conducted in Northern Manitoba using a new type of aircraft, the Vickers Viking.

The expedition had been carefully planned the preceding year. Fuel had been cached along the intended route, transported north in four-gallon cans, two cans to the case so as to be manageable by canoe. A Fairchild aerial camera was supplied, equipped with a mechanical film drive. There were 25 roles of film in 100-foot lengths and four film magazines. The Viking was stripped of all excess weight prior to departure. This included removing its wheels and tail skid, a 200-pound saving.

Everything that went into the Viking was weighed — 720 pounds for four crewmen, 212 pounds for emergency survival gear, 840 pounds for 112 gallons of gas and so on. Weight was critical, for there was a long way to go in an airplane with marginal performance capabilities. The Viking might run for three or four

Ground crew at work at the Jericho Beach air station in 1921, readying an F.3 for a fisheries patrol. By 1923 this type had been phased out of service in Canada.

Aviation and Space Division, National Museum of Science and Technology (1177)

The crew of the Viking used during the 1924 aerial survey in northern Manitoba. From left to right are Cpl Alex Milne, S/L B.D. Hobbs, R.D. Davidson and F/O J.R. Cairns. For several years, Alex Milne, survivor of this historic crew, has been active in the Canadian Aviation Historical Society in Toronto.

Public Archives of Canada (C25910)

miles before getting airborne; then there was the hour long climb to reach 5000 feet. In all, 2063 pounds were loaded onto the plane, giving an all-up weight of 5863 pounds. On July 18, the Viking set out from Victoria Beach on a northwesterly course.

It arrived at The Pas on the first day. The 325-mile trip took nearly 4 hours. Next day the crew was out on its first photo survey. The expedition's objective was to conduct a photo survey in the Reindeer Lake-Churchill River region, some 15 000 square miles in all. Over the next two weeks the Viking was to log 49 hours and cover over 2000 line miles. Cameraman Jimmy Cairns made 1800 exposures which were to form the basis of the first accurate map of the region.

Surveying methods were typical of the day. The cameraman, riding in the nose, was lashed in lest he be tossed overboard in turbulent air. Film magazines were changed in flight inside an eiderdown which was someone's sleeping bag at night. Camera repairs were made as required by Cairns and engineer Alex Milne. This entailed total strip-downs and rebuilds.

The expedition returned to home base 25 days after departure, mission accomplished. Reporting later on the operation, Major Basil Hobbs, pilot of the Viking commented, " . . . the operation was completed by factors not stressed in this report, such as flying in directions which would put the sun behind us as much as possible, as well as getting weather clear of clouds . . . . There was also the fact that we were over quite unknown country where landings had to be made on unfamiliar water, with the added difficulty of getting altitude quickly in spite of a heavy load, in order that we could start photographing as soon as possible. That these, and many other adverse conditions, were overcome

... gives assurance that even longer journeys may be planned with every prospect of success.''

For the fiscal year 1925, the RCAF flew a total of 5111 hours, about equally split between military and civil duties. On July 17, the first Vickers Vedette flying boat was taken on strength. The same year, the twin-engine Vickers Varuna flying boat was being evaluated by the Air Force. The usual forestry patrols, aerial surveying, treaty-money flights, mercy flights, and training continued. Each flying boat station by this period was equipped with a fire detection aircraft and an HS-2L "suppression" aircraft. The latter was ready to fly fire-fighting crews out to fires, along with such gear as pumps, hose, and collapsible canoes.

The following year was highlighted by the famous McKee-Godfrey trans-Canada flight, as well as budget cutbacks which curtailed certain activities. No. 4 Squadron at Dartmouth could not operate that year while No. 1 Squadron at Vancouver was forced to reduce fisheries patrols, and be content with its two aging HS-2L's. The only modern military aircraft serving in Canada that year were two Siskin fighters involved in cold weather testing at Edmonton.

Another significant operation in 1926 was a major survey conducted along the proposed route of the Hudson Bay Railway. Between September 17 and October 5, a Viking covered 24 000 square miles along the route, at first operating from Cormorant Lake, then moving to Norway House before having to fly back south as freeze-up approached.

The Hudson Strait Expedition
While Western Canada Airways and RCAF aircraft were assisting in the federal government port scheme on lower Hudson

Bay, far to the north, at the entrance to the Bay, another phase of the same program was under way. A seaport at Churchill would depend on safe navigation between it and the open waters of the North Atlantic. Hudson, Baffin, Radisson and Grosseilliers, and other adventurers had known these waters centuries earlier; but for them, the vast inland sea was forever mysterious and full of dangers. If it was to be guaranteed safe to modern shipping, these elements would have to be studied and understood. In 1927, then, Ottawa launched a scientific expedition into the Hudson Strait region.

The expedition was assembled at Halifax. Included were six open cockpit Fokker Universals and a Moth. There were also prefabricated buildings, tractors, launches, over 15 000 gallons of fuel and aviation spirits, coal, sand, cement, scientific gear and the thousand and one other items needed to sustain the 44-man party for 16 months. Everything, over 5000

The crated Fokker Universal "Saskatchewan", arrives at Nottingham Island, Base "B," August 1927. All aircraft on the Hudson Strait Expedition were registered to the Department of Marine and Fisheries, but flown by the RCAF.
Public Archives of Canada (PA 55522)

tons in all, was loaded aboard two vessels which sailed on July 17. Within ten days, both had reached Port Burwell on the northeast tip of Ungava Bay. Here a base camp was established. The ships then sailed on to set up two other camps at Wakeham Bay, and on Nottingham Island at the western extreme of Hudson Strait. The

Home-spun entertainment. This impromptu little group was known as the Wakeham Bay orchestra, and included, from left to right, F/O Carr-Harris, pilot; Romeo Lemieux, storekeeper; A.E. Axcell, wireless operator; S/L T.A. Lawrence, pilot; and Dr. W.J.K. Clothier.
Public Archives of Canada (PA 55643)

British Columbia damaged on takeoff from Eric Cove. The expedition had its woes.

Public Archives of Canada (PA 55613)

camps extended over the full 450 miles of the Strait. The task of locating sites for them had been facilitated by the float-equipped Moth, providing aerial reconnaissance.

By early September the camps were established. Each was equipped for Arctic survival, with personnel including a doctor, an RCMP constable, and a number of Inuit who served as helpers and advisers. By early November the Fokkers were beginning their work. One of their tasks was to determine the feasibility of using aircraft to help ships navigate the Strait. Each plane was equipped with a radio transmitter but no receiver, and on each flight the pilot's routines included checking in with home base every few minutes as a safety precaution.

There were day-to-day problems in flying in such a region. The only navigation aids available consisted of 100-year-old Admiralty charts. That increased the seat-of-the-pants aspect of getting around. Film of the expedition shows problems encountered recovering the float-equipped Fokkers during open water operations. This was tricky as they had no water rudders. Also shown, though, are various forms of entertainment enjoyed by the party during its stay. There was baseball in the snow and on Dominion Day, such fun as three-legged and wheelbarrow races, and a find-your-shoes-in-the-pile competition.

On February 17, 1928, Flying Officer A. Lewis became lost on a flight from Port Burwell in G-CAHG. He had come up against the kind of snow and fog conditions that plague the region and have ever since been the bane of fliers. With Lewis were Flight Sergeant Terry and Bobby Anakatok, an Inuit. When he realized his predicament, Lewis set down on the ice. He wasn't certain where they were, but felt it must be in the general area of home base. As the plane was damaged, and almost out

of fuel, the trio set out on foot, pulling along a life raft and survival kit. At first they struggled eastward, but after two days reversed their course towards what appeared to be land on the horizon. They had already abandoned their raft, using ice pans where necessary. Lewis describes one harrowing experience with open water:

" . . . Next day we breakfasted on frozen walrus squares, biscuit, chocolate and tea. Feeling like normal men again, we set out on our way.

"Though this day passed uneventfully enough, the one that ensued did not. We had been walking for about two hours when, sure enough, we came to a lead. It was impossible to determine how far it stretched in either direction, but, since we now had no raft, there was nothing for it but to walk north in the direction of the drift.

"After walking for about an hour, we decided to pry loose a pan of ice sufficiently large to support the weight of the three of us, and to use it to ferry across to the other side.

"After we had separated a fairly large pan from the main pack, Bobby took a flying leap onto the centre of it and kept it level while we in turn jumped on. The pan, under our combined weights, sank into the water at least three inches, and our feet, awash in cold water, rapidly became numb. We crouched down as low as we could to prevent the pan from capsizing, and quickly paddled our way across the few feet that barred our way to deliverance. When we hit shore, Terry in his hurry to get off, slipped and fell into the water. His immersion gave us some concern, but the water had not penetrated sufficiently to cause him any great discomfort. We bivouacked in the lee of an ice-ridge and there we remained until dawn, drinking tea and sipping brandy . . "

On the ninth day the trio finally reached land. It turned out that they had not been on Ungava Bay at all, but on the frozen Atlantic. Once ashore, they were rescued by local Inuit and on March 1 they

arrived at Port Burwell.

Throughout the Hudson Strait Expedition, 227 flights were completed. Information gathered related to navigation in the Strait, and permitted the updating of maps and charts. A better understanding of spring break-up in Hudson Strait was one specific factor better understood after the expedition had been completed.

Three radio navigation stations were eventually set up as aids to vessels using these waters. Valuable experience in northern aircraft operation was also gained, although little was heard afterwards of a proposed scheme to directly use aircraft to assist shipping. On November 14, 1928, most of the expedition arrived at Quebec aboard the CGS *Montcalm*. Included were the Fokkers. It had been hoped to fly them back to Ottawa, but float fittings were found to be badly corroded by salt water. Thus they were dismantled and loaded aboard ship, except for the Moth which had been sunk in a mishap. While the expedition was successful, it should be remembered that civilian operators were flying in the remote North at the same time. Their activities were carried out regularly and safely without the logistic support afforded the RCAF along Hudson Strait.

Into the Thirties

Aerial photography remained for years one of the RCAF's prime activities. In 1928, using Fairchilds, Vikings, and Vedettes, 64 400 square miles were covered by eight specially formed photo detachments. Starting at this time, D.H.60 Moths began replacing the Avro 504's as basic training aircraft. The following year nearly 23 000 hours were logged on military and civil flying duties. New types taken on strength during this period were the Avian trainer, Bellanca CH-300 utility aircraft, Curtiss-Reid Rambler trainer, Fleet 7B trainer, and Vancouver flying boat.

In 1931 the RCAF participated in the Trans Canada Air Pageant. It provided the famous Siskin demonstration team, supported by Fairchilds and a Ford Trimotor. By 1932 the effects of the Depression began to be felt in the RCAF. Two hundred eighty-eight staff were cut, thus representing 20 per cent of its strength. As well, the purchase of new aircraft and the construction of new facilities were severely cut back. Total time flown for 1933 was just 10 762 hours. That year the RCAF listed on strength nine Siskins, the only fighters and already obsolete; five Vancouvers; and 82 trainers. Fairchilds, Vedettes, D.H.80 Puss Moths, and Bellancas for use on Civil Government Air Operations numbered 83.

The Armstrong Whittworth Siskin IIIA was the first modern fighter used by the RCAF. They were taken on strength between 1927-1931 but were soon rendered obsolete. Some were still active when war broke out in 1939. These were photographed at the Toronto Flying Club, in 1929 or 1930.

James Collection, City of Toronto Archives

Coastal Operations

Some typical operations during these years have been related by J.D. (Jack) Hunter. In 1932 he was stationed at Havre St. Pierre with two Vancouvers being used to support the Imperial Economic Conference under way in Ottawa. The Vancouvers were used to fly mail and documents from the *Empress of Britain*. The liner was intercepted in the Strait of Belle Isle where mail bags were taken onboard the flying boats to be flown to Rimouski. From there other aircraft carried them to Ottawa. On July 24 Hunter's Vancouver, VU, was forced down onto the Gulf of St. Lawrence. This left F/L de Niverville and Sgt. Hunter in some dismay. This was worsened when someone dropped an oil pressure relief valve overboard. As there was no replacement, the crew had to improvise. Jack came up with a 1/4-inch aircraft bolt and after several hours of filing had produced a facsimile valve. It fitted nicely and the Vancouver got away. Some time after, the troublesome engine was sent to be overhauled. When it came back, Jack discovered that his hand-made valve was still in place, apparently deemed quite serviceable by the overhaulers!

F/L F.J. Mawdesley also had problems and was forced down one day. To get the mail to Rimouski he hailed a passing rum runner which agreed to deliver it. The sacks were dropped on the dock at Rimouski and the rum runners went on their way.

Rum runner patrols were conducted during these prohibition years with the RCAF and RCMP working as a team. Their combination of air and sea patrols made it difficult for the rum runners to make an honest living. RCMP agents on St. Pierre and Miquelon would often be able to radio the exact minute of departure of rum runners heading for the mainland, and a patrol plane and/or vessel would be waiting to intercept them. Jack Hunter intercepted one of these vessels, then called in the RCMP patrol boat *Alachasse*. It was soon being outrun by the speedier rum runner, and proceeded to launch a small hydroplane. This boat fired on the rum runner, which then hove to. Jack had had a bird's eye view of these activities from his Fairchild 71, observing that, as the rum runner sought to escape, its crew did its best to dispose of the evidence by dumping cases of contraband overboard.

Similar activities were conducted on the West Coast; but in addition to spotting for rum runners, RCAF aircraft conducted narcotics patrols. One type of patrol was to meet liners arriving from the Orient. A patrol aircraft would begin circling a liner perhaps 20 miles out to sea, watching for tin cans being tossed over the side. A practice of ship's crews had been to toss cans containing heroin into the sea for pick-up by a nearby contact vessel.

After one West Coast patrol near Port Renfrew, September 3, 1931, Jack Hunter had set down and tied up to an RCN destroyer. Around noon a storm blew up and the ship began drifting. It pulled up anchor and steamed off into the wind, towing the big flying boat behind. Jack found that, given his speed on the water and the strong head wind, he could pull back on the control column and actually get airborne. It was 9:00 P.M. before conditions subsided enough for the destroyer to stop and allow the flying boat crew, by then blue with cold, aboard.

One of 24 Westland Wapiti IIA army cooperation aircraft acquired by the RCAF in 1936. They had previously been used by the British in tribal warfare in regions like Palestine and Mesopotamia. The Wapitis were assembled in Canada by Ottawa Car and one test pilot at the time recalls that they were full of sand and carried the distinct odour of camels! The Wapiti was called the "What a pity" by airmen who knew it.

Jack McNulty

Occupational Hazards

Another incident from the early thirties involved a Vedette which had just taken off from its northern photo detachment base. Soon after liftoff power dropped. The crewman decided to check out the wind-driven generator. To do this he had to crawl from his forward position to the pilot's cockpit, then climb the struts to the top wing. This he managed, but on reaching the top wing he had the misfortune of losing several fingers in the whirling generator blades.

He quickly descended and informed the pilot of his trouble. The pilot made a quick turn around and headed back to land. He chose to land downwind and towards the head of a bay. This didn't work out too well, and the Vedette soon ran out of bay before even touching down. The pilot, F/O Bob Barker, pulled back to avoid trees. He skimmed the first of these but more loomed up. At the sight of these, the crewman, Sgt. Stan Greene, stepped into space. The Vedette crashed, and men from the camp raced to the scene. Barker was extricated safely from the wreck, but it took some time to pinpoint Greene. He was atop a tree, quite alive.

Modest Growth

In 1935 budget restraints were eased somewhat, enabling the RCAF to procure its first new aircraft since 1931. These were Atlas fighters. The following year procurements included Wapiti army cooperation aircraft, four Sharks, three Avro 626's, ten Fleets, three Deltas and two Super 71's. Even so, strength had dropped to 135 aircraft that year.

In 1937 the RCAF's budget suddenly rose to over $11 000 000 enabling the purchase of 104 new aircraft and a 50 percent increase in personnel. Nearly 20 000 hours were logged, although Civil Government flying dropped off to 2360 hours. These events coincided with growing tension as Europe rearmed.

World War II — Return to Action

It was 1939 before the RCAF finally retired its ancient Siskins and acquired its first modern fighters. In February, No.1 Squadron took delivery in Vancouver of its new Hurricane Mk.I's, and ferried them back to Calgary. Meanwhile the world situation was worsening, and by summer it was evident that war was near. In August the Air Force began taking precautions by repositioning squadrons to wartime stations. No.3 ferried its seven Wapitis from Calgary to Halifax; No.1 moved to

A Canadian Vickers-built Delta II of No. 8 (GP) Sqdn preparing to fly from Ottawa to Sydney, Nova Scotia in preparation for war, August 1939. The Delta, used mainly in the photo survey role, was the RCAF's first all-metal aircraft.

Public Archives of Canada (PA 63532)

St. Hubert; No.2 moved its Atlases from Trenton to Saint John; and No.8 moved its Deltas from Rockcliffe to Sydney.

Other squadrons were already strategically placed: No.4 with flying boats and No.6 with Sharks at Vancouver; and No.7 with Fairchilds and Norsemans at Rockcliffe. There were also 12 Auxiliary Squadrons either formed or being formed, but five of these never became operational.

On the eve of war, RCAF strength was 4061 officers and men and less than 300 aircraft. The inventory of "front line" aircraft included 13 Atlases, 10 Battles, 12 Deltas, 19 Hurricanes, 20 Oxfords, 11 Sharks, 5 Siskins, 9 Stranraers, 4 Vancouvers, and 22 Wapitis. General purpose and training types included 14 Avro trainers, 9 Bellancas, 23 Fairchilds, 41 Fleet Fawns, 1 Grumman Goose, 14 Harvards, 2 Hawker Tom Tits, 30 Moths, 4 Norsemans, and 9 Vedettes.

Throughout 1939 the RCAF stepped

An RCAF Stranraer coastal patrol aircraft off the West Coast.

DND (WRF-158)

up training. This included primary instruction provided by the civilian flying clubs. Interim and advanced training centred on Camp Borden and Trenton; a Flying Instructors' School was opened at Camp Borden. The significance of such activity became clear when Germany invaded Poland on September 1. Two days later England and France declared war on Germany, with Canada following suit a week later.

On September 14, as it was ferrying to Sydney, a No.8 Squadron Delta, No.673, crashed in the forests of New Brunswick killing Flight Sergeant J.E. Doan, and LAC D.A. Rennie. These two airmen thus became the RCAF's first World War II fatalities. Their remains and the wreck of their plane were not discovered until 1969.

It was immediately clear that Britain would need plenty of aid to stave off German might. In the air war thousands of aircrew and aircraft would be needed, and Canada was to be a major contributor.

No. 1 Sqdn Hurricanes at Vancouver. Twenty of these were accepted by the RCAF between February and August 1939. Three had been lost in Category A (serious) accidents by November and the last taken out of service the following June.
Aviation and Space Division, National Museum of Science and Technology (5269)

Canadian-built Grumman Goblins of No. 118 Fighter Sqdn in formation near Halifax early in the war. These served in the RCAF from late 1940 to early 1942.
DND (PL5954)

The British Commonwealth Air Training Plan

On December 17, 1939, the British Commonwealth Air Training Plan agreement was signed. Through this scheme Britain was to be provided with the aircrews it so desperately needed. The rationale behind the Plan was similar to that of the RFC Canada 22 years earlier. Canada was seen as a natural training ground for airmen. It had the manpower, natural resources, plenty of space, suitable climate, and immunity from enemy interference. Some of these assets were included by Air Marshal Robert Leckie in his 1936 air training proposal. Although he described Canada's climate as one of extremes, he noted, ''None of these conditions are comparable to the adverse flying weather experienced in England, and the flying can be continued with very few interruptions throughout the year . . . . A Flying Training School formed in Canada

may be said to be practically immune from enemy action . . . . I cannot visualize any circumstances under which the United States would tolerate the intrusion of a European Power into Canada . . . . '' He concluded by pointing out that there was a tradition of sympathy among middle-aged Canadian men towards the RAF.

On March 15, 1940, the first trainees for the BCATP were taken on strength and within a year it comprised no less than 67 training installations plus ten advanced schools. By late the next year the scheme peaked at 97 schools. These included Elementary Flying Schools, Service Flying Training Schools, Bombing and Gunnery Schools, Air Navigation Schools, Flying Instructors Schools, General Reconnaissance Schools, Wireless Schools, and Operational Training Units. These were spread from coast to coast, from Comox

on Vancouver Island (6 OTU); to Pearce, Alberta (36 EFTS); North Battleford, Saskatchewan (35 SFTS); Fingal, Ontario (4 B & G); Montreal (3 WS) and Charlottetown, P.E.I. (32 ANS).

Aircraft operated by these schools included many types of which the Anson and Harvard were certainly the most ubiquitous. Besides these, however, there were Battles, Bolingbrokes, Cranes, Cornells, Fawns, Finches, Forts, Oxfords, and Yales.

Typical of the BCATP stations was

A high altitude view of RCAF Station Dauphin in Manitoba, showing the typical lay out of a BCATP field. Many of these stations became civil airports after the war and are still in use. With the exception of a Harvard on a taxi strip, all the aircraft in the photo appear to be Cessna Cranes.

DND Via Ken Nicolson

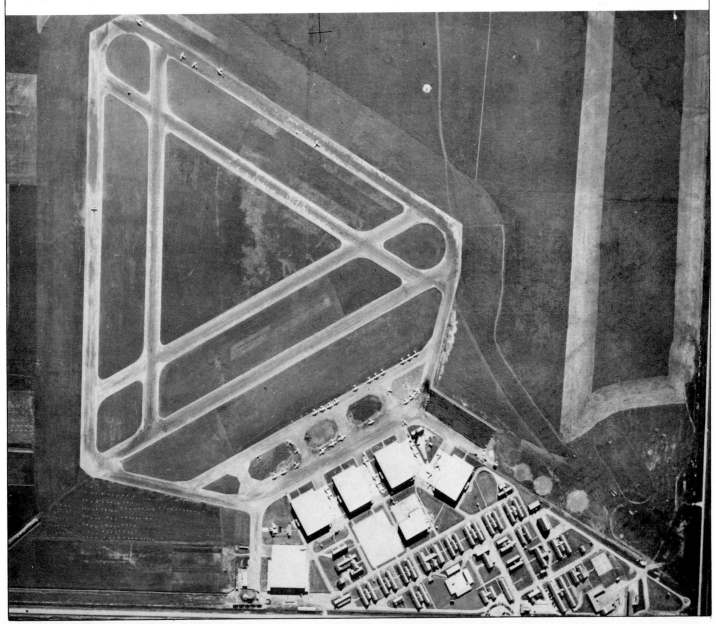

One of several piggy back landings that have occurred in Canada over the years. This accident involved Ansons of No. 7 SFTS, McLeod, Alberta.

DND (PL 988)

Aylmer, Ontario. Its history has been documented by M.L. McIntyre in the *Journal of the Canadian Aviation Historical Society*. Aylmer, home of NO.14 SFTS, received its first personnel in March, 1941. At this point the station was far from being operational and McIntyre notes, "The men got their meals at Fowler's Tea Room in Aylmer and took baths in private homes, transportation being provided in the local undertaker's panel truck . . . ."

The station diary begins July 3, 1941. Entries to the end of that month read: "Station Strength — 40 officers, 376 airmen, 27 civilian employees. First course of students arrives. All flying done from No.2 hangar as aprons not finished for other hangars. July 14th, first damage to aircraft; Harvard 3175 ran off runway into

Hardly any pilot's favourite airplane. This Fairey Battle was photographed while on a bombing and gunnery training flight.

DND (PL2451)

mud and damaged wing. Harvard 3222 had belly landing on field due to engine failure. Student landed downwind on wrong runway, overshot and nosed up in 3225. Officers' Mess opened. First night flying for instructors. Six Harvards arrive from Montreal. Harvard 3064 had aileron lockup on Uplands to Aylmer flight, F/O Grant landed at Trenton. Radio tests to runway control truck. Three Moths and one Anson arrive from D.H. for storage. July 31st, Station Strength 53 officers, 499 airmen, 103 civilians."

On June 19, the station's C.O. arrived. This was W/C G.N. Irwin of Whitby. During his tenure at Aylmer he was to introduce such improvements to station life as a truck converted as a mobile control tower, a swimming pool, well-kept and productive flower beds and garden patches, and rabbit shoots. About the latter, McIntyre writes, " . . . among the well-remembered activities were the C.O.'s regular evening rabbit shoots when no flying was in progress. Standard procedure was to have a man on each front fender and perhaps two in the back seat of the C.O.'s Buick, all with shotguns, while they cruised around the field banging away at the Jacks.

Fortunately, the only casualties were among the Jacks."

For the last year of the war, No. 14 SFTS operated at Kingston, and by the time it was disbanded in September, 1945, it had graduated 4144 pilots for the RCAF, RAF, RAAF, RNZAF, and Fleet Air Arm. The level of activity can be gauged by flying figures for March, 1944. Total hours flown were 11 901. Landings for March 1, numbered 642. Throughout its four years of operation, the school was not without accidents, though the rate was low. There were 26 fatal crashes in which 38 instructors and students died. As well, there were many other crack-ups, some of which have been documented by McIntyre: " . . . On 23 September, 1941, LAC Reynolds while night flying spiralled in from 600 or 700 feet and 3211 cartwheeled, the engine rolling about 100 yards beyond the rest of the wreckage. Reynolds was found wandering down the road by a farmer who brought him back to the station — his most serious injury: two broken ribs. . . ." On another occasion a Harvard had forced landed on the Lake Erie shore: "The plane was undamaged, but in the attempt to fly it out, an instructor had the misfortune to hit an outhouse on his takeoff run. Luckily the outhouse was unoccupied at the time . . . ." On August 13, 1942, an Anson from Aylmer was involved in another unusual incident. While hedge-hopping along the Lake Erie shore, it collided with a gunnery observation tower. Aboard were the pilot and one passenger, Ben Gazel (later well known as a long distance swimmer). McIntyre notes that when the collision occurred, "Gazel jumped out of his seat, scrambled to the back door and

A North American Yale in a quaint reflection photo. The Yale was forerunner of the Harvard on which thousands of pilots trained in the BCATP.

DND (PL 1427)

Liberators and Mitchells of No. 5 OTU Boundary Bay, British Columbia.

DND

Students at No. 10 SFTS, Dauphin by one of the school's T-50 Cranes.

DND Via Ken Nicolson

snapped on a chest pack 'chute which had been lying on the floor. By this time, the pilot was yelling that he had the airplane under control and not to jump. Gazel couldn't hear what he was saying, and wouldn't have believed him anyway. All he could see looking forward from the back door was water and the raw edge of the cliff. Gazel was a strong swimmer and never thought of the parachute until he dragged it ashore behind him. The pilot, meanwhile, had bellied the Anson in a field, run to a farmhouse and called the station to report the accident and the loss of his passenger.'' The accident later appeared in the station diary described as a case of ''Possible Gross Carelessness''!

At its peak, the BCATP was turning out 3000 graduates per month. By mid 1944 it was evident that the supply was beginning to exceed the demand, and training operations began to slow down. The entire Plan came to an end in March, 1945. Overall, 131 553 aircrew had been trained for the RCAF, RAF, RAAF and RNZAF. Of these, 49 808 were pilots, and 29 963 navigators. Included in the RCAF and RAF totals were some 12 000 Americans, French, Norwegians, Poles, Czechs, Dutch, and Belgians. The RCAF total was 72 835, who by war's end manned 46 overseas and 24 home-based squadrons.

SUMMARY OF AIRCREW GRADUATES OF THE BRITISH COMMONWEALTH AIR TRAINING PLAN
October 1940 - March 1945

	Pilot	Nav B	Nav W	Nav	Air Bomb	WOAG	AG	Naval AG	Flt Eng	Total
RCAF	25 747	5 154	421	7 280	6 659	12 744	12 917	—	1 913	72 835
RAF	17 796	3 113	3 847	6 922	7 581	755	1 392	704	—	42 110
RAAF	4 045	699	—	944	799	2 875	244	—	—	9 606
RNZAF	2 220	829	30	724	634	2 122	443	—	—	7 002
Total	49 808	9 795	4 298	15 870	15 673	18 496	14 996	704	1 913	131 553

Notes:

1. Figures include 407 BCATP Pilots who received SFTS training in RAF Transferred Schools prior to July 1, 1942, as follows: — 332 RCAF, 9 RAF and 66 RNZAF.

2. Figures do not include 5 296 RAF and Fleet Air Arm personnel who received training in RAF Transferred Schools and were graduated prior to July 1, 1942, when these schools became part of the BCATP, as follows: — 4 058 Pilots, 1 006 Navigators ''B'' (Observers), 151 Navigators ''W'', graduated from RAF Schools, and 81 RAF Pilots who received their ''Wings'' at RCAF Schools.

3. Included in Wireless Operator (Air Gunner) totals are 641 who were graduated in March, 1945, without Bombing and Gunnery School training, as follows: — 478 RCAF, 21 RAF, 94 RAAF, and 48 RNZAF. The RAF, RAAF and RNZAF personnel were graduated as Wireless Operators (Air).

4. Included in Flight Engineer totals are 207 who were graduated in Canada without type training, and proceeded to England for that phase of training.

Nav B — Navigator Bomber
Nav W — Navigator Wireless
Nav — Navigator
Air Bomb — Air Bomber
WOAG — Wireless Operator/Air Gunner
AG — Air Gunner

Naval AG — Naval Air Gunner
Flt Eng — Flight Engineer
RCAF — Royal Canadian Air Force
RAF — Royal Air Force
RAAF — Royal Australian Air Force
RNZAF — Royal New Zealand Air Force

As they were in World War I, some Canadian military aircraft were sponsored by the people. These Kitchener school children raised $12 000 to help purchase this Cornell.

York University, Scott Archives

Ferry Command

By early 1940 England was alone in Europe facing the Nazi might. It was desperate for all types of aid, especially aircraft. These could be procured from America, but obtaining delivery was a problem. Because of its neutrality policy, the U.S. could not ship aircraft direct to England. Red tape was circumvented however by a novel process. As long as aircraft were not flown to England or a Commonwealth nation, delivery could be effected by other means. Thus a scheme was initiated whereby aircraft were flown to airports in the U.S. near the Canadian border. From these they were towed or pushed into Canada!

Meanwhile the CPR had organized its Ferry Command Department to deliver aircraft overseas. It procured crews and trained them, especially in celestial navigation. It must be emphasized that at this time trans-Atlantic flying was still in its infancy. Except for Imperial Airways' and Pan American's proving flights in the late thirties little experience had been gained in flying the Atlantic.

On November 10, 1941 one of the historic events of World War II took place when Air Vice-Marshal D.C.T. Bennett led a flight of seven Hudsons from Gander. All of these arrived safely in Ireland, showing that trans-Atlantic ferrying was indeed possible.

From here on, aircraft began streaming across the ocean from Canada and Newfoundland to Britain. New routes were developed across the ocean, one being the Crimson Route. It originated in Vancouver and headed northwest through stopovers like The Pas, Churchill, Southampton Island, Baffin Island, then on to Greenland, Iceland, and Prestwick. For an aircraft flying Vancouver-Prestwick via Dorval nearly 5400 miles would be covered compared to 4400 miles via the Crimson Route.

Hundreds of civil and military crews joined Ferry Command. One pilot was F/L W.H. (Wess) McIntosh, posted to Ferry Command November 2, 1942. On the seventh he began training at Dorval on the Baltimore, Boston, Hudson, Mitchell, and Ventura. In three weeks he logged 40 hours 50 minutes, then, on December 14 took off on his first delivery. Copilot was P/O J. Bird, and crewman, Sgt. Hamlyn. The aircraft was the Boston, BZ262. The first leg was six hours to Jacksonville, thence over to West Palm, Borinquen Field in Puerto Rico, and Trinidad. On December 19 they flew to Natal in Brazil and next day to Yundum airport in Bathurst, Gambia. This was the longest leg, taking 10 hours five minutes. From Bathurst it was on to Gibraltar on December 27. After a few days grounded by mechanical problems the Boston took off for Prestwick where it arrived safely. The pilot's log for the entire trip shows 81 hours 45 minutes in the air.

A speedier and more typical trip was made April 8-April 10, 1944, by Fred Hotson and Don Murray, two civilians. Their aircraft was a Mitchell, FW271. They left Dorval and flew to Goose Bay via Mt.

Venturas, Hudsons, and Mitchells dominate this scene at Dorval, nerve centre of Ferry Comand. Along with a B-17 and B-24 they await delivery overseas by Ferry Command crews.

DND (WRF 621)

Joli and Mingan; thence to Bluie West 1 in Greenland; Iceland; and then Prestwick. Total flying time was 19:55 hours.

Many trans-Atlantic ferry flights never reached their destinations. Hundreds of aircraft were seen for the last time when they headed eastward from places like Gander and Natal. One of these was piloted by "Duke" Schiller, the famous bush-flying trailblazer. He died when the Catalina he was ferrying crashed into the Atlantic near Bermuda, March 13, 1943. More fortunate was another old time bush pilot, George Phillips. After ferrying a Hudson across the South Atlantic, he experienced radio trouble and became lost along the west coast of Africa. He located an airstrip and set down, only to learn that he was at Cotonou in Vichy French

KA387, a Canadian-built Mosquito F.B.26 being flown by a civilian ferry crew between Toronto and Montreal. The aircraft was destined for the RAF but the war ended before it could be delivered overseas. It was then taken over by the RCAF until struck off strength in the summer of 1947.

Don Murray

territory. George was taken prisoner and moved inland to Bamako to a POW camp. Nothing more was heard from him and he was presumed lost.

The fact that George was alive was discovered on a routine photo reconnaissance flight by an Allied P-51. The pilot photographed Cotonou and when his film was processed and analyzed it was noted that the tail of a Hudson was protruding from a hangar. The numbers on the tail matched those on George Phillip's Hudson. The 2-1/2 month wait was over for George's family and within a year of the incident, he was repatriated and back on active duty in Natal working for Ferry Command.

The Air War: Fighter Operations

From the beginning, Canadian fliers were in action over Europe. On January 2, 1940, the *London Gazette* announced the first two Canadians decorated for aerial combat. These were P/O S.R. Henderson and W/C J.F. Griffiths, both of whom received the DFC. On February 14, No.110 City of Toronto Squadron became the first RCAF squadron to embark for Britain and the first of 22 fighter squadrons to eventually serve overseas.

On May 23, 1940 the RCAF recorded its first successful aerial combat when S/L F.M. Gobeil, flying with 242 Sqdn. RAF, destroyed a Bf 109 over France. Two days later he downed a Bf 110 over Belgium. The first RCAF victory of the Battle of Britain took place August 11 when S/L E.A. McNab, flying with 111 Sqdn, RAF, destroyed a Dornier Do 215. On August 26, No.1 Sqdn's Hurricanes attacked raiding Dorniers, shooting down two. These were the first victories for an RCAF fighter squadron. In the same action, the RCAF suffered its first combat fatality when F/O R.L. Edwards was shot down. By the time No.1 was taken off operations in October it had accounted for 30 enemy aircraft destroyed and 43 damaged. It had lost 10 Hurricanes and three pilots in action.

The Battle of Britain whetted the appetite of Canadian fighter pilots. Thereafter squadron diaries relate thousands of sorties. One of the busiest days early in the war was August 19, 1941, over Dieppe. That day, in efforts to support the

Canadian fighter ace F/L Robert Wendell (Buck) McNair of 411 Sqdn. Between October 1941 and October 1943 McNair destroyed at least 16 enemy aircraft and was himself shot down twice. On another occasion he was catapulted from a training plane. He had dozed off without his harness on and the other pilot chose this time to do some aerobatics! After being rudely awakened travelling through space without his aircraft, McNair pulled his ripcord and cheated death.
Public Archives of Canada (PL 4988)

Field maintenance on a 442 Sqdn Spitfire IXb. A scene in Normandy, August 14, 1944.
Public Archives of Canada (PL 31363)

The 440 Sqdn Hawker Typhoon Ib "Pulverizer IV." The Typhoon was the scourge of German transport facilities, such as trains and rail yards, bridges, barges, road convoys, and airfields. This Typhoon is seen at Goch, Germany, April 2, 1945.
Public Archives of Canada (PL 42817)

On January 1, 1945 the Luftwaffe conducted mass air strikes on Allied targets. These were begun early in the morning and caught most Allied units completely unprepared after celebrating New Year's eve. The raids had a devastating effect, but were not the knock-out Germany had hoped for. This photo shows some of the damage inflicted upon 143 (RCAF) Wing at Eindhoven, Holland. Some 45 aircraft at this base were hit in the hour-long raid, including four Typhoons in readiness, prepared to take off in case of just such an attack. In this view taken just after the raid, Canadian Typhoons lie under clouds of black smoke coming mainly from fuel caches.

D.J. Davies

disastrous Canadian landing, the RAF experienced its greatest losses of the war. The RCAF itself lost 13 aircraft. One Canadian squadron over Dieppe was No.414, tasting its first real action. Hereafter it and other Canadian fighter squadrons became a scourge upon the enemy, flying "rhubarbs" against trains, trucks, bridges, troop columns, and other tactical targets, as well as flying photo reconnaissance over targets including V-1 launch sites, rail yards and road junctions, and the D-Day beaches. On December 24,

1944, one of its pilots, F/L W. Sawyer engaged 12 Bf 109's, downing three. The following May 2, F/L D. Hall downed three Fw 190's and a Bf 108. By the end of hostilities, 414 had chalked up 6087 sorties, and accounted for 29 enemy aircraft destroyed along with such targets as 76 locomotives, and 13 vessels. It had lost 19 pilots.

In August, 1944, the ground attack Spitfires of 403 (Wolf) Squadron accounted for 427 enemy transport vehicles, 13 tanks, 1 locomotive, 10 freight cars and three barges. By war's end, 66 of its pilots had shared in the destruction of 123 enemy aircraft. Four pilots, F/L H.D. MacDonald, F/L J.D. Lindsay, S/L L.S. Ford and S/L H.C. Godefroy downed 25 of these.

On July 20, 1944, S/L H.W. McLeod, C.O. of 443 Squadron won his twentieth victory when the pilot of an Fw 190 bailed out before McLeod even had a chance to fire at him! McLeod made one more kill before being lost himself in a dog fight over Rees.

F/L G.W. Johnson of 411 Squadron recorded a Bf 109 shot down June 7, 1944:

"Went down with Red Leader on two e/a chasing a Thunderbolt on the deck.

They split and I took the port one. First burst from 600 yards dead astern knocked small pieces off. Fired several bursts during a steep turn without seeing results. E/a straightened and I noticed strikes on cockpit and engine. Smoke poured from e/a and it crashed into a farm house." A single day's record for a Canadian fighter pilot occurred on December 29 when F/L R.J. Audet of 411 Sqdn personally accounted for two Bf 109's and three Fw 190's while engaging 12 enemy aircraft.

Several Canadian squadrons specialized in night fighter operations. One of these was 409 Sqdn, with its motto "Midnight is our noon." It had formed at Digby, Lincs., in June 1941, originally equipped with Defiants. These were soon exchanged for Beaufighters, and on November 1, one of these, crewed by S/L P.Y. Davoud and Sgt. T. Carpenter accounted for the squadron's first kill. Part of Davoud's report on the action reads, ". . . I increased speed and turned to port and obtained a visual at 6000 feet, silhouetted against the clouds in bright moonlight. I throttled back and lost height until slightly above and 400 yards to rear of enemy aircraft, who dived for cloud cover. I closed to approximately 200 yards, identified bandit as a Dornier 217 and fired a short burst observing hits on starboard mainplane. The Dornier returned fire and having closed to about 100 yards, I fired two long bursts, seeing the second burst hit his starboard engine. Just before Dornier entered cloud, a big explosion blew his right engine and wing off. I pulled up to avoid collision, and the Dornier fell burning, straight into the sea.''

Eventually, Canadian night fighter squadrons converted to the famous Mosquito. On December 10, 1943, F/O R.D. Schutz, flying one of these, destroyed three Do 217's. These were hazardous operations for hunter as well as for hunted. One night in 1943 S/L Moran and Flt/Sgt G.V. Rogers of 418 Squadron were on a "flower," or bomber escort operation. They fired on an enemy fighter which exploded so close in front that it damaged the Mosquito. The crew bailed out, but only Moran was picked up from the sea. The following week, a 418 Mosquito crashed when it ran into the barrage balloon defences at Dover, while the same night another of the squadron's Mosquitos barely escaped similar destruction over Canterbury.

Mosquitos flew many specialized night operations. Three from 418 Squadron escorted eight Lancasters on a raid against the Dortmund-Ems Canal. Their task was to suppress flak, searchlights, and enemy aircraft. In spite of their efforts, five Lancasters were lost that night.

To illustrate the unpredictability of fighter operations, it took 418 Squadron its first 22 months to down 22-1/2 enemy aircraft (the other half of this airplane was claimed by another squadron); while during the 23rd month, it downed 24! Evidence of just how things could pick up is given by the crew of Kipp and Huletsky which notched the squadron's 100th, 101st, 102nd, and 103rd kills on May 2-3, 1944. The four victims were all Fw 190's.

On June 13, 1944, the first V-1 "buzz bomb" fell on England. These deadly missiles, it was soon learned, were being launched from sites inland from the French coast. They were small and very fast, and as such presented a special defence problem. To counter the threat, three RCAF squadrons were put to work. These were Nos. 406, 409, and 418, each equipped with night intruder Mosquitos.

On June 16 W/C Russ Bannock of 418 Sqdn made what was probably the first night spotting from a fighter of a V-1. While on patrol, he and his navigator sighted what they thought was a burning aircraft. They watched it cross the English coast then noticed that anti-aircraft guns began firing on it! Later on they learned

Year		Aircraft		Pilot, or 1st Pilot	2nd Pilot, Pupil or Passenger	Duty (Including Results and Remarks)
Month	Date	Type	No.			
						Totals Brought Forward
						Summary for Month of June at 418 Sqdn.	{ 1. Mosquito VI 2. Oxford } A/c Types
						F/Lt ___ O.C. "B" Flight
						___ W/C C.O. 418 Sqdn	R. Bannock - S/L
7	1	Mosquito	P	Self	F/O Bruce	Ford - Base
	3	Mosquito	Z	Self	F/O Bruce	N.F.T.
	3	Mosquito	Z	Self	F/O Bruce	Cris Nez - Dieppe Ops. Anti-Diver
	5	Mosquito	Z	Self	F/O Bruce	Practice Attacks
	6	Mosquito	Z	Self	F/O Bruce	N.F.T.
	6	Mosquito	Z	Self	F/O Bruce	Cris Nez - Dieppe Ops. Anti-Diver
	7	Mosquito	Z	Self	F/O Bruce	N.F.T.
	7	Mosquito	Z	Self	F/O Bruce	Le Havre - Dieppe Ops. Anti-Diver
	10	Mosquito	Z	Self	F/O Bruce	N.F.T. Cannon Test
	11	Mosquito	Z	Self	F/O Bruce	N.F.T.
	11	Mosquito	Z	Self	F/O Bruce	Boulogne - Le Havre Ops. Anti-Diver
	13	Mosquito	Z	Self	F/O Bruce	N.F.T.
	14	Mosquito	Z	Self	F/O Bruce	N.F.T.
	14	Mosquito	Z	Self	F/O Bruce	Cris Nez - Dieppe Ops. Anti-Diver
	15	Mosquito	X	Self	F/O Bruce	N.F.T.
	5	Link		?	Self	B.A. Practice

Grand Total [Cols. (1) to (10)]
RCAF - 2371 Hrs 15 Mins.
Grand - 2492 15
Totals Carried Forward

that what they had been observing was a V-1. The next night 418 Sqdn downed three V-1's.

Night intruder crews soon devised techniques for attacking the V-1. It was observed that after launch they rose to about 500 feet then proceeded across the Channel at 350-400 mph depending on atmospheric conditions.

At that level, the Mosquito could manage 360 mph-370 mph, not enough to cope with their prey. This considered, the Mosquitos would stooge around the French coast at about 10 000 feet, watching for the tell-tale launch of a V-1. The target could easily be observed thereafter by the glow from its engine exhaust. As soon as a V-1 came under a Mosquito, the fighter dove steeply on it, reaching about 440 mph. Generally, the idea was to fire from about 300 yards, for it was dangerous getting much closer because of the chance of

A typical page from Russ Bannock's log while he was flying Mosquitos with 418 Squadron. Activities shown include anti-V1 operations and show nine July 1944 V1's ("divers") destroyed during three July 1944 sorties along the French coast. Also recorded are night fighter training (NFT), searchlight cooperation (S/L co-op), single-engine practice (S.E. practice), and beam approach practice (B.A. practice).

Russell Bannock

The team of Russell Bannock and Robert ▶ Bruce who destroyed more V-1's than any other crew.

De Havilland Aircraft of Canada (21033)

SINGLE-ENGINE AIRCRAFT				MULTI-ENGINE AIRCRAFT						PASS-ENGER	INSTR/CLOUD FLYING [Incl. in cols. (1) to (10)]		LINK TRAINER
DAY		NIGHT		DAY			NIGHT						
DUAL	PILOT	DUAL	PILOT	DUAL	1ST PILOT	2ND PILOT	DUAL	1ST PILOT	2ND PILOT		DUAL	PILOT	
(1)	(2)	(3)	(4)	(5)	(6)	(7)	(8)	(9)	(10)	(11)	(12)	(13)	(14)
					11:25			21:35					
								1:15					
3 DIVERS DEST.					.20								
					.20			3:50					
								2:00					
4 DIVERS. DEST.					.05			2:25					
DIVERS DEST					.15			1:45					
					.20								
					.15			3:05					
					.10								
					.15			3:55					
					.40								1:00
71:55	1486:35	5:20	57:15	19:40	495:50	36:00	4:40	91:50		87:30	27:00	50:55	52:25
(1)	(2)	(3)	(4)	(5)	(6)	(7)	(8)	(9)	(10)	(11)	(12)	(13)	(14)

TOTAL OPS. HOURS — 26:20

FOLLOWING TRAINING EXERCISES COMPLETED DURING MONTH OF JUNE
CINE GUN — 1
LOW LEVEL X COUNTRY — 2
S/L CO-OP — 1
S.E. PRACTICE — 1

explosion. One crew had a V-1 explode just 50 yards away. They survived, but their aircraft had most of its paint scorched off!

Another hazard of "Divers," as the V-1 interceptions were called, was that the explosion of a target ruined a pilot's night vision. To counter this, crews used the standard practice of closing one eye as they fired, thus preserving partial night vision if a bright explosion occurred.

Over 14 weeks, 418 Sqdn flew 402 sorties against the V-1, destroying 83 of them. W/C Bannock and F/O Bruce topped the list for individual effort, downing 18-1/2. On one 1-1/4 hour sortie they destroyed four! On another occasion, Bannock assumes he damaged a V-1's auto pilot, for it turned around after he fired on it, and flew back to France.

Eventually air strikes eliminated fixed V-1 bases. The Germans then began using mobile launchers as well as launching from bombers off the English coast. Bannock, then C.O. of 406 Squadron, intercepted such a mothership one night. It was over the water at about 250 feet and apparently in the hands of an expert pilot who jinked his plane so skillfully that he evaded the Mosquito.

On landing from patrols, night intruder crews usually had breakfast, then went to bed. Not so F/O Bruce. As an accomplished musician, the first thing he did after debriefing was to sit down at the piano and put the mission to music! After the war, Bruce continued his musical career and on visiting Canada from Wales in 1975 presented his wartime pilot with a copy of the Bannock-Bruce Symphony.

The V-2 followed the V-1 and the first of these fell on Britain in September, 1944. There was no direct defence against it. Once again, 418 Sqdn was put to work, this time on reconnaissance watching for V-2 launchings. These operations were known as "Big Bens" and the first success came October 10 when W/C Bannock reported a launch. By war's end, 418 Sqdn had flown 3492 sorties, logged 11 248 hours and destroyed 178 enemy aircraft, 105 in aerial combat. It had lost 59 aircraft and 94 crew. Its 62 decorations included 43 DFC's.

Another advanced German weapon which Canadian fighter pilots faced were jet aircraft. From September 28, 1944, Canadian pilots fought many duels with the Me 262 fighter, and occasionally encountered the Arado 234 bomber. They destroyed at least 10 Me 262's and three Arado 234's. On January 23, 1945, F/L R.J. Audet of 411 Sqdn destroyed two Me 262's. Another was destroyed by S/L Dave Fairbanks whose wartime score was to total 15 enemy aircraft. Later he became a well-known de Havilland of Canada test

S/Lt. D.J. Sheppard landing his Corsair aboard HMS *Victorious* in January 1945.

Via D.J. Sheppard

pilot and the 1976 posthumous winner of the McKee Trophy.

While RCAF fighter pilots took a heavy toll of German jets, they did not get off lightly themselves, for the Me 262's were often used as ground attack bombers against Canadian fighter bases. Grave in Holland suffered several of these attacks, losing men killed and aircraft destroyed.

Naval Fighter Pilots

One Canadian fighter pilot was awarded the Victoria Cross during World War II. On August 9, 1945, Lieutenant Robert Hampton Gray led a flight of Corsairs off the deck of HMS *Formidable,* and headed for Onagawa Bay on northern Honshu. The Corsairs were met by AA fire as they bore in upon ships at anchor in the bay. Gray was hit, but continued on to bomb and sink a destroyer. He then crashed into the bay. In the official history of this action the following appears:

" . . . Peeling off from the section, the leader dived towards one of the destroyers and was soon surrounded by exploding shells.

"The Corsair burst into flames but held steadily to its course until within fifty feet of the target when Gray released his bombs. The warship was struck amidships and sank below the surface of the bay to follow its attacker to a watery grave . . . ." Gray's aircraft is today commemorated by the Corsair owned and flown by the Canadian Warplane Heritage.

Other Canadians also featured prominently in the Fleet Air Arm of the Royal Navy. Sub-Lt. D.J. Sheppard became its first fighter ace in the East. He joined the Royal Navy in January 1942 and went to England for basic naval training. That August he returned to the United States for a year's flying training. In September 1943 he joined 1835 Sqdn, RN, flying Corsairs, then transferred to 1836 Sqdn aboard HMS *Victorious*. In April 1944 he participated in the attacks on the German battleship *Tirpitz* in Norway. In June, *Victorious* sailed to the Indian Ocean and to waters around Sumatra.

On January 4, Sheppard shot down two Japanese Oscar fighters and on the twenty-fourth participated in a raid on an oil refinery at Palembang, Sumatra. This resulted in another Japanese aircraft falling to Sheppard's guns. For his action on this occasion Sheppard received the DSC. Five days later he shared in the destruction of two more enemy aircraft, and on May 4, he recorded his fifth official "kill," thus becoming an ace.

Following the war, Sheppard joined the RCN. He took jet fighter conversion on Meteors with the RAF and in June 1946 became senior pilot with 883 Sqdn. He retired from the Canadian Forces in January 1974.

The second pilot to become an ace with the Fleet Air Arm of the Royal Navy in the East was another Canadian, Lt. W.H.I. Atkinson. He shot down at least five enemy aircraft while flying Hellcats with 1844 Sqdn.

Bombing Operations

The first Canadian airman known to have flown over Europe in World War II was P/O S.R. Henderson. He participated in a 206 Sqdn Wellington raid on a German target on September 4, 1939. Then, on November 8, while patrolling in an Anson he engaged and shot down a Dornier Do 18 flying boat and damaged another.

On June 12/13, 1941, RCAF squadron bombers made their first raid on Germany.

A lucky crew. P/O E.T. Jones and F/O E. Hooke peer through a gaping hole in their Lancaster ND329.

Via E. Hooke

Three Wellingtons of 405 Sqdn delivered 11 160 pounds of bombs onto a rail target near Dortmund. Another early raid sent the 405 Wellingtons over Brest to bomb the German battleship *Gneisnau*. Its nine aircraft were among the last to reach the target. Two were quickly shot down and another two did not make it home. Nonetheless two Bf 109's fell to the Wellingtons' 303's.

In May 1942 the RCAF participated in the first 1000-bomber raid over Europe.

Thousands of Canadian airmen flew with British squadrons during the war. Pictured here under the nose of one of their 226 Sqdn Mitchells are seven Toronto fliers: Bob Fowler, Russ Hunter, Mel Hammel, Jack London, Johnny Irvine, Joe Ouelette, and Jack Chinnel.

Via R.H. Fowler

Part of the destruction in Stuttgart, a target often visited by Canadian heavy bombers.

DND (52655)

Lancaster KB869 of 428 Sqdn back in Canada in 1945, 21 missions to its credit and wearing a fine example of Canadian war art.

DND (PMR 71-550)

Cologne was the target and participating bombers included 15 Halifaxes of 405 Sqdn. From this night onward the RCAF was to mount tens of thousands of heavy bomber sorties against Europe. As of January 1, 1943, RCAF bomber squadrons were part of No.6 Group, RAF Bomber Command. Many crews never returned from the largely night-time operations. Others made it home on a wing and a prayer. One of these close calls is recorded in the 433 Sqdn diary, June 29, 1944, and refers to operations over Metz: "This night was marked by a wonderful bit of work by Warrant Officer H.G. McVeigh, who was captain of 'C-Charlie.' He was attacked four times by fighters, and evaded them all until he was finally hit while in a corkscrew. The starboard fin and rudder were completely shot off, the starboard elevator, aileron, and wingtip were smashed, and the starboard flap and mainplane were badly damaged. The aircraft went into a tight spin at 13 000 feet, and McVeigh told his crew to abandon aircraft. Two members of the crew (the bomb aimer and the mid-upper gunner) baled out before the captain managed to level off at 6000 feet. He had barely set course for England when his port inner engine packed up. However, he managed to reach Woodbridge, where he landed. A good thing it was this station with its long runways, as it was necessary to land at 155 mph to hold the starboard wing up . . . ."

On April 4, 1944, 432 Sqdn Lancaster, E-Easy, collided with another aircraft during a raid on Noisy-le-Sec near Paris. In his haste to bale out, mid-upper gunner Sgt. G.J. Shaunghnessy disabled his parachute by pulling his rip cord before leaving the aircraft. He prepared for the worst, but actually survived the crash. He was immediately collared by German soldiers, but in the confusion of bombs falling around them, Shaunghnessy escaped. In a nearby shelter he located a first aid kit to dress his wounds, and found a pair of overalls which he donned. He was then harboured by some French fire-fighters, and eventually became a successful evader, returning to Britain in July. Another 432 Sqdn crew member, P/O D.A. McCoy, became an active member of the Resistance while awaiting repatriation. F/O Peter Holmes of the same squadron melded into the local French community he had parachuted into. He made his connections and posed as a photographer, working in a studio next door to the local Gestapo headquarters. He even attended parties with Gestapo officers!

Another 432 Sqdn action involved a Lancaster piloted by P/O J. McIntosh on a raid to Berlin. McIntosh's report of the incident typifies many a night experienced by RCAF bomber crews:

"Just after we turned for home . . . the rear gunner (Sgt. L. Bandel) spotted an Me.110. The enemy and my two gunners opened fire at the same instant. Cannon shells hit our aircraft like sledge hammers. The gunners scored hits on the Me.'s port engine and cockpit, and the fighter went down, burning fiercely. All this happened within five seconds. Meanwhile, my control column had slammed forward (the elevator had been hit), putting the aircraft into a near-vertical dive . . . By putting both feet on the instrument panel, one arm around the control column, and the other hand on the elevator trim, then hauling back with every ounce of strength while trimming fully nose up, I managed to pull out of the dive at about 10 000 feet (13 000 feet below bombing height). My compasses were unserviceable, the rudder controls had jammed, and I could get very little response from the elevators. I still had to wrap both arms around the control column to maintain height . . . .

"We were now far behind the rest of the bombers, and our only hope was to stay in the cloud-tops and take our chances with the severe icing we were encountering. Fighter flares kept dropping all around us and the flak positions en route were bursting their stuff at our height, but the fighters couldn't see us in that cloud . . . . My navigator took astro fixes and kept us away as much as possible from defended areas . . . . We had been losing a lot of fuel from the starboard inner tank, but enough remained to take us to Woodbridge . . . .

"About 70 miles out to sea, I let down through cloud, experiencing severe icing, then levelled off when I broke through . . . . The aircraft now was becoming very sluggish, and only with difficulty was I able to hold height. I detailed the crew to throw out all our unnecessary equipment and to chop out everything they could. This considerably lightened the aircraft and made it easier to control . . . . The navigator headed me straight for Woodbridge . . . .

"I used all the runway and felt the kite touch down on our port wheel . . . . It rolled along until the speed dropped to about 30 mph, then settled down more on the side of the starboard wheel, did a half ground loop, and stopped . . . . I shut down the engines, got out, and took a look.

"Both starboard engine nacelles were gone; the hydraulics were smashed and twisted; two large tears were in the starboard wing near the dinghy stowage; and the dinghy was hanging out; the starboard fuel jettison sac was hanging out; the tailplane was riddled with cannon and machine-gun fire; the fuselage had five cannon holes through it; . . . there were two cannon holes in the rear turret; there were hundreds of holes of all sizes in the kite; every prop blade had at least one hole in it, one being split down the middle; the starboard outer oil tank was riddled, and the starboard tire was blown clean off . . . but nobody was injured . . . ."

An incident with 434 Sqdn has been recorded by the late W/C F.H. Hitchens, RCAF Historian:

"When the captain told the crew to jump, Sgt. J.L.N. Warren, the rear gunner, did not hear the order because his intercom had been shot away. Thinking that the Halifax was on its way home, Warren remained at his post for a while until, becoming uneasy, he climbed back into the fuselage, found that the rest of the crew had gone, and was shocked to see that the altimetre read only 950 feet. He hurried back to the turret for his parachute, but before he could clip it on, the Halifax struck the ground and burst into flames. Despite injuries, Warren got free and hobbled away from the flaming wreckage . . . . In the spring of 1944, after one unsuccessful attempt, he escaped from prison-camp, reached Holland in a freight train, and made contact with the underground movement." Warren was free for about six months, then was recaptured and harshly treated by the Gestapo for his efforts. He was next put on board a train for Germany, but escaped en route. He was sheltered by the Dutch and finally liberated in April 1945.

Many Canadians flew with RAF squadrons throughout the war. Two of these were P/O E.T. Jones of Edmonton and F/O E. Hooke of Toronto. On January 30, 1944, they were pilot and navigator of a 103 Sqdn Lancaster, on a raid to Berlin. At 2010 hours while at 20 000 feet and about 25 miles northwest of Neuruppin, they were attacked by a night fighter. The bomb bay was hit by cannon fire, exploding some incendiaries. The official report on the incident goes on:

"Thirty seconds later a second attack, also from an unseen point, hit the starboard tailplane and made control difficult, put the mid-upper turret out of action and shot up the navigation aids. All power had ceased in the starboard outer engine. The filter on the mid-upper turret was hit and oil was sprayed all over the fuselage. A shell went through the runners to the mid-upper turret narrowly missing the mid-upper gunner. The servo feeds to the rear turret were completely severed by cannon fire and were hanging loose, several rounds firing off. By this time fire was getting hold in the bomb bay, the glow being seen outside the aircraft, and the smoke was filling the cockpit. The captain therefore opened the bomb doors and ordered the bomb aimer to release bombs as soon as possible at a suitable target if there was one. The bomb aimer delayed only long enough to estimate the position of batteries putting up a small concentration of flak on which the aircraft was

running up and let the bombs go. The bomb doors were left open and the aircraft put into a dive to try and extinguish the fire, 'stand by to bale out' being ordered.

"Not a minute later, mid-upper gunner sighted a Fw 190 coming in from port quarter down and at once gave evasive action to port. The Fw 190 fired a lengthy burst which overshot, and broke away up. It was not seen again . . . . '' As the fire went out, Jones elected to carry on rather than abandon the aircraft. Hooke worked out a route via the Danish coast which would take the crippled plane over a relatively safe path, and C-Charlie made it back to Elsham Wolds. For their efforts, Jones and Hooke each received the DFC.

In all, 16 Canadian bomber squadrons served overseas in World War II. The eight squadrons of 6 Group dropped 126 122 tons of bombs, and flew 40 822 sorties. Typical of its squadrons, No.432 flew 3130 sorties 2787 of which were successful. It dropped 8980 tons of bombs, lost 71 aircraft and 282 crew, and accounted for eight enemy aircraft shot down. Of 18 463 Canadian airmen who became casualties in World War II, over 10 000 of them were from Bomber Command.

Coastal Command

Several RCAF squadrons were kept busy on coast duties. At home, there were squadrons on both coasts flying the Beaufort, Bolingbroke, Canso, Digby, Hudson, Liberator, Shark, and Stranraer. Combatting the U-boat was their main preoccupation. Overseas squadrons like 162, 407, 422, and 423 performed similar work. No.407 formed in England in May 1941. It trained on Blenheim IV's then became operational with Hudsons. Its first operations were night patrols along the Dutch coast seeking enemy convoys. By late 1942 it had completed 180 shipping strikes. These were dangerous operations, and 24 Hudsons and 91 men were lost on them. In early 1943 the squadron reequipped with Wellingtons, 12 of which were eventually lost along with 72 crew. By war's end, 407 had recorded four U-boats destroyed and seven damaged.

An important event early in the war was the first sinking of a U-boat by the RCAF. This happened July 31, 1942, when an Eastern Air Command Hudson of 113 Sqdn sank U754 off Cape Sable, Nova Scotia. On October 30, two more U-boats were sunk, one by a Hudson of 145 Sqdn, the other by a Digby of 10 BR.

In March, 1942 Canada entered another theatre of the air war when 413 Sqdn flew from Scotland to Ceylon. No sooner had its Catalinas arrived there than

one of them saved the day for Ceylon. The Japanese were sweeping through the Indian Ocean and their fleet was on Ceylon's doorstep. On April 4, a Catalina flown by S/L L.J. Birchall sighted the enemy fleet and radioed its position even as his aircraft was being shot out of the sky by enemy fighters. The message got through, enabling the British to pull back lest their fleet fall prey to the superior enemy force.

On April 9 another Catalina relocated the enemy and got a message off before it too was shot down. Its crew perished but later it was determined that Birchall and his crew had survived and was in a POW camp. After this dramatic period, the squadron settled down to the routines of anti-submarine patrols and search and rescue which resulted in the rescuing of hundreds of shipwrecked sailors.

Nos.422 and 423 Sqdn flew Sunderlands between Iceland and Gibraltar. Oddly enough, 423's first combat was an aerial one, a duel with a Ju 88. On March 19, 1943 U-boats sank 19 ships from two convoys in the North Atlantic. A surviving tanker was saved when a Canadian Sunderland appeared to chase off a shadowing U-boat. Next day F/L Brady's Sunderland probably sank a U-boat and landed back at base after 17 hours 20 minutes aloft and with less than 100 gallons of fuel remaining.

May 12 saw F/L Musgrave's Sunderland engaged in a long duel with a surfaced U-boat. As the fight developed HMCS *Drumheller,* a corvette, and HMS *Lagan,* a destroyer, arrived. This forced the U-boat to dive and enabled Musgrave to make an attack unmolested. Then a Swordfish joined the fray. In a joint effort, aircraft and ships brought an end to U456. This was the first confirmed "kill" by an RCAF anti-submarine squadron overseas.

On July 22, 1943, another 423 Sqdn Sunderland was attacked in flight, this time by a Focke-Wulf Fw 200 maritime patrol aircraft, which greatly outgunned the Sunderland. The Canadians were on the receiving end not only of cannon fire, but also of air-to-air missiles which crippled their machine. They were lucky to find cover in the clouds before the Fw 200 could finish them off.

Another hard-fought combat occurred on August 4, 1943, when F/O Bishop's crew engaged U489. Bishop managed a successful run in against the surfaced U-boat, but in the process his Sunderland was damaged by fire from the enemy's deck guns. This forced Bishop to ditch. His report on this reads, " . . . We bounced once, twice, three times on the swell, and after the third bounce the port wing dropped . . . . The float was torn off, the

Sunderland Mk.III, EK591, of 422 Sqdn. On March 10, 1944 this aircraft sank U-625 at 52° 53'N 20° 19'W. This was the squadron's only U-boat kill.

Public Archives of Canada (PL 40996)

wing-tip dug in, and the kite cartwheeled into the sea. One second there was a crash and the next we found ourselves in the water . . . . The port wing had disappeared and a fire blazed where it should have been. The starboard wing (now also on fire) and the fuselage were still afloat. One of the boys sat on the tailplane for awhile but soon had to swim for it as the Sunderland went down within five minutes of hitting.''

Five of the plane's eleven crew were lost in the ditching. Along with 23 survivors of the U-boat, the six survivors from the Sunderland were picked up by HMCS *Castleton*.

On the whole, maritime patrols tended to be long and uneventful. By the end of the war, 422 and 423 Sqdn had logged 29 623 hours on operations, lost 17 aircraft and 82 crew, and sunk four U-boats. Few crews ever came face to face with the enemy. One fellow from 423 Sqdn commented after the war, "I flew like a son-of-a-gun, never saw anything, nobody ever shot at me, not even my friends, and I never saw a German." Even so, Canadian squadrons destroyed at least 22 U-boats.

The Victoria Cross

Of three Canadian airmen who earned the Victoria Cross in World War II, one was from Bomber Command, one was from 162 Sqdn on loan to RAF Coastal Command, and the third was a member of the RNVR.

On June 12, 1944, a 419 Sqdn Lancaster on a raid to Cambrai was attacked and disabled by night fighters. As mid-upper gunner P/O A.C. Mynarski prepared to leave the aircraft he noticed the tail gunner, F/O G.P. Brophy, trapped in his turret. He tried to free Brophy but was forced back by flames. Before he could jump, his clothing and parachute had caught fire. He survived his jump but died soon after of his burns. The Lancaster crashed but Brophy was thrown clear and survived.

The Coastal Command V.C. was awarded to F/L D. Hornell. On June 24, 1944, he attacked U1225 in the Atlantic north of the Shetlands. Hornell sank the enemy but his Canso was so badly shot up that he had to ditch. The starboard wing had been set ablaze and its engine had dropped into the sea. Upon ditching, the plane sank immediately. Only one dinghy was saved, forcing the eight crew to take turns in the icy water. Two men eventually succumbed, but the six others were rescued after 21 hours afloat. Hornell died soon after being picked up.

Air Transport

Several general purpose communications flights and transport squadrons operated in the RCAF during the Second World War. The former provided a variety of light duties throughout Canada using such aircraft as the Barkley-Grow, Beech 18, Fairchild 24, Goose, Lockheed 10, 12, and 18, and Stinson 105. Providing transport at

home were 12 Sqdn (Ottawa), 164 Sqdn (Moncton), 165 Sqdn (Vancouver), 168 Sqdn (Rockcliffe), and 124, and 170 (Ferry) Sqdns. These squadrons were operated under the Directorate of Air Transport Command, W/C Z.L. Leigh commanding.

A major undertaking on the home front in 1942 was the establishment in October of the Northwest Staging Route between Edmonton and Alaska. It was set up to strengthen this flank of North America against the Japanese who were active in the Aleutians. The project came about through the Canada-U.S. Joint Board of Defence. Prior to this time, Alaska and the Yukon had been relatively inaccessible. The only air service from Edmonton had been a limited one provided by Yukon Southern Air Transport. Otherwise the region counted mainly on coastal steamers and the narrow gauge railroad between Skagway and Whitehorse.

The Northwest Staging Route was to be a string of airports northwestward from Edmonton. The first contracts were let in February 1941 for airports at Fort Nelson and Watson Lake. Moving supplies into such isolated places was gruelling work often involving tractor trains, bushplanes, and rafts, but by year's end several airstrips were operational. At the same time the Alaska Highway and Canol pipeline were being built in the region. Eventually ten airstrips were completed along the Northwest Staging Route, seven under DOT, and three under RCAF control.

Once established, the Northwest

Staging Route was serviced by a very busy No. 6 Communications Flight with a Lockheed 10 and a handful of Norsemans. This unit was eventually relieved by 165 Sqdn, operating from Edmonton and Whitehorse. The construction of Namao airport near Edmonton was another direct result of operations on the Northwest Staging Route. It had become necessary due to excessive overcrowding at Edmonton's municipal airport. The men and material required for the defence of Alaska and for the campaign in the Aleutians were flown out of Namao; as well as thousands of warplanes from American factories destined for the Soviets.

No.168 was formed at Rockcliffe in October, 1943 as a heavy transport and V.I.P. squadron. F/L W.H. McIntosh delivered its first aircraft that month, when he flew Lodestar 552 from Vancouver to Ottawa. Training began immediately, and the squadron was soon accepting its B-17's. These were for use on a trans-Atlantic mail service. The first crossing by W/C R.B. Middleton was made December 15: Prestwick via Dorval and Gander. B-17 9204 made the trip with 189 bags of mail weighing three tons. This trip almost met disaster when the crew realized that fuel was not flowing from the reserve tanks into the main tanks. 9204 barely made it to an emergency field in Ireland. It was later determined that the fuel lines from the reserve tanks had been cut while the plane had been with the USAAF. The problem hadn't been detected by 168 Sqdn as the plane had had to be rushed into service

upon its arrival in Canada. The first complete round trip took place December 22, with F/L W.R. Lavery taking a B-17 eastbound and F/L W.H. McIntosh bringing it back to Rockcliffe.

Overall, 168 Sqdn completed 636 Atlantic mail crossings. These were not always uneventful operations. As the aircraft were unarmed, there was always the chance of falling prey to enemy fighters, though this never occurred. On January 23, 1944, however, one of the squadron's B-17's collided almost head on with a Coastal Command Wellington while en route Prestwick-Gibraltar. After surveying the damage, F/O H.B. Hillcoat discovered one engine knocked out, and bent and otherwise damaged propellers on the remaining three engines. Everything, mail included, was dumped overboard and the "Fort" was able to limp back to England. On another trip, March 3, 1944, F/L McIntosh was flying 9202 from Gibraltar to Prestwick. One engine failed over the Bay of Biscay. The propeller wouldn't feather, and the aircraft began losing altitude, dropping from 6000 to 1500 feet. Once again, the mail went overboard. McIntosh contemplated a forced landing in Portugal. Because all "visitors" to Portugal had to be officially civilians all buttons, flashes, and sidearms joined the mail in going overboard. Eventually McIntosh turned his plane around and made it back to Gibraltar. On landing, the crew found that one sack of mail had avoided a dunking by clinging to the stabilizer. By another stroke of luck, most of the jettisonned mail was fished out of

Flying mailmen. One of the 168 Sqdn B-17's taking off from Rockcliffe on the first RCAF Overseas Airmail Service flight December 15, 1943.
Public Archives of Canada (PL 23355)

the sea by friendly warships.

Three RCAF transport squadrons operated overseas during the war. No.437 served in Europe while Nos.435 and 436 operated with Dakotas in Burma towards the end of the war. Their main function was to supply British troops fighting the Japanese in jungle warfare. Dakotas were used exclusively. Crews with these squadrons soon realized that they were flying in a region of the world which, during monsoon season, presented the wildest weather conditions imaginable. As very limited meteorological facilities were available in the region, W/C R.A. Gordon of 436 Sqdn organized a unique weather reporting service known as Watchbird. A Dakota would take off and remain airborne for 14 hours each day flying over the whole operational region. It observed and reported on weather and airstrip serviceability half-hourly for the benefit of operations officers and aircraft in the air at the time. Watchbird actually sought out the worst weather and flew into it to ascertain feasible routes and then broadcast these. This service was made more effective through the efforts of S/L F.E.W. Smith who brought his knowledge of instrument flying to the operation.

F/L W. Cornell of 436 Sqdn one day experienced the monsoon at its worst while flying through a region of extensive cumulus. Part of his report on the

happenings of the day reads,

" . . . The airspeed indicator was reading 300 mph, the vertical speed was at 6000 feet-per-minute down, and the altimeter was unwinding at a frightful rate. I can't say how much altitude I lost, as my one idea was to pull out of the dive before the aircraft went into the ground. It finally did pull out, and in a fraction of a second the vertical speed read 6000 feet-per-minute up. I frantically applied more "Down" trim and forward pressure on the control column, but by then the aircraft was on its back and I was hanging on my safety belt. I applied full aileron and kicked the rudder . . . the aircraft must have half-rolled and ended up in another dive. This time I was able to level out, and I suddenly came into a clearing . . . . ''

Besides the hazards of nature, 435 and 436 Sqdn crews also had to contend with the enemy. On January 12, 1945, S/L H.L. Coons was attacked four times by a Zero. He dove to tree-top level in avoiding each of the attacks. Though his aircraft was badly shot up and had lost four feet of wing to the trees, Coons made it back to base. Two other Dakotas were not so lucky that day as they fell to the Zeros.

During their Burma operations, 435 and 436 Squadrons flew over 25 000 sorties and over 60 000 hours on operations. They delivered 56 460 tons of cargo and carried 29 000 passengers. Six aircraft and 20 aircrew were lost on operations.

The Last Days

Germany surrendered to the Allies on May 8, 1945. This signalled an immediate winding down of RCAF operations. Within days, most crews had flown their final sorties. There were last minute activities, however, ranging from food drops to Victory fly pasts. No.418, for example, took part in a 1400 plane flypast June 10 over Frankfurt to honour Marshal Zhukov.

Final "ops" sometimes led to spontaneous overreaction. On returning to base from his last trip over Europe, F/O Bruce Campbell of 405 Squadron observed celebrations below in the streets of Gransden Lodge. He put his Lancaster into a steep dive and thundered over the proceedings, releasing flares to add to the fun of it all. Fortunately there were no repercussions, other than a mild reprimand, and a complaint from a tavern owner who claimed the roar of the four Merlins had broken every glass he owned!

F/O Campbell's last few trips included two on Operation Exodus, flying Allied POW's home. On each of these, one from Jouvencourt, France, and the other from Brussels, 24 liberated prisoners were

squeezed into the Lancaster. The trips were full of emotion as some of the returnees had been prisoners since Dunkirk. Even so, there was some levity, for some of the POW's carried along loads of personal booty, fur coats included! In all, 6 Group flew 189 missions May 8-May 10, evacuating 4329 men.

Also in F/O Campbell's log late in the war are some trips flown to Holland. These were relief flights, with food being dropped onto a race course at The Hague. Although the war was still on, an agreement had been made with the retreating Germans that they not fire on the Lancasters as they flew in to drop sacks of flour and potatoes from 200 feet.

Soon after V.E. Day, eight RCAF bomber squadrons were assigned to Tiger Force, established to step up the war against Japan. In all, 165 Lancasters were ferried back to Canada for this purpose. One squadron involved was No.405. By the end of the first week of June it had flown the Atlantic in mass formation via the Azores to Scoduc, New Brunswick. All aircraft made the crossing in routine fashion except F/O Campbell's E-Easy. It had engine trouble and landed at Gander. After an engine change it completed the short hop to Scoduc. As with thousands of wartime pilots around this time, this was to be Campbell's last trip as pilot in command. The capitulation of Japan on August 14 put an end to Tiger Force and

most Canadian airmen were demobilized and soon back on civvy street.

Within a few weeks of V.J. Day the majority of Canadian squadrons had been disbanded. No.420 (Snowy Owl) Sqdn disbanded at Debert, Nova Scotia, September 5. Aircraft were quickly struck off strength, then taken over by War Assets Corporation for disposal. In the case of 420 Sqdn this meant one last flight to the disposal base. On September 13 the squadron's Lancasters took off from Debert and headed west. They landed at Montreal; then, on the sixteenth, carried on to Winnipeg. Here followed several days of what one crewman recalls as "rounds of continuous partying."

On September 24 the squadron took off for the final leg of its trip. Destination was Pearce, Alberta, from where the Lancasters were to be sold off or destroyed. This leg has been described by one participant as "how World War II came to the Prairies." Once out of Winnipeg, the gaggle of Lancasters set about terrorizing the countryside between there and Pearce. Aircraft, even as big as they were, flew under telegraph wires; one, flew so low over a farm, it collided with a barnyard duck. Another pilot buzzed a train and recalls his last impression as

Breaking up Lancasters at Pearce, Alberta after the war.

N.K. Found

seeing the startled look of disbelief on the engineer's face as he pulled down his blind!

After 4 hours and 15 minutes, the Lancasters arrived at Pearce. The first aircraft down was deliberately rolled off the end of the runway into a slough. It was followed by as many Lancasters as could be squeezed into the mire. After demobilizing all this government equipment the culprits were all taken on charge, though soon afterwards let off with a reprimand. Thus did the Snowy Owl squadron end the war!

Post-War Clean-Up

Just as had happened after World War I, Canada was flooded with surplus military aircraft in 1945. Disposing of all these posed a major challenge. So it happened that acres of aircraft from Finches to Liberators were burned on site; bulldozed into trenches and buried; and hauled off by farmers, scrap dealers, and other speculators. These were the times when fighter planes could be purchased for $50; Ansons and Bolingbrokes became almost as common on the rural landscape as silos and windmills.

Within months of war's end, War Assets' advertisements were cropping up in newspapers and journals across the country, describing aircraft available, conditions of sale, and so on. A typical ad read, "They are offered to the public strictly for their salvage value and parts or components dismantled or removed from them must not be used in licenced aircraft." Other aircraft, mostly trainers, were offered in flyable condition. There were Cornells and Cranes for $800 each, Harvards for $900, Ansons V's for $5000, and Cansos for $25 000.

Buyers soon appeared to cart or fly away their choice of a dozen aircraft types. Scrap dealers had a field day, purchasing acres of aircraft at a time. One bought up most of the Battles, Bolingbrokes, Lysanders, and Hurricanes he could find between the Lakehead and the Rockies. His Bolingbroke collection was equal to a dozen wartime squadrons! These aircraft he would quickly resell at a profit to farmers who in turn stripped them, or sold and traded them to neighbours or local scrap dealers. By the time a plane had made the rounds, there usually wasn't much left of it.

Another Western scrap dealer purchased 150 Battles at MacDonald, Manitoba. These had already been stripped of their tires by a local auto dealer, making it impossible for them to be towed away. For this reason the Battles were not a "hot item" among the farmers. The scrap dealer was able to corral the entire consignment at a dollar apiece! Two bulldozers were brought in to flatten the Battles so they could more readily be transported to Winnipeg. In so doing, various types of metal were mixed and hence contaminated. The 14 cents a pound the squashed Battles were supposed to bring in, dropped to a mere 1-1/2 cents.

All in all, it wasn't too long before War Assets had rid itself of a huge burden. Its vast clip-winged airforce faded into history at a rate that would surely have impressed the Luftwaffe a few years earlier.

Since this aircraft disposal process was shortlived, it didn't receive too much publicity. Some articles appeared decrying the colossal waste. One Winnipeg Free Press article was headlined, "Aircraft Are Suffering Post-War Let-Down Too," and read in part, "Where blue-clad mechanics and armourers used to swarm around her on the tarmac servicing and bombing up for the next flight, now chickens roost on her tailplane, cows scratch their backs on her rudder and the farmer's dog lies out of the sun beneath her wings.

"It's getting to be almost a common sight now — one that would have caused a minor sensation a few years back — to see one of these big yellow bombing trainers

Two aircraft which survived the war to fly in civilian roles. Photographic Survey's Supermarine Walrus, CF-GKA, dubbed Putsy-Putsy, is seen at Goose Bay on a survey contract. The Stranraer in Siple markings was photographed at Kenora.
C.H. Parkin and Norbert Millar

John H. Turnbull, one of the Canadian instructors in China in 1948, stands by the wreck of a Canadian-built Mosquito. A tire had blown while he was taking off and he was fortunate to walk away from the resulting prang. The accident occurred at Hankow. Carl "Moose" Fumerton and George Stewart were the other two Canadians who trained Chinese Nationalists on Mosquitos at this time.

George Stewart

A collection of aircraft in the early post-war years. Seen at RCAF Station Greenwood are Lancasters, Dakotas, Cansos, Sea Furies, a Norseman, and a Mustang.

Via Fred Lake

taking up space between the barn and the farmhouse."

"Barnyard bombers" were well worth the fifty dollars asking price. To begin with, a farmer could count on recouping his investment by simply draining gas and antifreeze from his plane. Tires were just fine for a farm wagon. A tailwheel fit the wheelbarrow. For years to come the carcass would be a veritable hardware store of nuts and bolts, piping and wiring. In the meantime it made a suitable chicken coop or storage shed. One farmer converted the nose of his Anson into a snowmobile. Big Waco gliders were hauled away just for their packing cases. The actual gliders were probably put to the torch.

While there were few civil flying roles for the bulk of War Assets aircraft, many still managed to survive the post-war housecleaning. The RCAF retained enough to see itself into the fifties, as it awaited conversion to more modern types.

Meanwhile, some types made the transition to civilian life. These were primarily Tiger Moths, Cornells, Anson V's, and Cranes. They were bargains at first sight. One ad offered Cornells at $385 and noted optimistically, "Overhaul at your local shop should not exceed $300." In fact, people buying these aircraft, if they had no ability to perform aircraft maintenance, soon found that running their aircraft was prohibitively expensive.

Nonetheless, the availability of war surplus aircraft did much to put flying clubs and private fliers back into the air. Various types were suitable for recreational, club, and commercial use and were available at a time when the industry had not made the transition back to civilian production and when money was not plentiful.

In the case of the Tiger Moth, 215 airplanes and spares were given to the Royal Canadian Flying Clubs Association.

The RCAF's standard fighter after World War II. These two Mustangs are carrying different styles of national marking. They are seen at Grande Prairie, Alberta, August 6, 1949 during Exercise Eagle. Seventy aircraft participated, including 9 Mustangs.

Public Archives of Canada (PL 53930)

Larger commercially valuable types like the DC-3 and Canso were limited to sales to major Canadian airlines and for export. Even so, many unorthodox sales were made. Oxfords were supposedly unsaleable for commercial use as they were technically bombers. Yet two appear on the civil register in this period as CF-BZH and CF-BZI, ex-RCAF EB456 and EB484. These were purchased by Algoma Air Transport and ferried from Swift Current to Winnipeg, but according to a letter of August 21, 1945 from E.W. Ahr of Algoma, they were then dismantled.

Another aircraft was the Lysander II, No.700. It was sold for $50 at Suffield, Alberta, to Westland Dusting Service with

EE311, one of two Meteor fighters acquired by the RCAF in 1946 and Canada's first jets.

Public Archives of Canada (PL 48690)

the stipulation on the bill of sale, "For Salvage Only." The aircraft later appeared as CF-GFJ and operated throughout Alberta for at least three years.

Expediting this disposal operation was the Babb Company, world's largest used airplane dealer. It operated from Montreal, also home for Siple Aircraft, Canada's largest such dealer. These companies purchased all sorts of aircraft in bulk and recycled them all over the world. In 1950 a partial list of Babb sales of ex-Canadian aircraft included 18 Cansos sold to Argentina and Brazil, and over 200 Harvards sold to Holland, Norway, Sweden, and Switzerland. Among Siple's many procurements were all remaining RCAF Stranraers.

Canadians in China

Also during this post-war period, 205 ex-RCAF Mosquito fighters were sold to Chiang Kai-shek's Chinese Nationalists. Fifteen Chinese pilots arrived in Canada and began training on the Mosquito at de Havilland in Toronto. After wrecking several aircraft and not really making too

much progress, the students returned home. The Mosquitos were shipped to Shanghai by sea, assembled under de Havilland supervision, then flown to Hankow where three Canadian instructors and several Canadian ground crew carried on with the training.

Communist forces overwhelmed the Nationalists before the ex-Canadian Mosquitos could see any active service in China.

Post-War Reorganization and Growth

While War Assets was disposing of most Canadian military aircraft in the immediate post-war period, the RCAF and RCN were reorganizing for peacetime roles. Early in 1946 this reorganization proposed eight regular and 15 auxiliary squadrons for the RCAF. One of the new regular squadrons was No.435 at Edmonton, flying Dakotas. Another was No.412 at Rockcliffe, initially equipped with Liberators, Dakotas, and Expeditors. These two squadrons had been formed from elements of 12 (Comm.) Sqdn and

164 Sqdn. New transport squadrons were now under 9 Group. Two other Rockcliffe-based squadrons were No.413 and No.414 tasked with photo survey primarily in the North. These squadrons flew Norsemans, Dakotas, Cansos, Mitchells, and Lancasters; through 1946 they photographed over 400 000 square miles. Their operations were actually to result in changes to the map of Canada.

An early post-war northern operation was Exercise Musk-Ox between January 1946 and May 1947. This was an army exercise with RCAF support. During it, 48 soldiers using snowmobiles trekked over 3100 miles across the Barren Lands, first northward to the Arctic coast, then southward to Edmonton via such towns as Norman Wells and Yellowknife. During the exercise, the RCAF provided six Dakotas, three Norsemans, a B-24 as well as some Waco gliders. Also at this time, the RCAF operated its Winter Experimental Establishment at Namao, testing such aircraft as the Lancaster X, Lincoln, Meteor, Vampire, Sea Hornet and Firefly IV.

In 1947 the RCAF took delivery of two new aircraft types. In April the first Sikorsky S-51 (H-5) arrived at Trenton, thus providing the Air Force with its first helicopter; and in September the first North Star transport was delivered.

In 1946 auxiliary Air Force squadrons were approved for Montreal, Toronto, Hamilton, London, Winnipeg, Saskatoon, Edmonton, and Vancouver. These used Harvards at first but within two years had converted to types like the B-25, Mustang, Vampire, and Expeditor.

Rescue activities between January 1 and 4 opened 1948. A 103 Search and Rescue Unit Canso was called out on two difficult East Coast emergencies. Each time it was piloted by F/O R.B. West. In the first case he flew from Halifax to evacuate a pneumonia patient from Harrington

In 1948 the de Havilland Vampire became the RCAF's first operational jet fighter. 17053 of 410 Sqdn is shown in this photo taken at Whitehorse during Exercise Sweetbriar in February 1950.
Public Archives of Canada (PL 50693)

RCAF activity at Golden Lake, Ontario in May 1953. Shown are a 408 Sqdn Canso and a 412 Sqdn Goose, No. 386. Both these aircraft continued flying after they left the RCAF. The Canso became CF-PQI, a water bomber owned by the Quebec government, while the Goose became CF-HUY and is still active with Parsons Airways of Flin Flon.
DND (PL 57162)

North American B-25 Mitchell's of 406 Sqdn bombing up at Goose Bay during Exercise Sun Dog in 1952.

DND (PL 53538)

Harbour on the Quebec North Shore. No sooner had the patient been evacuated than the Canso was en route back to the North Shore, this time to Mutton Bay for another medivac. In spite of rough water which damaged the Canso, West successfully removed the patient to Halifax, and for these flights was awarded the McKee Trophy for 1948.

In January 1948 the RCAF accepted its first operational jet fighter, the de Havilland Vampire. Previous to this it had gained some jet experience with two Meteor F.Mk.3's. The Vampires were shipped to Toronto from England and assembled by de Havilland. Test pilot Russ Bannock made the initial Vampire flight on January 17 and on January 23 the first Vampires were turned over to the RCAF. In December, 410 Sqdn at St. Hubert became Canada's first jet fighter squadron.

On April 1, 1948, Air Transport Command was formed and on June 15 it made its first trans-Atlantic crossing using a North Star. Aerial surveying was increased for the year. One flight resulted in additional territory being added to the map of Canada when a 413 Sqdn Lancaster charted two previously unnoticed islands with an area of 5000 square miles. These are today Barnett and Tomkinson Islands, named for the pilot and navigator of the Lancaster.

Air Transport Command completed two famous flights in 1949/1950. On one

of these, North Star No.17512 took off from Vancouver on January 14, 1949, and flew non-stop to Halifax in 8 hours 25 minutes at an average speed of 329 mph. This was the first ever non-stop aerial crossing of Canada. From January 2 to February 8, 1950, a North Star carried Lester Pearson to Columbo, Ceylon, then flew on to complete ATC's first 'round-the-world flight.

In March, 1950 the first post-war maritime patrol squadron, No.405 was formed. Based at Greenwood, Nova Scotia, it was equipped with newly refurbished Lancasters.

Notable acquisitions during this period included large numbers of P-51's and Avengers. The Mustangs were to equip RCAF auxiliary squadrons; the Avengers were for use aboard HMCS *Magnificent.* By late 1950 P-51's were equipping 402 Sqdn (Winnipeg), 403 Sqdn (Calgary), 420 Sqdn (London), and 424 Sqdn (Hamilton). Vampires were flying with 400 Sqdn (Toronto), 401, 410, and 438 Sqdns (St. Hubert), 421 Sqdn (Chatham), and 442 Sqdn (Vancouver). B-25's equipped 406 Sqdn (Saskatoon) and 418 Sqdn (Edmonton). The following year, the last two reserve squadrons were formed with Vampires, these being 411 Sqdn (Toronto) and 443 Sqdn (Vancouver). Meanwhile, reserve squadrons were being joined by newly formed regular ones including 404 Sqdn (Greenwood) with Lancasters, 416 Sqdn (Uplands) with P-51's and 441 Sqdn (St. Hubert) with Vampires.

In all, the post-war RCAF was to have on strength 130 P-51's, 86 Vampires and

146 B-25's; and the RCN 35 Seafires, 57 Fireflies, 75 Sea Furies and 125 Avengers. The Harvard continued as the basic training aircraft. Meanwhile, the Canadian Army had acquired 42 Austers for use as observation aircraft. On a regular basis aircraft of all three services exercised together at the Canadian Joint Air Training Centre at Rivers, Manitoba. Experimental flying was taken over by the Central Experimental and Proving Establishment at Uplands.

Search and rescue in 1950 included an operation to locate a downed U.S. bomber. On February 13 a Strategic Air Command B-36 disappeared off B.C.'s North Coast. It had been en route Fairbanks-Fort Worth when it flew into bad weather. Forty search aircraft were soon in the air, including a Norseman, Expeditor, S-51, two Dakotas, seven Cansos, and a Lancaster of the RCAF. On February 15, 11 crewmen who had parachuted from the B-36 were discovered and rescued from Princess Royal Island. They had been located by the fishing vessel *Cape Perry* and were picked up by HMCS *Cayuga.* Another crewman was saved the following day. The previous month a search had failed to turn up any sign of a USAF C-54 lost over the Yukon with 44 aboard.

Canadian Naval Aviation: The Post-War Years

During World War II many Canadians had flown with Royal Navy squadrons. Some of these had become fighter aces, and one had earned the Victoria Cross. Canadians had largely manned two aircraft carriers,

Avenger 86233 of VS 881 overflies HMCS *Magnificent*.
Public Archives of Canada (MAG 3177)

HMS *Nabob* and HMS *Puncher*. Towards the end of the war negotiations were completed between Britain and Canada whereby two light carriers, *Warrior* and *Magnificent*, would be turned over by Britain to the Royal Canadian Navy. This led to the formation of Canada's first naval air squadrons.

By mid 1945 arrangements were being made to form squadrons for service aboard the carriers *Warrior* and *Magnificent*. Aircrew were drawn from the Royal Navy Fleet Air Arm but also from the RCAF and RCN. The first squadron, No.803, was formed at Arbroath, Scotland, on June 15, 1945. It was followed by 825 at Rattray, Scotland, on July 1. These squadrons were equipped with Seafires and Barracudas respectively. By September, two more squadrons had formed, 826 with Barracudas, and 883 with Seafires. By early 1946 the torpedo squadrons had exchanged their Barracudas for Firefly Mk.I's.

On January 24, 1946 *Warrior* was commissioned into the RCN at a ceremony in Belfast. After completing trials, she took aboard 803 and 825 Squadrons, the two other squadrons having been temporarily disbanded. On March 31, *Warrior* arrived at Halifax. Her aircraft were flown off and landed at their shore base, the RCAF station at Dartmouth. Dartmouth was by this time home for the RCN's first shore-based flying unit, Fleet Requirement Unit 743 equipped initially with Swordfish, then with Harvards, and Ansons.

had not been winterized; the *Magnificent,* just completed, had been. Due to manpower restrictions imposed at this time by Ottawa, the RCN could not afford to operate both carriers, so opted for the more suitable of the two. By mid summer, *Magnificent* was involved in exercises off Canada's East Coast with the 19th CAG aboard. These took her as far north as Wakeham Bay on Hudson Strait.

In December, 1949 the RCAF turned Dartmouth over to the RCN, at which time the station was renamed HMCS *Shearwater*. Throughout this period squadrons aboard *Warrior* and *Magnificent* had taken part in many exercises, including some with allied forces. One such occurred in 1949 when a large force of U.S. Navy Mariner and Neptune patrol bombers operated from *Shearwater* and the Eastern Passage alongside Canadian squadrons. As well, RCN squadrons visited U.S. Naval air stations mainly along the East Coast. Certain Canadian pilots also did tours with Royal Navy and U.S. Navy squadrons.

Hawker Sea Fury F.B.11's of 803 Sqdn, 19th CAG (Carrier Air Group).
Public Archives of Canada (DNS 2731)

In late 1946, early 1947 *Warrior* completed a cruise to the West Coast and back. While at Esquimalt a major refit was undertaken. Once back on the East Coast, training operations continued with 803 and 825 Sqdn, by now designated 19th CAG (Carrier Air Group); and the reactivated 826 and 883 Sqdn, or 18th CAG.

In March of 1948 *Warrior* returned to Belfast where she was handed back to the Royal Navy. This had been required as she

One of these was Lt. Commander K.S. Nicolson who flew such American aircraft as the Hellcat, Bearcat, Corsair, Panther, and TV-2 during these early years of Canadian naval aviation. These exchanges provided RCN pilots with their first jet experience. Also during this period RCN squadrons were participating in annual tri-service exercises held at Rivers, Manitoba. Besides many Sea Fire sorties flown at Rivers in the summer of 1948, the Nicolson log shows flights in a Dakota, Waco glider, and Auster AOP aircraft. Otherwise, RCN aircraft performed at many air shows in the late forties.

Early in 1948 the RCN began reequipping with the Hawker Sea Fury, No.803 being the first squadron to convert. With the Sea Fury the RCN was flying the best performing propeller-driven fighter in Canada, and one easily comparable to the U.S. Navy's Bearcat, at the time a front line fighter.

Further updating began in 1950 with replacement of Fireflies. The Firefly was not as rugged a deck plane as the Navy required, so was gradually phased out in favour of the Avenger. The Avenger, though slower than the Firefly, was easier to fly, had a longer range, could accommodate a bigger ASW load, and was generally more reliable. Other changes during this period included a renumbering of squadrons in 1951 — 803 and 825 became 870 and 880 respectively, of the 31st SAG (Support Air Group); and 883 and 826 became 871 and 881 respectively, of the 30th SAG. Another innovation took place September 1, 1951, when the Navy formed its first helicopter unit, No.1

Landing prangs aboard the "Maggie." An 825 Sqdn Firefly V hung up in a Bofors gun position, and (left) an Avenger just as stuck. An H04S plane guard stands by behind the Avenger.
Public Archives of Canada (MAG 1355, MAG 7330)

Helicopter Flight under command of Lt. Commander J.D. Lowe, and equipped with three Bell HTL-4's (Bell 47's).

Korea
When the Korean War broke out on June 23, 1950, the RCAF made an immediate commitment to the U.N. by placing at its disposal the North Stars of 426 Sqdn. Six of these left Dorval on July 25 and flew to their new base at McChord AFB, Washington. This was the beginning of Operation Hawk which would see the North Stars flying the Pacific to Japan for the next three years. The inaugural flight began on July 28. Three aircraft completed their round trip in an average time of 81 flying hours. By mid August the North Stars were averaging one return trip per day. Their route included stops at Elmendorf AFB at Fairbanks, Shemya in the Aleutians, then on to Haneda, Japan. The return trip was 15 000 miles. In 1954 the weather facility at Shemya was closed down, and this signalled the end of Operation Hawk. On June 9, 1954, it was officially concluded at Dorval, with the arrival there of the 599th round trip. In all, the North Stars had carried 13 000 personnel and 3500 tons of cargo across the Pacific and logged 34 000 hours.

Canadians were even more directly involved in Korea. A handful of RCAF pilots served combat tours with the USAF there. F/L J.A.O. Levesque became the first of these to engage in an all-jet combat while flying with the 4th FIW. On March 30, 1950, he became the first Canadian to shoot down a MIG-15. In all, 22 RCAF pilots served with the USAF during the war. Six scored victories, for a total of nine enemy aircraft confirmed. One of these pilots, F/O S.B. Fleming, flew 82 combat missions. S/L A.R. Mackenzie was the only one shot down. He was a POW until December, 1954 having spent 465 days in solitary confinement.

One RCN pilot, Lt. J.J. MacBrien, served as an exchange officer with the U.S. Navy in Korea. He flew 66 sorties in Panthers from the USS *Oriskany* and received the American DFC.

NATO
On August 24, 1949, the North Atlantic Treaty Organization came into existence. Under the NATO agreement, Canada was to provide a European air contingent. No.1 Air Division was formed and came under the 4th Allied Tactical Air Force. The Air Division comprised four wings of three squadrons each of F-86's. No.1 wing formed at North Luffenham, England on November 1, 1951. The first squadron to arrive there was No.410. Its Sabres had

Leapfrog I. Twenty Sabres of 439 Sqdn just prior to their departure from Uplands for North Luffenham, U.K. The operation extended from May 30 to June 15, 1952. The Sabres sport their squadron's emblem, a sabre-toothed tiger.

DND (PL 54272)

been transported overseas aboard HMCS *Magnificent,* as were those of the next squadron. Thereafter the Sabres were flown across the ocean. The first such movement occurred May 28-June 15, 1951, when 21 Sabres of 439 Sqdn flew from Uplands to North Luffenham on Operation Leapfrog I.

No.1 Wing spent the next year in the U.K. awaiting completion of its base at Marville, France. Meanwhile the other wings began taking shape. Other bases being constructed for the Canadians in Europe were Grostenquin, France and Baden-Soellingen and Zweibrucken, Germany. H.Q. was set up at Metz, France. The first RCAF squadrons to arrive on the Continent since 1946 were those of No.2 Wing. They had flown to Grostenquin September 28-October 11, 1952, on Operation Leapfrog II.

On March 1, 1953, 444 Sqdn formed at St. Hubert as the 12th and last Air

Logistic support for the Air Division in Europe was provided by the RCAF's Bristol Freighter, an anachronous airplane when compared to the sleek Sabre. Freighter 9698 of No. 137 Transport Flight is pictured loading supplies at Langer Notta, England, August 1954. After being struck off strength in May 1967 it was purchased by Wardair, becoming CF-WAC.

York University, Scott Archives

Division squadron. It flew to Baden-Soellingen with 414 and 422 Sqdn. This operation included 63 Sabres which departed from Uplands August 24, 1953, and flew to Goose Bay. From there, 60 of them, shepherded by a North Star, flew to Bluie West, Greenland, where one aircraft was damaged. The other 59 flew on to Iceland. On the eighth day, 62 Sabres flew to Lossiemouth, Scotland, and next day to Germany. Later in the year, No.1 Overseas Ferry Unit was formed to handle the task of ferrying Sabres and T-33's between Canada and Europe.

The Hectic Fifties

Canada added a variety of new military aircraft to its inventory during these years. In April 1952 the first of six Bristol Freighters was delivered for use by the Air Division. In September the first C-119 Flying Boxcar was accepted. This type reequipped 435 and 436 Sqdns and gave ATC its first heavy lift capability and a transport capable of accommodating 65 troops.

The first of two 40-passenger de Havilland Comets arrived at Uplands May 29, 1953. Thus the RCAF became the

The only one of its kind ever built, the Canadair C-5 served from 1950 onward with 412 Sqdn as the RCAF's primary VIP aircraft. When disposed of in 1968 the airplane which had flown prime ministers, monarchs, and presidents brought $49 000 from an American buyer.

DND (PL 52721)

world's first air force to operate jet transports and the first operator to make scheduled trans-Atlantic crossings with jets. Also in 1953 the DHC-3 Otter joined the RCAF. All in all, the RCAF accepted 796 Canadian built aircraft in 1953, plus those imported.

Auxiliary squadrons continued their

For many years the basic heavy transport in Air Transport Command, these C-119 Flying Box Cars were photographed at Great Whale, Quebec in March 1955 while on Mid Canada Line operations.

Public Archives of Canada (PL 101657)

fighter and tactical roles into the mid fifties. One exercise in June, 1953 was headlined "Huge Craft 'Shot Down,' City Saved." The story described how P-51's and Vampires from reserve squadrons had successfully intercepted USAF B-29's and B-36's during simulated raids on Ontario cities.

Other new aircraft types to come on strength were the first Orenda-powered Sabres, delivered to Europe in 1954, and CF-100's, by now being regularly delivered. Six CF-100 squadrons were formed during this period, these being 419 Sqdn (North Bay), 428 Sqdn (Uplands), 425 Sqdn (St. Hubert), 432 Sqdn (Bagotville), 409 Sqdn (Comox) and 433 Sqdn (Cold Lake). Also in 1954 the first S-55 and H-21 helicopters were delivered to the RCAF. Preliminary work was being done for a new maritime patrol aircraft

The RCAF's first Comet upon its arrival at Uplands on May 29, 1953. It had made the crossing from London to Ottawa in 10 hours 20 minutes. The RCAF became the first operator in the world to schedule trans-Atlantic jet service.

DND

based on the Bristol Britannia, the go-ahead was given for the CF-105 interceptor and construction was started on the Mid Canada radar line. A historic retirement was that of the Anson from RCAF service.

In 1955 it was decided to build the Distant Early Warning Line across the top of the continent while new aircraft acquired were the P2V Neptune maritime patrol bomber, H-34 helicopter, T-34 trainer and Cessna L-19 Bird Dog army observation plane.

In 1956, a change in NATO policy saw the first CF-100's sent to Europe. Each

NORAD duo, a 410 Sqdn CF-100 and a USAF F-102.

DND

A fine study of a Canadian Forces CF-104 ▶ belonging to the Aeronautical Engineering Test Establishment, CFB Cold Lake. It carries AETE's red X on the tail and is on a test flight with LAU-3 rocket pods underwing. Though one of the oldest CF-104's in Canadian service, 104704 has relatively few hours, having spent its lifetime as a test rather than an operational aircraft. The photo was taken in November 1975.

Rae R. Simpson

wing in the Air Division relinquished one Sabre squadron for a CF-100 squadron, thus giving the Canadians in NATO all weather capability. Sabres returned from Europe at this time were turned over to auxiliary squadrons which were finally able to retire their P-51's and Vampires.

Two other events of 1956 deserve note. On January 16 an RCAF T-33 flew from Vancouver to Shearwater in 5 hours 52 minutes on the first jet crossing of Canada; in support of U.N. peace keeping in the Middle East, 435 Sqdn deployed to Capodichino, Italy.

In 1957 the aerial mapping of the North was finally completed, having had its start in 1944. Largely flown by Nos. 413, 414 and, later 408 Sqdn supported by civilian operators, the mapping had been expedited by SHORAN (Short Range Aid to Navigation), a distance measuring system using ground stations. SHORAN reduced photo errors to as little as 25 feet in 100 miles. To this time the Arctic had been photographed to the northern tip of Ellesmere Island and mapped to a scale of one inch to eight miles.

On July 31, 1957, the DEW Line became operational, on schedule 32 months after initiation. In this the RCAF had been a major participant, flying such aircraft as the Canso, Dakota, Flying Boxcar, and North Star. Also that summer the Overseas Ferry Unit was disbanded, having delivered over 800 Sabres and T-33's without fatality, living up to its motto, Deliverum non Dunkem! Another phasing out was that of the NATO Air Training Plan. Since 1950 the RCAF had trained and graduated 4600 pilots and navigators from ten NATO countries. This activity had been largely financed by Canada as a Mutual Aid Plan contribution.

Some 28 Vampires and 87 P-51's that were no longer required were declared surplus in 1957. These were gradually disposed of, mostly in the United States. Of the Vampires, 15 were then resold to the Mexican Air Force, becoming Mexico's first jet fighters. A large number of the P-51's were converted to civilianized, 2-seat Cavalier Mustangs by Trans Florida Aircraft of Sarasota and are still active.

On November 1, 1957, the RCAF resumed use of its two Comet jet transports. These had been grounded in January, 1954 following Comet crashes overseas, while de Havilland investigated reasons for these disasters. When the trouble had been pinpointed, the Comets, after two years in mothballs at Uplands, were ferried to Hatfield for structural modifications, then returned to 412 Sqdn for regular operations.

Growth of Naval Aviation

In the mid fifties Canadian naval aviation centred on HMCS *Magnificent*. Her annual cruises took her to the Caribbean, throughout the Atlantic on exercises with ships and planes of NATO allies, and into the Mediterranean. One such exercise was dubbed "Mariner." It lasted three weeks and involved some 300 ships and 1000 aircraft of nine nations. Otherwise, the *Magnificent* was often engaged in RCN exercises and keeping her pilot's deck qualified on their Sea Furies and Avengers. There were also occasional good will visits and annual refits.

In late 1952, the Sikorsky HO4S-2 was taken on strength and placed in service with VH 21, Shearwater. Meanwhile Avengers kept on arriving until a total of 125 had been accepted. In May 1953, the first RCN air reserve squadron was formed, this being VC 920 at RCAF Station Downsview. Initially equipped with Harvards, it later added Avengers, and in 1955 became deck qualified on the *Magnificent*. Other reserve squadrons formed at this time were VC 921 at Kingston; VC 922 at Victoria; VC 923 at Quebec; and VC 924 at Calgary. New regular squadrons formed were VU 32, previously FRU 743; and VT 40, a training squadron. In 1955 VT 40 received four T-33's, the RCN's first jet aircraft. In July that year HS 50 was formed with six HO4S-3's to become the Navy's first ASW helicopter squadron. In the meantime, VF 870 had relinquished its Sea Furies and awaited reequipment with the McDonnell F2H-3 Banshee. Other RCN aircrew began familiarization training at U.S. Navy bases on the Grumman Tracker, the intended replacement for the Avenger. Another development during this era was the acquisition of six "Guppy" conversions of the Avenger. These aircraft were fitted with radar housed in a bulbous belly pod. The radar was intended to seek out aircraft that might threaten the fleet, and as such became the RCN's first and only AEW (Airborne Early Warning) aircraft. Throughout this period, HMCS *Shearwater* was being constantly updated to serve the growing needs of Canadian naval aviation.

On November 1, 1955, VF 870 reformed and by month's end had accepted the first of 39 Banshee fighters. These were required for fleet defence with a secondary ground attack role. The same month, one of the best known RCN rescue operations was successfully undertaken when an HO4S-3 piloted by Lt. Cmdr J.H. Beeman and Lt. Cmdr F.R. Fink with two crewmen flew to the rescue of a freighter, the *Kismet II*, which was hard aground and being battered by high seas along the coast of Cape Breton Island.

High winds and the fact that the ship was cast up against a cliff complicated rescue procedures. Eventually its crew was

Buffalo 452 of 116 Air Transport Unit ▶ receives one of its frequent scrub downs at Ismalia in the Sinai Desert. The Buffalo and other de Havilland of Canada designs have proven themselves time and again as rugged, adaptable transports wherever United Nations emergencies have called for air support.

D.J. Veale

signalled to clear a landing space astern, and Beeman and Fink brought their helicopter in for four landings to rescue the 21 crew plus the ship's dog and cat. For their efforts on this operation, both pilots were awarded the George Medal.

Two key events occurred in October 1956. One was the Navy's acceptance on October 12 of its first CS2F Tracker ASW aircraft. The other was the last operational landings aboard the *Magnificent*. These occurred October 10 with the landing of the Avengers of VS 880. Hereafter the aircraft were flown ashore and the carrier assigned to her final duties. On December 29 she sailed for the Middle East transporting Canadian soldiers with their vehicles and supplies for service with the United Nations Emergency Force. On January 20, 1957, *Magnificent* set course from Port Said, docked briefly at Glasgow to take on RCAF Sabres, then sailed for Halifax. On June 14 *Magnificent* reverted to the Royal Navy.

The Sixties
In March 1958 the Avro CF-105 Arrow made its first flight. Soon five pre-production machines were involved in a busy flight test program and from that

A superb photo of a CF-100 Mk.IV taken by Avro photographer Hugh Mackechnie.
Hawker Siddeley Canada Ltd. (61857)

Another fine view of the CF-100, this one by RCAF photographer Cpl. W.D. Frickelton. The photo was taken at Uplands during .50 calibre gun pack tests. Just before the firing began someone thoughtfully reminded the firing crew to retract the nose gear unless they intended to shoot it off!
Public Archives of Canada (PL 59889)

An RCAF CF-101B Voodoo at Trenton in the early sixties. With the arrival of these interceptors, the CF-100 passed from the front line fighter scene in NORAD. Later, these Voodoos were exchanged for more up-to-date CF-101's. They were stored in the Arizona desert for a time, then reactivated as reconnaissance aircraft for use by the USAF in Viet Nam.

Larry Milberry

A Maritime Air Command P2V-7 Neptune on fisheries patrol off the East Coast.

DND (PCN 4764)

point of view things progressed successfully. S/L Jack Woodman of CEPE became the first RCAF pilot to fly the Arrow and the Air Force eagerly looked forward to equipping with the impressive new fighter. But less than a year after first flight, the government cancelled the Arrow and modified its air defence philosophy.

Henceforward, Canada, a partner in the North American Air Defence agreement signed May 12, 1958, would provide a combination of Bomarc missiles and manned interceptors. The Bomarc was ordered in September 1958, and an agreement was made whereby the USAF would provide the RCAF with Voodoo fighters from its surplus inventory.

Another major shift in policy at this time was the decision to redefine the role of auxiliary squadrons. By late 1958 these had given up their Sabres, and taken on a less glamorous role, that of transport, and search and rescue, flying Beech Expeditors.

Other interesting developments in 1958 included the delivery of the first Argus to 405 Squadron, Greenwood, and the retrofitting of J34 jet engines to the RCAF's Neptune patrol aircraft. In the summer of 1958 the Air Force accepted its first operational missiles. These were Ryan Firebee KDA-4 recoverable drones for use as targets at Cold Lake. In preparation for their entering service, two Lancasters, KB 848 and KB 851, were converted by Fairey Aviation at Dartmouth to serve as launch aircraft.

In 1959 Canada marked its 50th anniversary of powered flight. To celebrate, the RCAF made a flying replica of the AEA's Silver Dart. Construction was done at Trenton led by LAC "Mac" McCaffrey, and the aircraft was test flown at nearby Mountainview by W/C Paul Hartman of CEPE. It was then transported to Baddeck, Nova Scotia, and on February 23 was flown by Hartman before an audience that included J.A.D. McCurdy, the year's McKee Trophy recipient.

Cold Lake-based Lancaster KB851 lifts off fitted with two Firebee target drones.

DND (PL 120072)

Sabre 23600 of the Golden Hawks at Trenton, June 1, 1963.

Larry Milberry

Another great event of the year was the formation of the Golden Hawks flight demonstration team, with S/L J.F. Villeneuve commanding. Pilots for the team were selected from the Sabre OTU at Chatham, and each had had operational experience with the Air Division. They practiced three times daily for two-and-a-half months, before putting on their initial display at Torbay, Newfoundland, the first of 63 shows across the country that year. Many of these also included a performance by the RCAF's Red Knight in his T-33.

The RCAF accepted a new NATO role in 1959, that of strike/reconnaissance. For this a new fighter, the F-104, was chosen to reequip eight squadrons. Meanwhile, the Lancaster gave up the ASW role with the departure from Comox on May 13 of FM219. Later that year, the RCAF accepted its first Yukon, the largest type ever to serve in Canada at that time.

Throughout these years Air Transport Command continued its global operations. The North Stars of 426 Sqdn assisted earthquake victims in Morocco and Chile in 1960, while flying regular troop rotation between Canada and Europe. After the Belgiums granted independence to the

The North Star was still hard at work with Air Transport Command in the early sixties. This shows 17504 wearing the United Nations flag landing at Malton, June 29, 1960.

Larry Milberry

The Yukon replaced the North Star beginning in 1961. 15927 of 426 Sqdn was photographed at the Trenton air show, July 1, 1961.

Larry Milberry

Congo in June of that year, the North Stars began support missions for the U.N. forces rushed there to control civil war. In this case, they staged out of Trenton and flew to Gander, thence across the Atlantic usually via Lajes in the Azores, and on the Pisa. There followed the long run south to Kano and Leopoldville with very few navigation aids en route. Flight time Trenton-Leopoldville was a gruelling 42 hours.

In the Congo proper, the RCAF and Canadian Army helped coordinate air movements and communications for the U.N. This was a major undertaking in such a vast undeveloped country and was not always safe for those involved as illustrated by the deaths of 13 Italian airmen. They were taken off their two C-119's, killed and cannibalized by rebels at Brazzaville. On a later occasion a Canadian crew was held and their aircraft impounded by Congolese who mistook them for Russians!

A variety of new aircraft entered RCAF service in 1960 including the CC-109 Cosmopolitan, Grumman Albatross, and C-130B Hercules. As well, the 33rd and last Argus was delivered, four Caribou transports were ordered, and Otters began serving with the Reserves.

The first Canadair-built CF-104's were accepted by the RCAF in March 1961; while in July, 425 Sqdn became Canada's first CF-101B Voodoo squadron. These coincided with gradual phase-out of the CF-100 from NORAD operations. On the Congo scene, Yukons began replacing

Ten Grumman Albatross amphibians formed the backbone of Search and Rescue operations in Canada through the sixties. With their coming, the ancient Canso was retired from RCAF service.

DND (CF66-463-4)

North Stars. These could haul four times the North Star's payload, faster, farther, and without a doubt quieter! They flew non-stop Trenton-Pisa and Pisa-Leopoldville.

A historic retirement took place August 18, 1961. On that day the final flypast of the B-25 was made at the Air Navigation School, Winnipeg. Hereafter Dakotas replaced the ANS B-25's, although the type remained in limited service until 1962.

In December 1962 427 Sqdn became the first Air Division squadron to convert to the CF-104, while the same month Canada's four NATO CF-100 squadrons were disbanded. Completing Canada's NORAD requirements, a second Bomarc squadron was formed. These squadrons were based at North Bay, Ontario, and La Macaza, Quebec.

In conjunction with a 162 Sqdn reunion at RCAF Station Downsview, the Canso was finally retired. The date was April 6, 1962. The venerable amphibian was replaced by more up-to-date Albatrosses. On October 30 the following year the RCAF Comets were flown to Mountainview for disposal.

Disastrous floods struck East Pakistan in 1963, again calling for assistance from ATC which sent Yukons loaded with emergency aid. U.N. requirements that year led to the formation of 134 Air Transport Unit in support of peace-keeping in Yemen. This unit was equipped with six Otters and two Caribous. Commonwealth and NATO air training in Canada in 1963 included graduates from Nigeria, Denmark, and Norway. New aircraft types delivered were the CL-41 Tutor trainer and the CH-113 helicopter.

In 1964 No. 102 Detachment was

formed with Caribous for service in mountainous Kashmir. Another U.N. operation sent ATC Yukons and Hercules to Cyprus as fighting flared there between Greek and Turkish elements. On June 30 ATC completed its 392nd and last scheduled trip to the Congo. In all, 11 746 passengers and 2000 tons of freight had been moved on that operation.

In April, 1964 the Lancaster was phased out of service. Afterwards, the remaining Lancasters were either scrapped at RCAF Station Dunneville or sold as historic monuments. One was converted to a water bomber, then sold to a historic collection in Scotland.

Disbandings in 1964 affected the Golden Hawks, five auxiliary squadrons, two Voodoo squadrons, and No.2 Wing of the Air Division. These reflected austere financial times. Meanwhile, a dispute within NATO concerning the control of U.S. atom warheads in France forced the Air Division to consolidate its squadrons at its two German bases.

The Harvard retired from the RCAF in 1965, where it had served since July 19, 1939, and through World War II some 19 000 airmen in Canada were trained on it. New Harvards were still being built in Canada during the mid fifties and nearly 2400 were eventually delivered. In post-war years 6000 Canadian, NATO, and Commonwealth pilots learned to fly on Harvards. The last of these graduated from RCAF Station Penhold on May 21, 1965.

The C-119 also left the RCAF in 1965, being superseded by the Hercules. They were stored at Saskatoon, then sold off. Several went to the U.S. to be converted to water bombers for use in the American West.

On July 30, 1965, the two Comets were sold from Mountainview. The purchaser was a party apparently ready to sell one to the Peruvian Air Force. The other was cannibalized. The resulting rebuild became CF-SVR. It was stored at Mount Hope airport near Hamilton for some time, then, in January 1968 ferried to Miami as N3735.

On December 8, 1965, North Star No.17506 roared down Runway 15 at Downsview and made the brief run to Trenton in cloud and snow. Its landing at Trenton completed the last official RCAF North Star flight. Later in the day a formal retirement service was held. Presiding at the occasion was Air Marshal W.A. Curtis.

To this date the North Star had served 18 fatality-free years in the RCAF. It had served on the Korean airlift and with the U.N. in the Middle East, Congo, Yemen, and Cyprus. It operated in Indo-China with the truce commission, carried medical

HMCS *Bonaventure* under way with Trackers and HO4S's on the deck. The *Bonaventure* was 720 feet long with a flight deck 112'5'' wide. Its overall weight was 20 000 tons and full speed 25.5 knots.

DND (BN 4595)

supplies to Vienna to help those affected by the Hungarian revolt of 1956, and operated in the SAR role from Torbay. The last North Star service flight was one which returned from El Arish in the Sinai on November 14, 1965.

In December 1965 four RCAF Hercules began airlifting fuel into Zambia which had been temporarily cut off from resupply by the Rhodesian declaration of independence. A total of 247 operational trips were flown. Hercules logged 2726 hours and Yukons 143 hours on the operation.

There was also tragedy in 1965. Argus No.20727 crashed while on a night ASW exercise March 23 about 60 miles north of San Juan. The accident took all 16 men aboard to their deaths. This was the first fatal Argus mishap since the type entered service in 1958.

Centennial Year

Aviation featured in Canada's centennial celebrations in 1967. A new flight demonstration team, the Golden Centennaires, was formed with Tutors, a CF-101, a CF-104, and two Avro 504K's. During their 184 day trans-Canada tour, the team performed 100 times, as well as

eight times in the United States. These shows were viewed by an estimated 4 000 000 spectators.

Another centennial year story is that of W/C R.A. White, senior test pilot with the Canadian Forces Aerospace Engineering Test Establishment, Ottawa. As a centennial project he headed a venture to capture for Canada the world absolute altitude record. This had been held by Russia since 1961 and stood at 113 892 feet. All things considered, including favourable high level winds down the St. Lawrence Valley, the record appeared within Canada's grasp. The aircraft used was 12700, a lighter than usual CF-104. A flight program was devised and worked through. In all 42 flights were made, including 25 zoom climbs, 12 of which exceeded 95 000 feet. The last flight was made December 14, during which White reached Mach 2.4 and an altitude of 100 110 feet. Though short of the world record, this achievement became a Canadian record and demonstrated the sophisticated capabilities of AETE. W/C White received the 1967 McKee Trophy for his contribution on this project.

In August 1967 the RCAF supported an expedition to King William Island to search for remains of Sir John Franklin's

expedition. Franklin had gone to the Arctic in 1845 but he and his 129 companions were never seen again. The expedition 122 years later involved 51 men supported by two Voyageurs and a Hercules. A T-33 provided photo requirements. The expedition turned up no new clues as to Franklin's fate.

Another accomplishment of centennial year was the restoration to flying condition of a World War II vintage Lysander. This project was headed by Bernard Lapointe, an instructor at the Air Navigation School at Winnipeg. The remains of a Lysander had been located on a farm in Saskatchewan and taken to Winnipeg to be rebuilt. It made its first flight on December 29, a last minute historic event of this exciting year.

On the United Nations scene, an incident on May 17, 1967, illustrated the dangers inherent on peace-keeping operations. That day an RCAF Caribou was flying in the Gaza region when it was intercepted by a pair of Israeli fighters. These made two gestures of "follow me," but F/O R.J.V. Simpson, aircraft commander, ignored these. The Israelis next tried to force the Caribou out to sea, and fired warning shots, but Simpson again held his course and landed at Gaza.

The next day the situation in the Middle East deteriorated to the critical point and U.N. forces were ordered to evacuate the Sinai region. Between then and May 31, the Yukons of 437 Squadron, and the Hercules of 435 and 436 Squadrons pulled all Canadian elements in the Sinai back to Trenton.

Centennial year acquisitions included the Dassault Falcon, basically for VIP transport, and the Buffalo for tactical and SAR duties. By this time the Air Division had been reduced to six squadrons. One type retired from service in 1967 was the H-21 helicopter.

A Banshee about to be launched from the *Bonaventure*. The aircraft has been centred on the catapult by lateral rollers, the hydraulic chocks are up, and the nose gear extended to provide a flying attitude. Within moments the Banshee will be shot down the 113 foot catapult and launched into the air at 120 knots.

DND (BN 3752)

Unification

On February 1, 1968, the Canadian Forces Reorganization Act, introduced as a Bill earlier, came into effect. By this Act the RCAF, RCN, and Canadian Army ceased to exist, although their integration had been gradually effected in preceding months. Soon Canada's military aircraft began appearing in the markings "Canadian Armed Forces/Forces Armées Canadiennes."

In late 1968 the Sabre Transition Unit at Chatham closed and on November 29, the Sabre was retired from service. It had spent 17 years with the RCAF. Also retired that year was the Neptune. Like some of the C-119's, a number of ex-RCAF Neptunes later turned up in the U.S. as water bombers.

Crown Assets disposals for 1968 included the famous C-5 VIP transport. In service since July 1950 it had cost $1.2 million, but was sold to a U.S. buyer for $49 000. Another bargain that year was the 82 T-33's bought by Northwest Industries for $1000 each. Wardair acquired the last four Canadian Forces Bristol Freighters, plus spares for $40 000; Boeing in Washington purchased two F-86's with two spare engines for $28 488; and a Saskatoon buyer became the owner of five Harvards

for $9000. The perennial debate over reequipping Maritime Command continued during this period. A November 1969 editorial in *Canadian Aviation* noted, "Replacing the CP-107 Argus with a new long-range ocean patrol aircraft is described as the first priority in aircraft procurement. Introduced 11 years ago, the Argus will be at the end of its programmed life in 1973. By then these aircraft will literally have been flown to death . . . ."

HMCS *Bonaventure*

On January 17, 1957, HMCS *Bonaventure* joined the Royal Canadian Navy as replacement for HMCS *Magnificent*. The new carrier was built to Canadian requirements with such innovations as angle deck, steam catapult, and mirror landing system. On April 2 the *Bonaventure* underwent its first flight trials, and three days later the first Banshee fighter landed on and made its first "cat" launch. The ship sailed for Halifax from British waters in June, and by mid September was busy with flight training, VS 880 (Trackers) and VF 870 (Banshees) being aboard.

For the next 13 years the *Bonaventure* served as a vital component in Canada's fleet, NORAD and NATO elements

ranging throughout the Atlantic, Caribbean, and Mediterranean. With a capacity for just 34 aircraft, no more than two squadrons at a time could serve aboard. Others were land based when not at sea.

In 1958 the Banshees were given a combat boost with the addition of the Sidewinder air-to-air missile, Canada's first operational-guided missile. Though obsolete, the rugged and reliable Banshee provided good service aboard the *Bonaventure*. It had all-weather capability, an 800-mile tactical radius and speed of Mach.8. Its versatile armament range included four 20 mm cannons, two Sidewinders, 16 rockets, or six 500-pound bombs. Perhaps most importantly, pilots found the Banshee to be a good aircraft on the deck.

The Banshee was to serve nearly seven years in the RCN, flying with VF 870 and VF 871 until the latter was amalgamated with VF 870 in 1959. Activities were varied and included annual exercises at Rivers or Gagetown. In 1961 they spent five weeks at Rivers during which they flew 506 sorties; expended 10 000 20-mm shells; fired 1092 3-inch and 5-inch rockets; dropped 912 11 1/2-pound practice bombs; and 30 500-pound bombs. They also spotted for 450 rounds of 105 mm artillery fire. Ground crews expedited 720 snags and maintained a 70.5 per cent aircraft serviceability rate. As well, the squadron logged 16 200 holes of golf!

On August 3, 1962, VF 870 took off from *Shearwater* for its last operational flight; and on September 30 it was disbanded. The Banshee was not replaced and hereafter only Trackers and HO4S's served on the *Bonaventure*.

In 1966 the carrier began a major refit at the Davie Shipbuilding yards opposite Quebec. This was intended to maintain the vessel in service until at least 1975. In 1969, however, after having spent $17 million on the refit, the government mothballed the *Bonaventure* as an austerity move. The last landing on its deck had occurred December 12, 1969, when an HO4S set down.

The *Bonaventure's* final task was supporting a NATO exercise in Norway. Its final docking before being taken over by Crown Assets was at Halifax on April 25, 1970. That summer it was put up for sale and purchased by a Taiwan scrap dealer for $851 700.

The Seventies
In 1970 Air Transport Command was involved in global activities, everywhere from Malaysia, training Malaysian crews on the Caribou; to Lima, on earthquake relief; to Cuba, where it delivered FLQ terrorists. On the Peruvian operation 424

Sqdn Caribous flew vital relief operations carrying food and medical supplies to devastated communities in the rugged Andes and evacuating some 2000 inhabitants. The operation also involved Canadian Hercules and Yukons.

A major development with Canada's NATO forces in 1970 was the reduction of the Air Division to three squadrons based at Baden. After July 1 these constituted the newly formed No. 1 Canadian Air Division. New equipment ordered that year were 4 Boeing 707's and 74 Bell Kiowas. The 707's replaced the Yukons, while the Kiowas replaced the Hiller CH-112 helicopters, L-19's and L-19L's. The following year the Beech Musketeer was acquired to replace the Chipmunk; the first CC-138 Twin Otter was delivered to the Canadian forces for service in Kashmir.

The major reequipment project for 1971, one which had begun the previous year, was the acquisition of 66 rebuilt F-101F interceptors. These replaced Voodoos in service since 1961 and by this time outmoded.

On April 3, 1971, the Yukon retired after over nine years of service. After a distinguished career, the fleet was flown to Saskatoon for disposal. By this time the 12 aircraft had logged 169 046 hours with the low and high time aircraft having 8247 and 17 266 hours. Within three years all 12 had been sold, bringing a mere $1 350 000. Most of the Yukons took up new careers as freighters in Africa and South America.

Also in 1971 the H-34 departed the Canadian Forces. The last three had served as rescue aircraft at Cold Lake. They retired with a total of 15 577 hours and also went to Saskatoon for disposal.

The Search for CF-RLD
A key event for 1972 was the search for a Beech 18. This story began November 8 when Gateway Aviation's CF-RLD departed Cambridge Bay for Yellowknife on a mercy mission. Aboard was pilot Martin Hartwell, two Inuit patients, and a nurse. There were six hours of fuel for the 3 1/2-hour flight.

CF-RLD, on a VFR night flight plan, failed to arrive at its destination. This immediately triggered a search with a 435 Sqdn Hercules and RCMP Twin Otter airborne shortly after the alert. These did track crawls listening for the Beech's Emergency Locator Transmitter. The following day a full-scale search was mounted and SAR HQ established at Yellowknife. Activity was intense, as illustrated by November 11. That day five Hercules and three Twin Otters flew lines at 1000 feet at three-mile intervals (1000/3). Search time was scarce as there was only 2 1/2 hours of usable daylight at this time of year. Next day the search focused between Contwoyto Lake and Bathurst Inlet with lines of 500/1/2. This was the main search area until the fifteenth when it was broadened. During this period, many leads were investigated and many aircraft were involved, including the Buffalo, Dakota, Voyageur, and Argus, as well as many civil types.

Not a fun job. Spotters at work during the search for the Gateway Beech 18, CF-RLD. The spotters are strapped to litters on the ramp of a Hercules and in the bitter Arctic cold were restricted to only a few minutes of exposure before being relieved.

DND (IE 72-163-5)

On November 27 the search was suspended, but under public pressure, resumed three days later, though still with no luck. Then on December 7 a Hercules on a service flight to Inuvik reported an ELT on the air. It acquired a fix on the signal and next day two Hercules searched the area. They returned next day with an Argus and Twin Otter. At 1040 hours local time, Hercules No. 325 reported a crash site at 64° 52′N, 119° 02′W with one survivor evident. Shortly after noon rescue specialists Cpl. Harvey Copeland and Pte. Al Williams were paradropped to the scene. Their Hercules dropped rescue gear while a Twin Otter landed on a nearby lake. At 1315 hours a Voyageur arrived. By this time the wreck had been identified as CF-RLD and the survivor as the pilot. The others aboard had died, though a young Inuit had survived for 23 days.

The search for CF-RLD had entailed 1478.9 flying hours on the part of the Canadian forces and covered 1 1/4 million square miles. It was later determined that the Beech had taken off into conditions beyond the capabilities of both pilot and airplane. At first the flight had maintained 4000 feet, then began descending. The pilot had been studying his map when the plane crashed. It was 185 miles west of its inland course.

A C-130 Hercules of 435 Sqdn Edmonton, demonstrating LAPES (Low Altitude Parachute Extraction System) at the 1976 Abbotsford International Air Show. A bulldozer has just been deposited from five feet above the grass with the Herc maintaining a steady 120 K.

Larry Milberry

Further Modern Developments

In 1972 Canada terminated its nuclear strike/reconnaissance role in NATO and retasked its CF-104's as tactical strike aircraft with conventional weapons. The Canadian Forces assisted in the training of Venezuelans on the CF-5, several of which Canada had sold to that country; and a formal committee was established to study various possible replacements for the Argus. This was the LRPA (Long Range Patrol Aircraft) Management Group. New squadrons formed were No. 406 at Shearwater with Trackers and Sea Kings and No. 444 with Kiowas at Lahr, West Germany. Historical passings were of the Hiller CH-112, and of the Bomarc missile.

On December 8, the wreckage of a Hurricane and the remains of its pilot were discovered in the woods near Bagotville, a 30-year-old reminder of World War II. Also discovered was an Avenger in Bedford Basin where it had crashed in 1953. It was recovered by the Canadian Forces submersible, the SDL-1, and restored at Shearwater where it is today on view along with a Tracker and Banshee.

Canada's Hercules and 707's operated through 1973 in such areas as Viet Nam, the Middle East, and Africa. A five-year drought in sub-Sahara Africa had left that enormous region at the brink of disaster. An urgent call by the United Nations Food and Agriculture Organization brought aid from many countries. Hercules of 435 and 436 Squadrons were soon at work flying food supplies from Lagos into distribution centres like Dirkou, Arlit, and Agades in Niger. Three Canadian "Hercs" were hauling up to 120 tons of relief supplies

daily. Operations were made challenging by unpredictable dust storms, severe turbulence along the intertropical convergence zone, and temperatures of 120°F with only 2 per cent humidity. Bird strikes were another hazard. Major Bob Beaton's Hercules took 15 strikes on one landing at Agades. On 137 trips through July and August, 1973 the Canadian Forces "Hercs" accounted for some 2750 tons of sorghum, powdered milk, and cattle feed delivered on Operation Foodlift Africa.

Two 707's of 437 Sqdn, equipped with in-flight refuelling drogues, supported the Atlantic crossing of eight CF-5's in June. The aircraft flew from Bagotville to Andoya, Norway, in 5 1/2 hours, the first non-stop trans-Atlantic crossing by the CF-5.

New aircraft ordered in 1973 were eight CH-47 Chinook helicopters, while disposals included 22 CF-104's sold to Norway. There were 32 aircraft lost in accidents including five CF-104's, three CF-101's, one CF-100, two T-33's, three CL-41's, one Tracker, one Twin Huey and one Sea King.

A historic flight during 1974 was made by Argus No. 711. On a combination ASW/SAR flight May 30/June 1 it remained aloft from its Comox base for 31 hours 1 minute. The T-33 was taken out of its training role in 1974. The last T-33 wings parade took place at Cold Lake on June 20. Meanwhile Captain W.M. "Turbo" Tarling had established an individual record for T-33 flying. On March 10 he surpassed 5000 hours on type.

An interesting SAR operation for 1974 was one flown by a 442 Sqdn Buffalo from

Buffalo 115458 of 442 Sqdn Comox, with one of the squadron's Rescue Specialists making a training jump.

DND (PCN 71-105)

Comox. It is briefly outlined in an official dispatch to Air Transport Command HQ, Trenton: "Despite heroic efforts of flight crew and medical staff, a healthy 7 lb 8 oz baby girl was born on Medivac 5458 29 April, 1975 . . . And they were in doubt, saying to one another, What meaneth this?" Some time later Buffalo 5458 appeared sporting a pink stork and the title "We Deliver".

Through this period the Canadian Forces continued its participation in the program begun in 1969 to build and upgrade airstrips in the high Arctic. Two strips were completed at Whale Cove and Pangnirtung in 1974, and work progressed the following year at Eskimo Point, Cape Dorset and Pond Inlet. Each of the strips, of which 26 will eventually be completed, is constructed of packed gravel 4000 feet by 300 feet, capable of Hercules operations. Construction throughout the program has been supported logistically by 424 Sqdn, Trenton. Twice weekly it dispatches a Buffalo for Winnipeg where four tons of freight is loaded for points north. By the time it returns to Trenton it has been five days on the move, weather cooperating, and has logged 40 hours.

An important event occurred September 2, 1975, with the formation of Air Command to coordinate and administer all phases of military aviation in Canada. Air Command HQ was established in Winnipeg and Lt. Gen. William K. Carr was named its first commander. Also at Winnipeg that year, the Air Navigation School bid farewell to the Dakota when it received three Hercules.

Security and transport requirements occupied the Canadian Forces during the '76 Olympics in Montreal. Kiowas, Chinooks, Sea Kings, CF-5's, and Buffalos were some of over 50 aircraft committed to the variety of tasks during this international event. Hercules and 707's responded to the disastrous Guatamala earthquake that year, and CF-5's made the deepest probe ever made into the Canadian Arctic. This exercise had its beginnings in March 1976 when an Argus on a NORPAT (Northern Patrol) discovered a Soviet scientific installation floating inside Canadian territory. This was subsequently identified as Soviet base NP-22. Upwards of 15 aircraft were observed there. These came and went using a 1700 metre ice strip and modern approach aids.

Considering the scale of this operation, National Defence H.Q. and 10 Tactical Air Group met and devised a plan to deploy fighters to NP-22. This culminated on September 21 when three CF-5's took off from Yellowknife, and rendezvoused with a 707 tanker. One CF-5 then returned to base, being a back-up aircraft, while the others flew on to their target. At the time NP-22 was at 84° 50'N, 127° 40'W, or 320 miles SW of the North Pole. The Soviet base was readily located and the CF-5's spent 12 minutes making recce passes before returning to Yellow-knife.

As a result of the LRPA studies, Ottawa finally selected its Argus replacement. This was the Lockheed P3C Orion, delivered to specific Canadian requirements. Eighteen were ordered, but in mid 1976 this deal fell through on account of financial difficulties. A new order was subsequently placed for 18 aircraft designated CP-140 Auroras.

Once delivered, the Auroras will perform a variety of activities including ASW, pollution detection, fisheries patrol, ice reconnaissance, oceanographic research, SAR, and general transport.

In 1977 SAR was again prominent in Canadian Forces activities. In November, the search for a missing Rockwell Commander 112A which disappeared in Northern Ontario involved as many as 20 military aircraft per day and resulted in 1405 hours of flying. The aircraft was not located.

442 Squadron

As usual, SAR was most important on the West Coast, a region of 690 000 square miles covered primarily by 442 Sqdn Comox. The land area is 98 per cent mountainous. Of 6399 SAR incidents in Canada in 1975, 2937 of them occurred there. For the period January-June 1977, 240 SAR missions were flown from Comox by 442 Sqdn's three Buffalos and three Labradors. Others were flown by the 408 Sqdn Twin Huey detachment at Comox. During the period, 155 lives were saved, 31 recorded as lost and 10 people were not located. Buffalos logged 530.2 hours; Labradors 857.8 hours, and Twin Hueys 298.2 hours.

The busiest time of year for 442 Sqdn is during the annual herring fishery that opens in February. The rush for the herring sends hundreds of small vessels into potentially treacherous waters and always results in numerous emergencies. In 1975 16 herring boats were sunk and 14 lives lost.

A typical fisheries patrol flight saw Buffalo 115456 depart Comox mid morning, March 18, 1977. It patrolled the inside passage between Vancouver Island and the mainland, then landed at Port Hardy to deliver equipment for the Labrador detached there. It then flew across Queen Charlotte Sound, passed

NP-22, the Soviet scientific base photographed by Canadian Forces CF-5's September 21, 1976.

DND

Sandspit and across Hecate Strait to Prince Rupert where a lunch stop was made. The flight then returned direct to Comox. While no incidents had been reported, the crew was ready to assist any vessel on the spot. Aboard were two Rescue Specialists, and gear included four 10-man life rafts and two portable pumps of 500-gallon-per-minute capacity. The patrol had been six hours in the air.

SAR activities for July involved 442 Sqdn in many different incidents. On July 1 a Labrador flew a mother with her premature baby from Campbell River to Victoria. July 4 a Buffalo conducted an ELT search and discovered a crashed Jet Ranger near Toba Inlet. Three survivors were lifted to Comox. Two days later a Labrador flew a bomb disposal team and RCMP to Texada Island where an 11-pound practice bomb was recovered and exploded. On July 11 two Buffalos and a Labrador joined a Hercules and T-33 on a search for two single-engine Cessnas overdue on a flight from Dawson Creek to Fort Nelson. Both aircraft were located, crashed close to one another. None of the eight people on board had survived. On July 15 an injured fisherman, taken

onboard HMCS *Gatineau,* was ferried from the *Gatineau* to Victoria by a Labrador. A fallen climber was rescued by a Labrador on July 24 and flown to a waiting ambulance. Next day a Buffalo investigated an ELT signal near Grand Forks, and traced it to Jet Ranger C-FYVV. The ELT had accidentally been activated. The Buffalo advised the helicopter pilot who turned the ELT off. The month closed as it had begun, with another medivac of a premature baby, this time from Alert Bay to Vancouver.

Northern Patrols

Through 1977 Canada continued its weekly NORPATS throughout the Arctic. Each of these performs a number of tasks from sovereignty declaration, to environmental reconnaissance, to serviceability checks of remote airstrips, to population checks of small Native communities. A typical NORPAT began March 21, 1977, at 0700 hours in the briefing room at 407 Sqdn, Comox. At 0815 Argus 10718 was rolled out and an hour later was airborne for Cold Lake, its staging base.

Two patrols were scheduled for the week. The first got under way at 0500 next

The Argus Mk.I 10718 whose NORPAT mission is described here.

Larry Milberry

morning. After the briefing, the crew headed for their aircraft but were soon back in the hangar as '718 would not start. The morning was too cold, requiring ground crew to thaw the engines. This done, the Argus got away on its 12-hour patrol. First objective was a mine where polluting was suspected. It was on Prairie Creek, a tributary of the South Nahanni River in the Northwest Territories. The mine was found to be shut down. Next target was a point on the Upper Bonnet Plume River to spot for caribou, then to its junction with the Peel River where a large caribou herd had recently been reported. Results of both reconnoitres were summed up by a crewman: "No caribou as advertised." The sixth and final target was a bridge being constructed by Canadian Forces engineers across the Eagle River in the Yukon. Three photo passes were made, the last one with the rumbling Argus full out at 230 knots.

All targets covered, '718 turned onto a southeasterly course for Cold Lake. At 190 knots there were several hours of flying to go. This gave time for cooking supper in the galley, and, for those adept enough at the trick, some rest in the noisiest of Canadian Forces aircraft. At 2140 hours, '718 landed back at Cold Lake.

After a day for crew rest, '718 was again on patrol. It started up routinely this time, having spent the night hangared. Patrol two took it northeast with ten targets to cover. These included "recces" (reconnaissance flights) of Bathurst Inlet, the Hope Bay mine along Melville Sound, the tiny Perry Island settlement on King William Island, the DEW Line station at Gladman Point on King William Island,

Gjoa Haven, Spence Bay, and Shepherd Bay. The people at Gladman Point were informed of the impending arrival of '718 and warned to spruce up to have their picture taken! After the Shepherd Bay "recce", '718 headed for Cold Lake where the 2457-mile patrol terminated with a "Welcome back" from the tower. Next day it returned to Comox, having logged 32 hours. The crew debriefed, and '718 went into the hangar for servicing. Film from the week's efforts was processed by Base Photo and flown on to Northern Region H.Q. at Yellowknife for interpretation.

To this point the Argus fleet had flown some 400 000 hours, with the average aircraft being around the 13 000 hour mark. Only one fatal accident had occurred. But on March 31, Argus 10737 of 415 Sqdn crashed at Summerside, P.E.I., while returning from a SAR in aid of a stricken trawler. Heading home, it had had to shut down one engine. While on final it suddenly pulled up, descended, and bounced on the grass. It struggled through the air briefly, then sliced into a Nordair Electra and crashed. The Argus was destroyed and three members of the crew died. With this accident, the Argus fleet was reduced to 25 aircraft.

CFB Cold Lake

The Canadian Forces' largest air base is located in northeastern Alberta near the Saskatchewan border. This is CFB Cold Lake, established in 1954 primarily as a fighter pilot training base. This role continues today. Cold Lake enjoys the benefits of isolation, unlimited room for its aircraft to operate, and good year 'round weather conditions.

Cold Lake trains all Canadian fighter pilots at the basic level and all No. 1 Canadian Air Group pilots at the advanced level. There is a weapons range for training

with bombs, rockets, and cannon; another for high explosives; and the Primrose Lake range. The latter is operated by AETE (Aerospace Engineering and Test Establishment) and is instrumented with tracking radars, theodolite cameras, telemetry equipment, and a data processing centre.

Over 100 aircraft operate from Cold Lake. These belong to 417, 419, and 434 Sqdns, AETE, and Base Flight. No. 417 operates CF-104's and during an 18-22 week, 75-hour course trains pilots in the low-level tactical role. The CF-104, not a good dog fighting aircraft, has proven itself as a tactical fighter as its low level stability makes it an excellent weapons platform, though its ordinance load is small. CF-104's on training missions from Cold Lake fly at 450-540 knots down as low as 100 feet.

No. 417 Sqdn also provides support to NATO as an augmentation force. Because of this its pilots spend two weeks a year with 1 CAG to maintain their familiarity with the European environment. It also supports NATO maritime forces where, on exercises, its CF-104's are used to simulate enemy aircraft and cruise missiles. No. 419 Tactical Fighter Training Squadron's prime role is advanced flying and weapons training for pilots flying the CF-101, CF-104 and CF-5. Pilots begin the course after 200 hours of jet training on Tutors at CFB Moose Jaw. Initially 40 hours of conversion flying are done in low level navigation, day and night formation, visual "recce", basic fighter manoeuvres and air combat manoeuvres. Tactical flying training is gradually phased in as the course progresses. Fifty-two missions are flown before a student graduates.

A fighter weapons instructor's course is also given by 419 Squadron. This is the PhD of fighter courses, offered to above average pilots. Included is adversary

CF-5 "duals" of 419 Sqdn on the flight line at CFB Cold Lake.

Larry Milberry

The Dakota is the longest serving military aircraft in Canada. In the early sixties three were modified as CF-104 navigation trainers and operated from Cold Lake. These were dubbed *Woody Woodpecker*, *Pinocchio*, and *Dolly's Folly*, pictured here in a photo taken in March 1974. The only Dakotas still in regular Canadian Forces service are five based at Winnipeg.

Base Photo, CFB Cold Lake (CKA 137)

A CF-101F Voodoo of 416 Sqdn landing at Trenton. The Voodoo is one of three types to be replaced by the NFA. Designed for NORAD needs of the fifties, it can hit high flying bombers, though its outdated nuclear-tipped Genie missiles might destroy not just target but also interceptor in an actual firing. The Voodoo is ineffective against low-flying enemy bombers and cruise missiles which would be likely weapons in a future war.

Larry Milberry

Though fast at low level and a good weapons platform, the CF-104 is outclassed by the latest in Warsaw Pact fighter aircraft. CF-104 pilots do not have the black boxes which equip modern tactical fighters, and would have to rely on seat-of-the-pants flying skills in reaching and destroying targets in any future European conflict. This CF-104 "dual" is being serviced at Baden-Soellingen, West Germany.

Larry Milberry

training: air-to-air combat flying using Warsaw Pact doctrine and tactics. Several CF-5's at Cold Lake have been painted in different camouflage to simulate schemes on aircraft of potential enemies. Several 419 Sqdn instructors have received aggressor pilot training with the USAF. Since the mid seventies, 419 Sqdn has also been training fighter pilots for Holland which operates a version of the CF-5.

Also based at Cold Lake is 434 Sqdn with its 16 CF-5s. These are tasked for both North American and NATO roles and have operated overseas in such countries as Norway and Denmark.

Because of Cold Lake's favourable training environment pilots from 1 CAG periodically return there for refresher training. This is much preferred to training in Europe where weather and air traffic congestion pose limitations.

AETE operates a variety of aircraft at Cold Lake — CF-104's, CF-5's, T-33's and Hueys included. As the Canadian Forces' basic test and evaluation operation, it is responsible for research projects and the acceptance of all aircraft, from new ones direct from the factory to those re-entering service after maintenance, even if all that has been involved is a new paint job.

AETE's projects have recently involved testing an equipment carrier for the CF-5, launching laser-guided bombs from the CF-5, conducting a vertical stabilizer flight load survey on the CF-5, and investigating vibration on the "recce" nose of the CF-5 during 20 mm cannon firing. Other tests have involved aerial delivery systems using the C-130, long-range fuel tanks on the Tutor, and a search light fitted to a Voyageur. AETE conducts all escape systems work for the Canadian Forces and evaluated contenders for Canada's New Fighter Aircraft. It also has done preliminary work leading to acceptance in 1980 of the first Aurora.

116 Air Transport Unit

For over 20 years Canada has been involved with United Nations peace-keeping activities in the Middle East. Its present contribution includes 116 Air Transport Unit, based at Ismailia in the Sinai. The unit was formed late in 1973 and

its two Buffalos left Trenton for Cairo on January 2, 1974. To mid 1978 it shared its present base with Canadian land elements, the Egyptian army, an Australian helicopter unit, a Malaysian contingent flying a Skyvan, and contingents of Poles and Swedes. Its 47 men and women rotate back to Canada every six months. Of its nine officers, seven are pilots, drawn mainly from Buffalo squadrons at Comox, Trenton and Summerside.

Ismailia has a 4000-foot runway, generally for daytime VFR flying. The tower is operated by the Egyptian Air Force. A large hangar is shared by 116, the Aussie Hueys and Skyvan, though day-to-day maintenance is carried out on the tarmac. Living quarters are tents and barracks, and much of the unit's recreation

The NFA will help bring Canada's air defences up-to-date. One of the types considered in 1978 was the McDonnell Douglas/Northrop F-18L. The F-18L is an outgrowth of the YF-17 developed by Northrop for the USAF's Air Combat Fighter competition of the mid seventies. That competition was won by the F-16. The F-18 has since been adopted by the U.S. Navy as an air superiority fighter. The example shown here is actually one of the YF-17's in pseudo Canadian markings.

Larry Milberry

focuses on its famous centre, The Barn.

A weekly schedule takes the 116 Buffalos to Tel Aviv, Jerusalem, Damascus, Cyprus, Ras Sudr, and Abu Rudeis, the latter two places being south of Ismailia on the Gulf of Suez. A typical

For the latter part of this century, Canada's ASW patrol aircraft will be the Lockheed P-3 Aurora, a version of the P-3 Orion, widely used by the United States and its allies. The Aurora will be equipped to carry out a variety of tasks besides ASW, these including environmental and fisheries patrol. This photo shows a Royal New Zealand Air Force Orion with a Argus of 407 Sqdn, taken at Barbers Point Naval Air Station, Hawaii, during RIMPAC 76, a joint U.S., Canada, Australia, New Zealand ASW exercise.

U.S. Navy Via Dave Breese

day's operation occurred April 20, 1978. It began shortly after sunrise with ground crew readying Buffalo '452. By 0800 the air crew had arrived: Lt. Col. Doug Veale, Aircraft Commander; Capt. Ian Stenberg, First Officer; M/Cpl Gary Dentremont, Flight Engineer; and M/Cpl. Claude Caron, Loadmaster. The aircraft loaded 1033 pounds of baggage and freight, and 278 pounds of mail, then 26 passengers. These were Canadians, Poles, and Finns bound for their postings. At 0835 designated as UN Flight 57, the Buffalo was airborne and headed for Damascus, 357 miles away.

It flew north at 3000 feet holding carefully to the 10-kilometre wide corridor reserved for the UN between Ismailia and Port Said. Cruise speed was 220 knots.

Below lay the desert and the Suez Canal, but also the scars of war: bomb craters, razed towns, abandoned fortifications with their knocked out vehicles, the wreckage of a downed Mirage fighter. Port Said passed off the wing tip, then the great fleet moored offshore awaiting passage southbound through the canal.

Out to sea, the Buffalo climbed to 9000 feet, all the time navigating by its onboard Omega system programmed for this leg with 14 course changes.

Soon Cyprus and the Lebanese coast showed up on radar and the aircraft swung east and climbed to clear the Lebanese coastal highlands. Passing Beirut the scenery changed from Mediterranean green to snowy peaks, parched and rocky slopes, and the verdant Litani valley. As the

aircraft entered Syria near the town of Diemas a fighter strip appeared below. Beside the runway were circular arrangements of surface-to-air missile launch pads. On August 9, 1974, Buffalo '461 under command of Capt. Gary Foster had been brought down by a salvo of three SAM's fired from this very spot. All nine Canadians aboard died in this bizarre and unexplained incident.

UN Flight 57 arrived at Damascus at 1020 hours. Most of the passengers deplaned and 20 others, mostly Poles, boarded for Ismailia. Also on board were 912 pounds of baggage and freight, and 483 pounds of mail. The flight was airborne again at 1125 after the pilots had flight planned and obtained their clearances. Destination was Tel Aviv, 260 miles away. The Ben Gurion International Airport way station was intersected at 1248, and shortly afterwards the Buffalo was shutting down at the terminal. While Canadians were allowed to deplane, the Poles, being persona non grata in Israel, had to wait out the stop over aboard the aircraft. The 397 mile leg back to Ismailia began at 1333 and was covered in one hour and 39 minutes. Arrival was routine and as the 116 technicians took over the aircraft, its crew headed to The Barn for a well-earned beer.

Next day '452 operated Ismailia-Akrotiri (Cyprus)-Jerusalem-Akrotiri-Ismailia. On the homeward leg word was received of sand storm activity at Ismailia. On arrival there, visibility was found to be poor. The first approach was abandoned as the runway disappeared from view while on final; but the second was successful, the aircraft plunking down solidly on the runway under near-maximum cross winds of 40 knots.

More prevalent during winter and spring, sand storms are just one of several unique features in 116's day-to-day operations. During a storm the sand may rise to 15 000 feet and remain suspended in the air for lengthy periods even when the winds subside. Winds of 10-20 knots will produce a haze which, in the Sinai, is very common. This can escalate to IFR conditions within minutes. Sand also

Buffalo '452 of 116 Air Transport Unit being readied at Ismailia, April 20, 1978.

Larry Milberry

A typical scene aboard the 116 ATU Buffalos. Poles, Finns, and Canadians high above the Mediterranean.

Larry Milberry

causes technical problems by causing wear and tear on the Buffalo's T64 turbine engines and adds noticeably to basic aircraft weight.

Other challenges faced by Canadians in the desert are the changing political and military climate throughout the Middle East; temperature extremes ranging from 5°C to 50°C; no frills accommodations; water infested by parasites; and various types of insect pests to be endured. Balancing off these are The Barn, nightly films, a Canadian radio station, the messes, enclosed swimming pools, and R and R to places like Aquaba where the Scuba diving is reportedly outstanding.

Thus do Buffalos manage to survive in the Sinai!

Current Developments

Selecting a New Fighter Aircraft highlighted events in Canadian military aviation in 1978. The need to replace CF-101's, CF-104's, and CF-5's had already been apparent for several years. These aircraft are designs of the fifties and are now obsolete. By mid 1978 the NFA selection process included five types being evaluated: the General Dynamics F-16, Grumman F-14 Tomcat, McDonnell-Douglas F-15 Eagle, McDonnell-Douglas/Northrop F-18, and Panavia Tornado. In November the list had been shortened to the F-16 and F-18.

Various concepts have been evaluated throughout the NFA selection process. Technical ones included whether Canada needed a one- or two-engined fighter; a single- or two-seater; a specialized or multi-role aircraft. As to roles, Canada required an aircraft for NORAD interceptor duties as well as one for tactical strike with the NATO forces. With the November decision it appeared as though the government had opted for the cheaper of the products being offered so as to procure the most aircraft for the money available.

Besides preparing for the NFA, the Canadian Forces continue planning to accept the first Aurora sometime in 1980, and has taken delivery of two DASH 7's (CAF designation CC-132). The latter are for use with Canada's NATO forces and will replace the Cosmopolitan long resident at Lahr, West Germany. While such modern aircraft are being purchased, the CF-100, in service since 1953, has celebrated its 25th anniversary with the RCAF/CAF. It flies with 414 Sqdn, North Bay, in the Electronic Warfare role, though it is now being phased out in favour of EW-modified Falcons.

Rotary Winged Aircraft

Walter Leavens at the controls of the Pitcairn PAA-1. The photo was taken at Barker
field, North Toronto in October 1944. At the
time ASQ was powered by a 125 horse
power Kinner B-5.

Reprinted by permission of the Toronto Sun Ltd.

The Kellett gyroplane at Mt. Hope, Ontario in September 1952. This aircraft was 25 feet long and had a 40 foot rotor diameter. It was powered by a 225 horse power Jacobs L-4. Note the banner stowed beneath the fuselage.

Jack McNulty

Gyroplanes

The first rotary winged aircraft in Canada were two Pitcairn gyroplanes imported from the United States in 1931 and 1932. These stub-winged machines, with their free-wheeling rotors and conventional propellers had exceptional STOL capabilities.

The career of one of the Pitcairns, CF-ARO, was brief; but that of the other, CF-ASQ, lasted two decades. It became a trademark of Leavens Brothers throughout Southern Ontario, and proved its versatility by crop dusting, forest spraying, banner towing, photography, and barnstorming.

In 1950 another autogyro entered Canada. This was a Kellett KD-1A, CF-GTO. At first it operated in the Ottawa-Montreal area; then was purchased by Leavens Brothers. They flew it until October, 1954 when it was destroyed in an accident at Hamilton airport.

During the sixties three other types of gyroplanes appeared in Canada. One was the indigenous Avian, several test versions of which were flown before the company went broke. Another was the Umbaugh, a few of which were imported from the U.S. before they too faded from the scene. The third was the Bensen B8 series gyroplane from the U.S. These have been built in large numbers by Canadian homebuilders, with almost 100 being currently on the Civil Aircraft Register.

The Froebe Brothers Helicopter

The beginnings of the helicopter in Canada are usually associated with the Bell 47, Hiller, and Sikorsky S-51 which began appearing in Canada in the early post World War II years. The story of the helicopter in Canada, however, dates back to the previous decade.

During the thirties, the three Froebe brothers, Nicholas, Theodore, and Douglas, lived on a farm at Homewood, Manitoba. They were an inventive trio, and especially interested in flying. Long prairie winters provided ample time for tinkering and the brothers eventually put together

CF-LKF-X, the prototype Avian 2/180. At the controls is Ron Peterson. Peter Payne is riding as observer. LKF was later destroyed during a high-speed taxi run when it inadvertently became airborne.

Via Canadian Aviation Magazine.

An example of the popular Bensen gyroplane of which about 100 have been built in Canada. *Doc's Rock* awaits taxi clearance at the Toronto Island Airport.

Larry Milberry

their first aircraft, a Heath Parasol built from a kit. After picking up the basics of flying at the Winnipeg Flying Club, Douglas test flew the Heath. The little homebuilt's career was to be brief, however, for it was wrecked on its second flight.

Soon after this episode, the Froebes

Douglas Froebe at the controls of the Froebe Brothers Helicopter in 1938. The fuel tank was later moved aft to improve balance. At a time when efforts to build helicopters anywhere in the world were still in their infancy, this machine was a very credible effort and no less awkward in appearance than other designs.

Douglas Froebe/Manitoba Archives (WCAM 100)

procured a derelict Barling NB-3. They restored it, but it too was wrecked. Meanwhile, the Froebes had been reading whatever aviation material they could, including some magazine articles written by Bill Stout, the designer of the Ford Trimotor. Their research led them to the decision to build their own helicopter. After all, they had the rudimentaries: one designer, one machinist, and one welder.

Before beginning their project, Douglas went on an information gathering trip. He thumbed his way to Detroit where he met briefly with Stout and had a tour of his operation, after which he was given a dollar and sent on his way.

Back in Homewood, the Froebes set to work. They erected a shop, with a flat roof, in anticipation of VTOL rooftop operations. Besides an airframe, the Froebes needed an engine. This sent them on a trip

to California where they located a suitable Gipsy II. They paid $100 for it and toted it home in their house trailer. Through the following months the helicopter took shape. The Froebes continued researching whatever they could about helicopters, and hired professional help where necessary. This included MacDonald Brothers in Winnipeg which supplied chrome molybdenum specially cut and bent for construction on the rotor blades.

Actual flight testing began in November, 1938 and after several attempts the helicopter was urged into the air, and flown horizontally for a short distance. Test pilot on this and subsequent flights was Douglas Froebe who, in 1977, recalled that, "The first time it left the ground I was at the stick. The tail lifted off first. I'd say two or three feet. Then I pulled back and the front wheels left the ground one at a time. My two brothers were very excited, but I was sort of scared. After the flight we immediately realized the machine was somewhat nose heavy, so we moved the gas tank back behind the seat and filled it half way to balance things off."

While the Froebe brothers' helicopter was controllable, at 1400 rpm's a serious torsional problem would develop. This led to the bearings in the rotor hubs giving out, an unresolvable problem which soon forced abandonment of the project. The whole venture had developed unknown to people beyond Homewood. Neither the Department of Transport nor the Canadian military were ever informed of its existence.

The Froebe brothers returned to flying conventional airplanes. Theodore was killed in the crash of a Heath in 1943;

One of Okanagan's S-61N's at work. These versatile helicopters perform a wide range of duties including offshore oil support, commuter passenger service and logging. Here, C-GOKA is seen lifting a Trilander survey aircraft from the ice of Nighthawk Lake near Timmins, Ontario on January 7, 1977. The Trilander had made a precautionary landing on the lake a month earlier. Its recovery resulted in a major salvage operation. It was eventually lifted by OKA to Timmins Airport at a speed of 50 knots, below that at which it could itself start flying. Spruce boughs on the Trilander's wings dampened lift. Pilots on the operation were Vic Scheibler and Don MacKenzie.

Larry Milberry

Nicholas died in a crop dusting accident in 1959. Douglas retained his interest in flying through the years, and in 1974 returned to Homewood from his home in California. This time he was trying out another novel idea, a manual-powered "ornicopter," part ornithopter and part helicopter. He writes that, "The CBC television people came out to Homewood and took pictures of me trying to pedal it. This was shown on the national news with the comment, 'Well, back to the drawing boards.' I'm sorry I didn't have more success with it as I had hopes of coming up with a totally new concept of flight that would be efficient, safe from stalls, and noiseless."

Fortunately the Froebe brothers' helicopter has survived as a noteworthy piece of Canadian history. Both it and Douglas' "ornicopter" are part of the collection of the Western Canada Aviation Museum in Winnipeg.

Canadians in the Royal Navy

Mid way through World War II the Royal Navy procured its first helicopters, these being early Sikorsky R-4's. They were originally intended to perform convoy patrol duties. Among those chosen to train as the Royal Navy's first helicopter pilots was a handful of Canadians, perhaps no more than four men in all. Two of these were Dennis Foley and Eric Marshall. Training was centred at a joint Royal Navy, Royal Air Force/U.S. Coast Guard helicopter school at Floyd Bennett Field, New York. Lt. Commander Dennis Foley

A historic pair of Autair helicopters photographed at remote Mould Bay in the Canadian Arctic. The S-55, flying a surveying party, was forced down with mechanical problems in the spring of 1968. The Bell 204, one of the first in Canada, came to its aid. The S-55 represented a dying breed of helicopters; the Bell the symbol of things to come. This S-55 was later converted to turbine power and served with Nahanni Helicopters. The Bell, CF-AHA, was still active in 1979 with Northern Wings Helicopters.

Hans Pulkkinen

The first helicopter rescue in Canada. On May 19, 1945, a U.S. Coast Guard Sikorsky R-4 was used to rescue the downed crew of this 162 Sqdn Canso. The Canso was located 130 miles SW of Goose Bay and otherwise inaccessible for rescue. The R-4 flew out the crew one at a time. The military censor has blocked out the helicopter's serial which was 43-28234.

Public Archives of Canada (PL24540)

made his first helicopter flight from here on November 28, 1944, in a YR-4. After 6 hours 30 minutes of instruction he soloed, December 2. At month's end he was posted to NAS Norfolk where there were two R-4B's, but only himself as helicopter pilot. For the next few months he flew these on various tasks including communications, deck landing qualifications, search and rescue, experimenting with a bull horn for possible use on invasion beaches, and investigating uses of the helicopter in such roles as mine sweeping and medivacs.

During this period, Foley was involved in a noteworthy search and rescue operation. On a May night in 1945 a Corsair disappeared into the Dismal Swamp. A U.S. Navy blimp was assigned to the search for the pilot, but high winds forced its withdrawal. At first light, Foley set off with an observer, and found the Corsair. Unable to land because of trees, he located a ground party and guided it to the crash site.

For this and other contributions Lt. Commander Foley was awarded the United States Legion of Merit on March 28, 1946. The citation reads in part, "For exceptionally meritorious conduct in the performance of outstanding services to the Government of the United States while serving as British Naval Liaison Officer for Air in the Hampton Roads Area from March 1944, to November 1945.

Demonstrating outstanding tact and a fine spirit of cooperation in solving the many problems incident to the procurement, acceptance and delivery of lend-lease aircraft for Great Britain, Lieutenant Commander Foley maintained close liaison with Commander, Air Force, Atlantic Fleet, to supervise the loading of planes aboard carriers for ferrying to the United Kingdom and also participated in a program for qualifying Royal Navy pilots in landing aboard aircraft carriers. . . ."

Mentioned in his citation are several air-sea rescue operations, including the one for the Corsair.

For the rescue of the Corsair pilot, Foley also received the "Winged S" Air Rescue Emblem from Sikorsky for "having been pilot of a Sikorsky Helicopter during a successful life saving operation on May 11, 1945."

J.C. Charleson

Another Canadian who gained early experience flying helicopters was J.C. (Jack) Charleson of Ottawa. During World War II he was a pilot with the Department of Transport and one evening while attending a gathering in Ottawa found himself discussing the Northwest Staging Route with an American official. The American began praising Canada's great contribution to the war effort by maintaining this vital transportation, communication and ferry route. He also mentioned that he would like to see Canada repaid in some way. Jack half jokingly suggested that America could begin demonstrating its gratitude by making certain he got included on the next U.S. Army helicopter training course.

Not long after this, and to Jack's surprise, he received official notice that he was being called up for Army service and

was to report to Sheppard Field in Texas, to learn how to fly helicopters. So it happened that on July 17, 1945, Jack had his first helicopter ride. The course proceeded and soon the novices were getting the drift of this novel art. Their R-4's were rather marginal performers in the hot Texas climate, resulting in most of the flying being done early in the morning.

Within a few days Jack Charleson was deemed competent enough to fly his first operational "mission." He was aimed in the general direction of Oklahoma and instructed to fly there to pick up a high priority cargo — a case of moonshine. This was a vital operation as the county where the pilots had been training was dry. The trip was dutifully carried out and Jack graduated from the course July 31 with 17 hours 10 minutes logged on R-4's.

Helicopter pilots like Dennis Foley and Jack Charleson were aviation pioneers. To celebrate this, an international association was formed — the Twirly Birds. Original members must have flown helicopters before VJ Day. To this day, the Twirly Birds meet annually, at the Helicopter Association of America convention.

Other Pioneering

The initial flurry of helicopter activity in Canada took place immediately after World War II. At this time Bell Helicopters began operating a training school at Buffalo, New York. This soon attracted several Canadians, the earliest of these being Sten Lundberg, Paul Ostrander, Tommy Noakes, Jimmy Sampson, and Al Soutar. For such fliers the helicopter represented a new frontier, as well as the opportunity of employment in Canada where jobs in aviation were restricted on account of the post-war glut of pilots.

Lundberg was trained as a pilot for his father's mineral exploration company. He graduated as the only Canadian on the first course at Buffalo, and shortly afterwards went to Lapland to fly a Bell 47 on mineral exploration.

Like Lundberg and Ostrander, Soutar had been a World War II fighter pilot. Right after the war he joined the newly formed Photographic Survey Corporation. In 1947 he graduated from the second course at Bell. On March 12, 1947, he ferried the first Canadian-owned Bell from Niagara Falls to Toronto. This was CF-FJA, a Bell 47B-3, Bell's fifth production machine. On March 17, Soutar was issued the first commercial helicopter licence in Canada.

Photographic Survey had paid $27 000 for their Bell. Company president D.N. Kendall envisioned a great future for the helicopter in Canada, especially in the North. CF-FJA was soon at work in Northwestern Ontario, chartered by Ontario's Department of Lands and Forests to evaluate the effectiveness of the helicopter in forest protection.

On its first patrol, with Al Soutar and a forester aboard, a fire was spotted. The forester evaluated the situation and reported by radio to Fort William. A Norseman was dispatched with fire-fighters and equipment. As the nearest open water on which the Norseman could land was 15 miles from the fire, Soutar ferried the men the rest of the way, flying six trips in three hours. The fire was soon quelled, this being the first time the helicopter had been used operationally in fire-fighting in Canada.

Another task performed by CF-FJA in 1947 was crop dusting in Southwestern Ontario. This was undertaken under the name of Airspray Limited, with Al Soutar as pilot.

Paul Ostrander made his first flight at Bell on March 15, 1947. He already had a helicopter flying job, and his $2500 tuition had been paid by Skyways Services of Winnipeg. He passed his Civil Aeronautics Administration flight test April 17, having completed his course with 21.40 hours dual, and 8.20 hours solo. During this time he flew four Bell machines including NC1H, the world's first commercially licenced helicopter. This machine was later acquired by Viking Helicopters of Carleton Place, Ontario and will eventually be restored for historical purposes.

Skyways Services had imported two Bell 47's, CF-FQR, and CF-FQS. These were used on a variety of jobs and flown by Paul Ostrander and Jimmy Sampson. During June, Ostrander was operating CF-FQR on a timber cruising contract in

The world's best-known light helicopter is the Bell 47, first flown in late 1945. It was in continuous production for 31 years. Some 4000 were built. CF-FJA was the first Bell 47 in Canada, having arrived here in May 1947. In this photo taken at Oshawa FJA is being flown by Al Soutar and is rigged for spraying. Its bubble was removable for open air flying. There are still about 240 Bell 47's of all versions flying in Canada.

Claude Fournier

Northwestern Ontario. On June 19, while flying from Red Lake to Fort Francis, cylinder temperature in the Bell's Franklin engine rose well above normal. The pilot set down at Red Lake Station to wire Winnipeg about the problem, but then decided to push on. Shortly after taking off, the temperature again shot up and a precautionary landing was attempted in a lake. Ostrander later reported, "The lake was small and sunken and had a mirror effect. I can distinctly remember my right pontoon hitting the water. The next thing I knew I was upside down in the water. Releasing my seat belt, I came to the surface to find that my passenger was also up." Thus did Canada's first helicopter accident enter the records.

Shortly after this, on July 13, CF-FQS met its end. Jimmy Sampson was busy dusting the farm of Stan Walker when he crashed. Part of his report on the incident reads, "I just started one of these strips and was crabbing the machine at a southwesterly attitude shooting the dust into the edge of the field on my left when the tip of the main rotor struck one of the telephone poles and broke about one foot off the end of the blade. Immediately a violent vibration was set up in the machine and it went out of flying control."

Both these early machines were later salvaged and rebuilt by Spartan Air Services and had brief second careers, before being lost in accidents. CF-FQR crashed in Labrador, August 15, 1955.

In 1949 Ostrander moved to the West

Coast. His first job there was ferrying supplies to a mine site along the Squamish River. On his initial trip in he noticed that the site was very confined, but he landed regardless. Surveying the situation, Ostrander was amazed that he had made it in at all and was doubtful that he could get out. Nonetheless, he did, after ten minutes of careful jockeying on what he calls "my longest flight ever."

Carl Agar and Okanagan Helicopters

The most innovative of Canada's post-war helicopter pioneers was Carl Agar. Carl was born in Bruce County, Ontario, in 1901, but his family moved to Edmonton in 1905. It was here that Carl grew up. Flying was something he took an early interest in. One of the family associates was "Wop" May, and Carl's brother, Egan, lost his life in World War I as a pilot in the RFC. Through the twenties, Carl spent most of his time farming, but in 1928 joined the Edmonton and Northern Alberta Aero Club and took his private pilot's licence.

The economics of the times precluded Carl doing much more flying and he stuck to agriculture through the thirties, but when war broke out in 1939, Carl attempted to enlist in the RCAF. Already 38 years old and with a mere 25 hours flying to his credit, he was at first turned down, but as training requirements increased, he was taken on as an instructor, working at Edmonton, High River, and Abbotsford. Such a success did Carl make of this part of his career that in 1944 he was awarded the Air Force Cross.

In 1945 Carl was discharged from the RCAF. He spent a few months raising poultry, then went into partnership with two other Air Force veterans to form the Southern Okanagan Flying Club at Penticton. This venture did not work out, but Carl and his partners soon formed another operation, Okanagan Air Service at Kelowna. Their charter included aerial spraying.

The exigencies of the mountain environment made great demands on pilots' skills, and there was, inevitably, a high accident rate among spray pilots. When Carl Agar heard that a helicopter was being demonstrated in nearby Washington, it occurred to him that the helicopter might be the solution for spraying in rugged terrain. He travelled to Washington to observe the helicopter in action, and was instantly convinced that this was something with great potential.

Carl convinced his partners that they should purchase a helicopter. As funds

Carl Agar on the right discussing the Omega helicopter with his good friend Bernard Sznycer. For his contributions to Canadian aviation, Carl was awarded the McKee Trophy for 1950.

Katherine Sergava Sznycer Collection

were short, the company went public, raised money through the sale of shares, and in August, 1947, imported a Bell 47, CF-FZX.

CF-FZX was soon at work on agricultural spray contracts in the Okanagan Valley, but it became evident that this specialty was not going to be enough to support the company financially; so Carl began investigating other possibilities. He was able to obtain additional work spraying insecticide over hemlock forests, as well as suppressing mosquitoes.

Another early contract related to topographic surveying. A team of surveyors wanted to be dropped at the 5300-foot level of Wahleach Mountain. This sort of helicopter flying had never been done before. Carl, though, was very familiar with mountain flying from his days at Abbotsford. He thought the trip to the 5300-foot level was feasible. He reconnoitred the ridge with a government surveyor, then returned alone to practice approaches and landing techniques he had developed in theory. Eventually he got down on the ridge. From this point, he put another theory to work to achieve liftoff in the rarified air. This too worked out. It involved use of full power, and effective ground compression in a running takeoff. As horizontal speed picked up, lift increased. Carl then flew over the edge of the ridge and dove into the canyon below with ample speed and lift to have full control. This was the beginning of helicopter mountain flying, an art in which Carl Agar was to become the world's most renowned practitioner.

Okanagan's operations continued to expand. They included timber cruising and mining activities. A flying training school was established at Vancouver. One of the greatest helicopter achievements at the time was the hauling of 400 000 pounds of materials, mostly cement, from the 1200 to the 3500 foot level at Palisade Lake where a reservoir was being constructed for the City of Vancouver. This took place in 1949. The entire lift was conducted using the Bell 47 which could lift a mere 400 pounds of cargo per trip. On a single day, Paul Ostander, flying for Okanagan, made 41 trips up the mountain, each flight being a straight climb. Not to be outdone by Paul, Carl took the first opportunity to make 42 trips in a day! Also at this time, Okanagan became the first company to operate a helicopter on the huge Alcan project at Kitimat in northern British Columbia.

In 1952 Agar formed Okanagan helicopters and introduced the first civilian S-55 to Canada. This was CF-GHV. The aircraft was delivered to Canadian Pratt and Whitney on April 18, 1952, and then turned over for $188,822 to the owner, Morrison Knudsen Ltd. of Vancouver. Carl Agar then ferried the aircraft to Vancouver in 35 hours of flight, averaging 82 mph. It then went to the Kemano River region in northern B.C. where Okanagan operated it on behalf of Morrison Knudsen on the big Alcan aluminum refinery construction project. Within a year of this, Okanagan was operating eight Bells in Vancouver; four on oil exploration at Fort St. John in the Peace River country; and three S-55's on the Alcan project.

In 1956 Okanagan became the first commercial operator in Canada to fly the Sikorsky S-58, when it imported CF-JIB for use on radar line contracts in the North. By 1957 the Okanagan fleet had grown to include 21 S-55's and 31 S-58's, most of these being at work on the DEW Line.

In 1951 Okanagan had purchased the veteran Bell, CF-FJA, from Kenting. Four incidents from the file of this aircraft indicate typical problems faced by helicopter pilots. On October 27, 1951, CF-FJA was rescuing two men stranded during flooding by the Kemano River. The men suddenly grabbed its skids and tried to climb aboard, sending it out of control and causing it to crash. Then, on February 2, 1957, it was busy hauling supplies to the top of Dog Mountain where a microwave station was being set up. While delivering a heavy load, the pilot had set his battery towards the tail to keep his machine in balance. After the load was dropped, he overlooked repositioning the battery. After takeoff, the Bell went out of control and crashed because of the change in the centre of gravity.

Later that year, while operating from Beaverlodge on Lake Athabaska, CF-FJA had an engine failure caused by carburetor icing, and dropped heavily on top of a Volkswagen! Another incident occurred the following April 6 when CF-FJA was badly damaged during an autorotation on Lulu Island, Vancouver. By the time it was sold in the United States late in 1963, it is probable that CF-FJA had no original part left in its battered old airframe!

Through the fifties and sixties, Okanagan Helicopters grew continually. Various competitors such as Canadian Helicopters were absorbed. Today, with a

One of Kenting's Hiller 360's on topographic survey work in the Yukon during the early fifties. Evolved from the original design by Stanley Hiller in 1944, this type has been used widely in Canada for over 30 years. About two dozen are currently active here.

C.H. Parkin

fleet of some 160 helicopters, Okanagan is one of the world's major helicopter concerns, a great honour to its founder and driving force, Carl Agar. Carl was to receive many honours as a helicopter innovator. One of these came from Igor Sikorsky: "A flying craft remains useless unless there also exist other pioneers with courage, foresight, and energy, who can visualize the usefulness of a flying machine and fulfill the final stage of development of the craft by putting it to work to prove its value and thus assign to it its rightful place in our modern life. Carl Agar, to my mind, is one of the most brilliant and outstanding pioneers of this type." Carl Agar died in January, 1968.

Helicopters Go North

In the post-war forties the Department of Mines and Resources undertook to survey and map all of Canada to the scale of 1:50 000 feet for developed areas; and 1:250 000 feet for inaccessible regions. The Surveys and Mapping Branch of the Department was to carry out all field surveys, and plotting, compiling and printing of maps. As well, it recruited and organized all engineering and technical staff; acquired or developed necessary instruments and techniques; and organized transportation.

Before this, surveying and mapping had been generally confined to southern and otherwise settled parts of the country. Only a small number of people had been involved, and there had been little attempt to develop a systematic program. Remoteness had always been a problem for surveyors, but with the appearance of the helicopter after the war, some foresaw a solution to transportation difficulties. One of these was A.C. Tuttle, former Chief Topographical Engineer, who noted that, "For those field officers who had worked with canoes, pack horses, and back packs, the helicopter appeared to hold immense possibilities."

In 1948 Tuttle, H.N. Spence, and K.G. Chipman of the Surveys and Mapping Branch organized the first use of the helicopter in Canada for survey purposes. First contracts were in the Yukon and demonstrated the viability of helicopters in transporting field workers, supplying campsites, etc. "The use of airborne parties," writes Tuttle, "was expanded in 1950 with Howard Spence again in charge of a large party in Northern Quebec, using two Bell helicopters from Spartan Air Services . . . while I took a similar party into the northern Yukon, with two Hiller helicopters from Kenting Aviation and a fixed wing aircraft for logistical support. Gordon Townsend was Chief Pilot for the Quebec operation, and Al Soutar was Chief Pilot for the Yukon party. In the

Yukon we found it necessary in some places to drop helicopter fuel by parachute because of the scarcity of lakes suitable for landing the support aircraft." Typical of these helicopter operations was one flown June 16-September 30, 1952, in the Yukon. The contractor was the newly formed Canadian Helicopters, with Paul Ostrander flying CF-FCO. Throughout this period the surveyors covered 52 000 square miles. The Bell experienced one engine failure on the job, and was unserviceable for only five days. When the contract was up, Ostrander noted in his log, "We're in business, I think."

Once surveying and mapping of the mainland had been completed, surveying began on the Eastern Arctic Islands. This time larger Sikorsky machines were used relying on fuel cached the previous winter. In the Western Arctic islands surveying was conducted by the Army Survey Establishment, R.C.E. with helicopters provided by such firms as Okanagan and Associated. The degree of helicopter utilization on survey work in Canada is indicated by figures from 1954 when two machines on contract logged 962 hours.

Another early survey employing the helicopter took place in Labrador in 1948. On this contract Kenting provided a Hiller piloted by Al Soutar. From July 24 to July 26 it was ferried from Oshawa to Goose Bay via Cartierville, Mt. Joli and Seven Islands, shepherded along by Kenting's Walrus crewed by Charlie Parkin and Claude Fournier.

Bernard W. Sznycer and the Grey Gull

While so much was happening with helicopters in Canada after the war, one of the great Canadian aviation ''firsts'' was quietly unfolding in Montreal. In the fall of 1945 Bernard W. Sznycer had come to Montreal from New York with his idea of designing and building a helicopter.

Sznycer had been born in Poland in 1904. After seeing his first air show at the age of seven, he determined to spend his life in aviation. As a young man he attended the Technological Institute of Warsaw, graduating in Mechanical and Aeronautical Engineering. He worked for Poland's national airline, LOT; then set up his own business as a consulting engineer. Here his genius shone as he invented, experimented with, and marketed numerous aeronautical products.

Sznycer's special knowledge of aircraft skis brought him to America in May 1938 to collaborate with Admiral Byrd prior to Byrd's second South Pole Expedition. Conditions in Europe precluded his returning there. When war broke out Sznycer took research and design posts that involved him in such projects as America's first air-to-ground missile, an assault glider, and an early helicopter.

Late in the war he was at work with Selma Gottlieb and Douglas Watson on theoretical research into helicopter vibration and control problems. The opportunity of applying some of the results of this research came when Sznycer made an agreement with a Montreal group operating as Intercity Airlines. This group was headed by J. Ernest Savard and was interested in the investment possibilities of

The SG-VI-C in flight at Dorval during 1947.
Katherine Sergava Sznycer Collection

Sznycer's concept. Miss Gottlieb, a mathematician, aided Sznycer in this project.

Sznycer was granted limited funds, forcing him to use all the ingenuity at his disposal. Nevertheless, he had designed and built a prototype by late 1946. This was the SG-VI-C, a small machine incorporating many innovations. These included unit construction to reduce manufacturing costs and simplify maintenance; a horizontally mounted engine, again to facilitate maintenance; a rugged airframe; a four-bladed rotor (the first ever); and a cockpit interior designed to minimize injury in case of a crash.

The new machine was the result of subcontracts let to 42 Canadian firms. Only the engine and tail rotor blades had been imported. The many components had been assembled at the plant of Engineering Products in Montreal. To Sznycer this was a realistic approach to manufacturing, and he claimed that it would reduce final assembly of one of his machines to 16 man hours!

The SG-VI-C was officially rolled out at Dorval on October 15, 1946. It was soon involved in pre-flight testing and found early on to be amazingly vibration free. Tethered flights followed with the machine tested for control and stability at heights not exceeding three feet. These developments were closely followed by the press. *Le Petit Journal* headlined a story February 16, 1947: ''Un nouveau chapitre de l'aviation canadienne s'ouvrira-t-il à Dorval?'' Any doubt there may have been concerning this was soon put to rest as Bernard Sznycer's flourish on a test report form shows: ''Really OK. She flies! History is made at night. Today, July 9th, 1947 the SG-VI flew for five minutes at

about 6-8 feet.'' Pilot on this first breakaway flight was Henry J. Eagle Jr.

A few days later the SG-VI was flown officially at Dorval. It was already apparent that this was a fine aircraft. Eagle reported on its positive and instantaneous control characteristics, and its freedom from vibration and stick shake.

Once the initial test program was completed and data from it was analyzed, the SG-VI was dismantled and Sznycer and Gottlieb set to work on their first production machine. This became the SG-VI-D, the Grey Gull. This aircraft was rolled out and flown for the first time on February 6, 1948. Two weeks later it was demonstrated to hundreds of guests, at which time Mr. Savard was quoted in the press as being eager to begin production.

The next thing Sznycer knew, however, his funds had been cut. His backers sensed a waning in the helicopter market; it wasn't until October, 1949 that the project was reactivated. Even so, Sznycer and his small organization soon had testing again under way. They were preparing for the Grey Gull's ultimate test — Type Certification by the Department of Transport.

In late January, 1951 the DOT's representative, J.C. Charleson, arrived at Dorval to supervise certification trials. He presented Sznycer with a set of rigorous criteria. These were based on existing U.S. ones but tightened up to suit Canadian conditions:

1) Five consecutive days of flying, regardless of weather, with no maintenance other than visual inspection and greasing.
2) Soloing the government inspector.
3) Three power-off landings at full gross weight (2400 pounds), from altitudes under ten feet, with the government inspector

The SG-VI in its refined version, the Grey Gull, hovers along the hangar line at Dorval. The Grey Gull symbol and Intercity Airlines crest are evident in this fine view.

riding as observer, and cutting the mag switch at will.

4) Six consecutive autorotative landings, two of them at full gross weight, from altitudes of 500 to 800 feet, with the government inspector riding as observer at his discretion.

Testing began January 29 with the weather at its mid-winter grimmest — snow, high winds, with temperatures as low as -26°F. In spite of this, Sznycer and company succeeded. Pilot Jack Godsy flew in such adverse weather that at times the Grey Gull was lost to sight. Jack Charleson soloed after four short familiarization flights, and reported on the event: "Temperature — 10 degrees below zero. Altitude — instrument covered with snow. Wind — terrible. Aircraft — normal in all respects." The Grey Gull passed with flying colours. It was February 21, 1951.

The Certificate of Airworthiness was granted March 15 with the comment from H.S. Rees, Chief Aeronautical Engineer for the DOT, "We are satisfied that the S.G. Mark VI-D meets all airworthiness requirements as a land helicopter at 2400 pounds gross weight." Thus did the Grey Gull become the first helicopter designed, built, and certified in the British Commonwealth.

To Bernard Sznycer, Canada, with its great variety of terrain and climate, was the ideal environment for the helicopter, and, as such, an ideal country in which to establish a helicopter industry. Of his beliefs and aspirations he wrote:

"During the period of building and testing of the SG-VI in Montreal, we had an opportunity to observe some of the Canadian shops, to talk to Canadian operators, pilots, and mechanics, and to learn a bit about the problems connected with operating in temperatures ranging from 95 degrees above to 30 degrees below zero. By working on this project with some 50 or so suppliers and subcontractors, we

also had the chance to learn about the sources and availability of such parts as bearings, gears, seals, and such other necessary components.

"These experiences, together with the evaluation of flight test data, led us to the conclusion which, intuitively, we had known since the beginning, that environmental conditions in Canada are of such importance that only an original design, a design which takes into account most of these factors, can, in the long run, be successful in this country . . .

"We are convinced that the Canadian helicopter will evolve in a specifically Canadian manner, very much as the Norseman and the Beaver fulfilled the particular demands for a bush airplane. We are sure that the helicopter evolved for the very rough Canadian bush conditions will find useful applications in many foreign countries, and will become an important article of export."

This philosophy had been carefully developed by one of the most dedicated aeronautical minds in Canada. And not

Certification day for the Grey Gull. Left to right are test pilot Jack Godsy, DOT Inspector Jack Charleson, Selma Gottlieb, DOT Project Engineer Michael Jelenick, and Bernard Sznycer. Standing behind are mechanics Roger Duquette and Kenneth Cook.

Katherine Sergava Sznycer Collection

only did Sznycer have a philosophy, but he also had a certified helicopter. Even so, his Grey Gull was never to reach production. Competition from Bell, Hiller, and Sikorsky was rigorous. They were producing hundreds of machines a year, while Sznycer as yet had no production capability. Coupled with this, there was a recession. As a result, Sznycer's financial backers, never overly generous, finally withdrew their support. In 1954 they sold their interests in the SG-VI to a firm in New York. By this time Sznycer had returned to the United States, where he continued his aeronautical pursuits.

Bernard Sznycer's second design was the Omega BS-12D, the world's first twin-engined civilian helicopter and the original flying crane. The Omega made its first flight on October 29, 1956, at New Bedford, Massachusetts. As with the Grey Gull, Sznycer had to operate on a restricted budget. On this he designed and built his prototype, two pre-production machines, and carried the project through to certification with the flying skill of his old friend and test pilot, Slim Soule. FAA Type Certification was awarded May 2, 1961. At this time Sznycer was praised by the FAA for his accomplishment and was described by the FAA's Jim Plackis, who had supervised certification, as "the best in the business."

Unfortunately the Omega was not to enjoy success. Soon after being certified, unforeseen factors emerged to cut its career short. One machine crashed; there were administrative problems concerning the supply of Franklin engines; and the financial backers, at odds with one another over the management of the project, suddenly pulled their money out.

When the Omega failed to reach production, Sznycer retired from aeronautics, and devoted himself full time to his great love, the Arts. He painted, sculpted, devised a new technique for translating Chekhov, and at the time of his death on November 30, 1970, was writing his third play. Many of Bernard Sznycer's documents and aviation artifacts are today available in the Public Archives of Canada, the National Museum of Science and Technology, and the Massachusetts Institute of Technology. One of his many inventions lives on in the form of Sikorsky's giant S-64 Skycrane. This, of course, is Sznycer's flying crane patent, U.S. Patent No. 2973923.

Al Soutar's certificate of merit signed by Bernard Sznycer and Selma Gottlieb. Al and Jack Charleson were the only Canadians to fly the Grey Gull.

A.F. Soutar

Helicopters Come to the Department of Transport

In 1949 Jack Charleson met Alex Watson, head of Marine operations with the Department of Transport. They discussed icebreakers and the problems and expenses in their operation. Mr. Watson pointed out how so much time was lost bashing through ice on routine operations putting people ashore, searching for open water, and so on. Jack told his colleague that he thought he could help with these problems. His solution lay with the helicopter, actually based aboard ship.

Just at this time the *C.D. Howe,* a new government ice breaker, was nearing completion at the Lauzon shipyards. The decision was made to use it in evaluating Charleson's idea and a fantail landing deck was fitted astern. Soon afterwards, the

of the ship so that courses could be readily determined.

Then, just as the program seemed to be moving nicely forward, trouble developed. On August 5, 1950, Parkin was about to fly to shore with two passengers. Just at liftoff, the S-51 went out of control and tipped overboard into the water. The pilot and one passenger escaped quickly, but although the helicopter remained afloat for a long time, the other passenger disappeared into the 29°F waters of the Koksoak River. As the wreck was being towed upstream towards the *C.D. Howe* the tow boat's motor overheated and the helicopter had to be cut loose.

An investigation was soon launched to determine what had happened to CF-DOY. The investigation was about to be closed due to lack of evidence when some local

representatives to talk over native problems. The flight was 45 miles, much shorter than the route the ship would have had to follow. Later on, when the ice breaker was stopped in heavy pack ice, a quick reconnaissance by helicopter determined soft spots and the ship was soon under way again.

On September 26, the *C.D. Howe* berthed at Quebec, her voyage complete. The Bell had flown 94 trips and clearly proven the value of ship-based helicopters in Arctic operations.

In 1952 the ice breaker *d'Iberville* was launched complete with its own hangar and an improved landing pad. The hangar accommodated two Bells with only the tail booms protruding. This was a vast improvement over facilities aboard the *C.D. Howe* where the only protection for

The ill-fated S-51, CF-DOY. At the left is pilot Charlie Parkin with his engineer Ken Wallingford.

Via J.C. Charleson

DOT ordered its first helicopter CF-DOY, an S-51. On June 2, 1950, Charleson ferried it from the Sikorsky plant at Bridgeport, Connecticut, to Montreal.

At this point Charleson's superiors decided that he had gone far enough with his manoeuvring between the department's aviation and marine branches, and would not allow him to sail north with the *C.D. Howe.* Instead, C.A. (Charlie) Parkin was hired as pilot. The year before, as Al Soutar's student he had become the first Canadian-trained helicopter pilot.

Once in Arctic waters, the S-51 began to show its worth. It could quickly shuttle men and supplies to or from ship; and conduct vital ice reconnaissance well ahead

Inuit came up with the wreck, and, as it turned out, with the secret to the cause of the accident. Examination showed that one of the helicopter's six tie-downs had been left secured. This situation led to loss of control at lift off. A minor scandal then emerged as it was shown that evidence of just such a cause had been suppressed by members of the ship's crew at the time of the crash.

So ended the career of CF-DOY. The future of helicopters in the DOT might have been in jeopardy now had not the short-lived S-51 already proven its worth. The following year the DOT purchased a Bell 47D-1, a smaller, more practical machine. On June 27 that year the *C.D. Howe* sailed from Montreal for further helicopter trials.

The new Bell performed well throughout the voyage. At Makkovik it flew in

Jack Charleson seated on the float of a Department of Transport Bell 47. Jack was the first Canadian civilian qualified on helicopters. He brought the first helicopter to the DOT, and later was closely associated with Carl Agar and Okanagan Helicopters.

Via J.C. Charleson

the Bell was layers of wax to ward off corrosive emissions from the stack, and slip-on covers to provide cocooning. The *d'Iberville's* shakedown cruise took her to England for the Coronation Naval Review, where, with her helicopter facilities, she was a major attraction.

Today the helicopter is an integral part of Coast Guard operations in Canada, with aircraft as large as the S-61 in service on Canada's three sea coasts and along the Great Lakes-St. Lawrence Seaway.

Commercial Growth

From the early beginnings with companies like Photographic Survey, Kenting, Skyways, and Okanagan, commercial helicopter operations began expanding. In 1952 Canadian Helicopters was formed. Its first helicopter, a Bell 47, CF-FCO was purchased in Rhode Island and trucked to Edmonton. From there Paul Ostrander flew it north on a survey contract. Another firm operating at this time was Ambank with Jack Godsy as chief pilot. In 1954 its S-55, CF-HHU, made the first known helicopter lift of another aircraft in Canada when it rescued a downed Aeronca from Onion Lake in Northwestern Ontario. In 1956 Okanagan took over Canadian Helicopters. At this point several Canadian Helicopters' personnel broke off and formed Dominion Helicopters opera-

light helicopters and the S-55 the popular heavy type. There were other contenders, however. In the light helicopter field, a Canadian, H.B. Picken, designed and built the Helicon. This was registered CF-GEM-X, but technical problems kept it on the ground.

Two interesting designs were imported into Canada during this period. One was the Bristol 171 Sycamore, a four/five seat machine. It arrived by ship at Montreal in June 1955, was flown to Toronto, then to Winnipeg where sling-load tests were done. The Bristol was promoted by MacDonald Brothers of Winnipeg which engaged Charlie Parkin to fly it on an extensive sales tour across Canada and as far south as Mexico City. In spite of this, none were sold in North America, and in mid 1957 the aircraft was returned to Britain.

military service over thirty years, but the rotary-wing concept goes back even farther. Probably the first official Canadian military reference to rotary-wing aircraft was made January 23, 1943. This is a Royal Canadian Navy memorandum dealing with the U-boat menace:

"We are building frigates in Canada and in one year's time should have nearly 34 of them in commission . . . Could not some of these be built as baby aircraft carriers? A flat deck could give them a landing area of perhaps 45 x 300 feet, which would not be enough for an ordinary plane; but this could accommodate gyro planes. Is it not possible that gyro planes because of their slow speed, would have advantages over the submarine that are lacking to the ordinary 'plane? . . .''

Although such a scheme was not

A Sikorsky S-61N of the Canadian Coast Guard. From simple beginnings, the helicopter has become vital to civil government aviation in Canada.
United Aircraft Corp., Stratford, Conn. (S-45569-B)

The Doman-Fleet LZ-5 helicopter, CF-IBG-X hovering at Toronto Island Airport.
Canadian Aviation Magazine

ting with the Leavens Brothers gyroplane charter, Canada's oldest rotary wing charter. Other helicopter operators through this period included Helicopter Explorations of Vancouver, Associated Helicopters of Edmonton and Spartan Air Services of Ottawa. In 1956 Paul Ostrander left Dominion and formed his own company, Western Helicopters, later to become Niagara Helicopters.

Other Early Ventures

By the mid fifties the helicopter scene in Canada was dominated by three major types. Bells and Hillers were the common

In 1954 Fleet Manufacturing Ltd. of Fort Erie was attempting to get back into aircraft manufacturing. It began assembling a few Helio Courier STOL aircraft, but also entered into partnership with Doman Helicopters of Danbury, Connecticut, with hopes of marketing and manufacturing the Doman LZ-5 helicopter.

Fleet considered the LZ-5 had good potential for civil and military operators, but like so many other efforts in Canada's aircraft industry, the LZ-5 did not develop beyond the initial stages. The sole aircraft, CF-IBG, returned to the United States, its registration being cancelled in June 1959. It next turned up in Italy as an abortive project with Aeronautica Sicula.

Helicoptors in the Canadian Military

The helicopter has been in Canadian

adopted by Canada during the war, the memo suggests advanced thinking and was a prophecy of things to come.

By the late forties the helicopter had reached a state of sophistication which made it a practical means of air transport. The RCAF recognized its potential and in 1947 sent W/C Pat Clark to Sikorsky to train on the S-51. Clark returned to Trenton where he checked out S/L R.T. (Bob) Heaslip. In a sense S/L Heaslip was an old rotary-wing hand. As a boy he had enjoyed a flip in the Leavens Brothers Pitcairn, much to his mother's dismay!

S/L Heaslip soloed in the S-51 on July 21, 1947, after 5:45 hours of instruction. Soon after he began work developing the

RCAF's first helicopter instruction program. He transferred to Rivers, Manitoba, and set up the Light Aircraft School, Helicopter Conversion Flight.

The S-51 was the first helicopter used at Rivers, but as it was not an ideal training machine due to its heavy controls, was soon supplemented by two Bell 47D's. Students began with 20 hours on the Bells before progressing to the S-51.

On September 13, 1948, a U.S. Navy Beechcraft with five aboard disappeared while en route from Churchill to The Pas. One passenger was the U.S. Navy's Attaché from Ottawa. A large-scale search and rescue operation was immediately set in motion — Operation Attaché. Thirty Canadian and U.S. aircraft were involved, including an S-51 piloted by S/L Heaslip. Flying from The Pas, his task was to check out leads from trappers and other northerners, many of whom claimed to have made sightings of the lost plane.

Although the S-51 spent many hours aloft, none of the leads proved out. Eventually a Lancaster located the downed party 250 miles northwest of The Pas. On September 25 the five men were flown by Canso to The Pas.

In 1950 S/L Heaslip was again called out on rescue operations. That year the Red River flooded and inundated much of Winnipeg and surroundings. This time the S-51 was used on such tasks as flying engineers out to inspect dikes, transporting reporters and photographers, and making the occasional rescue. On one flight, S/L Heaslip was amazed to see a new Ford sedan neatly suspended by ropes high in a tree, safely above the flooded barnyard below!

Another rescue operation involving the S-51 took place in 1955. A chimney inspector had become stranded atop a 156-foot high chimney after a ladder had given way. After six hours on his perch the inspector was rescued by F/O J.C. Smith in an S-51 from 103 Rescue Unit, Greenwood.

Naval Helicopters

The Royal Canadian Navy trained its first helicopter pilots in 1950. The first of these was Lt. George H. Marlow. He made his first helicopter flight from Rivers on February 6 in the Bell 47D, No. 9609. He soloed on February 14 after 7:10 hours and graduated April 3 with 23:15 hours. All his instruction had been provided by S/L Heaslip.

Soon after this Lt. Marlow and Lt. J.D. Lowe were sent on course to the U.S. Navy Helicopter Training Unit at Pensacola. The course there ended April 30 and both men were assigned to Helicopter Utility Squadron 2, U.S. Navy, Lakehurst,

An H04S hovering over HMCS *Magnificent* as Avengers warm up in the background.
DND

New Jersey. In July, 1951 Lt. Marlow accepted and test flew the RCN's first helicopters, three Bell HTL 4's, at Buffalo. These were delivered to Shearwater the following month and became No. 1 Helicopter Flight, RCN. Its initial pilots were Lt. J.D. Lowe, C.O.; Lt. G.H. Marlow; and Lt. Commander D.L. Foley, Air Engineer Officer. Of these, Foley was a real veteran, having flown helicopters with the U.S. Coast Guard while in the RNVR beginning in 1944. During this period he became the second ever helicopter pilot to land aboard an aircraft carrier. He had finished the war with 175 hours on helicopters, then continued to fly with the U.S. Navy.

The following spring two more pilots joined the squadron, these being Bill Frayn and John Runseman, and in April its first Sikorsky HO4S-2 was acquired. Marlow and Lowe made the first landing of this type aboard HMCS *Magnificent* on May 6, 1952. In August they ferried the Sikorsky to Toronto to demonstrate it at the Canadian National Exhibition.

In November the squadron was re-designated VH 21. On November 5 its Sikorsky was on its first plane guard duty from the *Magnificent,* a duty hitherto performed by warships. These stood by during aircraft launch and recovery, ready to assist in case of a crash or ditching. This day was not an auspicious one for VH 21 as its Sikorsky was involved in a crash on the carrier's deck. Just before year's end, VH 21 received two more Sikorskies.

On September 21, 1953, a Sea Fury of VF 871 had an engine failure while approaching to land on the *Magnificent*.

The plane ditched in the North Atlantic, but within 32 seconds its pilot had been picked up by a Sikorsky on plane guard. This was the first such rescue in RCN history.

In 1954 the RCN acquired its third helicopter type, the Piasecki HUP-3, purchased especially for use aboard HMCS *Labrador* in the Arctic. The first HUP-3 was accepted at the factory by pilots Marlow and Webster on May 4.

In March, 1955 VH 21 was called on to carry out another rescue. Sub Lieutenant J.V. Searle had been landing his Sea Fury at *Shearwater* when it torque-stalled, crashed into bush, and caught fire. Within minutes an HTL was on the scene, piloted by Lt. Commander Roger Fink. Co-pilot Sub Lieutenant Douglas A. Muncaster jumped from the chopper to help Searle from his blazing fighter. Later, Muncaster was quoted in the local press:

"There was a small hole in the canopy so I tried to kick and beat it with my fists to make the hole larger. After I cut my wrists in the process I realized there must be a quicker method.

"I looked around for something to use as a club and spotted a big rock. With the rock I smashed the canopy until I had enlarged the hole a bit, but I still didn't think a man could crawl through it.

"Searle had other ideas. He slipped out of his parachute harness and began to squeeze his way through. He pushed and I pulled but after he got his head and shoulders through he got jammed.

"After some rather vicious pulls he finally got through the hole and we both ran like the devil in case another fuel tank should explode." For his efforts in saving Searle, Muncaster was awarded the George Medal.

RCN helicopters were to take part in

many search and rescue operations over the years. They provided standby SAR during Operation Budworm in New Brunswick; assisted on forest fire operations, and at the Springhill mine disaster in 1956; and rescued people in distress from ships and isolated lighthouses. A single H04S, the *Shearwater Angel,* had rescued 32 people by the time it was retired. It is today preserved in the National Aeronautical Collection.

In April, 1955 VH 21 became HU 21. The following July 4 the RCN formed its second helicopter squadron, HS 50, an anti-submarine unit. Its first aircraft, an H04S-3, was accepted July 6. The squadron's six aircraft were especially fitted with SONAR to search out submarines. This equipment was dunked

the Mid Canada Line, 2600 miles in length from Hopedale, Labrador, to Dawson Creek in British Columbia, generally along the 55th parallel. As most of the proposed sites were isolated, the helicopter became vital to completion of the project.

As there was no civil operator in Canada at this time with enough heavy-lift helicopters to handle the task, the RCAF formed 108 Communications Flight, S/L Heaslip commanding. The unit was formed at Rockcliffe, June 1, 1954. While Air Force crews were being trained by Okanagan, S/L Heaslip was for a time its only pilot. One of his many duties was ferrying new helicopters from Sikorsky at Bridgeport, Conn. and Piasecki at Morton, Pa. It was November before the first RCAF helicopter pilots arrived at

like Moosonee, Winisk, and The Pas. In spite of the many problems that had to be faced, operations progressed smoothly. The greatest problem was the cold. This persisted for over half the year, with temperatures of 50°F below zero being common. At these temperatures it was difficult starting engines and very tough on crewmen handling sling loads. In the cold and with rotor blades creating a 100 mph downwash theirs was not an enviable lot. Under such circumstances they worked in pairs, one crewman handling the load, with the other keeping an eye on his buddy for signs of frostbite! This was just one of the many occupational hazards. One time a crewman grasped a crate's rope in his teeth. Unfortunately, the pilot released the crate too early and the crate left the plane taking

This Vertol HUP-3 prepares to sling a load to shore from HMCS *Labrador* during Exercise Shotgun at Cape Fisher, N.W.T., July 8, 1955.

Public Archives of Canada (LAB.958)

into the sea via cable while the helicopter hovered or flew along slowly. If necessary, the helicopter could launch torpedoes against the enemy.

The Mid Canada Line

In the mid fifties construction began on a series of defensive radar lines stretching east-west across Canada. One of these was

Winner of the 1956 McKee Trophy, S/L Bob Heaslip chats with Igor Sikorsky at the Sikorsky plant where he was taking delivery of an S-55 for use on the Mid Canada Line.

Via R.T. Heaslip

the crewman's front teeth with it!

Aircraft maintenance and repair was another challenging aspect of the Mid Canada operation. On one occasion an S-55 made a forced landing out of Knob Lake. Repairs called for an engine change, in the middle of nowhere. A spare engine was flown in by Canso to the nearest accessible point, then rafted several miles to the disabled chopper. Three days later the S-55 was back in service.

Many items of cargo slung by No. 108 were oversized, such as the big crates containing radar antennae. Sometimes these had to be slung for up to 60 miles. En route the crates would swing erratically, often forcing pilots to set down in order to

Rockcliffe to join No.108.

Operations soon moved from Rockcliffe to Bagotville where intensive training got under way on the S-55 and H-21. For ten months, crews perfected the techniques of lifting heavy and awkward sling loads and generally learned to master the helicopter in a rugged, sub-Arctic environment with few navigation aids available.

On May 3, 1955, No. 108 repositioned to Knob Lake. On June 2 the first S-55's began flying to sites, initially to Knob Lake and Great Whale, then westward to others

A 108 Communications Flight S-55 at a remote Mid Canada Line site. A tattered flag was frequently the only landing aid for pilots servicing sites like this one!

Via R.T. Heaslip

stabilize them. It was not unusual to spend three hours covering the 60 miles with such a load.

While No.108 flew most of the operations on the Mid Canada Line, at one time HO4S's of the RCN provided some back-up, hauling over 850 tons. Another time a squadron of U.S. Army H-21's operated with No.108 from The Pas.

Eventually No.108 had 25 S-55's, H-21's, and H-34's working the Mid Canada Line. Only one aircraft was lost during the whole operation, that being an H-21 which crashed on a training flight. Much of the credit for this record goes to rigorous training, excellent maintenance, and the fact that many of the pilots were "retreads" — seasoned World War II veterans reactivated for the job.

Statistics indicate the scale of the Mid Canada airlift. For 1956 No.108 logged 10 000 hours and moved 9000 tons of cargo and 14 000 passengers. It flew its last missions in August 1957. After 21 000

hours of flying it was redesignated as a training unit, and its helicopters turned over to civilian contractors — initially Okanagan in the west, and Spartan in the east. These assumed the task of transportation for the resupply and maintenance of manned and remote stations along the Line. For his contributions to the success of the Mid Canada operation, S/L Heaslip was awarded the McKee Trophy for 1956.

Search and Rescue

Helicopters have served many roles in the RCAF, RCN, Canadian Army and, today, the Canadian Forces. These have ranged from training, to reconnaissance, AOP (Air Observation Post), anti-submarine warfare, logistical and tactical support; and search and rescue. Search and rescue (SAR) was one of the earliest roles of the military helicopter in Canada; and over the past three decades S-51's, S-55's, H-34's, and H-21's, and more contemporary Labradors, Voyageurs, Sea Kings, Hueys, and Twin Hueys have saved the lives of hundreds of people, plucking them from mountain tops, sinking ships, crash sites, and other perilous situations.

One incident occurred November 26, 1955, when an HO4S of HU 21,

Shearwater, rescued all 21 crew from the *Kismet II* aground at the base of a cliff along Cape Breton Island. The rescue was effected by making four hazardous landings on the vessel's stern. On another occasion an H-21 of No.121 CU, Comox, was called out to aid the stricken Greek freighter *Glafkos* which had run aground off Vancouver Island New Year's Day, 1962. For two days the ship was pounded by heavy seas, then it was decided to take the crew off. On January 3, H-21 No. 9611 arrived on the scene crewed by F/L Dan Campbell, F/L John Thompson, Cpl. Victor Hodge and LAC K.O. Mason. One by one, 22 seamen were hoisted aboard the H-21 and, in fives and sixes, flown to nearby Ucluelet. Six remained aboard the *Glafkos* and eventually managed to save her.

On the night of May 4, 1971, disaster struck the Saguenay community of St. Jean Vianney, when a landslide 800 feet wide and half a mile long swept away 42 homes. At 6:30 next morning H-21 No.9642 from Base Flight, RCAF Station Bagotville was on the scene. It quickly effected the rescue of a woman stranded atop a car but as pilot Captain Maurice Roy noted, "She was the only person we saw over that half-mile of

On April 19, 1955 S/L Bob Heaslip flying a Piasecki H-21 made this lift of the Boreal Airways Cessna 180, CF-HCL. The Cessna had broken through the ice on a lake southwest of Chibougamau, Quebec. It was flown to another lake about 20 miles away at a speed of about 15 knots. A slow flight was necessary to keep the load from "flying" on its own. The salvage job required 2.20 hours of flying, but including transit to and from Bagotville, six hours were logged for the day.

Via R.T. Heaslip

mud and earth." Later Cpl. Rod Vercheres was lowered from the H-21 to look for survivors in several houses but none were found. The H-21 was soon joined by a Huey and a Voyageur all of which spent several days aiding in the post-disaster clean up. The St. Jean Vianney slide had taken 30 lives.

The H-34 also saw extensive SAR duty with the RCAF. The last three in service, Nos.9632, 9633 and 9635 all finished their careers at CFB Cold Lake. During this time they picked up at least 19 pilots who had had to eject from their aircraft.

Another SAR operation took place July 3, 1972. A mountain climber had been injured by falling rock and was stranded at the 7600 foot level of Mt. Slesse, B.C. He was located at a point 350 feet below the summit, and a Labrador of 442 Squadron, Comox, was dispatched to the scene. The Labrador arrived, and moved in close to the rock face, but there was nowhere for it to set down. Making do, Cpl. T.J. Miller was lowered from the chopper then swung back and forth by the flight engineer until he gained a footing on the slope. The climber was then hoisted aboard the Labrador and was flown to hospital in Vancouver. It was later reported that a civilian helicopter pilot had surveyed the scene but rejected a rescue attempt because of the obvious dangers. An alternate plan was considered — that a rescue party would ascend the mountain and bring the climber down via pulley-assisted litter. This would have taken 12 men 48 hours to accomplish and exposed the victim to further danger.

On March 30, 1975, a fierce storm blew up along the lower B.C. coast. At 5:45 A.M. 442 Sqdn dispatched a Labrador, and before the day was out its crew had rescued 16 people. These included four picked up from a sinking catamaran; a family of four

Master Corporal Walt Davis of 424 Sqdn practicing rescue techniques, being lowered into a wooded area from his Twin Huey. Flying the chopper are Captain Jim Kendall and Captain Cam Mathias. Corporal Roy Copeland is operating the winch on the starboard side. This exercise took place at Mountainview, Ontario, August 25, 1977.

Larry Milberry

Sea King 4003 about to touch down aboard a Canadian destroyer escort. Both probes and the bear trap can be seen in this photo.

United Aircraft Corp. Stratford, Conn. (40783-42)

formed its first squadron, HS 50, on July 4, 1955. Aircraft acquired at this time were Sikorsky HO4S-3's equipped with SONAR and torpedoes.

The Navy's ASW capability was enhanced in the early sixties with the acquisition of the CHSS-2 Sea King to replace the HO4S-3. The Sea King was an important step forward with its all-weather, day-night capabilities; twin turbine reliability; and greater speed, range, and payload. It was intended for use aboard the Bonaventure and a new series of ASW vessels.

In March, 1963 Lt. Buck Rogers trained on the Sea King at the U.S. Naval base, Key West, becoming the first RCN pilot qualified on this type. In May he transferred to Patuxent River, Md. where he spent three months converting other RCN aircrew to the Sea King. HS 50 spent the next year working up on the new helicopter at Shearwater and finally went operational in December 1964.

Two complementary developments at this time were the introduction to the fleet of nine new Destroyer Escorts equipped with helicopter landing decks and hangars and the fitting to the DE's of the RCN's unique haul-down helicopter recovery system. These developments greatly enhanced ASW capabilities within the RCN.

When landing aboard ship, a Sea King approaches from astern and lowers its landing gear and two ventral probes. Through the probe amidship a small messenger wire is lowered. This is grounded, then reels aboard a heavier cable for use in haul-down.

Haul-down is guided by a qualified Sea King pilot from a console aboard ship. This is the LSO, or Landing Signals Officer. He controls tension on the cable to gradually work the Sea King to within a few feet of the deck. Meanwhile the Sea King is flying against the pull of the cable with the pilot making no corrective manoeuvres. As soon as the motion of the ship is right the LSO orders, "Land now. Down. Down. Down." With 3000 pounds of tension on the cable the helicopter complies.

As soon as the landing is effected, the Bear Trap closes on the main probe. This secures the Sea King. Number two engine is shut down; rotors and tail pylon folded; number one engine shut down; and the helicopter remotely pulled into the hangar.

Haul down of a Sea King can be effected within 5 minutes, including hangaring the aircraft. High winds, pitching, and rolling frequently complicate the procedure.

United Aircraft Corp., Stratford, Conn. (40783-4)

from another boat in distress; a woman with a broken leg; two women injured by a falling tree; three men from an overturned boat in the Fraser River; and an elderly couple from their small boat. That day the Rescue Coordination Centre in Victoria recorded 179 calls for assistance.

The ASW Helicopter

The most extensive use of the helicopter in the Royal Canadian Navy was in the ASW role (anti-submarine warfare). This continues so today with the helicopters of the Canadian Forces, Maritime Command. The RCN began studying the ASW helicopter concept in the early fifties, and

The Commercial Helicopter Today

In little more than 30 years the helicopter in Canada has evolved from something viewed suspiciously — even at times ridiculed — to a versatile and ubiquitous feature on the air transport scene. Today there are over 1000 helicopters operating in Canada. These include light machines such as the traditional Bell 47, five-seaters like the Jet Ranger and Gazelle, workhorses like the Bell 205 and S-58T, and Canada's largest civil helicopter, the S-61. In every part of Canada they are performing tasks that serve to reinforce the helicopter's unique capabilities. Smaller machines are used to report rush hour traffic problems in big urban centres and are used on power line and pipeline patrol, agricultural spraying and dusting, forestry protection, and flight training. Larger types add further dimensions to these activities.

The Canadian helicopter has found an important calling in the North, where other types of transportation are inefficient or non-existent. This is particularly apparent in the Arctic where extensive environmental research and oil and gas exploration have made special demands on available forms of transportation.

Troops rappelling from a Huey of 427 Sqdn. Photographed at CFB North Bay, July 1, 1977.

Larry Milberry

Victims of progress, these H-21's once served with the RCAF and later with Dominion Helicopters on the Mid Canada Line. Time has passed by such early generation helicopters and few have escaped the bone yard. These were seen at CFB Mountainview in June 1971 not long before they were melted down for scrap.

Larry Milberry

A Boeing-Vertol CH-47C Chinook, six of which serve with 450 Sqdn, at Uplands. This photo of 147003 was taken during the 1978 Canadian International Air Show. The CH-47C has a maximum takeoff weight of 46 000 lb. It is powered by two 3750 horse power Lycoming T55's and can cruise at 160 mph. It is 51 feet long and has a 60-foot rotor diameter.

Larry Milberry

James Bay

From 1971 when the project got under way, the helicopter has been vital to the James Bay hydro development in northern Quebec. At first it was the only practical means of transporting surveyors, geologists, hydrographers, and others involved in preliminary work. As the construction of roads, work camps, dams, dikes, power houses, and airstrips picked up, helicopters became increasingly important. By 1975 there were 63 at work on the complex. That year helicopter contracts with SEBJ were worth $15 million.

The first use of a heavy lift helicopter in James Bay occurred in 1972 when supply barges became stranded off Ft. George. The supplies were urgently required to keep the project on schedule. This led to the chartering of an S-64 Skycrane. On two separate contracts it flew 383 trips and lugged nearly 3000 tons.

Today, smaller machines operate dawn-to-dusk throughout the complex transporting drillers, slashers, geologists, environmental experts, archaeologists, VIP's and anyone else requiring transport beyond the confines of the campsites. The larger Bells are primarily engaged in sling operations. Their pilots are widely experienced, one of these in 1977 being Roy A. Heibel. A 7000 hour veteran, Heibel earlier spent six years flying in Southeast Asia, with stints in B.C. and the Arctic.

July 14, 1977, saw Heibel working a typical morning on the James Bay complex. After checking with the dispatcher at Caniapiscau who provided a list of jobs he fired up his machine CF-IBT, and was off. The first task was delivering six sling loads onto a drilling raft anchored in the Caniapiscau River. To the observer ashore the deliveries appeared simple but Heibel later commented, "That was a tough job. As soon as I hovered over the raft it disappeared from view. Looking down all I could see was water. This was a bit disorienting as I had nothing to go on but my mirror. Things were complicated by the river current; and my downwash kept blowing the raft away."

From here it was over to a shoreline clearing for two more sling loads; then 30 miles into the bush to lift a disused helipad, required at another site where the lack of a pad had contributed to the crash of a 206. A crew flew in ahead to prepare the half-ton pad; then Heibel arrived, lifted it, but immediately realized that it would not fly. As he put it, this was "an unruly load." Nonetheless, the wind was favourable, and by hovering, the 205 was blown towards target and Heibel had soon delivered the load.

The helicopter will remain important to James Bay long after the construction phase is completed. With installation of power lines beginning in 1978, heavy lift machines will again be called on. To support transmission lines Hydro Quebec will use a 31 ton tower plus its own unique design of 19 tons. On the installation of an experimental line, an Okanagan S-61 was used.

Okanagan Today

After 30 years, the company founded by Carl Agar is Canada's largest operator of helicopters. Today it includes Okanagan, the parent company, plus several subsidiaries across Canada, such as Sept-Îles Helicopter Service, Canadian Helicopters, Dominion-Pegasus Helicopters, and Associated Helicopters. Associated, one of Canada's oldest helicopter operators, was acquired by Okanagan in 1977. Equipment within this large organization ranges from the ever-popular Bell 206 to the S-61. These may be found at work daily on such tasks as oil exploration, fire-fighting, water level surveys, wildlife counts, or on such specialized contracts as lifting meteorological equipment to the top of the CN Tower and training Canadian Forces crews in the art of mountain flying.

Besides Canadian operations, Okanagan Helicopters has equipment at works around the world. One period in 1977 saw five S-61's on off-shore oil exploration work. There was one each in Halifax, Alaska, Shannon, Bombay, and Invercargill in New Zealand. Another was flying on a logging contract on islands in the Strait of Georgia; while the seventh was operating a commuter service between Edson, Alberta, and a coal mine 39 miles away.

The Edson contract is unique in Canada. The owners of the Luscar mine had a transportation problem as their property was remotely located. Consideration was given to building a new townsite to house employees and/or an all-weather

CF-IBT, a hard working veteran of the James Bay hydro development in northern Quebec. IBT is a Bell 205A-1 of Trans-Quebec Helicopters Ltd. and is shown here slinging cement.
Société d'Energie de la Baie James, Chantier LG 2
(7510-08101CV)

highway over 50 miles of rugged terrain. After studying the options, the helicopter service was selected. Today a 28-seat IFR S-61 operates 18 round trips daily transporting the 250 workers required at the mine site. At a million dollars a year, the S-61 is providing the most practical and economical solution to a vital resource operation.

Offshore Work

Since the 1960's, helicopters have been involved in exploration for gas and oil off Canada's coasts. Their prime task is to provide logistic support to offshore drilling rigs and ships. Okanagan led Canadian companies in perfecting this specialized service and operated its first IFR S-61 offshore in 1969. This was based at Sydney and Halifax on long term contract to Shell Oil.

In July 1978 Okanagan was operating an S-61 from Halifax for Mobile Oil, servicing the 65-man drilling rig *Gulftide* at work off the west tip of Sable Island, 143 miles from the Halifax International DME. For June this aircraft, C-GOKZ flew 21 trips to the rig carrying 292 passengers and 7695 pounds of freight. There were also two medivacs. Of 62 hours flown 36 were VFR and 26 IFR. This was not typical as IFR conditions generally prevail in the region, fog being the main problem.

At the same time Heli Voyageur of Val d'Or had its Puma based at Halifax for Chevron Oil. This big machine, C-GUMP, is unique as the first Puma in Canada, and since its arrival here in 1976 has been most at home in offshore work. Its first jobs were off the Labrador coast and in the Beaufort Sea area.

From Halifax the Puma serviced the *Ben Ocean Lancer,* a 504-foot long, 100-man drilling ship at work 141 miles SSE of the Halifax DME. Flying in June totalled 20 trips with 241 passengers and 8500 pounds of freight carried. Hours flown were 53 with 32 being VFR and 21 IFR. As with OKP that month, no trips were cancelled because of aircraft serviceability problems. The only time lost was the result of weather.

Medivac Operations

The civilian helicopter is being put to more and more use as a flying ambulance as the need for medivacs is increasing annually in Canada. In Ontario alone some 1200

patients were carried by air in 1976. This led the Ontario government to establish a heli-ambulance pilot project the following year.

An IFR Bell 212 was acquired through a private consortium and operated by Viking Helicopters. It was fitted with medical support equipment found in a regular ambulance, and is capable of handling two stretcher cases, two critical care personnel, plus two pilots. Additional capabilities are a direct communications link with the province's ambulance dispatch centre, high intensity lights for night operations, tail lighting, siren, P.A. system, tape recorded music, and extra sound proofing and heating.

The aircraft began operations from Toronto-Buttonville airport covering a 115 mile radius. When on alert status it is rolled out and ready for flight within two minutes. The service is centralized near Toronto in order to take advantage of its large airports and hospitals. During its first 12 months in service beginning in September 1977 Viking's 212 carried 98 patients and operated as far away as Earlton in Northern Ontario. One of its trips began with one patient officially onboard, but finished with three! The patient gave birth to twins while in the air.

HAA Awards

In recent years Canadian helicopter pilots have twice received the Helicopter Association of America Pilot of the Year Award. In 1971 the recipient was Okanagan's Don MacKenzie. On April 30, 1970, he was pilot in command of the S-61, CF-OKP, operating from a drilling rig off Nova Scotia. An instant after liftoff tail rotor control was lost. MacKenzie closed the throttles and made an immediate landing. This resulted in undercarriage collapse and the helicopter rolling onto its side, but none of the two crew and 14 passengers was hurt.

Later investigation revealed that control had been lost due to tail rotor driveshaft failure, brought on by the tuliping or bending outward of the tail rotor blade tips. This condition may arise in helicopters given particular conditions, one for the S-61 being a wind from the right front quarter. The aircraft manufacturer had not provided S-61 operators with adequate information about this potential hazard.

The 1977 HAA Award was made posthumously to Okanagan's Chief Pilot Donald Jacques in recognition of his innovative contributions over the years to helicopter flying. One of these was the first

Toronto's CN Tower was topped off on April 2, 1975, using this Sikorsky S-64 Skycrane. It had made 56 ascents lifting "cans," or sections of the Tower's mast and lowering them into place. The delicate operation came off flawlessly. This photo, taken on March 25, 1975, shows a "can" about to be lifted. After completion of the mast, meteorological equipment was added to it. This job was completed by one of Okanagan's Bell 212's.

Larry Milberry

use of the helicopter in power line construction. Jacques lost his life in September 1976 in the crash of an S-58T in B.C.

Another Canadian honoured by the HAA was Dennis L. Foley. He was recognized in 1973 at the HAA's 25th anniversary. Foley, a helicopter pilot since 1944, was singled out as one of the pioneers of helicopter flight.

State of the Art

Though some of the Bell 47's imported to Canada in the early fifties are still active, the helicopter scene is now dominated by turbine-powered types like the Jet Ranger, Hughes 500, and Gazelle. Each of these becomes more sophisticated with successive model years as illustrated by the Bell 206L Jet Ranger and T-tail Hughes 500D. They are highly advanced compared to their ancestors of the mid sixties. For 1978 58 new turbine helicopters were brought into Canada.

A new series of helicopters is now being introduced. There are the Aerospatiale AStar 350C, Bell IFR 212, the 214B with its 2930 horse power engine, and the all new 222. Sikorsky's S-76 has now appeared in Canadian skies, the first ones in Okanagan colours.

Boeing has introduced a civilian version of its famous Chinook and Canadian interest in it is high. The Chinook would have viable applications logging, constructing power lines and transporting personnel. It has a hook capacity of 28 000 pounds and fully loaded it almost equals the weight of two fully-loaded DC-3's. Its passenger capacity is 44.

The state of the art as represented by such technology is the result of efforts begun barely 40 years ago. During this brief era the predictions and aspirations of men like Bernard Sznycer and Carl Agar have come to pass.

The most sophisticated helicopter operating off shore in Canada to 1978, Heli Voyageur's Puma. Here it is shown about to take off from the drilling ship *Ben Ocean Lancer* about 140 miles off Halifax. In 1979 the aircraft was taken over by Sealand Helicopters of St. John's, Nfld.

Larry Milberry

Preserving
Aviation History

One of the numerous World War I vintage aircraft in the National Aeronautical Collection, this Sopwith Snipe came to the United States after World War I and appeared in several films produced in Hollywood.

Aviation and Space Division, National Museum of Science and Technology (10203)

The National Aeronautical Collection

Canadians value their aviation heritage. It is preserved throughout the country in museums, archives, and private collections in the form of aircraft, artifacts, and other memorabilia. The centre piece of this heritage is the National Aeronautical Collection, one of the world's great collections of historic aircraft. The National Aeronautical Collection was formed in 1965 through the joint efforts of the RCAF, Canadian War Museum, and National Aviation Museum, and brought together for display at RCAF Station Rockcliffe where it took over three wartime hangars recently vacated by the Lancasters of 408 Sqdn. In 1967, as a result of the National Museums Act, it came under the auspices of the Aviation and Space Division of the National Museum of Science and Technology. Besides aircraft and aviation artifacts on display at Rockcliffe, others are maintained at the National Museum of Science and Technology, at the Canadian War Museum, and at Uplands Airport.

Aircraft in the collection date as far back as a 1911 Bleriot, and the McDowall Monoplane built sometime between 1912-1914 by the town engineer for Owen Sound, Ontario. There is a superb sampling of World War I aircraft, including originals shipped to Canada as gifts or war prizes after 1918 and a number

of fine replicas. Several of these aircraft were flown by the RCAF's "Snoopy Squadron" during Canada's Centennial Year. Included were original examples of the Sopwith Snipe and Avro 504, and replicas of the Sopwith Triplane and Nieuport 17. Other aircraft of this era in the Collection are a JN-4 Canuck, acquired from a New York State farmer who had had it stored in a barn for years; a SPAD VII, Junkers J-1, and a twin-engined German bomber, the A.E.G. GIV. Of all these aircraft, the prize is the Royal Aircraft Factory B.E.2c in which Lt. F. Sowrey downed the Zeppelin L.32. It and several other aircraft were shipped to Canada in 1919 through the efforts of Lt. Col. A. Doughty, the Dominion of Canada Archivist.

The inter-war years are represented by several aircraft synonymous with bush flying in the Canadian North: the Fairchild FC-2W-2, Fairchild 82, Junkers W.34, Bellanca Pacemaker, and Puss Moth. Some of these were still in commercial service shortly before going to the museum during the mid sixties. Prior to this period, no such aircraft had been preserved in Canada. The fine collection of early bush planes now held in Ottawa was acquired through the efforts of K.M. Molson, curator of the National Aviation Museum and later of the National Aeronautical Collection.

The collection of World War II aircraft includes key training aircraft of the

British Commonwealth Air Training Plan — The Anson, Battle, Cornell, Crane, Finch, Harvard, and Tiger Moth. Combat aircraft include the Hurricane, three versions of the Spitfire, the Mustang, Mosquito, B-25, Bolingbroke, Canso, Lancaster, and Liberator. The Spitfire IX was a gift of Mr. John Paterson of Thunder Bay who had flown it privately after acquiring it in Europe in 1963. The Bolingbroke was one of two purchased from War Assets by George Maude of Sidney, B.C.

After years of exposure to the elements, it was donated to the collection and restored. One of the two Lysanders from the collection was traded to India in 1968 for the B-24. World War II prizes are an Me 163 rocket fighter and an He 162 jet fighter of the Luftwaffe.

The National Aeronautical Collection holds a large number of aircraft from the post World War II era. There are such types as the Sea Fury, Vampire, Sikorsky HO4S, Dakota, North Star, T-33, F-86 and CF-104. Some of the Collection's other aircraft include two replicas of the *Silver Dart,* a Curtiss Sea Gull, Aeronca C-2, Lockheed 12A, Boeing 247, and Fleet Canuck. The Lockheed had served with the Department of Transport from 1937 to 1967 while the Boeing had flown with Chevron Oil primarily on mineral exploration work in the Yukon and Northwest Territories between 1958 and 1967. Its total flying career had spanned 34

The Spitfire IX donated to the National Aeronautical Collection by John Paterson. In this photo it is being flown by Mr. Paterson en route Sault St. Marie-North Bay in September 1963. It was on its way to Montreal and the Canadian Fighter Pilots Association reunion at St. Hubert. As with most rare aircraft in the Collection, the Spitfire is no longer flown.

Via John N. Paterson

This Stinson Reliant, restored on the West Coast, is one of dozens of vintage aircraft meticulously brought back to life by antique aircraft buffs. OAZ is seen taking off during the 1976 Abbotsford International Air Show.

Larry Milberry

The Curtiss HS-2L hull being constructed from scratch by craftsmen at Rockcliffe.

Larry Milberry

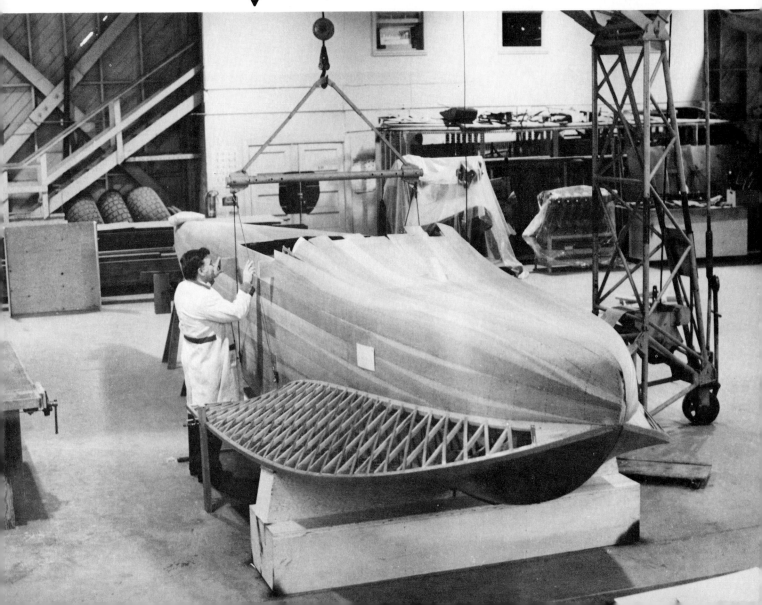

While many World War II military aircraft managed to survive the war, many more did not. Some types all but disappeared, as did the Fairchild-built Bolingbroke. Fortunately a few have reemerged, mainly from prairie farms. Harry Whereatt of Assiniboia, Saskatchewan has rescued this example of the Bolingbroke for future restoration.

Larry Milberry

years, including a stint in the RCAF during World War II.

The National Aeronautical Collection is much more than a static museum for aircraft and related historic material. Projects are constantly under way to refurbish aircraft. This can range from straightforward paint jobs, to complete rebuilding of aircraft and powerplants involving sophisticated wood and metal work. A long term project at Rockcliffe has been the construction of a Curtiss HS-2L hull. This will be mated to a set of original wings to provide Canada with an authentic example of this famous type. Once the HS-2L is completed, a Fokker D VII will be restored.

Another type of activity is the locating and recovery of wrecks in the field. Wrecks recovered have been a Northrop Delta from the forests of New Brunswick, a Fleet Freighter from Labrador, an HS-2L from Northern Ontario, and a Vickers Vedette from Cranberry Marsh near Trenton.

Close liaison is maintained with other museums in Canada and around the world. This sometimes leads to new acquisitions. An Atlas missile was acquired from the USAF museum for the loan of one of the collection's Me 163's for a 5-to-10 year period.

The collection also devotes a major portion of its meagre resources to a flying program using an Avro 504, Nieuport 17, Sopwith Pup, and Sopwith Triplane. These displays take the aircraft to air shows from coast to coast.

The National Aeronautical Collection currently houses 96 aircraft in addition to 200 aero engines and thousands of other artifacts. These latter include reminders of great Canadian achievements — there are the nose sections of the sole Avro Jetliner, and that of the sixth Avro Arrow. Although the collection is large, numerous other aircraft of importance to Canadian aviation history are yet to be preserved. For the time being the acquisition of new

Each year many older generation aircraft in Canada end their flying days. After a decade in service, most CF-100's had been grounded and scrapped. This large shipment of dismembered CF-100's was photographed on a siding at the Hamilton steel works, October 27, 1963. Many were Mark V's, built in the late fifties.

Larry Milberry

One of the last Lockheed Lodestars surviving in Canada. CF-SEQ's last flying role was as an airliner for Royalair, a Montreal-based carrier. It was grounded in 1969 and has since probably served its new owners better as a "patates frites" stand than it did Royalair. It was photographed on Rt. 125 south of St.-Julienne, Quebec.

Larry Milberry

Many historic aircraft are still earning their keep in Canadian skies. One of these in 1979 was TCA's first DC-3, a 33-year veteran, C-FTDJ. This plane was originally operated on TCA's Toronto-New York route, then was purchased by Goodyear in 1947. It has logged over 20 000 hours in the air.

Larry Milberry

aircraft poses a problem, for the facilities at Rockcliffe are not only antiquated, but also filled to capacity.

Other Preservations

Other than through the National Aeronautical Collection, aviation history is preserved elsewhere across Canada. This is done through the work of museums, archives, individuals, associations, and communities. One unique organization is Canada's Aviation Hall of Fame in Edmonton which honours the work of Canadian aviation pioneers. Aircraft have been preserved, restored and displayed through provincial auspices. The Fleet 2, CF-AOD, for example, may be seen in the British Columbia Provincial Museum in Victoria. The Western Development

Museum at Moose Jaw displays several aircraft such as a Norseman and a Cessna 195 formerly used by the Saskatchewan Government Air Service. In Ontario the Ministry of Natural Resources has restored its old Fairchild KR-34, CF-AOH. This aircraft was salvaged from the bush in Northern Ontario where it had been abandoned after an accident 16 years earlier.

Many individual aircraft are preserved throughout the country. At the Brome County Historical Society's museum in Knowlton, Quebec, a virtually original Fokker D VII is displayed. This is the sole survivor of a batch of D VII's shipped to Canada in 1919. Many aircraft have by now been mounted on pylons for outdoors display. These include a Hudson at

Canadians are more aware than ever of their aviation heritage. Historic aircraft are preserved in museums across the country. On April 10, 1979, this Found Brothers FBA-2C was presented to the National Museum of Science and Technology by Centennial College, Scarborough, Ontario. It was the fourth FBA-2 built and was originally registered CF-OZV.

Larry Milberry

Gander; an F-86 at Chatham, New Brunswick; a CF-100 at North Bay; a Lancaster at Toronto; a T-33 at Portage la Prairie; and a Bristol Freighter at Yellowknife. There is often a direct association between the type of aircraft represented and local community history.

Aircraft and collections are also maintained by private individuals and groups. Individually-owned flyable Canadian antique aircraft presently include such famous types as the Beech 17, Fairchild 24, Fleet Finch, Stinson Reliant, and Tiger Moth. One privately-owned collection is that of Harry Whereatt of Assiniboia, Saskatchewan. Another large collection of historic aircraft is being developed for display by the Western Canada Aviation Museum in Winnipeg. Presently its aircraft include several examples of early bush planes and types used in the British Commonwealth Air Training Plan. Many of these aircraft are best classified as in ruins, but a number are restorable. The WCAM has been responsible for the recovery of several historic wrecks from the bush.

Canada's most significant collection of flyable historic aircraft is operated by the Canadian Warplane Heritage of Hamilton. The CWH has as its prime objective to obtain examples of aircraft

McKee Trophy winners Walter Gilbert and Z.L. Leigh exchanging memories at the 1975 CAHS Convention.

Larry Milberry

flown by Canadians during World War II, and to restore these to airworthiness. Its large collection presently includes the Anson, Avenger, Corsair, Crane, Harvard, Lancaster, and Mitchell. Post-war aircraft like the Vampire and CF-100 have also been added. Each year the CWH sponsors one of North America's great airshows, at Hamilton, with World War II vintage warplanes from Canada and the United States being the big attraction.

The Canadian Aviation Historical Society

The Canadian Aviation Historical Society was formed in 1962 to stimulate interest in aviation history. Since then it has encouraged extensive research into Canada's aviation past, and, through its *Journal,* provided a forum for the dissemination of the results. Other significant material has been published in the Society's registers of early Canadian civil aircraft, its *Vintage Aircraft in Canada,* and the forth-

coming *Chronology of Canadian Aviation.*

The CAHS has chapters in Toronto, Ottawa, Calgary, and Vancouver which meet monthly to present talks covering all aspects of Canada's aviation heritage. A national convention is held annually which usually focuses on a central theme. The McKee Trophy was featured in 1975. Guests included many winners of the trophy, and Earl Godfrey himself. The efforts of the CAHS were formally recognized in 1977 when the Aircraft Owners and Pilots Association of the USA awarded its AOPA Award to CAHS president Fred Hotson, for his dedication to preserving Canadian aviation history.

Air Vice Marshal Earl Godfrey, winner of the 1977 McKee Trophy. He is seen here accepting a memento from the Canadian Aviation Historical Society at the 1975 CAHS Convention. Making the presentation is CAHS past president and historian John Griffin. Z.L. Leigh looks on.

Larry Milberry

Guest speaker at the 1979 Canadian Aviation Historical Society convention was Jim Floyd, who led the Avro Jetliner design team in the late forties. Here he receives a commemorative tray from Jetliner test pilot Don Rogers. Later Floyd was involved with the design of the CF-105, and the super-sonic transport in the U.K.

Larry Milberry

North America's first jet transport, the Avro Jetliner. Interest in this fine Canadian project was high in 1950. The USAF budgeted for 20 for use as navigation trainers. Several U.S. airlines were prepared to purchase the type. Howard Hughes wanted 30 for TWA but political decisions doomed the Jetliner. In Canada the federal government refused to allow production, citing Cold War tensions and the need to focus on CF-100 procurement. In the U.S. lobbying closed the door on Hughes' proposal to have the Jetliner built under licence by Convair.

Hawker Siddeley Canada Ltd. (35033)

Bibliography

The following books were used as reference sources in the preparation of *Aviation in Canada:*

Collishaw, R., *Air Command: A Fighter Pilot's Story,* Wm. Kimber, London, 1973.

Drew, George A., *Canada's Fighting Airmen,* Maclean Publishing Co., Toronto, 1931.

Ellis, Frank H., *Canada's Flying Heritage,* University of Toronto Press, Toronto, 1954.

Ellis, John R., *Canadian Civil Aircraft Register,* Canadian Aviation Historical Society, Toronto.

Goodspeed, Lt. Col. D.J., *The Armed Forces of Canada 1867-1967,* Directorate of History, Canadian Forces Headquarters, Ottawa, 1967.

Gordon, John, *Of Men and Planes, Vol. III,* Ottawa, 1968.

Griffin, John A., *Canadian Military Aircraft, Serials and Photographs,* Canadian War Museum, Ottawa, 1969.

Halliday, H.A. *Chronology of Canadian Military Aviation,* National Museums of Canada, Ottawa, 1975.

Harris, John Norman, *Knights of the Air,* Macmillan, Toronto, 1958.

Kealy, J.D.F. and Russell, E.C., *A History of Canadian Naval Aviation 1918-1962,* Naval Historical Section, Canadian Forces Headquarters, Ottawa, 1965.

Keith, Ronald A., *Bush Pilot with a Brief Case,* Doubleday, Toronto, 1972.

Kostenuk, S., and Griffin, John A., *RCAF Squadrons and Aircraft,* National Museums of Canada, Ottawa, 1977.

Main, J.R.K., *Voyageurs of the Air, A History of Civil Aviation in Canada 1858-1967,* The Queen's Printer, 1967.

Molson, K.M., *Pioneering in Canadian Air Transport,* James Richardson and Sons Ltd., Winnipeg, 1974.

Thomson, Don W., *A Story of Aerial Photography in Canada,* Information Canada, Ottawa, 1975.

Sullivan, Lt. Allan, *Aviation in Canada 1917-1918,* Rous and Mann Ltd., 1919.

Vincent, Carl, *The Blackburn Shark,* Canada's Wings, Stittsville, Ontario, 1974.

Vincent, Carl, *The Liberator and Fortress,* Canada's Wings, Stittsville, Ontario, 1976.

Other research sources have included:

Air Pictorial
Aircraft
Aircraft and Airport
American Helicopter
Calgary Herald
Canadian Aircraft Operator
Canadian Aviation
Canadian Aviation Historical Society, Journal
Canadian Civil Aircraft Register
Canadian Geographical Journal
The Chronicle Herald
Crowsnest
Le Devoir
Edmonton Journal
ESSO Air World
Financial Post
Flight
Flight Comment
The Globe
The Globe and Mail
Hamilton Spectator
House of Commons Debates
Imperial Oil Review
Maritime Advocate
Montreal Daily Star
North American Aviation News
Ottawa Citizen
The Roundel
Toronto Star
Toronto Telegram
Troy Daily Times
The Sentinel
Wings
Winnipeg Free Press

Index